THERE ONCE WAS A SHOW FROM NANTUCKET:
A COMPLETE GUIDE TO THE TV SITCOM

By Bob Leszczak

Published in the USA by:
BearManor Media
1317 Edgewater Dr #110
Orlando, FL 32804
www.bearmanormedia.com

Paperback ISBN: 978-1-62933-666-4
Case ISBN: 978-1-62933-667-1
BearManor Media, Orlando, Florida
Printed in the United States of America
Book design by Robbie Adkins, www.adkinsconsult.com

*Cover Photo: The "Jet Set" left to right Steven Weber, Crystal Bernard, Tim
Daly, Farrah Forke, Rebecca Schull, Thomas Haden Church, David Schramm
and Tony Shalhoub.*

Dedication

Dedicated to the memory of David Angell, Robin Chamberlin, Roz Doyle, Marcia Gould, William Hickey, David Lloyd, Noam Pitlik, John Ritter and David Schramm who have all earned their "wings."

Acknowledgements

Those wonderful people providing quotes for this book, this labor of love include (alphabetically) Caroline Aaron, Gregory Behrendt, Wendy Allen-Belleville, Ana Auther, Erick Avari, Tim Bagley, Sharon Barr, Derek Basco, Darryl Bates, Layne Beamer, Adam Belanoff*, Rick Beren, Andrew Bilgore, Jim Bock, Charlotte Booker, Kevin Brief, Jim Brochu, Barbara Bruno, Ellen Byron, Amanda Carlin, Clint Carmichael, Peter Casey, Jane Childerhose, Rick Copp, Tim Daly, Bill Diamond*, John Ducey, Steven Eckholdt, Van Epperson, Tim Fall, Farrah Forke*, Leonard R. Garner, Jr.*, Howard Gewirtz*, David Gianopoulos, Joyce Gittlin, Gilbert Gottfried, Jeff Greenberg, Ian Gurvitz*, Dave Hackel*, Kevin Haggerty, Brian Haley, Carolyn Hennesy, Tony Hicks, Suzanne Holmes*, Kaitlin Hopkins, Jim Hudson, Lissa Kapstrom, Ray Laska, David Lee, Robert Gary Lee, Ken Levine, Steven Levitan, Christopher Lloyd, Vince Lozano, Deborah May, Jim McCoulf, Christie Mellor, Bruce Miller, Craig Richard Nelson, Taylor Nichols, Robert O'Brien, Sam Pancake, Sy Richardson, Keith Rosary, Michael Saltzman*, Julia Sanford, Rebecca Schull, Robert Shafer, Eric Howell Sharp, Harris Shore, Jonathan Slavin, Michael Bailey Smith, Fred Stoller, Kirby Tepper, Christopher Vane*, Liz Vassey, Todd Waring and Steven Weber. Many of those same people also provided wonderful photographs for use in this book. Those providing assistance in other arenas include Al Aidekman, Mike Armijo, Clark Conrad, Paula Finn, Adam Greenberg, Jack E. Herman*, Dan O'Shannon, Richard Sackley*, David Schwartz, Joel Tator, Jason Thornton, and Vincent Terrace. To those with an asterisk (*) next to their name, thank you most of all for going above and beyond the call of duty! A tip of the wings and a lifetime boarding pass to all of you.

TABLE OF CONTENTS

THE FLIGHT PLAN: An Introduction

A TV Guide *listing touting the new NBC sitcom* Wings. *I think it's going to be a good sitcom. (Courtesy of Suzanne Holmes).*

Long before *Wings* was a blip on anyone's radar, its creators were making memorable Emmy-winning television with the NBC stalwart called *Cheers*. David Lee and Peter Casey said, "*Cheers* was a well-oiled machine and hailed as a hit. Being part of it was like being in a great rock band. David Angell was already working for *Cheers* when we were hired." They happily toiled together for three seasons before the trio decided to strike out on their own, forming their own production company. "It was called Grub Street Productions," Lee and Casey explained, "Grub Street, in London, was known in the 18th century for its writers who would turn out anything for money. Penny Dreadfuls mostly. The street is long gone but we thought it would make a delightfully self-deprecating name.

We were living in the [San Fernando] Valley at the time. One day we went to what used to be the Beverly Garland Hotel Coffee Shop and began tossing around this idea David Angell had about a sitcom based in a small airport." One might say they all then "co-piloted" a pilot script for this proposed series. Lee and Casey recalled, "NBC's Brandon Tartikoff didn't like the idea initially. He didn't get the airport setting. He said, 'I only see the backs of people in line.' He was envisioning a much larger airport than we had in mind. We had

WINGS SALUTE

Grub Street Gang

The production company's outstanding pedigree includes "Cheers" and "Frasier."

BY RICK SHERWOOD

Partners (from left): David Angell, Peter Casey and David Lee.

A t a party on soundstage 19 celebrating the 100th episode of "Wings," Paramount TV topper Kerry McCluggage decided to come clean. When asked to say a few words, he told cast and crew that he had noticed the Grub Street Prods. creative team that conceived the show long before he joined the studio and confessed to an attempted corporate raid.

"The truth of the matter is that, while I was still at Universal, I tried to get the original creators of this show to come over to my studio when their deal was up (at Paramount)," he recalls telling them. "I had been so impressed with what they did on 'Wings' that I wanted them to work for me."

But the mountain didn't come to Mohammed.

Unluckily then, but happily now that he's chairman of the Paramount Television Group, McCluggage has formed a relationship with the creative team that is working to everyone's advantage.

In addition to "Wings," the Grub Street team of David Angell, Peter Casey and David Lee has gone on to create and (in association with Paramount Network Television) produce last season's critically acclaimed new show, the multiple Emmy Award-winning "Frasier." Its principals count among their accolades some 12 Emmy nominations and two wins for their work as part of

the "Cheers" team of writers and producers as well as a People's Choice Award, the Television Critics Association salute for best comedy, an endorsement from the Viewers for Quality Television, and nominations for Golden Globe and Humanitas Prize honors.

Their track record has made them a credible force in the production business. "I think they are going to be an important company for the future, and certainly they will figure prominently in our future," says NBC's Warren Littlefield. "Not only are the three principals very strong, but almost like a magnet, they attract strong, creative talent."

Their business philosophy has enticed an impressive roster of talent to become a part of the growing Grub Street team. Creativity and individuality are not only encouraged by the principals, but pretty much required.

"Our ultimate talent is in hiring good people and letting them do what they are hired to do," says Angell. "We give everybody a lot of creative freedom here, including writers and actors, and that seems to be paying off in terms of the work they turn out."

The company was formed in 1990. The trio came together

through "Cheers," though members had individually worked or written scripts for a variety of shows over the years, including "The Jeffersons."

The name of the company is something of a joke unto itself. It was suggested by Angell's wife, who stumbled upon it during research.

"Grub Street was a street in 19th century London, no longer there, a street where for some reason what came to be known as hack writers came to live and write their poetry, dime novels and potboilers," says Angell.

"And whenever they put on a play it was called a Grub Street production, signifying that it was a rather shoddy work," says Casey with a laugh.

Obviously they haven't lived up to their name, turning out nothing but top programs. It has happened, they think, because of a guiding philosophy that stresses teamwork.

They also credit Glenn and Les Charles, producers of "Cheers," for showing them a better way. "They always were looking for a new angle to take each season," says Casey, "and by doing that you do generate more stories and keep the interest alive."

"Grub Street is a wonderful, supportive place to be," says Mark Reisman, "Wings" executive producer. "They let us take things where we think it should go, and that helps us in terms of creativity. This year, everyone made a conscious effort to take the season in new directions and get things off and running, and we have done that."

Wings *creators left to right David Angell, Peter Casey and David Lee – the Grub Street Gang from* The Hollywood Reporter. *(Courtesy of Suzanne Holmes).*

to explain that we wanted it to be a small airport and literally had pictures drawn to show him the look. Then the Charles Brothers, Glen and Les who created *Cheers,* read the pilot script and didn't get it. They told us that the expository information was too subtle. It needed to be much clearer to the audience. So we clarified. A lot." Tim Daly added, "We would play a beat many times and what I thought to be excessive was really solidifying the characters. The audience really knew who we all were." Casey and Lee added, "But even then it wasn't an easy ride. *Wings* was always a struggle. Every year we were kind of on the bubble, never at the top of the ratings but doing okay. We got moved around on NBC's schedule again and again. There was never a breath. We could never relax."

It wasn't titled *Wings* from the very beginning. The year was 1989 and the flight pattern changed a bit along the way. Casey and Lee shared, "The original working title was *Blue Skies*. We wanted to use the classic Irving Berlin song with someone different performing it each week. Berlin was still alive at the time in 1989 and surprisingly said, 'No.' We weren't able to use it, and the show's title became our second choice *Wings*." It should be noted that later a 1994 series did indeed utilize the title *Blue Skies* and the song. How? Berlin had passed on by that time. "Then our thoughts turned to the location of the airport. We considered many, including the Grand Canyon Airport, but eventually narrowed it down to three – Hyannis, Martha's Vineyard, and Nantucket. David Angell was from Providence so he knew the entire area very well. Nantucket eventually won out." Questions about Nantucket were sometimes answered by prolific artist and year-round Nantucket resident Marshall DuBock.

Casey and Lee continued, "Casting for *Wings* was extensive. Like *Cheers*, we wanted very talented people who weren't yet household names. These weren't people everyone had seen in a million things. Ours was a show filled with fresh faces."

Still, many famous names auditioned for roles including (per casting director Jeff Greenberg) George Clooney, Hank Azaria and David Duchovny (for Brian Hackett). Greenberg also let me know that Bryan Cranston was in the running for the role of Joe Hackett. Tim Daly got the nod for Joe, and Daly remembered another famous name who came close to snagging the role, "It came down to Kevin Conway, the voice of Batman and me. We both screen tested for it. I do think he would have made a great Joe Hackett." Actor Todd Waring said that he was also in the running for each of the Hackett Brothers' roles. Without doubt the toughest role to cast was Helen. Megan Mullally auditioned for the part (and was later used as a guest star on the show). Jeff Greenberg elaborated, "When we were auditioning for the pilot Megan Mullally did a great job as Helen but wasn't quite right for the role. However, then and there the producers thought she'd be great for an early episode as Cindy, 'the town pump' in 'There Once Was a Girl from Nantucket.' We made her a straight offer for the role." Lisa Kudrow and Julia Louis-Dreyfus tried out, too, but Peri Gilpin (also later a guest star) came the closest to the Helen they all had envisioned but Brandon Tartikoff didn't think she was yet ready to carry a series. Jeff Greenberg added these names to the Helen auditions - Rita Wilson (with a very pronounced Greek accent), Katherine Keener, Marcia Gay Harden, Mariska Hargitay, Marcia Cross and Julianne Moore. Lee and Casey reflected, "She was originally a dark-haired Greek beauty named Helen Trionkis. But then we were introduced to Crystal Bernard. We conjured up a flimsy excuse for her Southern accent – she was born in Texas, but moved to Nantucket when she was ten - which nobody ever really bought - nor did we expect them to." Greenberg added, "Crystal got the part because she was really funny and really cute. Didn't matter at all that she had been on another series. We were fine to go with a total unknown, like our first choice, Peri Gilpin, if they were best for the role." Casey and Lee added, "When Thomas Haden Church read for Joe and Brian we knew that, even though he wasn't quite right, we had to come up with something for him. His delivery and his voice were so unique. Thus Lowell was born." Greenberg elaborated, "When we were casting the pilot there was originally a role for a cab driver. I had brought in Stephen Tobolowsky, whom everyone loved." Oddly enough, Tobolowsky was one of the stars of that aforementioned 1994 sitcom titled *Blue Skies*. Greenberg continued, "However, Stephen had some other offers on the table, so because we didn't want to lose him we immediately brought him to the network for approval, even before we had brought any of the other characters. Well, he got approved but it felt a little horse-before-the-cartish, as we didn't know who any of the leads would be. As it turned out, after he was approved he changed his mind and decided he didn't want to do it, after we had gone to a lot of trouble to accommodate him. But it was a blessing because shortly after that we found Tommy Church for Lowell. I had cast Tommy on *Cheers* as a deadpan hockey player and he stole the show. I brought my *Wings* producers over to see him and they then created the role of Lowell the mechanic just for him. With Lowell now in the cast they didn't feel like they needed the cab driver character. That is, until Tony Shalhoub came along guesting in Season Two as Antonio the waiter, becoming a regular in Season Three as the cab driver – a character who you could explain being at the airport all the time." About the actress behind the ticket counter, Casey and Lee said, "Rebecca Schull was perfect for Fay. Incidentally, we gave the character three names, Fay Evelyn Cochran because every woman associated with the history of aviation seemed to have three names."

Instead of "Blue Skies," the theme song chosen was a lovely, classy classical piece by Franz Schubert from his "Piano Sonata in A Major, D. 959, Fourth Movement (Rondo)." It was the opening theme song for the sitcom's first two-and-a-half seasons (making a triumphant return for the series finale in 1997 titled "The Final Approach").

The back story is, before becoming Sandpiper Air in 1987 it was called Siasconset Air and the previous owners were drummed out of business by the island's wealthy and powerful Kingsbury Family (of whom we get a glimpse in the episode titled "Death Becomes Him"). Ever since childhood Joe and Brian Hackett were intrigued by flight. They used to run along the Nantucket beaches with outstretched arms pretending to be airplanes. Aviation lessons came next and when Siasconset Air went belly up, Joe saw this as his chance to live out his dream. He was able to scrape up just enough scratch to get Sandpiper Air off the ground. His original vision was to have fiancé Carol run the ticket counter, but she ran off with his younger more devil-may-care brother Brian and plans were placed in a holding pattern. It was on a large commercial flight to Hawaii (escaping the Carol conundrum) that Joe met Fay Evelyn Cochran, a disgruntled flight attendant who was being forced into retirement. She and several mini bottles of hooch convinced Joe that they should work together, and Sandpiper Air soon came to be. Joe's plane is a Cessna 402C. Its F. A. A. tail number is N121PP (which, in correspondence with the tower was "Nevada One Two One Papa Papa," sometimes Cessna Nevada One Two One Papa Papa) – fairly consistent throughout the program's eight seasons. However, what we see on the screen varies. The original N121PP was destroyed in 1996, so despite what is said in the cockpit, occasionally we see

N121PB (usually on the ground) and N160PB (in flight). The Cessna with the tail number of N121PB was still used for charters by a company called Cape Air after the series ended. Joe's only competitor on the island is brash, conniving and snarky Roy Biggins, owner of the larger and more profitable Aeromass. Instead of the typical "living room-based sitcom," *Wings* has a fresh perspective, having its base in an airport where countless zany people come and go.

Upon the death of the Hackett Brothers' institutionalized father Donald, a suitcase with instructions was left for them in the will. Even though estranged because of the Carol incident, Joe is talked into contacting his wayward brother, Brian. They open the suitcase together only to find a sea of keys that leads them on a wild goose chase. Also enclosed – the words "You're rich" attached to a photo of the Hackett Boys in their youth. Those words, the photograph, and the fact that Carol ditched Brian too, helps reunite them. Also present in the terminal is Joe and Brian's childhood friend, the formerly calorically-challenged Helen Chappel who has crushed on Joe since moving to the Island. In their youth, Joe, Brian and Helen were the Three Musketeers. Their daft savant-like airport mechanic is Lowell Mather. He works for both Aeromass and Sandpiper. Additional characters such as Antonio Scarpacci - the cab driver, Alex Lambert – the charter helicopter pilot, Budd Bronski – Lowell's replacement, and Casey Davenport – Helen's down-on-her-luck sister all find a home in the terminal in later seasons.

Shooting took place on the Paramount Studios lot on Stage 19 (where *Happy Days* had been filmed). Rebecca Schull recalled, "Roy Christopher designed our huge set. It was wonderful, perfect, and very comfortable." It had to be large to contain Joe's plane in the hangar. As big as it was, the wings of the plane still had to be disassembled to get it in there. The terminal set was rather large, too. What impressed me, your author most about it was that it had a functioning second level. Many sitcoms have staircases that lead to nowhere, but the one on *Wings* was useable. The second level contained the restrooms, the observation deck, lockers and another staircase that allegedly led to the tower (although that staircase did not really lead anywhere). About those lockers on the upper level, Brian Haley shared, "There was one locker up there that had obscene photos plastered everywhere on the inside. The guys thought that was hilarious to send people up there to open that locker. I'm still traumatized from the event." About working on that second level, Executive Producer Dave Hackel said, "Very few scenes were done up there because it was difficult to get cameras up there, space was very limited, turnarounds were hard, and there was rarely a crane available for use." Director Leonard R. Garner, Jr. shared, "We didn't use the upstairs often, but we did in the series finale when Brian and Joe toss the money from the suitcase to the terminal below them. I loved the challenge of blocking with such a big set. We used an unprecedented four dollies. That's quite rare. The huge space allowed a great flow of business. Plus there were three stations – Helen's counter, Roy's counter, and Fay's counter. It was very shootable and one could still get to see Roy, Fay, Helen, Lowell, etc. in the background doing their jobs while focused upon other actions." Conversely, writer Lissa Kapstrom stated, "We were writing for an amazing ensemble and their movements were very important. Comedy is generally easier in a closer and smaller space." Director Rick Beren added, "And scenes from behind Helen's counter looking out over the terminal were a little clumsy. There wasn't much room back there." Ken Levine added, "The set was big and at times unwieldy. There was a whole second story to the terminal that was hardly ever used. Hard to get cameras up there. Also hard to get cameras deep into the terminal set. The problem with the hangar is that it took up precious space you'd like to have for swing sets."

The *Wings* pilot sold, and as Lee and Casey remembered, "The Charles Brothers who created *Cheers* lobbied for us to be on after them. There were only six episodes produced in that first season because it was a mid-season replacement." The program premiered on NBC on April 19, 1990 to mixed reviews as many critics saw *Wings* as a *Cheers* clone. That early stigma is likely the reason this cleverly-written, brilliantly-acted, intelligent, laugh-out-loud funny sitcom was always riding the coattails of *Cheers* and *Frasier* like a red-headed stepchild, never receiving the accolades and applause it so richly deserves. About the yearly Emmy snubs, Tim Daly said, "That rankles me to this day. We were a Top 20 show but got no push from NBC. We'd see promos for *Friends*, *Frasier* and *Seinfeld*, but none for us. Maybe it's all because initially critics weren't fond of the show. That is, until the USA Network reruns. Then opinions changed. However, the die had already been cast and it's very hard to break out of that first impression." Lee and Casey said, "Yes, even though it was a very crowded field at the time the snubs were a mystery. We agree with Tim Daly, early reviews for the show weren't great and it's hard to correct that." Director Leonard R. Garner, Jr. said, "The Emmy snubs? That may have been related to the show's blue collar workers and blue collar image." Farrah Forke's take on this is, "The Emmys were always the elephant in the room. We knew we would be snubbed each year so we really didn't have any expectations that it would change." Rebecca Schull added, "The only Emmy nods were for guest stars and I thought that was so wrong. Our cast had no weak links and amazing chemistry." Even though the show wasn't nominated (except for guest stars), writer Michael Saltzman shared, "I was particularly proud of the fact that in the two years Bill Diamond and I were writing for the show three of the four episodes that Lee, Casey and Angell submitted were ones that we'd written. That was a real honor for us."

Speaking of writers, *Wings* had a writers room filled with some of the very best in the business, as Adam Belanoff recalls, "It was a veritable murderer's row of the best comedy writers then working in the business. Not just David Angell, Peter Casey and David Lee but David Isaacs, Ken Levine, Christopher Lloyd, and his father David among so many others. Imagine that being one's first staff job. What a standard was set."

Taking a look at the *Wings* calendar, Executive Producer Dave Hackel said, "A typical week on *Wings* usually consisted of a table read on Monday. Sometimes rehearsals would begin on Monday, but not always. There would be some rewriting on Monday evening. Tuesday was rehearsal day with more rewriting and punching up at night. Wednesday was more rehearsing, and if we hadn't solved all the problems inherent in the script we'd do still more rewriting. On Thursday we did camera blocking, and still more script polishing. Friday was more rehearsing, then a big dress rehearsal, and at 7 PM the audience came in for the shoot. There were often a few pickups shot after the audience was gone." Later in the show's run when the third regime was running things shoot night moved to Tuesdays.

The real Nantucket Memorial Airport can be found at 14 Airport Road, approximately 5.7 miles from Tom Nevers Field (formerly Ackerly Field) - a real place at 130 Tom Nevers Road, Nantucket, Massachusetts 02254. Somehow over the years, the possessive apostrophe in the name of the field was lost. The man for whom the field, the street, a pond, and a swamp are named was actually Tom *Never* with no "S." In some old Nantucket records it's said to have been spelled Nevar and even Neavar. Never may have been a Native American employed by a whale lookout station in the South East Quarter of Nantucket circa 1745 when he was about 20. That area later became known as Tom Never's Head. At one time in the late 1800s there was even a whale oil company bearing his name. Information about the man is sketchy at best. From 1990-1997, his name appeared in all 172 episodes of *Wings*. The Club Car, the gang's favorite hangout on Nantucket Island is a real but seasonal restaurant at One Main Street. And Madaket Way or Road, the location of Brian and Joe's childhood home is also a real Nantucket thoroughfare.

There was great chemistry on screen, but also behind the scenes. Writer Lissa Kapstrom said, "Everyone was happy to be there. They didn't really hang out together, but all got along very well. They were a nice family." Steven Weber added, "Like any family, we had *moments* like all families do, but for all intents and purposes we had a great time and every day was a joy." Director Rick Beren remembered, "Going to cast and crew parties on season premiere nights was a lot of fun. And we all used to take trips to Las Vegas together – actors, writers, directors. Most of the guys were in their early 30s and single. And Steven Weber was my neighbor. He was like a real wacky sitcom neighbor. He would barge in through my back door in the Hollywood Hills. Very charming. Tim was the rock of the group and Amy Yasbeck was just wonderful." Many cast and crew members over the eight seasons were invited back for the series finale and some were used as extras in the show's final scene in the terminal with Fay on the microphone.

Have they kept in touch? Tim said, "I had lunch with Rebecca a short while ago. I see Weber a lot. We talk and text regularly. Tommy is rather private, and I haven't heard from Crystal in many years. Tony and I are in touch frequently. We both do a lot of theatre so we see each other's plays. I saw him in *The Band's Visit*." Weber said, "I see Andy Ackerman from time to time. In fact, I saw him when he directed an episode of my recent sitcom *Indebted*. I also stay in touch with Tommy Cole, the show's key makeup man. Tommy and I did a couple of other projects after *Wings*, like *The Weber Show* and a couple of pilots – an amazing guy and a former Mouseketeer." Director Rick Beren added, "I worked with Steven Weber again recently. I was the Associate Director on the pilot for his recent sitcom *Indebted*. When he saw both Andy Ackerman and me he smiled and said, 'Oh, gees.'" Rebecca recalled, "I spent a lot of down time with David Schramm as neither of us was a lead character on the show. We went to the opera together during the run of the series and even after it ended." Farrah Forke said, "I've kept in touch with Adam Belanoff. We've been friends for years. Oh, and Caroline Aaron who played Mary Pat Lee – she, David Schramm and I had dinner parties together." Executive Producer Dave Hackel added, "I'm still in touch with Peter Casey, Rebecca Schull, Steven Weber, Tim Daly, and Tony Shalhoub." Ken Levine shared, "David Schramm did a play reading of mine in New York a number of years ago. I bump into Tim and Steven occasionally. I've directed Tony and Steven in other shows. Farrah Forke did a wonderful thing. She was later on *Lois and Clark* which I watched with my kids who were young at the time. Her character dies in an episode and my daughter was very upset. I called Farrah and she spoke to my daughter assuring her it was just make believe. What a sweetheart! I've stayed friendly with all the writers and directors as well as casting and editing. I'm Facebook friends with the writers' assistants as well. There is no one on *Wings* I wouldn't love to see again."

The *Wings* guest star list over eight seasons is rather impressive as well – highlighted by (in alphabetical order) Brooke Adams (Shalhoub's real-life wife), Kirstie Alley, Carol Alt, Clint Black, Dan Castellaneta, Ray Charles, Lana Clarkson, Robert Culp, Tyne Daly (Tim's real-life sister), Calvert DeForest, Chris Elliott, Anne

Francis, Peri Gilpin, Gilbert Gottfried, Kelsey Grammer, William Hickey, George Kennedy, Phil Leeds, Jay Leno, Peggy Lipton, Norman Lloyd, Valerie Mahaffey, Rose Marie, Sam McMurray, Josh Mostel, Megan Mullally, Bebe Neuwirth, Edwin Newman, Oliver North, Michael J. Pollard, Maury Povich, John Ratzenberger, Debbie Reynolds, John Ritter, Soupy Sales, Cathy Silvers, The Real Don Steele, David Ogden Stiers, Peter Tork, Amy Van Nostrand (Tim Daly's wife at the time), Abe Vigoda, George Wendt, and Steve Young. It never aired, but there was also a PSA (Public Service Announcement) with bowling legend Dick Weber made in conjunction with Southwest Airlines and an Australian charity called Angel Flight.

The souvenir seat cushion from the Wings, *Southwest Airlines and Angel Flight bowling event. (Courtesy of Suzanne Holmes).*

The retro cable channel known as Antenna TV, which specializes in classic TV, aired a *Wings* marathon celebrating the program's 30th Anniversary (April 19, 2020) and provided many much-needed laughs during the early stages of the Coronavirus pandemic. Rebecca Schull said, "I was in Rochester, New York during that marathon and caught a couple of episodes. I hadn't seen the show in some time and it had aged so well. I got to see one of my favorite episodes, too – the one about Helen and Joe's wedding where his hand is stuck in the toilet. Still so funny." Leonard R. Garner, Jr. added, "The 30th Anniversary is a big deal. It's so great that Antenna TV did that weekend marathon honoring the anniversary." Writer Lissa Kapstrom said, "This was a golden age of sitcoms. *Wings* was and is great comfort food."

It's important to note that *Wings* and its cast are mentioned in *The Simpsons* episode titled "Whistle While Your Wife Works" in which Quagmire and his friends are immersed in beer at the brewery. Quagmire confesses how much he loves *Wings*. There is also mention of *Wings* in an episode of Tony Shalhoub's *Monk* titled "Mr. Monk and the Airplane" with guest star Tim Daly.

The *Wings* cast was never on the cover of *TV Guide*, but they are well *covered* in this volume. The purpose of this book is to finally shed light upon an underappreciated sitcom gem that was "must see TV" for so many, including me. It must have been an absolute blast working on this show. I've written ten books prior to this one and I've never encountered such enthusiasm and appreciation from so many interviewees about *Wings* and this behemoth undertaking of mine. Thank you for making it so much fun. Many will keep in touch long after publication, as we've become good friends. The largest section takes the reader through all 172 episodes. Now, just anyone can binge watch the entire run of the show and write about it. My aim in writing this book is to bring what can't be seen on the screen into focus. There's more to tell about every episode and the behind-the-scenes stories are unveiled in this volume by the cast, crew, writers, directors, producers, guest stars, casting personnel, composers, and even the show's warm up guy, Robert G. Lee. Other sections of the book focus on the makeup of the characters, and the actors and actresses who portrayed them. There's also a glossary of terms unique to the show called "*Wings* Things." Even with a very diligent continuity department certain factual minutiae can sometimes fall through the cracks and to the wayside, only to be contradicted in later episodes – there's a section for that. And there's a thank you section, a dedication, an extensive index, a list of the episodes that aren't in syndication, a list of your author's Top

20 favorite episodes, a list of celebrities who are mentioned (but do not appear on the show), and countless photos of cast, crew, staff and *Wings-related* items and souvenirs (many provided by the interviewees and even many who aren't quoted in the book). So order up a "big sandwich" (I recommend the Cordoba), munch on some honey-roasted "Wingnuts" from your flight on Sandpiper Air, and savor some of Helen's coffee as you come fly with *me*. We're about to take off, so be certain that your belts are fastened, and your seats and tray tables are returned to their upright positions for takeoff. Ignore the exit signs – once you start reading, you won't want to leave.

THE PRINCIPAL ACTORS (in alphabetical order)

Crystal Bernard

Crystal Bernard was born on September 30, 1961 in Garland, Texas to Gaylon Fussell Bernard and Jerry Wayne Bernard. Crystal loved the skits performed on variety shows on TV and loved to reenact those sketches. Both Bernard and her character, Helen were born in the Lone Star State, and both are very musical. Crystal, sister Robyn and father Jerry formed a gospel group, the Bernard Trio. By the time Crystal was in her early teens, they had recorded twelve albums together. Bobbie Gentry of "Ode to Billie Joe" fame used them on one of her Las Vegas tours as background singers. In 1983, Crystal appeared on an NBC variety show called *Fantasy* as

Crystal Bernard as Helen Chappel

Crystal Bernard as Helen Chappel being "counter" productive on the set of Wings. (Courtesy of Suzanne Holmes).

an up-and-coming vocalist. On *Wings* Crystal plays a classical cellist, and as the show's creators David Lee and Peter Casey recalled, "Although very musical, she did not actually play the cello but was tutored and practiced hard to look as though she did and carried it off brilliantly."

She studied acting at Houston's Alley Theater and then was a drama major at Baylor University at the age of 18 and immediately headed off to Hollywood to pursue a career in modeling. She quickly found work in commercials. Garry Marshall liked her and used her first in the 1982 theatrical film *Young Doctors in Love* wherein Crystal played Julie in a spoof of hospital soap operas. Marshall then cast her in the 1982 season of *Happy Days* on which she portrayed Richie's cousin K. C. Cunningham. This was followed by a four-year run on the syndicated version of the sitcom *It's a Living* on which she played Amy Tompkins. Since she already had playing a server down to a science from that experience, she then snagged the toughest role to cast on *Wings,* that of Helen Chappel who ran the lunch counter at Nantucket's Airport. The role was completely rewritten for her and she played it to a tee. Her Southern accent on the series was attributed to Helen spending the first ten years of her life in Texas before moving to Nantucket Island. Guest star in the three-part "Wingless" episodes Jonathan Slavin recalled that she entertained the crowd with her singing as part of the audience warmup. Speaking of which, the warmup man Robert G. Lee said, "The cast was uniformly great – Tim Daly, Steven Weber, Tony Shalhoub and Crystal Bernard – they all stand out as being very friendly and gregarious to me. Stars don't have to be kind to the guy in the stands, but this cast was and it made my job that much more enjoyable." During this time of success on TV, Crystal never lost interest in her musical aspirations and eventually focused on recording. For a time she was making demos in her own home studio, and eventually got to record a duet with former Chicago lead singer Peter Cetera, and parlayed that into two albums for his record label. This led to a brief tour. She and Jim Messina also teamed up for a lovely tune titled "Watching the River Run." Several of her music videos can be viewed on You Tube.

Thomas Haden Church

Thomas Haden Church was born Thomas Richard McMillen on June 17, 1960. Like Farrah Forke and Crystal Bernard he has a Texas connection. Although born in Woodland, California, when his parents divorced (oddly enough, he would later co-star in a TV series titled *Divorce*), his mother took him along in her move to Texas. It was there he discovered a love for surfing. After briefly working in the Lone Star oil fields, he opted to finish high school and then attended the University of North Texas. His mother remarried and for a time his last name was Quesada, but he changed it to Haden Church, inspired by family members with those surnames. His dulcet tones led to a start in the radio business, and that went so well he decided to pursue acting and tried his luck on the West Coast. His star quality was obvious almost immediately and he was cast in the role of Gordie Brown on an episode of *Cheers* titled "Death

Thomas Haden Church as Lowell Mather

Thomas Haden Church as Lowell appears ready to raid Helen's cookie jar. He will do anything for a sugar cookie. (Courtesy of Suzanne Holmes).

Takes a Vacation on Ice." Director Rick Beren recalled, "He was so good and impressed so many on that guest shot, the *Cheers* people wanted us to see his work as we were readying the pilot for *Wings*. He is so unique, and that voice!"

Indeed, a very short time later, Thomas got to audition for the new Grub Street project titled *Wings*. He originally auditioned for the roles of Joe and Brian Hackett. David Lee and Peter Casey added, "He was so special we had to come up with something for him and that something was Lowell Mather. His delivery was unique." Steven Weber said, "Tom Church could reduce me to hysterical laughter, and both of us had a blast." Writer Lissa Kapstrom shared, "The character of Lowell was easy to write for. Kind of a savant and yet dim. He would say some really profound things among the stupid. Great comic relief." Director Leonard R. Garner, Jr. recalled, "I had one mix up with Thomas. He wanted to go to the gym after lunch. I told him it was fine but that he would have to be back on time. When he wasn't I got a bit upset with him. The next day he gave me a bottle of champagne as an apology for acting up. He played that Lowell role like no one else possibly could. He had a unique rhythm. Also, I don't know how he negotiated it but he always got paid in cash. I've never seen that happen before or since." Well, after six seasons of "winging it," Thomas wanted to leave *Wings*. He kept telling everyone that it wasn't a ploy to get more money, he just wanted to move on. He really wanted out a season earlier but was contracted through Season Six. When the pilot for his next series, *Ned and Stacey* sold and was to air on the Fox Network, the writers and producers had to adapt. Despite now being in his own starring vehicle with Debra Messing, Church agreed to come back for one final *Wings* episode to find closure (after initially being against the idea). In that episode he witnesses a mob hit in a Boston restaurant while Antonio is in the restroom and Lowell then decides to enter into the Witness Protection Program after testifying. Farrah Forke recalls a guest shot on Tom's new show, *Ned and Stacey*, "I always got along nicely with Thomas, and one day he called me and asked why I'd turned down his invitation to guest star on his new series. I knew absolutely nothing about it and called my agent to ask why they turned him down. I wanted to do it. I played a nymphomaniac in the episode, and Tom and I kissed for the first time ever. We never had reason to kiss on *Wings*. He was like a big brother to me at times. While both of us were still on *Wings*, we did a press junket together on Nantucket. It was so much fun. It was very memorable." Rebecca Schull shared, "He went on to great things, including an Oscar-nominated role in the movie *Sideways* with Paul Giamatti. We had an amazingly talented cast." While he didn't win the Oscar, he did win a "Best Supporting Actor" Emmy for an AMC project titled *Broken Trail*. He also portrayed a villain called the Sandman in *Spiderman 3*, and Robert in the aforementioned HBO series *Divorce*. He lives on a huge ranch in Kerryville, Texas and has two children from a former relationship.

Tim Daly

Tim Daly has been an actor for 40 years. He is the recipient of Theatre World, Golden Satellite, GLAAD, Gracie, and Peabody

Wings *star Tim Daly as Joe Hackett, nicknamed*
"Binder Boy" is taking copious notes.

Tim Daly on Madam Secretary, *surrounded by planes and author Bob Leszczak portraying a high-ranking Air Force man in the episode titled "Strategic Ambiguity."*

Another angle in the airplane hangar on Madam Secretary *with Tim Daly and author Bob Leszczak.*

Awards. He has been nominated for Emmy and SAG awards. He is known for the long-running comedy *Wings, Private Practice* and *The Sopranos,* and as the voice of Superman for the animated series. He most recently starred in *Madam Secretary* on CBS and the web series *The Daly Show* on YouTube. Daly has worked extensively in the theatre on and off Broadway and regionally. He is on the board of the Putney School, Inside Out Writers, and currently serves as the president of the Creative Coalition.

Farrah Forke

Farrah Forke was born a Capricorn on January 12, 1968 in Corpus Christi, Texas – yet another of *Wings'* Texas connections. Forke shared, "I was named after Farrah Fawcett. True story. And I was a huge fan of hers, thinking as a child, 'If she can do it so can I.'" Farrah attended an all-girls private school – the Hockaday School in Dallas and became a cheerleader in high school. She got the acting bug while appearing in a Lone Star production of *The Rocky Horror Picture Show* and pursued it as a career after studying at the famous Lee Strasberg Institute in New York. After appearing in her first film, *Brain Twisters* in 1991 she got to join the cast of the already-established NBC sitcom *Wings* as helicopter pilot Alex Lambert in 1992. About her character, Forke said, "I am really nothing like her but the toughness I got to display as a real bartender in New York at closing time prepared me for the role of Alex. I would lower the tone of my voice to show I meant business and I used that in my

Farrah Forke as helicopter pilot Alex Lambert joined the cast in the episode titled "Two Jerks and a Jill" in Season Four.

audition. I knew I could play her." She added, "I was so green and so nervous. There were so many people around, and four cameras. My hands used to shake in the early episodes. You'll see me holding coffee cups with both hands to control the shaking." She added, "It was a great learning experience. I learned so much, especially from Steven Weber and Tony Shalhoub." Writer Rick Copp said "The Alex character played by Forke was difficult to write for. She was still relatively new at the time and I remember having a tough time nailing down the voice and giving her jokes. It had nothing at all to do with her performance. I just felt that the character was not clear, at least to me." When she wasn't asked back for Season Six of the sitcom, Forke said, "It was a surprise and very painful then. It still hurts today. Although I did get to go back one more time for one of the Mary Pat Lee episodes. By the way, the woman who played Lee, Caroline Aaron is a dear friend." After *Wings* Forke kept very busy with a role in Robert DeNiro's *Heat* and Barry Levinson's *Disclosure;* a couple of sitcoms – *Dweebs* and *Mr. Rhodes;* a recurring role as Mayson Drake on *Lois and Clark;* and a guest shot with her old *Wings* co-star Thomas Haden Church on his Fox sitcom *Ned and Stacey*. Forke's fondest memory of *Wings* is, "Meeting the father of my children, Mark Layton Brown. He worked in the Art Department." Forke says, "I have no plans to return to Hollywood. I love my life here in Texas, raising my twin boys. Life is good."

Brian Haley

Brian Haley was born on Abraham Lincoln's birthday, February 12, 1963 in Seattle, Washington. He was the fifth of sixth children, and he would later have a large family with five children of his own. He is of Irish and Italian descent, the latter explaining his middle name of Carlo. Coincidentally, his father was an airline executive (foreshadowing his airline role on *Wings*) and the family briefly lived in Quebec, Canada. While still in his early teens he had his first experience as an extra on a small Connie Stevens film titled *Scorchy*. The acting career was placed on the back burner for a stint in the Green Berets. About his military years, Haley shared, "I went through Special Forces training in the regular army from 1980 to 1983, in the reserves after that for a few years, but my stand up career started to take off so I got out of my commitment early. Nothing was going on. I was in at a time when there were no conflicts (1980 - 86). I tell people I did a lot of pushups and jumped out of a lot of aircraft, that about sums it up. I was a medic and that has come in handy. The SF medical course is very intense. Our doctor instructors didn't care much for us because we were doing after six months what took them twelve years to accomplish. They called us gorillas with scalpels. Ops, baby."

After his tour of duty he became a headliner who eventually got his big break on *The Tonight Show Starring Johnny Carson*. Success at stand-up led him back to acting, and numerous movie roles. His *Wings* break came when he replaced Thomas Haden Church as the new mechanic for Sandpiper Air and Aeromass. Director Leonard R. Garner, Jr. called Brian, "A really great actor."

Along with numerous other roles on the small screen, Haley's big screen credits include *Gran Torino, The Taking of Pelham 123, Mars Attacks, The Departed* and *Pearl Harbor*. As of this writing, his most recent credit was *Escape at Dannemora*. Did he get to work with any of the *Wings* gang again? Haley said, "I worked with Tony Shalhoub on The Coen Brothers' movie *The Man Who Wasn't There*, but we weren't in any scenes together."

David Schramm

David Michael Schramm was born in Louisville, Kentucky on August 14, 1946. It's not well known, but his father was a bookie and young David and he spent a lot of time at the track. Acting was a way of life for Schramm since his teen years and he garnered a lot of experience in his native Kentucky's many large outdoor productions. He studied acting at Western Kentucky University and earned a full scholarship to the prestigious Julliard School. Actor John Houseman took him under his wing after seeing him in *King Lear*, saying it was the best adaptation he'd ever seen. David didn't begin to pursue film and TV work until he was already in his 40s. He co-starred alongside a couple of heavyweights in 1989 – *Let It Ride* with Richard Dreyfuss, and *A Shock to the System* with Michael Caine.

Next came his defining role, that of snarky, conniving, brash, frugal, loud, larger-than-life and yet insecure Roy Biggins on *Wings*.

David Schramm and Charlotte Booker in a 2018 production of Cat on a Hot Tin Roof *at the Baltimore Center Stage. (Courtesy of Charlotte Booker).*

While others were a bit skeptical, Schramm is said to have been certain of *Wings'* success right from the start. About Schramm, nicknamed "Schrammy," Tim Daly said, "He was hilarious. A quirky, funny guy. If you notice, in many scenes he's holding a clipboard. One day I approached him about it and looked at what was on there – it was his lines. What a brilliant comic actor. Watching him was like a comedy clinic. That song and dance routine he did to 'Buttons and Bows' in the episode titled 'Try to Remember the Night He Dismembered' was simply awesome. He knew how to squeeze every last drop of juice out of a scene. A reliable comic actor who could always find the funny." Creators David Lee and Peter Casey said, "Paramount had lined up auditions in New York for Schramm, Weber and Schull. We had previously seen Schramm at the Pasadena Playhouse in *Born Yesterday* and he was amazing." Rebecca Schull said, "I spent a lot of down time with David Schramm as neither of us was a lead character on *Wings*. We were very good friends. We went to the opera together often during the series, and even after it ended." Farrah Forke shared, "We were close friends. He could always make me laugh. He loved to shop. In fact, almost every piece of furniture in my house he encouraged me to buy, even when it was something above my pay grade. He got chills going into a fabric store. I didn't need a coffee table, but he talked me into it. His own house was extraordinary. He should have been a decorator. He, Caroline Aaron [Mary Pat Lee] and I often had dinner parties." Even though she was not part of the *Wings* cast, actress Charlotte Booker of TV's *Hi, Honey, I'm Home* was among the last people to work with Schramm on stage. She shared, "I first met him in 1992 in a Cleveland Playhouse production of Ayckbourn's *Man of the Moment* with Howard Hesseman. We became fast friends and we went to many NBC parties and Julliard fundraisers together. I was always amazed at how starstruck he could be. We didn't work together again until 2018 in *Cat on a Hot Tin Roof* at Baltimore Center Stage, directed by Judith Ivey who had played opposite David on Broadway almost 40 years earlier. David was born to play Big Daddy, and I was lucky to play his long-suffering wife, Big Mama. We had more fun onstage than anyone. There was always a twinkle in Big Daddy's eye when he was especially cruel to Big Mama – he elevated the rest of us with his commitment, skill, generosity, and passion. He was having some physical problems then, but I honestly expected him to be around much longer by strength of sheer will. I miss him profoundly and am sorry we'll never attack the other projects we'd planned – like playing Charles Laughton and Elsa Lanchester together. He'd have been transcendent. I'm glad you're writing this book, Bob, so that David will be remembered." David Schramm died of a heart attack on March 28, 2020 during the height of New York's Coronavirus outbreak. Tim Daly added, "He was very kind – a human being. It was an honor and a pleasure to have been able to work with him."

Rebecca Schull

Rebecca Schull was born in New York City on February 22, 1929 as Rebecca Anna Wattenberg. She shares that birthday with "the father of our country," George Washington. Coincidentally (or not) her three ex-husbands on the long-running NBC sitcom *Wings* were named George (and she almost married a fourth). In real life, she married Gene Schull in 1951. Rebecca studied acting in Dublin at the Stanislavski Studio and her first professional work was at the Focus Theater there. She returned to the U. S. in 1975, and the following year earned a role as a nursemaid in Dore Shary's *Herzl* on Broadway. She turned most of her attention to television in the

Rebecca Schull as Fay Evelyn Cochran

That's the ticket – Rebecca Schull in front of her ticket counter at Sandpiper Air. (Courtesy of Suzanne Holmes).

1980s and quickly found a recurring role on the soap opera *One Life to Live* on ABC. In 1985 she had a role in the Lucille Ball TV movie *Stone Pillow* on which Lucy portrayed a homeless woman and lots of other film work followed. Her forte was comedy and she honed her comedic chops in guest starring roles on countless sitcoms including *Roseanne, Eisenhower and Lutz* (on which she had a recurring role), *Newhart* and *Hooperman* (with John Ritter who would later do a guest shot on *Wings*). In 1990, she secured her most famous role – that of Fay Evelyn Cochran, the ticket agent for Sandpiper Air on *Wings*. The show's creators, David Lee and Peter Casey said, "Most female aviators had three names, so we gave her three. We had seen Schull in *The Matchmaker* at the La Jolla Playhouse playing a great, funny elderly woman and knew she'd be perfect for Fay." Some of Fay's funniest moments on the series were her inappropriate announcements over the terminal microphone. Writer Ian Gurvitz said, "Rebecca really nailed the character and she was easy to write jokes for because she knew how to deliver them. She had a dry, understated wit and sly delivery." Several years after *Wings*, Rebecca got to work again with Steven Weber who said, "I had fun working on a show with her titled *Chasing Life* on the ABC Family Channel. It was a nice reunion." Rebecca recalled, "I got to work with one of our guest stars, Kelsey Grammer again on *Frasier*" [the episode is titled "RDWRER"]. She also had a recurring role on USA Network's popular *Suits* series. She added, "I've heard rumors about a possible *Wings* reboot." Coincidentally, Schull also co-starred in a post-9/11 film titled *United 93*. She said, "The movie was shot in England and was an amazing experience. Just fascinating. Director Paul Greengrass was so smart." She has three children and two grandchildren. Her husband Gene Schull passed on in 2008. Gene had a walk-on role as the man in lederhosen in the 1993 episode titled "Goodbye, Old Friend."

Before Wings, *Tony Shalhoub was a co-star in Broadway's female edition of Neil Simon's* The Odd Couple *starring Rita Moreno and Sally Struthers.*

Tony Shalhoub

Anthony Marcus Shalhoub was born the ninth of ten children in Green Bay, Wisconsin on October 9, 1953. It's an amazing parallel that his parents were named Helen and Joe (Steven Weber was astounded when I told him about that). His was an Arabic-speaking Christian household of Lebanese descent. His Master's Degree from the Yale School of Drama has served him well. Before joining this sitcom set in Massachusetts, Shalhoub spent four years in Cambridge with the American Repertory Theater. Next stop – Broadway

Tony Shalhoub's name appears in Playbill *as a cast member of the female version of Neil Simon's* The Odd Couple *on Broadway at the Broadhurst Theater.*

for a role in the female adaptation of *The Odd Couple* starring Sally Struthers and Rita Moreno at the Broadhurst Theater. Then came a guest shot on *Wings* as a character named Antonio Scarpacci, a waiter on the Valentine's Day episode titled "Looking for Love in all the Wrong Places" in Season Two. The one-shot role turned into much more. Creators David Lee and Peter Casey said, "He absolutely killed it as the waiter. We knew we had to write for him and add him to the cast. So many auditioned for the waiter but they were doing really bad Italian accents. Tony's was very subtle. He was brilliant. We found the way the bring him into the airport – as a cab driver." Rebecca Schull added, "Yes, we knew how good he was from that first guest shot. They signed him to join the cast almost immediately." Writer/producer Steven Levitan said, "We were all in awe of Tony's talents. Also, he's one of the nicest guys on the planet so when I was looking for a lead for *Stark Raving Mad*, I thought Tony was ready for his starring moment. That we had worked together previously made coming together that much easier." Guest star Jonathan Slavin from the three "Wingless" episodes said, "We didn't have any scenes together but in the short time we were around one another I could see that he was a great guy." Farrah Forke shared, "Tony taught me something very important. There were a couple of weeks there when he had only about three lines. I asked him if that bothered him. He told me that he still gets the same amount of money for those weeks, so every

SCENES FROM

THE ODD COUPLE

Top left: Rita Moreno. Top right: Sally Struthers. Center: Marilyn Cooper, Mary Louise Wilson, Jenny O'Hara, Kathleen Doyle and Rita Moreno. Bottom: Sally Struthers, Lewis J. Stadlen and Tony Shalhoub.

26

Tony Shalhoub and the cast of The Odd Couple *in* Playbill *at the Broadhurst Theater.*

'and' and 'but' that were part of his sides those weeks were especially profitable – worth even more than on weeks with a large amount of dialogue." Beginning with the second episode of Season Three titled "Is that a Subpoena in Your Pocket?" Shalhoub was cast as sad sack, down-on-his-luck, dateless/loveless cabdriver Antonio Scarpacci – a regular fixture. His restaurant closed after being sued by the family of a man who choked on a chicken bone, so he became a hack. He remained with *Wings* until its end in 1997. During his time on *Wings,* Tony also starred in highly acclaimed indie picture *Big Night,* along with an episode of David Lee, Peter Casey and David Angell's other hit sitcom, *Frasier* titled "The Focus Group" on which Tony portrayed an Arabic owner of a newsstand who is the only one who says he doesn't like Frasier Crane's radio program. After *Wings,* came the aforementioned NBC sitcom – *Stark Raving Mad* on which he co-starred for a season with Neil Patrick Harris. While that show wasn't a whopping success, his next venture was – *Monk* on the USA Network. As Adrian Monk, the obsessive/compulsive detective, he garnered three Emmy Awards out of eight consecutive nominations. Tim Daly guest starred on an episode of *Monk* titled "Mr. Monk and the Airplane" and *Wings* is referenced in the dialogue. Tony won a Tony for Best Actor in a Musical for *The Band's Visit.* Tim Daly said, "We both do a lot of theater. Tony comes to see my work, and I go to see his. I saw his Tony-winning performance." And still more Emmys and Golden Globes were to follow for his role as former math professor Abe Weissman, the father of Midge Maisel on Amazon Prime's *The Marvelous Mrs. Maisel.* Caroline Aaron, aka Mary Pat Lee also co-stars on that series as Shirley Maisel (and your author regularly plays a tailor on that show). After receiving a Grammy nomination for Best Spoken Word Album in 2008 it became obvious that it would be only a matter of time until he was an EGOT (winner of an Emmy, Grammy, Oscar and Tony). As of this writing he's halfway there. During the pandemic of 2020, both Tony and his actress wife Brooke Adams (who did a guest shot on *Wings* as a nun in the episode titled "All about Christmas Eve") were quarantined because of exposure to the virus, but fully recovered after a few weeks. With facemasks, hand sanitizer, rubber gloves and all forms of PPE, Shalhoub in his own words said that we are all Monk now

Steven Weber

A "salute" to Brian Michael Hackett and one of his trademark gaudy neckties.

Steven Robert Weber was born in Queens, New York on March 4, 1961. Show business "was in his blood" as his father was a theatrical agent for comedians and singers and his mother a singer in New York City nightclubs. He carried on the family tradition by attending the High School of Performing Arts and the State University of New York at Purchase. His early training was in theater, but he soon secured TV work on *As the World Turns* playing opposite Julianne Moore, and then came a film role in Garry Marshall's *The Flamingo Kid*. In the 1990 ABC miniseries *The Kennedys of Massachusetts* he gained acclaim for his role as a young John F. Kennedy. Speaking of Massachusetts, his next role kept him there for seven years. Others may have auditioned for the role of carefree skirt-chaser Brian Hackett, but Weber was the definitive choice. When asked how he is most like and unlike Brian, Steven Weber said, "I guess we are similar in that we both possess a good deal of snark and have a penchant for making – hopefully - amusing jokes. While I did my share of skirt-chasing back in the day, I don't think I was anywhere near the obsessive that Brian was. And the show never really explored any particular depth to the character, so it's hard to say how I'm like or unlike him beyond the obvious, 'I'm not a pilot!'" He elaborated, "I've never flown a plane. Not sure I have the intellectual capacity. There was a moment when an actual pilot came to the set to give Tim and me a quick lesson so we looked authentic pressing all the buttons and flipping all the switches in the cockpit, but even what the guy told us was quickly forgotten and any button-pushing/switch-flipping was strictly improvised. I fully expect some alien culture to have built their technology around our fake pilot behavior, like in *Galaxy Quest*." Brian is quite the sports fan. Is that also true of Steven? He said, "I lost the sports gene when I was young. My dad was a classic 'screaming at the radio/ TV while watching a game' type of guy and that didn't appeal to me very much. To this day I have very little pop sports knowledge." So, sports fan, no. Prankster, yes. Weber shared, "I have to say that I was probably the biggest upstart/prankster/joker on the set. There's a reason those blooper reels are mostly me laughing or messing around. But Tom Church could also reduce me to hysterical laughter and both of us had a blast being devilish." Were the love scenes on *Wings* with Farrah Forke awkward? Weber shared, "Well she is gorgeous so it was nothing other than enjoyable. And the scenes themselves weren't elaborate, so we kissed and moved on." What about Brian's loud neckties. Were they yours? Weber said, "I don't know why that was so prevalent, especially in the early seasons. They weren't mine, of course. Yikes! I think it was to illustrate that Brian was 'wild and crazy' in contrast to Joe's buttoned-up style. After a few seasons, the ties went the way of all things, though." David Lee and Peter Casey added, "Costuming did that, but likely Steven had some say. Because Joe was notorious for not paying his pilots well it's great that we had Brian reuse many of his out-fits." Weber is fondly remembered by cast and crew as gregarious. Farrah Forke said, "When I joined the show, Steven Weber took me around to visit the stage. I saw the bleachers there next to the stage and asked what they were for, not realizing that *Wings* was done before a studio audience. He was very kind and helpful. I also learned something very important from him. He talked to every-one and treated even those 'below-the-line' workers equally. He was kind to the extras. I'll never forget that." Guest star on the "Murder She Roast" episode, Andrew Bilgore recalled, "I remember Ste-ven Weber making me feel welcomed and even offering the use of his dressing room phone if needed. This made a big impression upon me and I always try to live up to his example toward guest cast." Director Rick Beren had a most unusual Weber anecdote, "He wanted to buy my high-top leather shoes that I had specially made by Converse. I got them to make the shoes under the guise of needing them for Sam Malone on *Cheers* on which I also worked. Weber loved them and offered to buy them but respected me for saying no." Writer Lissa Kapstrom said, "Brian was easy to write for – kind of goofy. Steven and I had an instant connection." After eight seasons on *Wings*, Weber earned his own starring vehicle on NBC. It was originally called *Cursed*, but the network stepped in and said, "You can't have a guy losing every week. There has to be some winning." So, the show was altered quite a bit and the title changed to *The Weber Show*. Steven shared, "The show started out one way, people wanted it to go another way and I was all swept up in the glory of it all, having my own show. But it needed to be much better than it was. It was cool to be with a lot of old friends, however. Quite a few of the people I worked with on *Wings* [Lissa Kapstrom, Ellen Byron, Tommy Cole] came over to the new show. It made for an easier transition." Brian Hackett was the only *Wings* character to surface on another series. He played Ajax's long-lost brother on an episode of the animated series *Duckman* (although Brian was not animated and the scene took place in Joe's office at the airport). Weber said, "I always loved doing voices for animation and even though I wasn't animated in this one, I jumped at the chance. I don't remember much about it beyond the fact that I did it." Providing the voices for multiple characters on the animated *Ultimate Spiderman* was much more memorable. His other series post-*The Weber Show* include *Studio 60 on the Sunset Strip, Happy Town, Chasing Life, NCIS New Orleans,* and most recently *Indebted* on NBC with Fran Drescher. Has he gotten to work with any of the *Wings* gang again? Weber said, "I saw Andy Ackerman and Rick Beren on *Indebted,* I've worked with Tony Shalhoub on *Monk* and *Stark Raving Mad,* Rebecca Schull on the ABC Family show *Chasing Life,* and Tim Daly on his hilarious on-line show *The Daly Show.*" Had *Wings* returned for a ninth season, or if there was ever a reboot Weber shared, "I would continue forever. Jobs like that are hard to come by – ones that are so much fun and are of great quality. In a heartbeat."

Amy Yasbeck

Amy Marie Yasbeck was born in Blue Ash, Ohio on September 12, 1962. Her father was a butcher, and like Tony Shalhoub, of Lebanese descent. Both parents were already in their 40s when they had Amy, and both passed on while she was in her very early 20s. Amy's first taste of stardom came as a child when she was featured with a shock of red hair on the box in which the famous Kenner Betty Crocker Easy Bake Oven came. After graduation she moved to New York to pursue an acting career. After guest shots on shows such as *Dallas* and *China Beach,* she briefly became a regular on *Days of Our Lives,* and then got to play the mermaid in the movie sequel *Splash, Too.* She joined the cast of *Wings* in Season Six as

*Amy Yasbeck with her suitcases packed for her move
back to her native Nantucket in "Twisted Sister."*

Helen's elder sister, Casey Davenport – the rich, snooty one. In an early episode of the series titled "Terminal Christmas" Helen's sister was referenced, but her first name was Lorraine (please see the inconsistencies section). Casey was short for Cassandra, and Helen's parents always tended to prefer Casey because she was married to the very successful Stuart who earned a fortune in the corn pad industry. When Casey returns to Nantucket, she is separated and penniless. Yasbeck joined the show in 1994 and remained until the very end in 1997. Over that time, she and Brian (Steven Weber) had a relationship that was based solely on sexual attraction – they had nothing else in common. About those episodes, Weber said, "The episodes where Amy and I were together were hysterically funny and we had a ball doing them." Her character eventually stops mooching off of Helen. She finds work first in the tourism industry and later in a department store. While they were still dating, Amy brought her significant other, John Ritter over to play her ex-husband, Stuart on a memorable *Wings* episode "Love Overboard." Director Leonard R. Garner, Jr. said, "John and Amy were brilliant together. He was an incredible physical comedian." Amy and John were wed in 1999, and only four years later on September 11, 2003, while on the set of his newest sitcom, *8 Simple Rules for Dating My Teenage Daughter,* Ritter suffered what was thought to be a heart attack. When he died later that day the cause was found to be a previously undiagnosed congenital heart defect. After *Wings* Amy co-starred in a couple of short-lived sitcoms – *Alright Already* and *Life on a Stick.* The once very busy actress recently chose to slow things down, taking a break over the past few years to focus on and spend time with her family.

THE MAIN CHARACTERS

He called everyone by their surname, so your author would have been simply "Leszczak." David Schramm as Roy Biggins behind the Aeromass counter. (Courtesy of Suzanne Holmes).

Roy Peterman Biggins

Played to perfection by the late David Schramm, Roy Peterman Biggins is the owner of Aeromass, the larger of two airlines operating at Nantucket Island's Tom Nevers Field. Instigator Roy has seven planes, compared to the one owned by his only competitor, tiny Sandpiper Air, run by the flighty Hackett Brothers, Joe and Brian. Roy's business was able to "get off the ground" because of money willed to him by an uncle. He wants to expand by having another hangar built, and never ceases to flaunt his success and business savvy to his "fly-by-night" competitors. His laugh resembles that of Muttley in the old *Dastardly and Muttley* cartoons. Despite his successes, he does feel threatened by Sandpiper and makes frequent attempts to purchase the company. He is jealous of Joe and Brian because of their youth, their looks, their success with the ladies, and their occasional charter flights (charters are the one nut he has yet to crack).

A doppelganger for Oliver Hardy, Roy's last name of Biggins is most apropos as he is big - a larger-than-life presence in the terminal who claims to have a cholesterol count of 325. The Oliver Hardy resemblance is reinforced in the episode titled "The Waxman Cometh." Roy's motto is, "If it's green it's trouble, if it's fried get double." He has chili for breakfast almost every morning. He played semi-pro football in his youth. Roy calls everyone by their surname (Hackett, Cochran, Chappel, Scarpacci, Lambert) and sometimes refers to zany Fay as Amelia Airhead, calls Joe "Sparky," refers to Antonio as "Pastahead" or "Spaghettihead," and sometimes uses the nickname "Sweetcakes" for Helen. He sees women as sex objects and has a collection of *Playboy Magazines* in his office. He is immediately aware if anyone has touched, taken or rearranged those magazines. He also has an erotic candle and decanter collection and often refers to women as chicks, dolls, skirts, dames, toots, babes and broads. He had a blow-up doll named Ramona – that is until she exploded. He loves the music of Slim Whitman and was born on Leap Day, February 29, 1948. Because his true birthday only comes around every four years he claims to be one-quarter of his actual age. His hairline has a bigger oil slick than the Exxon Valdez; his suits are cheap, tacky, loud and usually made of polyester. He wears Sansabelt slacks; and his home has orange shag carpeting and a picture of famous clown Emmett Kelly made out of macaroni shells. He is the butt of many jokes mostly from Brian, Helen and Fay.

Roy is the poster boy for insurance fraud and tax evasion - setting up fake charities and lying about having 26 children as dependents. He also lies about the presence of life jackets under the seats of his planes. He is dishonest, conniving, a practical joker, cruel to his employees, very manipulative and full of bravado. Roy loves to rub peoples' noses in their flaws, shortcomings, foibles and misfortunes but is not able to take doses of his own medicine. He is rarely invited to play in any reindeer games. He was married once to a woman named Sylvia (played by Concetta Tomei) and early on tells everyone that Sylvia is dead, but in reality she left him for a successful Boston plastic surgeon. Together Roy and Sylvia had a son, R. J. (Roy, Jr., played by Abraham Benrubi) who is gay and proud. At first the boy is shunned by Roy after coming out, but Roy eventually softens and becomes more accepting of the situation because he loves R. J. Roy's attempts to reconcile and reunite with Sylvia fall flat.

Roy has a metal plate in his head from an incident in the stands at a baseball game when he attempted to swipe his brother's Milk Duds and was hit with a brick. He wins a seat on the city council, but almost loses the election to Fay. He can play "Yankee Doodle" in pooty noises by squeezing his palms together repeatedly (and his version of "Yankee Doodle" is a dandy). He is a minister at the Church of Universal Harmony (a tax writeoff) and can perform wedding ceremonies. He loves Jane Pauley, Barbra Streisand, and has an autographed picture of Richard Nixon in his office. He is surprisingly light on his feet for a big guy. He can sing the National Anthem (except for that one high note). However, he was humiliated when he passed out because of nerves in his first attempt to sing "The Star-Spangled Banner" at a Boston Red Sox game – a scenario embarrassingly rerun on local TV for weeks afterward. To make matters worse he is introduced as Roy Baggins and Ray Buggins. His walkie talkie handle is "Raging Stallion." He pets a stuffed hamster when stressed, likes the Grateful Dead and pro wrestling, and makes the best pasta salad on the island (with tortellini and dill). He calls many different people as well as a pet rat "Cupcake." He was once arrested attempting to board Air Force One to meet President George H. W. Bush. He drives a bright purple El Camino, and cares for his cranky, crusty and demanding mother Eleanor "Bluto" Biggins. She lives in a nursing home and is only alluded to until the Eighth Season episode titled "Heartache Tonight" (when she is portrayed with much vinegar and volume by Rose Marie).

Roy's often venomous and vindictive personality is merely a way of compensating for a wealth of insecurities. He is the antagonist and seemingly unlikeable, and yet beloved by viewers — a tricky balance managed with much aplomb by seasoned professional David Schramm. Roy does occasionally try to be a nicer, better person - a ray or is that a Roy of humanity amidst all his vitriol is sometimes visible.

Budd Bronski

A scene from "The Big Sleep" in which Joe dreams that Budd Bronski has a crush on him. Left to right Steven Weber, Tim Daly, Brian Haley.

The character of Budd Bronski, portrayed by Brian Haley, was the replacement mechanic after Lowell Mather entered the Witness Protection Plan. He was hired by Brian and appears in only eight episodes of the series.

Information about Budd is scarce in comparison to the show's other recurring characters. He is a former Marine, and still sports a crew cut. He has an "incident" on his record about which he hates to talk. It involves a crash and a court martial (which is eventually reversed). Despite being exonerated he still harbors much guilt over this. As a result of "the incident," he double checks every bit of his work on the airplanes, often chiding himself and overreacting for failing to remember to do some small element of his job. He is shy, very skittish, awkward at parties, and has difficulty interacting with others but loves cats. He does a few tricks, including being able to hide a lit cigarette in his mouth.

Fay Evelyn Schlob Dumbly DeVay Cochran

She certainly made a "name" for herself. Fay Evelyn Schlob Dumbly DeVay Cochran gets ready to make another bizarre announcement on the terminal microphone.

Played brilliantly by Rebecca Schull for eight seasons, Fay lives at 205 Elm Street and handles the ticket counter and baggage check for tiny Sandpiper Air. She is also responsible for the flight announcements, many of which are bizarre, inappropriate and frankly alarming to the passengers. Upon reading what I had written about her character, Rebecca Schull said, "I think it's terrific. It's full of facts I had no recollection of at all. Thank you for doing this." Ms. Schull, the pleasure is all mine.

Fay grew up in a two-story rowhouse in Syracuse, New York, but is well-traveled and previously lived in New York City, Atlanta, St. Louis and Hawaii before settling on Nantucket Island. She spent a summer with the traveling carnival. While in Syracuse she was a soda jerk at Woolworth's and entertained the troops in the U. S. O. as a drummer in an all-girl band in Korea. She was at Cape Canaveral when they tested the first Mercury rocket. She is a former stewardess who sometimes pumped fuel and once had to kick down the landing gear. She also put in many years as a flight attendant who was forced into retirement because of her age. She was the first to use the emergency exit gesture on a flight. As a stewardess she was once snowbound in Butte, Montana. On her last day as a flight attendant she met passenger Joe Hackett and formed an instant bond. She has been married and widowed three times and each husband was named George. Two of the Georges passed on in the month of June. She woke up next to her third George in Reno and grew to love him. She almost unwittingly married a fourth George. She knew him as Lyle, but his real first name was George. We get to see the Georges (or at least their ghosts) in an episode titled "Fay There, Georgy Girl" in which Fay finally decides to let go of her late husbands' personal effects. In an earlier episode titled "The Faygitive" we learn all of Fay's amusing surnames. She was born into the humble, hard-working Schlob family, which Joe Hackett snidely refers to as a long line of "Poor Schlobs." Her first George, the dentist had the amusing surname of Dumbly which she took on only because it was better than Schlob. He was a Golden Gloves boxer and she was his "corner man." She didn't mind the bad language in the ring but despised the spitting. George Dumbly met his demise being hit by a truck. Next came the most amusing of all, George DeVay which led to Fay being asked such things as, "Will you show me DeVay?" and "Do you go all DeVay?" The best line in this scene is, "Old soldiers never die, they just Fay DeVay." Her third and final George, who liked to sew had the surname of Cochran, which might lead one to think of it as a tribute to the pioneer female pilot Jacqueline Cochran (for whom an airport in California's Coachella Valley is named), but Schull said, "No, I don't think so. I am aware of her and her story but I think this is merely a coincidence." George Cochran died in his favorite chair. They owned a boat together. She briefly dated a Funk of the Funk and Wagnall's Encyclopedia fame, and appropriately is a good speller and a member of the Historical Society. She once punched out Abbie Hoffman and her hand smelled of marijuana for a long time thereafter. She once weaved a basket out of an old lawn chair.

Over the 172 episodes of *Wings* we discover many things about Fay. She loves artichokes and scallops and some of her favorite entertainers are Lucille Ball, Regis Philbin and Barbra Streisand. She has impure thoughts about David Brinkley and had a pet rock named Engelbert. She shoots skeet, loves bowling, pro wrestling, boxing and all animals (and once had a dachshund/wiener dog who slept at the foot of her bed). She is a birdwatcher. When asked about some of these things Schull said, "I like artichokes and I like animals, but I'm not passionate about either one." She sometimes gives pedicures, belongs to a quilting club, occasionally tells fortunes, won the Volunteer of the Year Award for her roadside trash pickup work, was arrested in a 1966 anti-war rally, is taking psychology classes at the community college, plays in the senior tennis tournament, loves politics, plays canasta, makes great double fudge brownies but terrible lemon bars, loves the first name of Katherine, has experience in welding, and has touched every first lady since Eleanor Roosevelt. Her favorite color is blue, she is often teased about her large feet (gunboats), she drives a Plymouth Duster, one of her Schlob ancestors was on the Mayflower, she is an honorary Sioux Indian, belongs to a senior dance group, is a creature of habit, used to take in boarders, wants to be cremated and faints at the sight of blood. She has a sunny personality, is batty but kindly, yet can be quite manipulative. She does not take criticism well, cries easily, is often too honest, can be a busybody, and has a terrible handwriting (her fives look like eights, and the word overdue looks like omelet). When asked about the latter Schull admitted, "Yes, that is true, I have terrible handwriting." In the show's last two seasons Fay becomes a bit more controlling, surly, often barking out orders to the Hackett boys. Though years may pass, the smiles and laughs Rebecca Schull brought to the Fay character will never "Fay DeVay."

Cassandra "Casey" Chappel Davenport

Casey Chappel Davenport, portrayed by Amy Yasbeck is Helen's older sister. Her real first name is Cassandra and she was named for the Greek goddess. She was also raised on Nantucket Island, but was born in Texas to which she later returns. Unlike Helen, she managed to lose her Texas twang, as well as her husband, Stuart (played by Amy's real-life love interest and eventual husband John Ritter) and his money from success in the corn pad industry. Casey and Helen's parents opted to return to Texas to live near "the married one." Later, Casey and Stuart had a palatial home on Knob Hill where she was on the board of the San Francisco opera and once served Placido Domingo quiche. When the marriage falls apart and Casey's snooty, upper crust lifestyle comes to a screeching halt, she returns to Nantucket with her tail between her legs attempting to start a new life there. She has little money, Stuart has canceled her credit cards, and she has no skills necessary to earn a living - crashing and burning with almost every new employment opportunity. She manages to keep her tourism and salesclerk jobs the longest. She once had her hair cut by Lowell's cousin Beevo, a dog groomer (who also shaved animals for surgery).

Casey was a bit of a snitch in school, and later earned the nickname "Easy Casey" because of her sexual appetite. Lilies are her favorite flower, Snickers is her favorite candy bar, and she worships Oprah Winfrey. Antonio finds her irresistible, but never can conjure up the nerve to divulge his feelings or ask her out on a date (often just hemming and hawing, stammering and growling in her presence). For whatever reason, her red tresses become a bit browner in the show's final season. She and Brian have a loveless, purely sexual on-again/off-again fling that begins the night before Joe and Helen's wedding. During one of their hot romantic escapades her bra unknowingly lands near the fireplace and ignites (and quickly burns down) Helen's house. As a result, Joe, Helen, Brian and Casey all begrudgingly live under one roof (Joe and Brian's house).

Estranged husband Stuart is spotted in the audience at a televised sporting event and has a connecting flight at Tom Nevers Field where he runs into Casey and she discovers that he lied about being broke. In fact, Stuart still has his yacht and a goodly amount of cash (which she throws into the ocean). Their divorce is eventually finalized. Casey takes over Helen's lunch counter in the final episode.

Brian Michael Hackett

Brian Michael Hackett, played by Steven Weber is a Pisces and is the younger brother of Joseph Montgomery Hackett, owner of tiny Sandpiper Air, a one-plane airline in a one-seahorse Massachusetts sea town. When Brian returns to Nantucket Island he arrives via Sandpiper's competitor Aeromass. Joe and Brian have been estranged for six years with good reason – Brian stole Joe's fiancé, Carol (Kim Johnston Ulrich) and married her. His first date with Carol was at the top of the famous Prudential building in Boston. After she left and eventually divorced him, Brian threw a Hail Mary pass at a reconciliation by meeting Carol in that very same location but was unsuccessful. When the brothers make up after so many years apart, Brian is hired to take some of the piloting burden off Joe and comes in especially handy when Joe is temporarily grounded for having high blood pressure. The brothers could not be more different – Joe is tidy, by the book, very OCD. Brian flies by the seat of his pants. He is irresponsible - a free spirit who worms his way out of every predicament with charm and guile. There is a real *Odd Couple* dynamic to their relationship. When asked about that Steven Weber said, "It's a classic dynamic and has been around a long time in one form or another, the two contrasting characters who nevertheless compliment and even love each other. They are definitely related, but Brian isn't as sloppy nor dark as Oscar." Brian once painted his brother blue. He has been known to sit in the park while letting pigeons eat popcorn out of his mouth. Brian sometimes wears Robert Parish tee shirts in early episodes. About sports fan Brian Hackett Weber said, "I lost the sports gene when I was very young. It's just one of the ways Brian and I differ." When he wears a tie (especially in early seasons), it is usually one with two large commas on it. By wearing very loud, colorful shirts and ties with high top sneakers he conforms to the professional climate of

Sandpiper Air in the least possible conformist way. Each brother has the same Achilles heel – pretty girls.

Brian and Joe's mom Mae Hackett ran out on them at an early age. This left Joe, the elder to become the responsible one – even more so when their dad, Donald became increasingly unstable. Donald's last words were, "Sit on my lap, Eydie" – thinking his son was singer Eydie Gorme. Donald did leave behind one priceless gift willed to the boys – a suitcase full of keys which incited a wild goose chase. The chase was not totally in vain, however, as it helped the estranged brothers heal and reunite. Brian wore braces and had acne in high school. In their youth the Hackett brothers slept in bunk beds. For a time Brian slept underneath said bunk beds after his mom deserted the family. He used to tell people that his mom was Shirley, the matriarch of *The Partridge Family*. In later years, Mae Hackett was found. She had been in prison for embezzlement and worked in the lockdown's laundry. Brian loved his Schwinn bicycle (a gift from his dad) and slept with it, dreamed of becoming a spy, and adored *Captain Kangaroo* whom he envisioned as somewhat of a father figure. He continued carrying a piece of his lucky childhood blue blanket with him well into adulthood. He never fully managed to outgrow the issues of his formative years, and squandered every opportunity afforded him – most notably a scholarship to Princeton University, a job at TWA, and acceptance into the astronaut program at NASA as their youngest trainee. Then came a stint as a charter pilot for Iguana Airlines ("We're ugly but we get you there") in Mustique, West Indies (where he lived with wife, Carol). When said marriage ended abruptly, Brian returned to Nantucket where slowly he got his life together and was promoted from pilot to partner. There were numerous speed-bumps along the way, including relationships with helicopter pilot Alex Lambert (and after the breakup he sought counseling from a psychiatrist named Dr. Grayson); a purely sexual tryst with Helen's elder sister, Casey; the sinking of Lowell's houseboat; a plane crash and a couple of major fires. It could happen to anyone.

Brian's addresses include 427 Madaket Way and 627 Cherry Street. He is a practical joker, cocky, fickle and confident. His poker face is case study worthy. Often self-serving, he does possess a good heart and a kind and caring soul. He lives for the conquest of women, only to toss them to the curb a short time later. He is often disrespectful to the opposite sex and has been known to refer to them as skirts or "chickage." His dream girl would be a six-foot tall red-headed Asian woman. He considers Kevin Costner to be the world's handsomest man. His nicknames include "Slick" and "Glandzilla." He is a Three Stooges fanatic, loves the film *Mandingo*, hates S'Mores, voted for Michael Dukakis, and can make his pecs wiggle independently of one another. On the animated *Duckman* series, Ajax envisions Brian Hackett as his long lost brother in an episode titled "Role with It" which combined film and animation as the two characters embrace.

I am eternally grateful to the kind and generous Steven Weber for agreeing to answer a bevy of questions I had about the program and his role on it. In return I was taken by his being impressed and inspired by my enthusiasm for this project. When asked how he is most like and unlike Brian, Weber contributed, "I guess me and Brian are similar in that we both possess a good deal of snark and have a penchant for making hopefully amusing jokes. While I did my share of skirt-chasing back in the day, I don't think I was anywhere near the obsessive that Brian was. And the show never really explored any particular depth to the character so it's hard to say how I'm like or unlike him beyond the obvious 'I'm not a pilot.' I guess I've lived more real-life than Brian because, well, Brian is fictitious!"

Helen Chappel Hackett

The role of Helen was the most difficult to cast. Peri Gilpin was an early contender for the role, as were Megan Mullally, Julianne Moore and Julia Louis-Dreyfus, among others but Executive Producer Dave Hackel said that it was a "meshing well with the other characters" that led to the character being reinvented and recast. Once the creators and casting directors decided upon Crystal Bernard for the role, Helen, a Libra (although in one episode it's said that her birthday is August 3rd) became a former Texan who moved to Nantucket Island with her parents at the age of ten and later took over the family business – a lunch counter at Nantucket's airport at Tom Nevers Field. Although her Southern accent is more prevalent in the *Wings* pilot, it remained a big part of her character for the show's eight seasons, and even caused the breakup of her relationship in the episode titled "Exit Laughing." In later seasons, her sister Casey is questioned about why she, unlike Helen, has not maintained her Texas accent. The name Helen is a tribute to a lactose-intolerant aunt. *Close Encounters of the Third Kind* is one of her favorite films and she has always been a fan of *The Brady Bunch*. She has quite a temper and frequently jumps to conclusions and inappropriate actions (for example, driving a Jeep through Joe's office…twice). She is infatuated with men's buns and drives a black Jeep Laredo.

Helen Chappel lives (until marrying Joe and adding the name Hackett) at 612 Elm Street and got her first kiss at Kingsbury Point. Her vision of the "perfect man" is one who is solid, sensible, dependable. He must have a sense of whimsy and be a lover of music and children. He should want to be committed to a relationship and must have respect for her independence. He should be adventurous and yet be a homebody. All of these qualities can be found in Joe Hackett, whom she has secretly wanted to marry since childhood (might be one of the reasons her last name is Chappel), although she claims she "doesn't date pilots." She, her sister Casey, Brian and Joe grew up together on the island. They all frequent a local establishment (and a real business in Nantucket) known as the Club Car. Eventually Helen's mom and dad returned to Texas to be with "the married one," Casey. Now a pretty, petite blonde (she calls it highlights, while others say her roots are darker than Alex Haley's), Helen was morbidly obese as a child but lost 68 pounds after Brian married Joe's fiancé Carol. In school she was voted "Most Likely to Explode." She reverts to her calorically-challenged ways when depressed, ingesting everything in sight. She used to hide some of her girth behind the cello she began playing at the age of eight. Her license plate is Cello. Said cello is the cause of much consternation in her life as every attempt to finally achieve her goal of playing in an orchestra is thwarted (including a plane crash that keeps her from a job with the Boston Symphony). She comes to begrudgingly accept that her lot in life is to be a waitress at the airport lunch counter where she serves lackluster, stale sandwiches, sarcasm, and the occasional beer. She does obtain her real estate license and briefly dons a Bonnie Doone blazer in a career move that quickly fizzles (along with a brief attempt at stand up comedy). She has also been known to teach cello to youngsters, and briefly was a cocktail waitress in a New York strip bar. To keep her friend Antonio from being deported, she agrees to wed him – a decision she soon rues as immigration senses a fraudulent arrangement. Said marriage, during which she wears Antonio's mother's oversized wedding dress, also delays her eventual marriage to Joe because her divorce from Antonio is not legal as a result of her forgetting to mail in the documents.

The palpable sexual tension between Helen and Joe finally evolves into a fiery on-again/off-again physical relationship. During one of the off-again periods, Helen falls for a wealthy-but-undependable man named Davis Lynch. His last-minute cancellations and Helen's disappointment as a result become a running joke. Just as she is about to finally marry Davis and settle down, Joe steps in with a proposal of his own and wrests the fair maiden from Lynch's clutches. After many fits and starts, including a couple of major fires, Helen and Joe finally set up house. Joe fashions a music room for Helen in the attic of their new home – inciting renewed interest in the cello, leading Helen to new possibilities of fulfilling her dreams of a successful musical career when the opportunity to study in Vienna, Austria comes to fruition in the series finale.

Joe Montgomery Hackett

Joseph Montgomery Hackett, a Capricorn is the owner and founder of tiny, struggling, one-plane Sandpiper Air, based at Nantucket's Tom Nevers Field. Joe started the business with $5,000 and his own sweat and spit. He has been known to kiss his Cessna plane with the letters N121PP (sometimes PB) emblazoned upon it. Was his middle name Montgomery because of a mild resemblance to actor Montgomery Clift? When asked Tim Daly replied, "Bob, you're overthinking this." Creators David Lee and Peter Casey said, "We wanted a name that sounded great when yelled by an angry mother. However, now that you mention it, there is a resemblance to a young Montgomery Clift." He wanted to be a pilot ever since he asked a stewardess in his youth if he could fly the plane and she gave him the wings off of her uniform. He has a kind heart, and that often gets him in Dutch when he agrees to do things (against his better judgment) just to keep the peace. He is the elder of the Hackett boys, and by far the more responsible. His need for order, preparation and cleanliness border on *Monk*-like OCD, and over the eight seasons his anal-retentive condition becomes more prevalent. He is a self-admitted control freak. The need for neat is Joe's only real flaw. He re-cleans silverware before he eats, orders a BLT every Tuesday from Helen's lunch counter, keeps the tags on his mattress because "it says to," can't fall asleep if his shoes in the closet are touching, faces all of his pot handles due north, affixes a label to an empty drawer in his office stating "empty drawer," files his food alphabetically, and irons his tee shirts. He is a risk taker "Only in a carefully controlled environment to a certain extent." He likes spontaneity as much as the next guy but, "He just needs a little warning so it doesn't come completely out of nowhere." He is constantly being told to "loosen up." Many around him joke that a humor-ectomy was performed on him at a young age. While some of the writers interviewed for this book stated that Joe was one of the more difficult characters for whom to write, producer/writer Steven Levitan said, "I remember enjoying writing for Joe because he was a bit nerdy and earnest." Joe was quite the jock in school and held the strikeout record at Siasconset High School for decades. Nicknames for Joe include Cindy, Skirts, Joey Bear, Sparky and Ace. He and his younger, much less responsible brother Brian run the airline. They were estranged for six years, however, when Brian married Joe's fiancé, Carol. During this time, Joe opted to leave his charter flight job and, at the urging of a flight attendant named Fay Cochran opened his own airline business (eventually known as Sandpiper Air). Despite their chronic sibling rivalry and one-upmanship, Joe hired Brian as a pilot at Sandpiper after Carol leaves and divorces him. Initially Brian is merely there to take a couple of flights each day but proves to be especially necessary when Joe is briefly grounded because of hypertension. Brian eventually becomes a partner in Sandpiper. Joe practically raised Brian because their mother, Mae flew the coop while they were still young, and their father went mad, believing he was a waffle who was often comforted when syrup was poured over him. They have an Aunt Fern who once broke her hip. In the off-season Joe delivers pizzas by plane to rich Bostonians.

Joe lost his virginity at Kingsbury Point. The late Chuck Yeager is one of his heroes. He has been friends with Helen and Casey Chappel since childhood. He has an old pilot friend named Danny McCoy. Joe has a "no blind date" rule, can't walk past a mirror without checking out his own clenched buttocks, used to drive an AMC Pacer, built his own patio furniture, says "It's all for the best" a lot, hates the circus, is afraid of elephants and pumping his own gasoline, used to have a dog named Ranger, loves Peaches and Herb songs as well as country music, thinks Peter Jennings is the sexiest man alive, thinks the eyes are the sexiest body part on a woman, has an autographed picture of Richard Roundtree as *Shaft*, is passionate about the Celtics, Red Sox and fly fishing, voted for Ross Perot and Michael Dukakis, and had a Monkees lunchbox. Strudel once sent him into anaphylactic shock. He is afraid of snakes and is said to have a birthmark on his thigh and a hairless chest (but the latter is proven false in bedroom scenes with Helen). He lost a bid for councilman to Roy Biggins. His dream is to one day make the cover of *American Flyer Magazine*. He almost loses Helen Chappel to Davis Lynch, but gets her to cancel that engagement after he proposes in an elevator. Helen and he unknowingly burn down Brian's house after Brian similarly burned down their home. Their wedding ceremony is conducted in a hotel bathroom because Joe gets his hand stuck in the toilet trying to retrieve Helen's wedding ring. He is not able to be freed from his dilemma in time to attend the ceremony, so it comes to him. After a year of being settled in their new home, Joe encourages Helen to resume pursuing her dream of becoming a concert cellist – a move which leads them to Vienna, Austria in the series finale. In the episode titled "Brother's Keeper," Tyne Daly, Tim's real-life sister guest starred as a wealthy woman who falls for Brian. She was nominated for an Emmy Award for that guest shot, oddly one of a very few nominations the show received. Daly said,

"Even though Brian has the most scenes with Tyne, our scene in my office is great and so well written." The two Dalys would again work together on an episode of Tim's long-running *Madam Secretary* series in 2019.

Alex Lambert

Writer/Producer Adam Belanoff with Farrah Forke near Fay's Sandpiper counter. (Courtesy of Adam Belanoff).

Alex Lambert, played by Farrah Forke, enters the fray in Season Four, Episode Six titled "Two Jerks and a Jill." Her mother's name is Adele, and while she is never seen on camera, her words, "You're not getting any younger, Alex" continue to haunt her daughter. Alex flew U. S. Army Apache Helicopters in Desert Storm. She also posed in *Playboy Magazine* for a beach shoot. Roy Biggins just happened to have that issue in the collection housed in his office at Aeromass. While in school Alex was turned in for smoking by the homecoming queen. Seeking revenge, Alex flushed her tiara down the toilet. She loves running and working out. She has a big, tough dog named Chopper.

Alex resides on Old Post Road in Apartment C and was once engaged to a man named Dan. Often donning a leather jacket or a vest, she is tough and takes no guff. The lovely Farrah Forke said,

"I am really nothing like Alex. However, I was a bartender in the West Village and upon closing up each night I sometimes had to deal with people who didn't want to leave the establishment. So I found I was able to lower my voice and act tough to get them to comply. When I heard what the role of Alex entailed, I knew I could portray that character because I had already been doing it some nights at the bar." Her favorite color is green. She sets up a helicopter tour business at Tom Nevers Field, bonds with Helen, and sees right through smarmy Brian and Joe, initially thwarts their advances, nicknaming Brian as "Slick" and Joe as "Ace." She eventually succumbs to Brian's undying charm and agrees to go out with him on Lowell's boat to watch the tall ships. In this episode, said boat, Lowell's home sinks because of Brian's carelessness. This tragedy necessitates Lowell taking up residence in the Hackett house. Alex is a country music fan and is led to believe that Brian is friends with Clint Black. Alex's favorite song is "I Can't Stop Loving You" by Ray Charles.

Alex and Brian get along swimmingly for a time, and they even move in together. That is, until Alex discovers that Brian just can't commit. Also, their idiosyncrasies drive one another to distraction. When she leaves, Brian becomes a basket case and has to seek therapy from a Dr. Grayson. After the breakup Alex traveled through Europe, became a personal pilot for a corporate CEO and flew medivac patients for Boston General Hospital.

Alex returns in a most memorable way – as a special guest on an episode of a popular local talk show hosted by Antonio Scarpacci's hero, Mary Pat Lee (Caroline Aaron). Brian is lured to be on the show without knowing that he is being set up and that Alex will embarrass him on live television. After this brief reunion, Alex leaves the inhabitants of Tom Nevers Field for good. Forke stated, "I was so hoping that after this episode they would once again bring me back as a regular, but it wasn't meant to be."

Actress Farrah Forke is an utter delight. She and I, your author quickly bonded while discussing her role in 35 of the 172 episodes of *Wings*, and quickly developed nicknames for one another. I began calling her Ace, and I was proudly crowned "Slick" – her nickname for Brian Hackett. I'm considering having my name legally changed to "Slick" Leszczak.

Davis Lynch

Financier Davis Lynch was portrayed by Mark Harelik in six episodes of the series. He meets with Joe and Brian Hackett for a possible business opportunity. He thinks he wants to invest in Sandpiper Air. However, after a few days of supervision he realizes that said investment would not be prudent, and instead turns his attention to competitor Aeromass, much to Joe's dismay. To make matters worse, Lynch has designs on Helen. She is available at this time, as her relationship with Joe had been broken off. She quickly falls for the man and is impressed by his considerable wealth. However, she quickly becomes the butt of her friends' jokes because of Davis' frequently canceled dates and nixed weekend getaways because of business obligations. She still professes her love for Lynch and agrees to marry him, only to be saved from that occurrence at the last possible minute by a proposal from Joe in an elevator.

Without being told about the new wrinkle in Helen's love life, Lynch finds himself under house arrest in Burma after an attempt to salvage his investments there. He falls in love with a woman who secures his release and returns to tell Helen, thinking they are still engaged so that he can get his granny's heirloom ring back (a ring that briefly gets stuck on Helen's finger) to present to his intended named Caroline.

Lowell Mather

Laconic Lowell is part of a fifth generation of Mathers living on Nantucket Island. He lives at 213 Church Lane (a play on the actor's last name, Church). He is extremely eccentric, naïve and at times appears not to be the sharpest cheese in the deli case, but is actually rather intelligent and, as Executive Producer Dave Hackel characterized him, "Somewhat of a savant." He certainly knows a lot about plane engines and is the mechanic and handyman for both Sandpiper Air and Aeromass. Lowell was crushed when his

*He's not an orphan, but his brother is. He's Lowell
Mather.*

inspiration, handyman Weeb Gilroy passed on at the age of 90.
Lowell's other hero, the one who made him want to be a mechanic
was his shop teacher, wacky Mr. Connolly. Lowell is a graduate of
M. I. T. No, not the Massachusetts Institute of Technology, but
rather Murray's Institute of Tools where he graduated Murray Cum
Laude. With a little more money from Lowell, M. I. T. could have
gotten him the title of Doctor Mather. He carries a large amount
of money with him because of Charles Keating who attained noto-
riety in the 1980s (the savings and loan scandal). The Lowell role is
alleged to have been written especially for Thomas Haden Church,
inspired by his guest shot on *Cheers* portraying a similar character –
a daft hockey player named Gordie Brown.

Lowell states that he is not an orphan, but his brother is. The birth
mother, who taught Lowell how to cook and keep house abandoned
him at the age of five on the first day of kindergarten. She also had

a fling with Communism in the 1950s. He has a sister, Trina, with webbed toes (and another who is very fertile), and an uncle who lost his nose in an industrial accident. Lowell's godmother is loud and scary Siasconset Sal. Some of his female relatives are strippers. His mother-in-law was abducted by aliens. His great aunt Jeanette used to date the annoying Carlton Blanchard. His great-grandfather Snooky Mather was very wealthy, having won a lawsuit against Joe Kennedy whose Duesenberg crashed into Snooky's ice truck in 1929. As a result, Lowell was willed a small fortune at the age of 31 ½. Said money was squandered in a business venture called "Lowell Mather's House of Wax," but after it burned to the ground it brought in a sizeable insurance check. As a child, Lowell was trapped under the ice for five hours at the Winter Carnival, and an article was written about the incident in *Time Magazine*. Lowell was named for an Uncle Lowell who was found dead in the well behind the Mather house. Although an adult, Lowell has many immature, wide-eyed child-like qualities. This may account for the surname Mather, as Lowell's world is filled with wonder, much like that of *Leave It to Beaver* star Jerry Mathers. Lowell has a bath toy named Mr. Squishy (which he accidentally leaves behind after a weekend away), he will do almost anything for a sugar cookie, he once put an entire kitten in his mouth, accidentally shot his brother-in-law in the leg because of his resemblance to an elk, thinks there are only 42 weeks in a year, and eats with a napkin tucked into his shirt. He has known Helen, Joe and Brian for many years. Brian is the only one who calls him "Lowelly."

Among his many eccentricities, Lowell loves shooting rats down at the dump, thinks Tom Petty is extremely handsome and that Ernest Borgnine is sexy, says the sexiest part of a woman's body is chest hair, claims to be a leg man and reads *The Ladies Home Journal*, says that nostrils are the window into the soul, names his golf balls, speaks fluent French, practices the ancient art of face reading and loves musical theatre. He is afraid of the city of Boston and the sound the soda can makes when it drops from the vending machine. He does get in touch with his feminine side and does needlepoint and cross-stitching, and gets manicures and pedicures. He loves figs, thinks the answer to every trivia question is

Ann-Margret, is a gourmet chef, learns to do the cha cha, listens to vocabulary tapes, and fears anything bad happening to his treasured orange baseball cap. He performs bad celebrity impressions. Speaking of impressions, his Aunt Freda did great chicken impressions (and once even laid an egg). We often hear about his odd Cousin Beevo who has many talents. Lowell has limited dating experience, and admits that his wife, Bunny was the first woman he ever dated. He first met Bunny while she was gutting a sea bass and he fell in love instantly. While he worships Bunny and their two children, he eventually leaves and divorces Bunny when it is proven to him that she is sleeping around with multiple men.

Lowell, a side character, is there for some wonderful, slow-moving, non-judgmental, oft-confused comic relief. He is a sweet, kind, shy and diligent employee who never takes a day off, although Roy sometimes calls him Slackass. Working at Nevers Field is his dream job. Some of this lovable scatterbrain's favorite songs are "That Old Black Magic," "Mona Lisa," "Isn't It Romantic" and "Moon River." He can be heard singing the latter two in multiple episodes. Lowell lives on a houseboat, and when Brian borrows and accidentally sinks it, Lowell moves in with the Hacketts and exhibits many mother-like qualities to the boys. After a year, the Hacketts kick him to the curb, even though he is a great housekeeper, he can be really demanding. The freckles on Lowell's back, when connected in a "connect the dots" manner resemble Mt. Rushmore without a nose for President Lincoln. He is allergic to ragweed. In one episode it is stated that he is deathly afraid of spiders, while in another he professes to love spiders.

After witnessing a mob hit in a Boston eatery, Lowell opts to do the right thing and testify against the killer, thus forcing him into the Witness Protection Program. Although he must then leave his dream job and his co-workers/friends, he could not live with himself knowing the killer was loose on the streets. He leaves his beloved baseball cap to Brian and Joe. As a loving tribute, the cap is then affixed to the wall outside Joe's office. This is how actor Thomas Haden Church was able to take "wing" and move on to a starring role on Fox's funny-but-short-lived *Ned and Stacey* sitcom.

Antonio Scarpacci

Antonio Scarpacci, the unwed, seemingly cursed, always down-on-his-luck, dateless/loveless cab driver from seasons three through eight on *Wings* was first introduced as a waiter at Pontrelli's Restaurant in the second season Valentine's Day episode titled "Looking for Love in all the Wrong Places." Antonio is an Italian immigrant from Pasitano near Appechio, the central region of Marche in Italy. He came to the United States packed in a small box. His parents were Annamaria and Angelo Scarpacci. Theirs was an "arranged marriage," but they grew to love one another. Antonio is always called Angelo by the annoying recurring elderly character named Carlton Blanchard (William Hickey). A cousin Giacomo (who later resides in Boston) is seen in the Valentine's Day episode referenced above. That restaurant, Pontrelli's at which Antonio was a waiter was closed because of a lawsuit filed by the widow of a man who choked on a chicken bone there. The chicken bone hangs from the rearview mirror of her car – a Lamborghini.

Antonio's character was created by Executive Story Editors Michael Saltzman and Bill Diamond. In fact, Saltzman recalled, "I almost played him. We hadn't yet found an actor in time for the table read, so I read it and Sheila Guthrie, our casting director asked if I'd be willing to do it in the show because she hadn't been able to find anyone. Any images of future stardom were immediately replaced with images of me tanking in front of a studio audience, humiliating myself and ruining the episode. I urged her to please find someone. She came in the next day with Tony Shalhoub and I received years and years of character payments." Antonio comes from very humble beginnings. While others were having turkey, every Christmas his family would carve the holiday eel. His grandparents were married for 81 years. His Uncle Bruno was on the *RMS Titanic*, his Uncle Paolo drives a rundown station wagon. Uncle Sal owned a girdle shop and Antonio worked there after school for a while. He does have one well-to-do living relative, an Uncle Giancarlo whose profession was cobbler, another made calf-skin gloves for ten bucks a pair, and in Season Six we get to meet his Cousin Dominic who manufactures gaudy leather goods and makes a great living.

Antonio is allergic to clams. They cause his tongue to swell up and before going into anaphylactic shock he must seek medical help. He drives a taxi (without insurance) and works out of Nantucket's Airport, often eating breakfast and/or lunch at Helen's counter. On days he forgets his wallet at home he lavishes Helen with compliments to get free food. Wednesday is usually his day off, and Friday is his most hectic day of work. He also briefly worked for Whispering Pines Mortuary, and at the department store with Casey.

For the most part he is timid, mild-mannered, kind and thoughtful (and yet bitter and resentful of others who have good fortune). None of his good deeds goes unpunished. He is a hopeless romantic, yet unlucky in love. He is deathly afraid of the opposite sex and stammers uncontrollably when attempting to converse with them, often sweating profusely (boy, can he sweat). He is an admitted "butt man." His first sexual encounter was with an elderly woman (he was 14). He is head-over-heels in lust with Casey Chappel, Helen's sister, but his feelings are unrequited. He is often bullied and ridiculed by Roy who calls him Scarpacci, Pastahead or Spaghettihead. Ridicule is nothing new to Antonio, having been caught trying on his sister's wedding dress by his friends on the soccer team. He has a *Baywatch* thermos and considers Sylvester Stallone to be the sexiest man on earth. He is a huge fan of fictional TV talk show hostess Mary Pat Lee (Caroline Aaron) and frequently says, "You go, girl." He knows only one song on the guitar, "Michael (Row the Boat Ashore)" by the Highwaymen.

To avoid getting deported when his visa expires, he marries Helen only to be investigated for fraud by immigration. He and Helen get a quickie divorce, only to find out a while later that the divorce is not recognized, thus delaying Helen and Joe's wedding license being drawn up. Roy connects Antonio and Helen with a contact in Mexico named Pepe, and their divorce is finalized. Antonio's sad and lonely existence is a recurring theme. He has been known to fill his lonely hours making shadow puppets on the wall. He can be an annoying, overbearing, weepy and needy roommate. A fair amount of his wardrobe consists of used 1970s leisure suits and Nehru jackets from one of Fay's late Georges. He often takes those outdated items to Jiffy Cleaners. Unlike Brian and Joe Hackett, Antonio sometimes wears bowties. His neighbor has a high-powered leaf blower called the Yard Demon 742 and the din it creates awakens him every morning. Likely his surname is Scarpacci because Antonio's daily life is scarred and jinxed.

THE CREATIVE CREW

D. A. Johnson (left). He's the background actor always seen at the Pilgrim Car Rental counter pictured here with his nephew, director Andy Ackerman (right). (Courtesy of Suzanne Holmes).

Andy Ackerman

Andy Ackerman was born September 19, 1956 in Los Angeles and is a graduate of Santa Clara University. His work in TV began as a videotape editor and he parlayed that into a long career. He was a co-producer on *Cheers* but is best known as a prolific sitcom director with credits including *Seinfeld, Curb Your Enthusiasm, Everybody Loves Raymond, Becker, Frasier, Two-and-a-Half Men,* and several seasons of *Wings.* He owes his success to following his instincts. Falling off a horse in the 1990s led to some time missed on *Wings.* It's an injury that still occasionally haunts him today, but that hasn't stopped him from directing. In fact, he and Steven Weber were recently reunited on Weber's most recent NBC sitcom titled *Indebted*. Thus far he has garnered three Emmys and two Director's Guild of America Awards.

David Angell

David Angell was born April 10, 1946 in Providence, Rhode Island. He studied English Literature at Providence College. He, Peter Casey and David Lee worked together on *Cheers*, and later formed their own company, Grub Street Productions. They created both *Wings* and *Frasier*. Angell wrote his scripts out longhand. He had the knack of being able to have his handwritten pages on yellow legal pads always coincide with the number of pages on the final typed script. Tragedy struck on September 11, 2001. David Angell and his wife of 40 years, Lynn were aboard one of the planes that crashed into the World Trade Center. *Wings* had ended its run four years earlier, but *Frasier* was still in production (incidentally, Frasier Crane's radio station was KACL – *A*ngell, *C*asey, *L*ee). *Wings* warm-up man Robert G. Lee shared, "I'll never forget that day. I was in bed that morning when my wife came in and said, 'Bob, David Angell's picture is on TV. I think something happened.' I ran downstairs and we all know the rest of the story. It was devastating to think of David and Lynn and what they must have felt in the last minutes of their lives. I don't know if I'll ever fully get over it." Tim Daly said, "I think of him every day. Because of him on every episode I was always tucked in, unlike Brian. He was very neat – a former Navy guy and he used to always say, 'Adjust your rack.' For those who don't know what that means, one's shirt buttons have to be aligned with one's fly. I was living in Providence at the time of his passing and he still had family there. He was a gentle and sweet man, and his wife Lynn was delightful. Looking back, I had taken that same flight many times. It's crazy and unforgettably sad." Casey and Lee added, "He was such a good guy with a dry, wicked sense of humor. We played many rounds of golf together and beat him only once. His librarian wife, Lynn was loaded with Southern charm. David Angell was often quiet. He would sometimes out of nowhere, pitch a great joke." Executive producer Dave Hackel added, "Angell's wife, Lynn was my wife's closest friend. So sad. To this day, none of that event makes sense. I still tear up when I think about it."

Kathryn Baker

Kathryn penned the "Ladies Who Lunch" episode – the final episode for Gretchen German as Joe's girlfriend Gail. Kathryn also wrote for *Melrose Place, Murphy Brown, The Adventures of Brisco County, Jr.* and *Coach.*

Larry Balmagia

Larry Balmagia was born September 1, 1953 in Los Angeles. He has a long history of producing and/or writing TV sitcoms. Among his impressive list of credits are *M*A*S*H, Rhoda, Cheers, Dear John, Barney Miller* and *Saved by the Bell.* He is credited with writing five episodes of *Wings* and producing or co-producing 44 more.

Darryl Bates

Darryl Bates is an editor and a director. He is probably best known for *Two Broke Girls, Becker, Just Shoot Me, Gilmore Girls, In Living Colour, Head of the Class, The Comeback* with Lisa Kudrow and *Wings.* He is listed as editor on 125 episodes and as director of three others including part one of the three-episode arc titled "Wingless."

Adam Belanoff

Adam Belanoff's credits as a writer and/or producer include *Star Trek: The Next Generation, Judging Amy, Murphy Brown, Cosby, Titus, The Closer* and *Wings.* He most recently concluded six years as a writer and Executive Producer of TNT's *Major Crimes.*

Prolific writer/producer Adam Belanoff. (Courtesy of Adam Belanoff).

Rick Beren

Rick has a long list of credits as a director, associate director, technical coordinator and writer. He has worked on numerous shows from Paramount Studios, including *Cheers, Frasier* and of course *Wings*. Beren said, "My job as technical coordinator was to help pick shots and relay them to someone in the booth. For a time I was working on both *Cheers* and *Wings*, but when they began shooting on the same night I had to make a choice and stayed with *Cheers*. After *Cheers* ended in 1993 I asked Executive Producer Dave Hackel if I could direct *Wings*. He said yes but was getting ready to leave the show at that time. He still arranged for what he had promised and I got to direct four episodes."

Peter Bonerz

Peter Bonerz was born August 6, 1938 in Portsmouth, New Hampshire, so directing a show set in New England was an ideal situation. Bonerz began his acting career in the 1960s with a guest shot on an episode of *The Addams Family*. Coincidentally, he was part of the cast of the 1970 film *Catch 22* with future co-star Bob Newhart. On *The Bob Newhart Show* Bonerz portrayed dentist Jerry Robinson for six seasons. He later had recurring roles on *Three Sisters* and the TV version of *9 to 5*. His credits as a director are staggering, and include *Friends, The Bob Newhart Show, Alf, Murphy Brown, Home Improvement, Just Shoot Me, Archie Bunker's Place* and *Wings*. The latter includes one of the famous Carlton Blanchard episodes, "Say Uncle, Carlton." He has been married to wife Rosalind since 1963 and they have two children.

James Burrows

James Burrows was born December 30, 1940 in Los Angeles. He is the son of Abe Burrows, a director/writer/composer and frequent game show guest star. James is a graduate of the Yale School of Drama. Tutored by sitcom directing legend Jay Sandrich, Burrows has become the director's director known for his complex shots and his use of four cameras instead of the usual three. His sitcom directing credits run a mile long and include *The Mary Tyler Moore Show, Frasier, Friends, Laverne and Shirley, Cheers, Will and Grace, Night Court, Two-and-a-Half Men, The Big Bang Theory,* and the pilot/debut episode of *Wings* titled "Legacy." His wife Debbie is a celebrity hair stylist in New York. He has three daughters and one stepdaughter. He has garnered five Emmy Awards. Cleverly, he often directs pilots and reaps the rewards by then garnering some extra residuals for being part of the creative process involved (even if he never directs another episode of the series).

Writer Ellen Byron is all smiles after penning yet another funny script, and because lunch will consist of "The Big Sandwich." (Courtesy of Ellen Byron).

Ellen Byron

Born in New York, she graduated from Tulane University. Ellen's *Cajun Country Mysteries* have won the Agatha award for Best Contemporary Novel and multiple Lefty Awards for Best Humorous Mystery. Her new *Catering Hall Mystery* series, written as Maria DiRico, launched with *Here Comes the Body* and was inspired by her real life. She's an award-winning playwright and non-award-winning TV writer of comedies like *Wings, Just Shoot Me* and *Fairly Odd Parents.* But she considers her most impressive credit working as a cater-waiter for Martha Stewart.

Peter Casey

Peter Casey began his Hollywood career in 1975 delivering pizzas for Two Guys from Italy. This led to other fascinating jobs such as liquor store clerk, radio survey taker, and peddler of turkey/avocado sandwiches out of a cooler at Paramount Studios. His television career began in 1979 when he and writing partner, David Lee, finally sold a freelance script to *The Jeffersons*. Soon after, they joined the show as staff writers. In 1985, Casey and Lee became writers/producers on the highly acclaimed comedy series *Cheers*. In 1989, they, along with fellow *Cheers* alum, David Angell, formed Grub Street Productions. The first show they created was the popular NBC sitcom *Wings*. 1993 saw the premiere of their second creation *Frasier*. An instant classic *Frasier* ran for eleven seasons on NBC garnering a record 37 Emmy Awards.

Rick Copp

Richard Copp, a native of Bar Harbor, Maine said, "I knew from a very young age that I wanted to be a writer. In fifth grade I began a tradition of writing original scripts based on old TV series, and then mounting them as plays. My productions included *Gilligan's Island* and *Charlie's Angels*. It was a natural assumption that I would someday begin my professional writing career in television, though given my questionable choice in material, nobody ever expected me to win an Emmy – and so far they've been right." Shortly after graduating from New York University's Tisch School of the Arts, Rick's career began. In the summer of 1988 during a prolonged writer's strike, an old friend and colleague named Gloria Banta sent a few finished scripts written by Rick and writing partner David A. Goodman to Tony Thomas of Witt-Thomas Productions. Because of the strike, Thomas

Copping a big smile from the co-writer of two of the famous Sandy Cooper "Joey Bear" episodes, Rick Copp. (Courtesy of Rick Copp).

had time to read the scripts and brought the fresh new writers out to the West Coast. When the strike ended, Rick and David were writing for *The Golden Girls* and *Empty Nest*. This also opened up the door to film and led to work on *Howard Stern's Private Parts* and *The Brady Bunch Movie*. For our purposes, Rick and David wrote two episodes of *Wings* involving one of the sitcom's most notorious characters, Sandy Cooper. Rick added, "Mark Reisman, with whom we'd worked on *Flying Blind* had recently started working on *Wings* and asked if we'd be interested in a freelance assignment. We pitched a few ideas to the writing staff and the one they liked the best involved this old high school friend who is so sweet to everyone, thus no one believes Joe when he tells about her crazy side." They wrote two very funny chapters in the Sandy Cooper trilogy, but, "We were developing a *Knight Rider* series when asked if we could do a third episode featuring her. We couldn't do it, but I did see it when it aired." Copp has remained very active writing best-selling novels and developing TV pilots for Nickelodeon and Lifetime.

Bill Diamond

Bill Diamond has worked in broadcast television for over thirty years, writing, producing and showrunning at all the major U.S. networks. He said, "I was raised in Canton, Massachusetts. Got my Bachelor's degree from the University of Pennsylvania and Master's degree from the Journalism School at Columbia. Michael Saltzman [his writing partner] and I were classmates and met there." A five-year veteran and executive producer of the Emmy Award-winning comedy *Murphy Brown*, he has written for such shows as *Doctor Doctor, Anything but Love, Emily's Reasons Why Not*, and *Wings*. On *Wings*, Diamond and Saltzman concocted a character you love to hate – TV's most annoying geezer, Carlton Blanchard. Diamond said, "If my writing partner Mike Saltzman and I ever had more fun writing for a character, I don't remember it. The best part was just Mike and I trying to top one another with bizarre questions for Carlton to ask." Diamond also worked closely with and developed pilots for CBS Studios, NBC/Universal, Warner Bros., Disney/ABC Studios, Sony Television, Paramount, 20th Century Fox, FX,

Line Producer Roz Doyle with Rebecca Schull at the 1991 wrap party.
(Courtesy of Suzanne Holmes).

Revolution, ATG and CMT. He also produced the TV series *Civil Marriage* and the full-length TV movie *To the Edge of the World* for the TNT Network in Russia.

Roz Doyle

The character played by Peri Gilpin on *Frasier* was named Roz Doyle as an homage to the line producer in the early years of *Wings*. Roz sadly received the terrible news that she had breast cancer on the same day the pilot episode of *Wings* was being filmed. A real trouper with a proper British accent, she worked on the show for its first two seasons (1990-91) before succumbing to the disease (a total of 28 episodes). Writer/producer/director Ken Levine said, "She was a lovely woman, a crackerjack producer, and taken from us way too soon." Lisa Kudrow was the original choice to play Roz Doyle on *Frasier,* but another great role awaited her on *Friends.*

Leonard R. Garner, Jr.

Leonard R. Garner, Jr. was born in Baltimore but raised in Scranton, Pennsylvania. He graduated from Syracuse University's School of Speech and Dramatic Arts. As an actor, early on he used the name Lenny Garner and earned roles on *Cheers, Moonlighting* and *The Blues*

The happy face of director extraordinaire (and all-around good guy) Leonard R. Garner, Jr. (Courtesy of Leonard R. Garner, Jr.)

Brothers Movie. At the same time, under the name Leonard R. Garner, Jr. he began as an Assistant Director and eventually sat in the director's chair for hundreds of episodes of great comedy television, and in 2012 won the prestigious NAACP Image Award for Outstanding Director of a Comedy Series for an episode of *Rules of Engagement* titled "The Set Up." He also taught multi-cam television directing at USC, and often spoke to high school and college groups about career opportunities in television. About *Wings,* Garner said, "I was there from the pilot episode which happened just after I'd gotten married late in 1989 [to Robin]. We had time for a honeymoon trip from Seattle to Los Angeles, and then I was ready to go to work. However, a family emergency took me away from a few early episodes, but I was back for the last few in that short first season. The *Wings* era was so important in my life – so many things happened then, my marriage, the birth of my children [two boys], the passing of my parents. Paramount was a wonderful place to work in that era – a big college campus of talent and creativity. So much fun." When director Andy Ackerman fell off a horse and had back problems, Garner was asked 'if he was ready.' Garner shared, "I said yes and then wondered, 'what have I gotten myself into?' The first episode I did was 'The Customer Is Usually Right.' Apparently they liked what I did because I got to do three more next season which turned into seven, and finally ten as I officially surrendered my AD [assistant director] job to devote my full attention to directing." Lenny currently does most of his directing for the Disney Corporation. About his name, "The union eventually made me choose one name, and I opted for Leonard R. Garner, Jr., although almost everyone calls me Lenny." About *Wings* Garner shared, "I was there the whole time. We had a great slice of time together. Towards the end everyone's frame of mind was about what happens after this? What's next? But *Wings* was a joy and looking back now it is appreciated even more now than when it was happening." About Garner, Tim Daly said, "He was there all the time. He deserves all the success he's having. Love that guy."

Howard Gewirtz

Howard Gewirtz said, "I was born in Long Beach, Long Island and got my BFA in film and television studies from New York University's Tisch School of the Arts. My son is entering his senior year at Rhode Island School of Design and my wife is an artist who regularly sells her paintings and digital artwork. We live in the Brentwood section of Los Angeles in a large house that *Wings* helped build." Maybe he should build a wing and name it the *Wings* Wing? As a producer, Gewirtz's credits include *Taxi, Just Shoot Me, Everybody Hates Chris, Bosom Buddies* and *Wings*. As a writer his credits include all of the aforementioned shows and *Three's Company, The Larry Sanders Show* and *The Simpsons*. At press time he was very busy writing his own book.

Joyce Gittlin

Joyce is a director and writer of many sitcoms and has had multiple films in development at major studios. She most recently wrote an original Lifetime movie *A Twist of Faith* starring Toni Braxton and published the novel *A Narrow Bridge* under the penname, JJ Gesher. On *Wings*, she directed the sixth and final holiday episode "All about Christmas Eve." She also wrote six episodes and was a creative consultant for well over 60 others.

David A. Goodman

David A. Goodman was born December 13, 1962 in New Rochelle, New York. He attended the University of Chicago and is the President of the Writer's Guild of America West. He is a writer/producer often paired with Rick Copp. Among his credits are *The Orville, Star Trek: Enterprise, Family Guy, Futurama, The Golden Girls,* and *Wings.* For the latter, he and Copp wrote two of the three very famous Sandy Cooper (Joey Bear) episodes.

Ian Gurvitz

Ian Gurvitz was born in New York City, but he has lived in Los Angeles for the last three decades working as a TV writer and producer. Before saying, "California, Here I Come" he earned his B. A. in Philosophy from Ithaca College, graduating cum laude and working toward an M. A. in Buddhist Studies from Colgate University which included living in Japan and studying Japanese. His credits include *Becker, The Wonder Years, Get a Life, Frasier,* and of course *Wings.* He has also written about politics and culture for *The Huffington Post* and Attn.com. He's penned five books so far – *Hello, Lied the Agent – and Other Bullshit You Hear as a Hollywood TV Writer; Deconstructing God – a Heretic's Case for Religion; Welcome to Dumbfuckistan – the Dumbed-Down, Disinformed, Dysfunctional, Disunited States of America; Death to America – How We the People Screwed Ourselves;* and *Freak Out – the 2016 Election and the Dawn of the American Democalypse.* He also wrote, produced and directed the independent feature film *L. A. Blues* released in early 2007. He has many published articles to his credit and he's a frequent guest lecturer.

Dave Hackel

Writer and Executive Producer Dave Hackel began his show business career as a disk jockey in high school and college in Ohio - spinning records as well as writing and reporting the news. Once out of college he was hired to produce and direct local TV in Columbus, Ohio.

In 1972 he moved to Los Angeles and worked for a small agency that supplied prizes for network gameshows. When the staff for a network sitcom pilot moved in across the hall from his office he was introduced to a whole new world - writing for television. "Getting to know those writers opened up new possibilities. Not only was writing more creatively satisfying, but it paid better, too."

So, after work each evening, he and a partner tried to break into this new part of show business by writing spec scripts. After many attempts, they finally got their first assignment on *Fish*, a spin-off of *Barney Miller* that starred Abe Vigoda. After that, slowly but surely, a career emerged.

In the beginning, they accepted any assignment they were offered - comedies, dramas or variety shows. As both they and their careers matured, Dave decided to put his efforts solely into sitcoms and his partner left to concentrate on detective dramas.

On shows like, *Webster, Dear John* and *Wings,* Dave worked his way up the ladder from staff writer, to story editor to producer and then Executive Producer. "Writing and producing television shows is a lot of hard work, but it also can be a great deal of fun. For instance, during my years on *Wings* I met a great group of people and am still in close touch with creators Peter Casey and David Lee, as well as most of the cast members."

Eventually Dave created his own show, *Becker* starring Ted Danson. He describes it as the show of which he's the most proud and calls it the most collaborative experience of his career. "Working with Ted was a pleasure. Not only is he a nice person, but he's one of those actors who improves every piece of material he's given." Dave explained that, by design, *Becker* was a comedy that could have dramatic elements. "As well as pure silliness, I loved that our stories also explored subjects like prejudice, death and religion."

Happily retired for the last fifteen years, Hackel still writes for his own enjoyment saying, "Being a writer is like having homework for the rest of your life." These days he's also expressing himself through painting. "I'm not a great artist but I thoroughly enjoy the creative process."

David Isaacs

David Isaacs was born October 26, 1949 and is usually credited in tandem with writing partner Ken Levine. His writing credits include *The Simpsons, Cheers, Frasier, M*A*S*H, The Tony Randall Show* and *Wings*. He was a consulting producer and writer for the award-winning *Mad Men*. Still active, he is a professor at the University of Southern California teaching screenwriting and comedy.

Lissa Kapstrom

Lissa Kapstrom was born September 29, 1958 in Sacramento, California. She is a producer and writer, often paired with Ellen Byron. Her many credits include *The Fairly Odd Parents, Still Standing, Just Shoot Me, The Weber Show, Fridays, In Living Colour* and *Wings*. Among the many episodes of the latter, she and Byron wrote three of the most famous – "Here It Is: The Big Wedding," and both of the Mary Pat Lee episodes. She and Byron also introduced a running gag on the series known as "the big sandwich."

Ken Keeler

Keeler was born in Cambridge, Massachusetts on December 2, 1961. His writing and producing credits include *Futurama, The Simpsons, The Critic, Late Night with David Letterman* and *Wings*. While he only wrote one episode of the latter, it is quite an important one titled "Fay There, Georgy Girl" – the episode in which Fay has visions of her three late husbands named George, while attempting to part with their belongings.

Lori Kirkland-Baker

Lori Kirkland-Baker went from working in a brush factory to a writer's assistant on *Perfect Strangers,* and was later a producer, writer and story editor for many other prime time shows such as *Desperate Housewives, Frasier* and *Wings*. On the latter she had involvement in over 50 episodes. *Frasier* garnered her an Emmy Award and a Writers Guild Award.

Shelly Landau

Shelly Landau is a co-producer, story editor and writer of numerous prime time shows such as *Step by Step, Growing Pains, Webster, The*

Facts of Life and *Wings.* She penned seven episodes of the latter with two focused on Fay ("The Faygitive" and "Gone but Not Faygotten").

Philip LaZebnik

Philip LaZebnik was born in Ann Arbor, Michigan on February 8, 1953, but was raised in Missouri. Like Helen Chappel, he is a very accomplished musician, playing violin for the Boston Pops and the Boston Ballet Orchestra. He's also written over 20 musical plays. His writing and producing credits for TV include *The Torkelsons; Star Trek: The Next Generation;* and *Wings.* On the latter, one will notice his name in some capacity on every episode of the show's first two seasons. He was also part of the planning sessions prior to the filming of the show's pilot. He is married with three children.

Janet Leahy

Janet Leahy is a showrunner, executive producer and writer who remains very active. Among her credits are *Newhart, Cheers, Mad Men, Major Dad, Gilmore Girls, Boston Legal* and *Wings.* Most recently, she produced Pete Holmes' series *Crashing* for HBO on which I, your author, was an extra on two episodes.

David Lee

David Lee is a native of Claremont, California, a graduate of the University of Redlands, and currently splits his time between homes in Los Angeles and Palm Springs. He has a successful post-television career directing and writing for the theater, working at many respected regional theaters around the country.

Robert G. Lee

Robert G. Lee was the warm-up man for the live studio audience on the nights that *Wings* was filmed. He got to appear in one episode of the show, too. The episode is titled "Take My Life, Please" and (credited as Robert Gary Lee because of another Robert G. Lee in SAG) he plays the emcee on comedy night at the Club Car. He also was invited to join the writers to pitch jokes for inclusion in the scripts. About getting the warm-up job, Lee said, "I got it being kind to the wives of the producers. Each show has its own vibe until the right warm-up is found. They had yet to find an audience comic that worked. I was called in, did my job and we hit it off. Why? Because the wives of the Executive Producers sat in the front row directly in front of me and I was smart enough to know where the power was. I later found out that I was hired because the wives liked me. They considered the other comics too pushy or rude." Lee added, "Most people think the warm-up does his opening ten-minute act and then goes away. The reality is we're there from the first scene until the very end. With costume changes and rewrites it can take four to five hours. That was my life for several years. It was a great job, and when people ask me about my favorite shows over my career, invariably I bring up this production."

Ken Levine

Ken is an Emmy-winning writer/director/playwright/major league baseball announcer. Full-length plays include *A or B, Going Going Gone, Our Time, Upfronts and Personal, America's Sexiest Couple, On the Farce Day of Christmas* and *Guilty Pleasures*. They've been performed in New York, Los Angeles and throughout the country. His many short plays have been produced around the world and have won numerous festivals and competitions. Ken has written over 200 episodes of television for such shows as *M*A*S*H, Cheers, Frasier, The Simpsons* and *Wings*. He has directed over 60 TV episodes and has been the play-by-play voice of the Baltimore Orioles, Seattle Mariners, and San Diego Padres and hosted *Dodger Talk* for eight seasons. He's done more, but that's enough (in Levine's own words).

Steven Levitan

Steven Levitan was born in Chicago on April 6, 1962. He attended the University of Wisconsin-Madison where he majored in journalism. He was a news reporter there until moving to Hollywood to pursue work in TV. He is a writer, producer and director whose credits include *Frasier, Just Shoot Me* (which he also created), *The Larry Sanders Show* and *Wings*. He wrote 15 episodes of the latter and produced almost 50 others. About working on *Wings*, Levitan shared, "*Wings* was my first television writing job. Thanks to [Michael] Saltzman and [Bill] Diamond liking a *Cheers* spec script I wrote, I had the chance to come in and pitch a freelance script. They liked my pitches so I got to write the script. I came into the office to turn it in. Someone saw me and invited me to the filming of the first episode of the season, the following Tuesday. I had never been on a sitcom set before so I was so excited and, for some strange reason, terrified. I was sitting in the front row and I waved to a few of the writers, including [Peter] Casey, [David] Angell and [David] Lee. That's when it hit me that they had invited me BEFORE they read my script. From that moment on, I became convinced that they hated it and they wanted nothing to do with me. After the curtain call, David Angell walked over and asked me to come down to the set. We walked over to the Sandpiper desk where he said, 'We really liked your script and we'd like to invite you to join our writing staff.' Truly, one of the best moments of my life."

His biggest success came with a long-running and award-winning series titled *Modern Family* which he co-created. He has three children.

Christopher Lloyd

Christopher Lloyd the screenwriter and producer is not to be confused with the famous *Taxi* and *Back to the Future* actor. This Lloyd was born June 8, 1960 in Waterbury, Connecticut. His first writing credits were for *The Golden Girls*. Then came *Frasier* and *Wings*. Christopher is the son of the late David Lloyd who also worked on *Wings*. Christopher is still very active, most recently working with Steven Levitan on *Modern Family*. Between *Frasier* and *Modern Family* he has won twelve Emmys. He is married to Arleen Sorkin and has two sons.

David Lloyd

David Lloyd was born in Bronxville, New York on July 7, 1934. Among his proudest moments was writing the Emmy-winning "Chuckles Bites the Dust" episode for *The Mary Tyler Moore Show*. He also wrote for *The Bob Newhart Show*, *Taxi*, *Cheers*, *Frasier*, *The Tonight Show Starring Johnny Carson* along with the underappreciated *Best of the West, The Tony Randall Show* and *Wings*. One of his five children, Christopher also worked on *Wings*. It is said that David spoke very quickly, making it a bit difficult for those typing the scripts to keep up with his constant flow of comedy gold. As of Season Four, unlike all of the other opening credits on *Wings*, David Lloyd's name is the only one that doesn't use the double propeller design. His "written by" credit appears only in typeface with no background. David died of prostate cancer on November 10, 2009.

Jim McCoulf

Jim McCoulf was born in Burbank, California and studied at California State University Long Beach. His TV writing credits consist of *Arli$$, The Single Guy, The Jeff Foxworthy Show,* seven episodes of *The George Carlin Show*, and the "Bye, George" episode of *Wings*. He has also penned several screenplays including *Lie, Cheat and Steal; I Love You Very;* and *Top Ten*. McCoulf shared, "Prior to *Wings* I had sold a couple of screenplays. One of them, *Top Ten*, was read by Carl Reiner. Carl liked the writing enough to recommend me to his manager, George Shapiro. George signed me as a client. Sam Simon, a friend of his from the days of *Taxi* (when George represented Andy Kaufman) was just starting *The George Carlin Show*. He hired me as a staff writer for two seasons. Sam had worked with *Wings* producer Howard Gewirtz on other shows. I don't know, but I suspect he may have let Howard know I could turn in a script quickly if needed. That might have helped getting the assignment."

Peter S. Mehlman

Mehlman was originally a sportswriter, and later a freelance writer for magazines until an opportunity to write for *Seinfeld* arose and he moved to Los Angeles. He remained with *Seinfeld* until the end. In between, he wrote one episode of *Wings* titled "The Tennis Bum." Most recently Mehlman was a contributor to *The Huffington Post*.

Jeff Melman

Melman was born May 18, 1947 in Harrisburg, Pennsylvania and attended San Diego State University. Still very active to this day, Melman has an amazing list of TV directing credits topped off by *Night Court, Everybody Loves Raymond, Frasier, Malcolm in the Middle, Desperate Housewives, Grey's Anatomy, Finding Carter, Two-and-a-Half Men* and *Wings*. For the latter he directed some 40 episodes, including the series finale, "Final Approach Part Two."

Bruce Miller

Composer, arranger and conductor Bruce Miller is a native of Detroit where he cut his teeth on the local jazz and R&B scene as a guitarist and saxophonist in his teens. He was in strong demand for much of the professional music scene including local showrooms featuring major acts, records, commercials, jazz clubs and whatever else was happening around town relating to the music business. Bruce found himself breaking out of Detroit to go out on the road as Paul Anka's guitarist. After his three years with Anka, Miller's experience and musical abilities began to catch the ear of many notables in the industry whose encouragement brought him to the West Coast where he began working in Los Angeles. Bruce's broad musical knowledge led him to doing orchestral arrangements for a long list of R&B artists including the Commodores, the Temptations, Rose Royce, and the Four Tops, as well as more contemporary artists such as Joss Stone and Rod Stewart. His first big break in scoring for television came when he was contacted by the composer for *Knots Landing*. Hiring Bruce to write an updated arrangement for the theme song, his new version won over the producers, who kept it for the rest of the series' run, and eventually got him included in the composer roster on the show for the next five years. It was through this initial offering that he started to meet executives from Lorimar Studios, as well as many other notable producers. Obviously, they were impressed, and work came quickly for Miller, whose credits would include *Frasier, Becker, Designing Women, The New Odd Couple,* and *Wings* to name just a few. He was nominated for an Emmy Award in 1989 for Best Arranger (Music Direction) for the *Sammy Davis Jr. 60th Anniversary Celebration*, and he garnered a second nomination in 1994 for Best Theme for *Frasier*. In addition, he has 16 BMI TV and Film awards and 14 SESAC awards. In 2012, he was awarded the prestigious SESAC "Legacy" award. Miller also boasts various gold and platinum records for his work with numerous A-list recording artists across many genres.

Bob Moore

Along with the warm-up man, Robert G. Lee, *Wings* had a live band to pump up the audience on show night. Lee recalled, "That was among the great aspects of working on this show. They were called Bob Moore and the Wrong Brothers – basically a bunch of session musicians who played for groups such as Paul Revere and the Raiders on classic rock tours on weekends, and then came to play for us. Moore was a great guy, a great drummer, and would play his heart out for very little money. I guess that's what musicians do." Moore also appeared in the episode titled "Remembrance of Flings Past" as the bandleader.

Judy Pioli

Judy Pioli (also known as Judy Askins) was born March 3, 1950 in Brooklyn. She is a retired actress, producer, writer and director who worked on a couple of Garry Marshall shows (*Laverne and Shirley, Blansky's Beauties*) early in her career. Other credits include *Step by Step, Valerie, Perfect Strangers* and *Charles in Charge*. She directed one episode of *Wings* titled "What the Cabbie Saw" in which Antonio testifies against a suspected criminal and then panics when the man is released on a technicality.

Noam Pitlik

Noam Pitlik was born November 4, 1932 in Philadelphia. His acting career began in the 1950s, first in an off-Broadway play and then as a busy character actor with credits including *The Andy Griffith Show, The Patty Duke Show, Get Smart, The Odd Couple, All in the Family, Barney Miller, I'm Dickens He's Fenster, The Bob Newhart*

Show and films such as *The Fortune Cookie, The Front Page, The Graduate* and more. As good as he was in front of the camera, he may have been even better behind it. He won an Emmy for directing *Barney Miller*. About his work on *Wings*, Tim Daly said, "He was so wonderful as we were just getting started on the series." Steven Weber said, "Noam was our first director and I had known who he was from his movie and TV appearances. What a sweet, hilarious and loving guy. I was going through a rough patch that first season and he was so sweet to me." Rebecca Schull shared, "I loved working with Noam – a sweet, caring, smart man." Guest star Amanda Carlin ("A Stand Up Kind of Guy" episode) said, "I had loved watching Noam Pitlik as an actor [*Barney Miller*], and really enjoyed his calm easy energy, and his sneaky dry wit. He had a physical grace about him, too. I was still new to L. A. - having moved from N. Y. C. a few months earlier and excited to land my first guest-starring TV role on this new comedy. I was SO eager to rehearse, ready to perform; also my character was high-energy, so I was 'a bit much!' On the second day, after rehearsal of our scene, Noam sidled up to me and said softly, 'Relax- you've got the job.'" Noam is said to have hated the many columns present on the terminal set. He said they always got in the way of his shots. Pitlik was married three times and succumbed to lung cancer on February 18, 1999.

Bruce Rasmussen

Rasmussen was born March 18, 1961 in Bridgeport, Connecticut. He is a writer and producer currently working for *The Conners* on ABC. *Wings* was one of his early TV jobs. While there he penned four episodes and co-produced another 21. He won a Peabody and a Golden Globe for his work on *Roseanne*. Although situation comedy is his forte, he did also work on dramas such as *Without a Trace* and the reboot of *Dallas*.

Mark Reisman

Often teamed with Ian Gurvitz, Mark Reisman is a writer and producer of such shows as *Frasier, Dear John, Saturday Night Live* and *Wings*. On the latter, he and Ian Gurvitz took the reins of the show when David Lee, Peter Casey and David Angell moved on to their next creation, *Frasier*, and Dave Hackel was getting ready to move on to *Becker*. Reisman's most recent credit is for creating, writing and producing *Sydney to the Max* for the Disney Channel.

Jeffrey Richman

Richman is a producer and writer known for his work on *Frasier*, *Desperate Housewives*, *Yes Dear*, all episodes of *Modern Family*, and of course, *Wings* with former writing partner Joyce Gittlin. He co-produced some 50 episodes while writing eleven. Currently Richman is paired with actor John Benjamin Hickey.

Michael Saltzman

Michael Saltzman began his career partnered with Bill Diamond after the two met at The Columbia University School of Journalism. They got their start working on the ABC sitcom, *Anything but Love*. Their second job was on *Wings*, which they joined in the show's second season. While there they wrote nine episodes and created the character of Antonio Scarpacci, so memorably played by Tony Shalhoub. After *Wings*, Bill and Mike went on to *Murphy Brown*, where they ultimately rose to be Executive Producers and showrunners of the hit CBS sitcom. After the two split up as a writing team, Michael revamped and ran the NBC comedy, *The Naked Truth*, starring Tea Leoni. He created the sitcom *Baby Bob* for CBS and *Misconceptions* (starring *Frasier's* Jane Leeves and French Stewart) for the WB (the latter show, unfortunately, never aired when the network went out of business before its premiere date.) Frustrated with the declining market for comedies at the time, Michael pivoted to writing drama, working on the acclaimed AMC shows *Mad Men*, *Hell on Wheels*, and *Halt and Catch Fire*, as well as the Amazon Prime shows *Sneaky Pete* and, most recently, *The Boys*. Not forgetting his comedy roots, Michael also did a stint on *Arrested Development* for Netflix, and created a show for Carol Burnett for ABC, which was, sadly, not picked up to series. The pilot was directed by longtime *Wings* helmer Andy Ackerman.

Michael Sardo

Michael Sardo is a writer and producer known for *Rizzoli and Isles, Fairly Legal, Caroline in the City, The Tracey Ullman Show* and *Wings*. On the latter, he was part of the latter regime and produced 24 episodes, wrote twelve, and was story editor on some 51 more.

Christopher Vane

Vane graduated from Wesleyan University and is a writer and producer famous for creating *Impastor* which ran for two seasons. He also wrote and/or produced *Dream On, Good Luck Charlie, The Love Boat, Suddenly Susan, Veronica's Closet, The Bill Engvall Show* and of course *Wings* on which he was a producer for Season Seven and Supervising Producer for Season Eight. He also wrote eight episodes of *Wings*, including the penultimate "Raging Bull*&@!." Coincidentally, Vane also wrote for the short-lived sitcom *Blue Skies* in 1994 - *Blue Skies* was the original working title for *Wings*. Christopher's son's name, Kyle Vane was used for the unseen character receiving love letters from the mysterious "R" in the episode titled "Ms. Write."

Bryan Winter

Winter's stay in TV was brief but he packed a lot of work in a short period. He wrote and produced many shows such as *The Fresh Prince of Bel Air, My Two Dads, The Cosby Show, Hearts Afire* and *Wings*. He was the story editor for two very popular episodes of the latter – "Murder She Roast" in which Brian thinks Fay is a wanted serial killer, and "Mother Wore Stripes" in which the Hackett Boys reunited with their long lost mother only to discover she'd been in prison for embezzlement.

THE EPISODES
SEASON ONE

A souvenir postcard from Nantucket – Approximately 56 square miles of smiles you'll enjoy, especially in summer.

A souvenir postcard with an aerial view of the real Nantucket Airport.

A souvenir postcard with a ground view of the real Nantucket Airport.

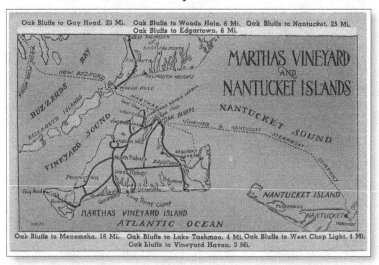

A postcard showing a map of not only Nantucket, but also of Martha's Vineyard.

Each episode began with 60 seconds of artsy soaring airplane footage underscored with the beautiful "Piano Sonata #20 in A" by Franz Schubert (arranged and adapted by Antony Cooke). Casting delays led to a truncated midseason order of only six episodes here in Season One. All six aired on Thursday nights at 9:30 on NBC.

"Legacy" (Season 1 Episode 1) Aired April 19, 1990
Written by David Angell, Peter Casey and David Lee
Directed by James Burrows

The cover of the Wings *pilot script.*

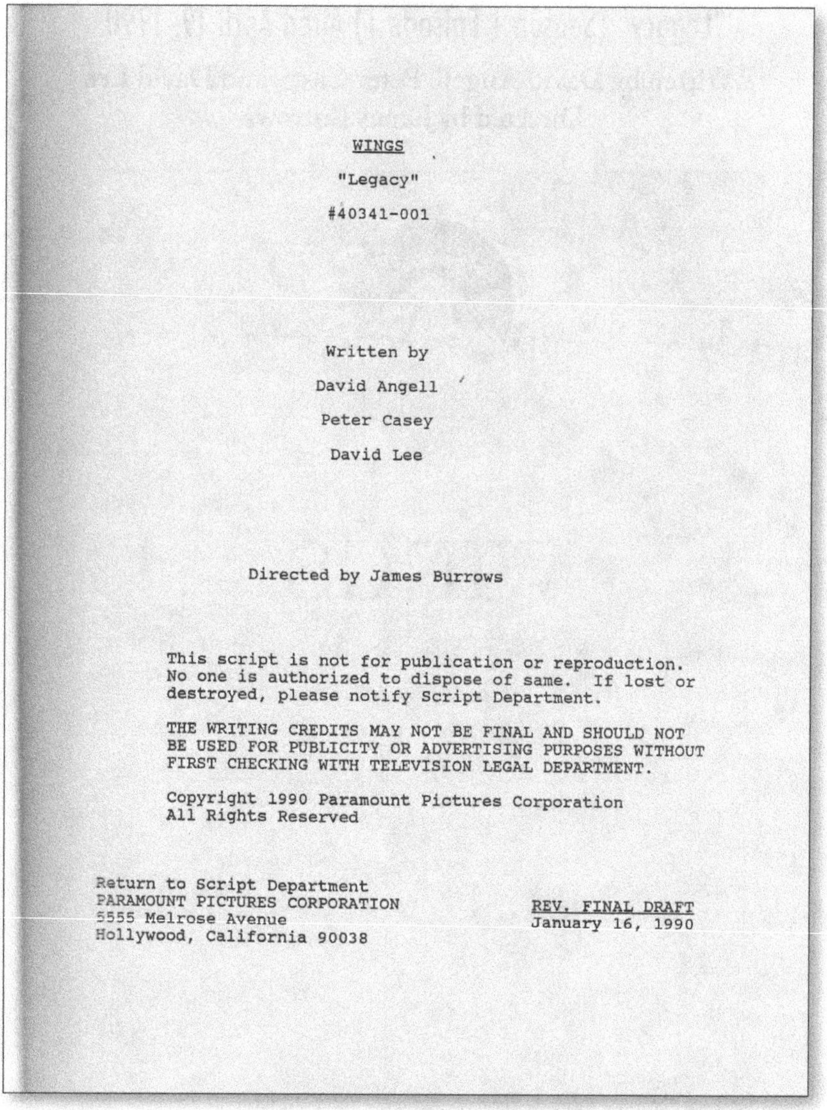

```
                        WINGS

                       "Legacy"

                     #40341-001




                     Written by

                    David Angell

                    Peter Casey

                    David Lee




                Directed by James Burrows




        This script is not for publication or reproduction.
        No one is authorized to dispose of same.  If lost or
        destroyed, please notify Script Department.

        THE WRITING CREDITS MAY NOT BE FINAL AND SHOULD NOT
        BE USED FOR PUBLICITY OR ADVERTISING PURPOSES WITHOUT
        FIRST CHECKING WITH TELEVISION LEGAL DEPARTMENT.

        Copyright 1990 Paramount Pictures Corporation
        All Rights Reserved


    Return to Script Department
    PARAMOUNT PICTURES CORPORATION
    5555 Melrose Avenue                    REV. FINAL DRAFT
    Hollywood, California 90038            January 16, 1990
```

The historic Wings *pilot script.*

This pilot episode (a pilot about pilots) was filmed on January 19, 1990 and aired exactly three months later. The show's star, Tim Daly said, "In the very first scene of the show, I'm kissing my plane." Yes indeed. This episode, the first of 172, opens with pilot Joseph Montgomery Hackett alone in the hangar at Tom Nevers Field in Nantucket, Massachusetts with his beloved Cessna airplane on which the letters N121PP are emblazoned. Well, at least Joe thinks

REVISED 1/18/90

                            WINGS

                          "Legacy"

                          #40341-001

                            CAST

JOE HACKETT...............................TIMOTHY DALY

BRIAN HACKETT.............................STEVEN WEBER

HELEN CHAPPEL.............................CRYSTAL BERNARD

LOWELL MATHER.............................THOMAS HADEN CHURCH

ROY BIGGINS...............................DAVID SCHRAMM

FAY EVELYN COCHRAN........................REBECCA SCHULL

WOMAN.....................................BRIGITTE KEMPT

PASSENGER.................................TORREY HANSON

RADIO (V.O.)..............................LARRY MCKAY

                            SETS

INT. HANGAR

INT. TERMINAL

INT. OFFICE

INT. AIRPLANE

*The episode's cast list and an unredeemed ticket to
the filming of the Wings pilot on January 19, 1990.
(Courtesy of David Lee and Peter Casey).*

he is alone. Upon verbally expressing his love for the Cessna, an answer can be heard echoing back – that of mechanic and handyman Lowell Mather who was in the cockpit executing some repairs. It is a Tuesday (we know this as Joe, a creature of habit, orders his usual Tuesday BLT at Helen Chappel's lunch counter in the airport terminal). Oh, but it is not just any Tuesday. A package addressed to Joe was mistakenly delivered to competitor Roy Peterman Biggins and, after several days of forgetting about it he's just getting around to giving the package to Joe. Biggins runs the larger and more profitable Aeromass out of the same terminal. Speaking of "terminal," the package contained information about Joe's late dad's legacy. The deceased Donald Hackett spent his final years in mental decline exacerbated when his wife, Mae abandoned the family. At the end, Donald thought that Joe, the son who looked after him in his final days was actually singer Eydie Gorme. The will has to be read with both Hackett boys present. The problem is Joe and his younger brother Brian Michael Hackett have been estranged for six years as a result of Brian stealing away and marrying Joe's fiancé, Carol. With much dread and trepidation, Joe contacts his wayward brother who is also a pilot allegedly working for a Mustique charter company in the West Indies (the truth is, Brian is no longer among the employed). Flying on Aeromass, Brian returns to his childhood home of Nantucket Island and is instantly surprised by his newly-svelte friend, Helen Chappel who has lost 68 pounds since last he saw her. Sibling rivalry instantly rears its ugly head as the brothers vie for the affections of that fair maiden. The relationship between the Hackett brothers is strained, but they attempt to work together harmoniously given the situation. Finding out that Carol has also left Brian for another guy aids in the reconciliation process. Where there's a "will," there's a way.

It soon becomes obvious that the late Donald Hackett was not only a loon, but also quite the prankster, leaving the boys a suitcase full of keys that sends them on a wild goose chase rife with more suitcases, more keys, several maps, and even some pop up snakes. Brian and Joe are in search of their father's alleged fortune, as one of the last things Donald ever said to Brian was, "You're rich." Those words are also written on an old photograph of them together in friendlier times found in one of the suitcases, and in true *How The Grinch Stole Christmas* fashion, their hearts grow at least three sizes that day when they see this photo. Speaking of "you're rich," the deceased Hackett had also alluded to having won a large sum of money but given his mental state in his latter years such comments were taken with a grain of salt. Joe, an old softie offers an olive branch and takes on the jobless Brian as a pilot – an act of kindness he will at times come to rue. Torrey Hanson plays the harried Sandpiper passenger, alarmed by Joe and Brian's mid-flight sniping.

"Across the World in Eighty Years" (Season 1 Episode 2) Aired April 26, 1990

Written by Philip LaZebnik
Directed by Noam Pitlik

The episode's title is a play on Jules Verne's *Around the World in 80 Days*. This episode does a wonderful job of providing expository information about the cast of characters. We see Brian's attempts to get Joe to loosen up and add more spontaneity to his rigid existence. Helen returns to her uninspiring lot in life - waitressing, after what she believes was yet another lackluster cello audition. Brian suggests that Helen should start dressing more provocatively for future auditions. When she gets a callback for a second audition, she opts to take Brian up on his suggestion and orders a more revealing frock. Her sexy dress is delivered just in the nick of time for takeoff (by actor Sam Pancake as the delivery boy). About the experience, Pancake shared, "I remember it all fairly vividly because it was my very first line of dialogue on an actual tv show. Woohoo. Other than commercials, *Wings* was my first television job and I was very excited and grateful they picked me. I had lived in L. A. for about two-and-a-half years and after booking this role, I felt like maybe I had a chance to make a living as an actor in Hollywood. And eventually, I did. I was brought in for the role in February or March (pretty sure?) of 1990 by the wonderful casting director Sheila Guthrie, whom I had met through a cold-reading workshop, and I recall it was a situation in which, right after my callback right there on the Paramount lot, they asked me to wait outside, then told me I had the role, and Sheila's

Wings *writers/creative crew from the early years. Front row left to right David Angell, Peter Casey, David Lee, Bill Diamond. Back row left to right Dave Hackel, Roz Doyle, Philip LaZebnik, Bruce Rasmussen, Michael Saltzman. (Courtesy of David Lee and Peter Casey).*

associate at the time, Jeff Greenberg, kindly walked me over (to Stage 19 where they filmed) for the table read. I was over the moon. Such a small part, I know, but it was a VERY BIG DEAL to this young kid (somewhat) fresh from West Virginia at the time. Also, somehow I knew or was told that they shot on the same stage that *Laverne and Shirley* [actually *Happy Days*] had been made on, one of my favorite shows from childhood. Extra thrilling. I remember that even though it was the second episode aired, it was the fourth or fifth one that was shot. That happens a lot with new sitcoms, as they find their groove. It was not only my first sitcom, but my first earthquake! During one of the rehearsal days, an earthquake hit and we all ran out of the soundstage. I remember looking up and seeing all the heavy lights above us swaying, the airport set shaking, and the plane rocking back and forth before hightailing it out of there. Crystal Bernard was lovely and helpful and kind, and I confided to her that I was nervous and it was my first job and she absolutely had my back. I really liked her. Steven Weber was a damn delight and we stayed friendly and I still see him over the years as we cross paths in good ole show biz land and through mutual friends. He's an ace and I'm always grateful for how good he was to me that week, when I was terribly anxious on my first sitcom job. David Schramm and Rebecca Schull were professional and kind and I just loved sitting around in the cast chairs and listening to them have 'veteran character actor conversations' as I thought of it. I kept thinking, 'that's what I want to be' I don't remember a whole lot about Richard Erdman, other than he was friendly and kinda quiet and clearly an old pro, or about the producers, other than I knew they were the *Cheers* guys, and that was a big deal. If I hadn't been so green, I would have known to pay more attention. I was a little starstruck around Noam Pitlik because I fully remembered him as an actor on the 70's shows I grew up on, and even remembered his distinctive name in the credits of shows as a director. (I knew I wanted to be an actor from a very young age and paid attention to those things even then). He was tall and handsome and charismatic and had a big moustache and I was kind of in awe. I learned a lot from him and the whole process very quickly that week, because even though I had a degree in theatre and had done lots of plays and by that time, a handful of commercials, sitcoms were a new adventure for me, and there was no Sitcom School one could go to. Multi-cameras situation comedies are a very specific medium with techniques, processes and a terminology all their own. I learned only by doing and hearing about experiences from other actors, and *Wings* was my first class. Noam Pitlik was a great teacher in that respect, even though I was only around him for a week. I soaked it all up like a sponge."

Helen returns to Nantucket from her cello audition confident that she will get the job, but the only correspondence she receives from the Maestro involves a phone call about a dent to his car caused by her cello case, leaving Helen to doubt both her cello playing and her quotient of sexiness in that revealing new dress. It is in this episode that we first become aware of Helen's fiery and destructive temper.

Meanwhile, busybodies Fay and Roy develop a curiosity about a man named Howard Banks (Richard Erdman) who has been lurking around the airport for days on end. When the man is confronted, he admits that he is a retired hat salesman from New Bedford and an Aries with his moon in Scorpio whose favorite color is blue. He has been flying around the world in a Stearman two-seater plane and fears that when his journey is officially completed, upon return-ing to New Bedford he will die. He opts to take his time and remain in Nantucket for the time being, reading his newspaper in the ter-minal. Then, instead of finishing his journey, he opts to backtrack in the opposite direction, returning to New Bedford so as to remain among the living. Fay refers to him as being, "Nuttier than a squir-rel's cheeks in October." Although fearful of dying in this episode, it should be noted that Richard Erdman lived to be 93.

"Return to Nantucket Part One" (Season 1 Episode 3) Aired May 3, 1990

Written by Philip LaZebnik
Directed by Noam Pitlik

Brian's old pilot friend Danny McCoy (William Bumiller) is briefly seen in this episode at Helen's lunch counter. It's part one of a two-parter on which Danny lets on that Brian's ex-wife, Carol (Kim Johnston Ulrich) has dumped her new beau. She has designs on moving to London, but on her way has a four-hour layover in Boston. Thinking it's a sign that she wants to reconcile, Brian sets up a reunion at the same place they had their first date – the top of the Prudential building (he calls her and leaves a message to arrange that meeting). There are a few wrenches in his plans, how-ever – repairs to the plane take longer than expected, and a dense fog grounds all flights (but once the plane is again airworthy Brian defies the tower and flies through the murky Massachusetts sky).

Instead of meeting with Brian directly, Carol has paid an African American cab driver named Luther Talbot (Sy Richardson) $30.00 to deliver flowers to Brian along with the message that she will not be able to attend but treasures the time they had together. About his funny role as Luther, Sy Richardson said, "As a character actor it is very rare that you work on a show you love to watch. *Wings* was my favorite sitcom. When I booked it I started screaming and shouting, 'Thank you, Jesus.'" About director Noam Pitlik, Rich-ardson said, "He was very personable and allowed me to create my character. He didn't tell me how to do it. And the cast, they were so professional and on the money. They made me nervous because they

were so 'on it.' My line 'Remember me fondly' came out differently than I had planned." Joe and Helen arrive just in time to console a crushed Brian who had set his hopes extremely high. The episode ends, however, with Carol having a change of heart. The elevator doors open to reveal her presence, much to the amazement of Brian and Joe.

Big smiles from the Hackett Brothers, Brian and Joe. They must be up to something.

"Return to Nantucket Part Two" (Season 1 Episode 4) Aired May 10, 1990

Written by David Angell
Directed by Noam Pitlik

After a recap of events in Part One, Brian discovers that he misinter-

preted Carol's (Kim Johnston Ulrich) layover in Boston. She intended to spend a little bit of time with her parents and their three-legged Chihuahua named Lucky while there. It was not meant as a signal to Brian. He does manage to lure her back to Nantucket for a trial reconciliation, much to

All three of these characters have some real baggage (left to right) Joe Hackett, Helen Chappel and Brian Hackett.

the chagrin of onlookers Joe and Helen. Carol seems to have no recollection of having ever met Helen. All seems well and good for Brian and Carol. That is, until Carol comes on to Joe in his office. Against his better judgment, Joe tells Brian what went down. These events almost renew their six-year estrangement. After they reject her advances in tandem, Helen has the last laugh by hitting Carol with a pie in the face, a la Soupy Sales.

"There Once Was a Girl from Nantucket" (Season 1 Episode 5) Aired May 17, 1990

Written by Dave Hackel
Directed by Noam Pitlik

For continuity sake, Tim Daly asked for a change in part of the script in this episode. Daly shared, "In the very first scene of the first episode [the pilot] I'm seen kissing my plane. So I confronted the writers about the opening scene of this episode. Brian wants me to go out on the town with him, but I said no, I was too busy washing the plane. They wanted me to appear put upon, but I thought that was inconsistent with what we set up previously. Staying home washing the plane would be something Joe *wanted* to do. He would be happy to do it – he loved his plane. They then agreed that this was the right way to do the scene."

With a show set in Nantucket, it was only a matter of time until the risqué old limerick "There once was a Man/Girl from Nantucket" came into play. This was the perfect opportunity to utilize said limerick as a woman with a "reputation" named Cindy McGrath (Megan Mullally) of Madaket Road is Joe's blind date – a fixup courtesy of Brian. Originally it was supposed to be a double date, but Brian reneges on his end of the bargain (but because of Joe's insistence goes along anyway and takes Helen for moral support). Ditsy Cindy works at the cosmetics counter at a local drug store. The date ends in disaster as one of Cindy's many jealous boyfriends, Jimmy (Ben Mittleman) sees her out with the Hackett brothers at the Club Car and punches both in their respective noses, egged on by Brian's bravado. Large, uncomfortable bandages were required in each case. Joe's nose also took the brunt of another jealous rage caused by Brian in the episode titled "Noses Off" in Season Four. Cindy breaks it off with Joe (the date, not the nose) and thinks he's following her out of the terminal to keep her from leaving, but he has to follow her – he's the pilot for her flight out of town. It's interesting to note that Megan Mullally was at one time considered for the role of Helen. Also of significance, this episode contains the first mention of Helen's credo, (albeit a temporary one) "I don't date pilots."

"All for One and Two for Helen" (Season 1 Episode 6) Aired May 24, 1990

Written by Dave Hackel
Directed by Noam Pitlilk

Animal lover Fay, an avid birdwatcher is attempting to save a family of short-eared owls living on the airport grounds. She watches them like a hawk with her own invention called, "The thing I use to peek around corners and look at birds with" (it's a stick with a mirror attached). Fay's attempts to save the birds anger Roy, as her actions hold up the building of a new hangar for his seventh airplane. Meanwhile, "the Three Musketeers" Joe, Brian and Helen have plans to see the Celtics host the Knicks in Boston. Joe is crestfallen when he is unable to go with them after all because Roy has called an emergency Airport Committee meeting about the standoff concerning the owls. Joe is upset, not only about missing the game, but also because Brian is alone with Helen and he fears the worst from his horndog brother. The meeting is held for naught as it is discovered that Lowell accidently crushed the owls with his truck. It turns out that Joe did have reason to be concerned about the actions of his brother, however. The game was called off last minute because of flooding caused by a burst waterpipe. Brian did intend to make a pass at Helen, but she intercepted the pass as it was being thrown and nothing happened. Upon returning to Helen's home, however, they become aware that they are being watched by Joe (in his car) and they put on quite a show to teach him a lesson.

The Three Musketeers, Brian, Helen and Joe (left to right) in "All for One and Two for Helen."

SEASON TWO

Season Two was the sitcom's first full season and consisted of 22 episodes. Bruce Miller was now the arranger and composer for the show and remained until the end in 1997. The first few episodes of the new season aired on Thursdays at 9:30. On November 9, 1990 the show moved to Fridays at 9:30. To start 1991, the program returned to Thursday nights at 9:30 where it remained for the rest of the season. Tony Shalhoub made his first appearance this season as Antonio Scarpacci, a waiter in the Valentine's Day episode titled "Looking for Love in All the Wrong Places"

A 1990 promotional flyer for Paramount TV shows, including Wings. (Courtesy of Suzanne Holmes).

The first page of the sheet music for the Franz Schubert theme song in the opening credits. (Courtesy of Bruce Miller).

"The Puppetmaster" (Season 2 Episode 1)
Aired September 28, 1990

Written by Philip LaZebnik
Directed by Noam Pitlik

The show's theme song is by Franz Schubert, and the composer's name is mentioned at Helen's lunch counter as a handsome young guy is heard humming the fourth movement of Schubert's Trout Quintet. Truth be told, he is an actor named Matt Sargent (Craig Bierko) hired by Brian to be Helen's dream date. He is also a Pan Am pilot – an attempt to trick Helen into dropping her "I don't date pilots" rule. As a result, Brian anoints himself "the Puppetmaster."

The plan backfires when Helen falls for the guy and Matt pretends to fall for Helen and lets her in on his scheme. When Matt and Helen make plans to run away and get married, Joe steps in and admits his feelings for Helen (he's in on their plan, too). Joe and Helen then kiss passionately (and each one is taken by surprise at how hot the kiss really is). A scuffle and a convincing prop gun Joe aimed at Matt soon makes Brian, the "Puppetmaster" look like the dummy as he gets a big dose of his own medicine, thinking that Joe has shot Matt.

Hangers-on in the hangar – rear left to right Thomas Haden Church and David Schramm. Middle left to right Steven Weber and Tim Daly. Front left to right Rebecca Schull and Crystal Bernard. (Courtesy of Suzanne Holmes).

Cast: L to R - Rebecca Schull, Thomas Haden Church, Steven Weber, Crystal Bernard, David Schramm, Timothy Daly.

The episode closes with Lowell singing "Moon River" for the first of several times during the run of the series.

The Wings *sheet music for the closing theme. (Courtesy of Bruce Miller).*

"The Story of Joe" (Season 2 Episode 2) Aired October 5, 1990
Written by Bruce Rasmussen
Directed by Noam Pitlik

This episode is the first of three on which *Cheers* characters visit the *Wings* gang. In this one Norm Peterson (George Wendt) and Cliff Claven (John Ratzenberger) fly on Sandpiper Air with Brian as their pilot. They're on their way to Nantucket to get in some fishing, but never quite seem to get themselves out on the water, instead opting to "perch" belly up to every bar on the island. Meanwhile, Joe is on edge because of an upcoming interview for *American Flyer Magazine*. His dream has long been to grace the cover of the magazine. It could also be a boon for business, as it has been for others.

When Ted Cobb (Charles Hallahan) from the magazine visits to interview Joe, jealous Roy attempts to horn in on the man's focus, but it is the carefree Brian who wins Cobb over and dominates the proposed magazine article (because Brian knows of Ted's previous work for *Mercenary Monthly* and because both of them used to live in the West Indies on Mustique). Ted hates flying, hates writing for the magazine, hates that his boss' aunt thought that writing about Sandpiper Air would make a cute story (after she flew on the tiny airline), but Brian's wild "flights of fancy" ignite Ted's interest in the project. Joe overreacts and crashes Brian's luncheon interview at the Club Car with Ted, only to discover that Brian has been singing his envious brother's praises, calling him the best pilot he's ever seen. After all that, the publisher opted to kill the story because it just didn't have enough substance and oomph, dashing Joe's dream.

"A Little Nightmare Music" (Season 2 Episode 3) Aired October 12, 1990

Written by Bryan Winter
Directed by Noam Pitlik

"A Little Nightmare Music" is a takeoff on the title of Stephen Sondheim's *A Little Night Music*. Fay is practicing to be Madame Zorko in the fortune telling booth at the upcoming VFW Carnival. Meanwhile, Helen spots Edward Tinsdale (David Ogden Stiers) walking through the terminal. He is the conductor for the Minneapolis Philharmonic, and he's on his honeymoon with the new Mrs. Tinsdale (Kelly Miller). In most of this episode's scenes, Mrs. Tinsdale is merely a loud voice emanating from the bedroom. Brian and Joe devise a scheme to detain a piece of Tinsdale's luggage only to then have Helen deliver it to his hotel room later with her cello in tow. When she arrives at his door, Tinsdale, in a bathrobe reluctantly allows her to audition, and his evaluation of her performance devastates her. Joe then arranges a second audition for Helen, but Tinsdale is still not wowed by the cellist.

In the meantime, Helen comes to terms with the rejection and decides to "move on" to an existence sans cello. She handles the rejection and the closure it brings very well. That is, until Tinsdale, prior to boarding his return flight to Minnesota has a change of heart, telling Helen that there is a "glimmer of talent" present in her work, reigniting her passion for practicing. It should be noted that

Stiers and David Schramm were both previously members of the famed theater group known as "The Acting Company."

"Sports and Leisure" (Season 2 Episode 4) Aired October 19, 1990
Written by David Angell
Directed by Noam Pitlik

Joe has to cancel numerous Sandpiper flights while awaiting a replacement strut for the airplane, much to the delight of Roy who gets to absorb all of those stranded passengers. Brian, Fay, Helen and Joe now have the rest of the day off as a result of the Sandpiper

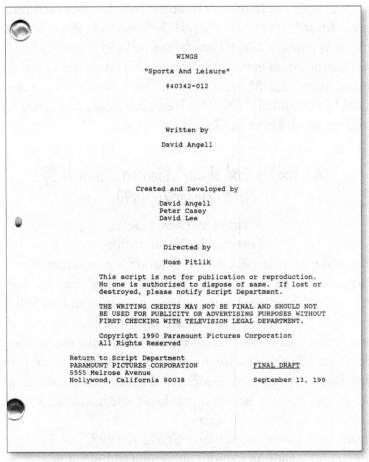

Cover page for the "Sports and Leisure" script. There was no guest star in this episode, but Ann-Margret does receive many an honorable mention.

cancellations and they plan to go fishing on Lowell's boat. To everyone's dismay, Fay invites Roy. While at sea Roy punks them into thinking the boat is ablaze and laughs hysterically when they all jump overboard and return to the terminal sopping wet. Roy begins to think of himself as "one of the guys" when Fay invites him to Trivial Pursuit night at Helen's. The only advantage to having Roy attend is that he plans to bring along his famous pasta salad made with tortellini, cheese, basil and dill. Joe uninvites Roy, and then feels bad when he sees how upsetting the news is to the big guy. None of them have never seen Roy cry before. Roy promises to try to be a nicer person in the future and gets re-invited to the gathering. In a very touching and humbling moment with Joe, Roy calls him Joe instead of just Hackett and sheepishly tries to make amends. Roy's attempts to reinvent himself are short-lived and go awry when he is paired for the board game with Lowell who answers every question with the name Ann-Margret. At first "New Roy" is able to contain himself, but eventually "Old Roy" rears his mustachioed head, and the bluster we all know and love returns.

"A Stand Up Kind of Guy" (Season 2 Episode 5) Aired October 26, 1990

Written by Dave Hackel
Directed by Noam Pitlik

Except for the debut episode in Season One on which Joe kisses his airplane before the opening credits, all other prior episodes of *Wings* immediately began with the opening credits and the Schubert theme. This particular episode kicked off the regular appearance of the short and funny vignette or "teaser" to start the show, followed by the theme. In this one we discover that Roy has a metal plate in his head from a childhood incident in the stands at a baseball game. We also find out that he has a prankster son named R. J. (but we don't yet get to see him on screen).

Meanwhile, a man named Jerry Starke (Kelly Connell) attempts to contact Joe, claiming to be an old school chum, but no one seems to remember him. Joe is too nice to tell Starke that he does not recall ever meeting him but in being nice allows himself to be talked into being Starke's best man at his wedding to Marilyn (Amanda Carlin). About her character, Carlin recalled, "I understood this character's eagerness to connect. I was grateful to the writers for making her someone with the annoying habit of finishing other people's sentences. It takes comic precision between all the actors in the scene, so it's a fun challenge to find the rhythm together."

Upon arrival at the terminal, the "stark" reality is that no one has any recollection of Starke, a dentist who met his intended at an automobile accident. After a slip of the tongue by Fay, Joe is then obligated to throw Starke a bachelor party, too. Strangely the only person who seems to remember Starke is Roberta (Leslie Cook), the exotic dancer Brian hired for that bachelor party (she also works in a gift shop). Starke was once madly in love with Roberta, and suddenly the old Starke spark is reignited, leading him to marry her instead of his intended, Marilyn. Carlin said about Kelly Connell who played her fiance in the episode, "A wonderful character actor, wonderful person. Met him there first, and then worked with him twice subsequently - once on stage, and once on another sitcom. I told him this was a new environment to me (we both came from theatre, but he already had a few TV jobs under his belt by then). He was so generous with his time ('want to run those lines?'), and also my personal Eskimo. He took care of me!" Was the cast just as nice? Carlin said, "Abso-damn-lutely true! Gracious, welcoming cast and crew. Turned out that both Tim [Daly] and Steven [Weber] had worked with my mother, actress Frances Sternhagen, and so they felt like 'instant brothers' to me. And David Schramm and I had multiple mutual theatre friends. It was like old home week." Even though the character of Jerry Starke is very clingy and promises that Joe will see him on a regular basis, he never again graces Tom Nevers Field. While watching the episode, take notice of the boom microphone briefly becoming visible in the corner by Pilgrim Rent a Car.

"It's Not the Thought, It's the Gift (Season 2 Episode 6) Aired November 9, 1990

Written by Peter Casey and David Lee
Directed by Noam Pitlik

Fay aids Lowell, helping to get his finances in order, urging him to get a refund for a rented tuxedo. Meanwhile Helen's birthday gift from her parents is a reel of great old home movies from her eleventh birthday party.

Speaking of birthdays, sibling rivalry runs rampant in this episode which focuses upon the Hackett brothers' attempts to win Helen over by purchasing the most expensive and impressive gift for her. It is a good thing they saved the receipts because each gift bought was returned in a vicious circle of one-upmanship. After exchanging a hand-knit sweater, a fondue pot, exorbitant perfume, a cassette player, a portable phone, a cappuccino maker, etc., the boys call a truce and promise to buy only a small, practical gift. Joe follows the truce, but Brian wins Helen's favor with a CD player (Joe got her a piece of driftwood with a seagull seated on top). Because of the thoughtful gift, Helen invites Brian over for dinner that evening. Her unceasingly giddy glee about Brian's gift causes a rift between Joe and Helen. The next day, Joe arrives are her place unannounced with the gift of a cameo pin. Joe shrugs it off as a mere trinket, but Helen later discovers the origin of the cameo pin while re-watching her old birthday movie. Joe's mother was wearing it. Valri Jackson makes a "cameo appearance" (see what I did there) in Helen's birthday movie as Mae Hackett.

"Hell Hath No Fury like a Policewoman Scorned" (Season 2 Episode 7) Aired November 16, 1990

Written by Bill Diamond and Michael Saltzman
Directed by Noam Pitlik

The title is a play on "Hell Hath No Fury like a Woman Scorned" which comes from a play titled *The Mourning Bride* by William Congrieve. Lowell is attempting to win a big money prize with his new camcorder for a program similar to *America's Funniest Home Videos* (*America's Wackiest Videos*). He attempts to stage a funny event with Roy's help but is totally oblivious to a spectacularly choreographed series of mishaps in the terminal involving golf balls, a group of ticketholders falling over like dominoes, and a faceplant in a large cake which would have won the $100,000 hands down. About that

intricate scene, co-writer Michael Saltzman shared, "All credit really has to go to the stunt people who choreographed it. They basically took what Bill [Diamond] and I wrote and executed it perfectly. They might have had to adjust some things for safety or practicality but they took what was on the page and made it happen. And all

Hanging in the hangar. A promotional still from the final scene of the episode titled "Hell Hath No Fury like a Policewoman Scorned."

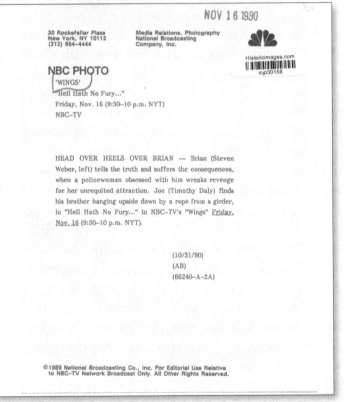

A promotional writeup for one of the show's early episodes, "Hell Hath No Fury like a Policewoman Scorned."

in one take. There was no trickery or editing. They just pulled off an insane physical stunt perfectly. We were as delighted as anyone when it played even better than we imagined."

In other developments an overzealous policewoman named Colleen Thomas (Sharon Barr) slaps handcuffs on Joe for parking in a handicapped zone as well as over 40 other such unpaid violations – all of which are Brian's fault. Attempting to rescue his brother, Brian turns on the spigot of smarmy charm, but the cop sees right through his ploy. She does, however, want to go out on a date with him and Joe makes sure it happens, just for spite. The date with the policewoman is such a disaster, Brian is certain he will never hear from her again, but he could not be more wrong. She is infatuated with Brian. To get out of his predicament, Brian tells her he is dating Helen…a "*cop*out" that might have worked if he had only warned Helen in advance. When Helen suddenly finds herself in Colleen's crosshairs, she gets even by telling Colleen that she is waving the white flag and stepping aside. Helen also spreads the news that she found out that Brian has planned a romantic getaway with Colleen to Vermont. Brian is now in quite a bind and Joe suggests that Brian try being honest with Colleen. Honesty is the best policy after all, and it works – *except* for that thing about Brian being hung upside down in the terminal by the scorned and spurned officer of the law. Executive producer Dave Hackel added, "Shooting that scene involved multiple takes, as Steven Weber could only hang upside down for so long. We were afraid he would pass out so it was all done in pieces. It took a while, but it was worth it." About the policewoman episode, Saltzman remembered, "It was our [with Bill Diamond] first episode and not our best. It was marred by some repetition. It also suffered from some early miscasting where the first actress hired to play the policewoman had to be let go in the middle of the week. The replacement was very good." Said replacement was Sharon Barr who recalled, "Yes, now that you mention it, I do recall that I replaced someone, but I have no idea why or who it was. Everyone in the cast and crew of *Wings* was lovely to me. I had the most to do with Steven Weber who is, was, and always will be a doll – such a nice person. I saw him at an art opening recently and he looks exactly the same. The funniest thing I recall was having a dressing room next to Thomas Haden Church, another amazing actor. The walls were paper thin, and he has such a fabulous deep voice that I could hear every word of his phone conversations. He must have been juggling about five girlfriends at the time. It was quite impressive. What a charmer! I didn't meet the great Tony Shalhoub but later became friends with him through his wife, Brooke Adams." Barr added, "Soon after I did *Wings* I began studying Chinese medicine and became a doctor, so TV work was curtailed dramatically. I've always written and have a novel *Like a Complete Unknown* with a great agent in hopes it will get published. During the Covid 19 quarantine I participated in comedienne Paula Poundstone's podcast *French Trump*. Perhaps someone will ask me to be in a film or TV show again, but in the meantime I'll amuse myself with my own work and fun things that come along."

"High Anxiety" (Season 2 Episode 8) Aired November 23, 1990
Written by Bruce Rasmussen
Directed by Noam Pitlik

Sharing a title with the Mel Brooks movie classic *High Anxiety*, this episode focuses upon Joe's being grounded temporarily by Dr. Bennett and the F.A.A. because of his hypertension. Joe blames his condition on Brian. Other goings-on include a blood drive held in the hangar, and Joe's search for the gold wings pin he lost (he had it since he was eight). It is a good luck charm and getting a new one just would not be the same. Between the high blood pressure, the grounding, and his car getting sideswiped in the parking lot, if it weren't for bad luck he would have none at all. Roy seizes the moment with feigned concern, and an on-going interest in buying Sandpiper Air.

With Joe out of commission, all of the flying onus now falls upon pilot Brian. After having an argument with Joe, Brian quits and heads to St. Louis and TWA Flight School, necessitating a search for a new pilot. All qualified applicants laugh at the available pilot salary. Within moments of Joe finally selling out to Roy and then opening a frozen yogurt shop, Brian comes back and begs to be rehired. He was accepted with TWA but went AWOL. Family responsibility and some amount of guilt led him back home to Sandpiper. This leads to a nice closing scene when Joe finds his gold wings pin in the pilot's seat, and the two brothers who used to spread out their arms, run around and pretend to be airplanes as kids recreate that moment in the hangar.

Harris Shore who portrays Dr. Bennett shared, "I studied acting with Rebecca Schull in Michael Howard's Studio in New York. When I came to Los Angeles, I got to stay in Rebecca's guest house. I was just starting out in film and television, having mostly done theater during my 18 years in New York. I asked Rebecca if there were any auditions I might attend for her series *Wings*. Thanks to her I got to read for the part of Dr. Bennett. My audition went well and I got the part. It was a very smooth week of work. Everyone was very welcoming and I was so fortunate to work with director Noam Pitlik. Thanks to him, great writing and a beautiful set-up by my 'patient,' Tim Daly, I got some great laughs. It was only the one scene, but Dr. Bennett grounding Joe set up the storyline for numerous episodes that followed."

"Friends or Lovers?" (Season 2 Episode 9) Aired December 7, 1990

Written by David Lloyd
Directed by Noam Pitlik

With Joe still grounded for hypertension, Sandpiper seeks another pilot to take up some of the slack from slacker Brian. The pickings are slim. Two of the three candidates/interviewees are immediately disqualified – Mr. Stubbs (Charles Dugan) is elderly and cannot fly at night, another dressed in army fatigues named Doug (Jeremy Roberts) is just "plane" terrifying and wacky. This leaves the 18-year-old Kenny McElvey (Michael Manasseri) who just got his pilot's license two weeks earlier – the same week he had his braces removed. He has a B-plus average and is a member of the Chess Club. He was the top young man in his flight class.

In other action it seems everyone working at Tom Nevers Field is feeling as though they are in a rut and need to break out and do something exciting and different. Helen despairs after attending another friend's wedding (always a bridesmaid never a bride).

If Joe and Helen date, can this trio still be the Three Musketeers? Watch the episode titled "Friends or Lovers" and see for yourself. Top to bottom Tim Daly, Crystal Bernard and Steven Weber.

After an abundance of verbal foreplay, Joe and Helen decide to go out on a date, but there is one problem – they've always included Brian. They are like the Three Musketeers. How will Brian handle the news? After all, Brian has been wanting to date Helen as well. Little do they realize that Brian already knows about their date because of a faulty pilot's radio that cuts in and out at will. Brian overheard their plans in the cockpit while Kenny was serving as co-pilot. Joe and Helen's date, although clumsy, goes rather well.

They end their first night at the big make-out spot known as Indian Point and fumble around until they finally get to kiss without laughing, only to be surprised by Brian who has been in the backseat the entire time.

"There's Always Room for Cello" (Season 2 Episode 10)
Aired December 14, 1990
Written by Peter Casey and David Lee
Directed by Noam Pitlik

The title is a play on a classic TV commercial that said, "There's always room for *Jello*." There is a true-life moment in the opening vignette in which Joe has difficulty deciphering a phone number on a note from Fay – her fives look like eights. When asked about her handwriting, Rebecca Schull stated, "That is accurate. I have terrible handwriting."

The first mention of Roy's son, R. J. (Roy, Jr.) occurred in the episode titled "A Stand Up Kind of Guy." However, in this episode we actually get to see the big guy played by Abraham Benrubi. Roy views him as a chip off the old block. He is 17, plays defensive tackle for Siasconset High's football team, and can bench press 350 pounds. When R. J. wants to take cello lessons, Roy thinks that it's because he has a crush on pretty Helen. He couldn't be more wrong – R. J. is gay. R. J. made up the story about being "horny for Helen" so his macho father would allow him to take the music lessons. R. J. feels relieved and free once he has told many people about his sexual preference, but Helen keeps him from telling his dad (temporarily). Roy eventually finds out and does not handle the news well and challenges his son to a game of basketball. If R. J. wins he can be gay, but if Roy wins he can't. R. J. returns to the series (with his boyfriend) in the episode titled "Sons and Lovers" in 1996.

"A Terminal Christmas" (Season 2 Episode 11)
Aired December 21, 1990
Written by Bill Diamond and Michael Saltzman
Directed by Noam Pitlik

Each holiday season the cast and crew were gifted with a different holiday pin. (Courtesy of Suzanne Holmes).

This is the show's first of six yuletide episodes, the title being a classic play on words. This one opens with a man (Chuck Sloan) attempting to carry a large wrapped package (new golf clubs) onto a Sandpiper flight. The problem is it's too large for the baggage compartment. The man then offers to buy a seat for it, but it seems the flight is sold out. The passenger is crushed but has no choice but to surrender the package to Fay and wishes her a Merry Christmas. Fay then carries the package into Joe's office, which is jam packed with other similar packages and says, "We're doing a lot better than last Christmas."

In other action, Brian wants Joe to cancel the Christmas day flight so that they can go skiing together in Vermont, but responsible Joe waits to see if anyone buys tickets as his airline is the only one making an available stop in New Bedford on the holiday. Sure enough, a ticket is purchased by a Mr. Tolbert.

Fay says she is carrying on the tradition of having friends over for Christmas dinner. She says she misses being with her third husband George and entering in the annual holiday boat parade. She's reminded of the annual event when the boat contest's usual winner, Frank (George Furth) stops by her ticket counter to say hello and gloat. It seems that Joe once entered a sailboat into the contest with lights arranged to resemble Rudolph the red-nosed reindeer, but at the last moment prankster Brian rearranged the lights so that a different part of Rudolph was illuminated (they didn't win). About George Furth, the episode's co-writer Michael Saltzman recalled, "Having him guest star on this episode was special because I'm a huge fan of musicals, and Furth wrote the book for both *Company* and *Merrily We Roll Along* – two of my favorite Stephen Sondheim shows." Helen's plans for the holiday include a visit from her parents who usually spend the day with her wealthy sister "Lorraine" in Hawaii (one of this long-running series' few inconsistencies as we find out in season six that Helen's wealthy sister is named Cassandra, Casey for short, and she returns to Nantucket from San Francisco penniless). However, Mr. and Mrs. Chappel cancel the trip at the last minute because a camel at a nativity scene accidentally fell on Helen's mom (she wasn't seriously injured but needed rest). Mr. Tolbert who bought the only ticket on Joe's New Bedford flight also changes his plans and cancels. Lowell's mother-in-law is in town for the occasion, and when he makes a pass at her after too many hot-buttered rums wife Bunny Mather kicks Lowell off the houseboat. Roy will be alone this Christmas – his son R. J. is with friends in Gainesville following the Grateful Dead's tour. Any plans of salvaging the Hackett's skiing trip are dashed because of heavy snowfall. The only thing left is for all of them to crash Fay's dinner party, which is no picnic as they find her sitting alone in the dark pining for her third George. Saltzman added, "I love the joke where Fay hasn't moved anything since her husband died, not even the glass his dentures were soaking in, and we reveal Lowell with his mouth full of water, having taken a drink from that glass. It's one of my favorites. The traditional move would have been to do a spit take, but instead we had him do a swallow take where he looks around with the mouth full of water not sure what to do. He decides to just swallow it. Tom was just hilarious with that." To help her move on, they all aid Fay in her quest to fulfill George's wishes to be buried at sea – although, after a mishap on Joe's plane the container (a teddy bear cookie jar) where George's ashes were stored is broken and his ashes are strewn about the plane. Eventually these ashes are hurled from the plane in a Dustbuster (Joe's brand new Dustbuster). Said Dustbuster crashes onto and sinks nemesis Frank's former prize-winning vessel mid-contest. Fay sees it as a sign from George that she did the right thing. Saltzman added, "I loved what the guys did in post-production with the little segment of 'I'll Be Home for Christmas' playing at the end. It was the perfect finish." About the episode, co-writer Michael Saltzman added, "It was very meaningful to me because it was an episode about Fay coming to terms with the death of her husband, and my brother had just died about six months earlier from Hodgkin's Disease. I was able to deal with some of my own emotions through the writing of that episode."

"Airport 90" (Season 2 Episode 12) Aired January 3, 1991
Written by Bruce Rasmussen
Directed by Noam Pitlik

This was the first episode aired in the New Year, 1991. It opens with Lowell on the telephone attempting to play the old "Prince Albert in a can" prank on Fay.

Meanwhile, Joe, Helen and Brian take a flight to dump trout into the bay – a way to make money in the off-season. Released a bit too early because of a miscue, the marine life landed in a wooded area. While airborne, Brian lets Helen briefly take the reins. It's such a rush, she begs the Hackett boys to teach her to fly, but Joe's teaching method is so dull and slow she is about to abandon the dream. Brian rescues Helen from the tedium and takes her up in the plane to be his co-pilot. When he hits his head and is knocked unconscious while moving about the cabin, poor frazzled Helen needs to be rescued as she is left alone in the cockpit to land the plane. When Joe finds out, he attempts to guide her to the runway from the tower, despite the presence of tower man Walter (Ralph Bruneau) who takes nothing seriously. Somehow she lands the plane successfully, and the scary incident leads Joe and Helen to then take their relationship to the next level, initially thinking they would never see each other again.

In other action Fay is babysitting for Roy's vicious dog while he takes a vacation in Boston. In the episode she says she loves dogs, but in real life Rebecca Schull said, "I like dogs, but I'm not passionate about them." While with Fay, Brutus the bulldog gets in touch with his feminine side and becomes a changed and docile canine, much to Roy's dismay. Brutus was portrayed by an English bulldog whose real name was Rascal.

"Love Is like Pulling Teeth" (Season 2 Episode 13) Aired January 10, 1991

Written by David Hackel
Directed by Noam Pitlik

The episode begins with Roy expressing some mild concern about his cholesterol level being at 325. Meanwhile, the Hackett boys are planning the menu for the guys who are coming over the house to watch the Boston College/Providence game. Among those in attendance, an old friend named Phil Meriwether who always wows them by doing a Letterman-esque "stupid human trick" called "the eye thing." He can now do this trick with both eyes, doubling everyone's pleasure, doubling everyone's fun. Helen throws a wrench in Joe's plans by scheduling the extraction of her wisdom teeth on the same day as the game. Joe wants to be there for Helen, but also wants to be there with his bros for the game. He and Brian concoct a scheme that will allow him to do both. Helen's pain pills cause drowsiness so as soon as she drifts off to dreamland, he can meet the guys and watch basketball.

All goes according to plan and Joe goes to be with the guys, but guilt brings him quickly back to Helen's side. When Joe attempts to watch the game at Helen's place, he discovers that her TV is in the shop. He then carries her groggy body with him to rejoin the fellows. Joe then panics when the pain pills lead Helen to wander off to parts unknown causing the formation of a search party. She is found safe and sound curled up with an Irish Setter on a neighbor's porch, and totally unaware of all that has transpired. Joe gets through the ordeal scot-free.

"The Tennis Bum" (Season 2 Episode 14) Aired January 24, 1991

Written by Peter S. Mehlman
Directed by Noam Pitlik

The episode begins with Brian's description of all the disgusting ingredients in the average frankfurter, paired with Roy's savoring of every last bite of his, laden with every condiment imaginable. Later, Roy wants to hire a new pilot, and Helen encourages him to hire a woman. He almost convinces Helen that the person he does hire named Audrey (Christopher Best) is a woman with very masculine features.

Elsewhere, Lowell has painstakingly built a miniature zeppelin that flies by remote control. Lowell plans to enter it in the model air show on the weekend. It took him six years to complete, everything is to scale and historically accurate. Even the toilets flush. There's even a tiny musical orchestra inside. Lowell trusts Joe to keep it safe in his office, but, "Oh, the humanity." Joe plays with the blimp after being ordered not to, and it gets crushed when Roy thrusts open the door to Joe's office. The dirigible is then unrecognizable - truly a LEAD Zeppelin. Co-Producer Bill Diamond said, "I recall fellow Co-Producer Bruce Rasmussen giving the blimp pilot a really funny name, Captain Jazzbo. We came up with this idea for Lowell to have this stupid blimp and then some poor props guy had to make it." Speaking of the prop blimp, memories are murky but most people involved with this episode think that there was only one or possibly two blimps created for the shoot, so it was imperative to try to get it all in one take. Tim Daly said, "I seem to recall there was only one blimp. That said, I have never known a props person to only make one of anything." Needless to say, Lowell was devastated by the loss of six of years of exacting work, exacerbated by having Roy step on Captain Jazzbo on his way out of Joe's office. Eventually Lowell does forgive Joe with the help of prayer and a sign from above.

Meanwhile Fay is upset with her performance at the senior tennis tournament. Fay has been the champion for five years, but this year she blew it. Brian attempts to renew her confidence by challenging her to a match. He used to play for the team at Princeton but discovers that Fay is quite good. He claims he "let her win," but was handily defeated. Brian even feigned injury in an attempt to save face. When asked if she plays tennis in real life, Rebecca Schull said, "No, I definitely do not."

"My Brother's Back and There's Gonna Be Trouble" (Season 2 Episode 15) Aired January 31, 1991

Written by Bill Diamond and Michael Saltzman
Directed by Noam Pitlik

Hey, Brian Hackett, the plane isn't missing. It's being guarded by Associate Producer Suzanne Holmes. (Courtesy of Suzanne Holmes).

This episode's title is a play on the lyrics of a 1963 number one hit by the Angels titled "My Boyfriend's Back." In this instance, "back" is used as a double entendre, referring both to the body part and someone's return. Joe throws out his back and has to be hospitalized in traction placing his irresponsible brother Brian and young pilot Kenny McElvey (Michael Manasseri) in charge. Before going to the hospital, orderly Joe instructs Brian to follow his detailed calendar (to be found in his desk) including the plane's scheduled 100-hour checkup, but free-spirited Brian pays no heed. Joe tries to explain his very specific system of how to run things to Brian, who, completely uninterested in Joe's detail-oriented approach, ignores him, preferring to run things his way.

While temporarily in charge of Sandpiper Brian attempts a promotional idea that benefits travel agents (thinking Sandpiper will become their airline of choice in the future), but the plan goes awry when the plane mysteriously disappears and the F. A. A. stages a surprise inspection (Jonathan McMurtry as Inspector Hanson) with a possible suspension and fine looming. Lowell hires a psychic (Karen Hensel) to find the plane, and a marching band for the Siasconset High Marching Mules to whom Brian has promised a flight has filled the terminal to capacity along with their mascot, a real mule named Esther. Had Brian followed his brother's orders he would have known about the plane's temporary disappearance because of its 100-hour checkup, and all of the ensuing chaos would have been avoided. Joe's early return to the terminal only exacerbates the pandemonium. Director Leonard R. Garner, Jr. was an assistant director on this episode and recalled, "The shoot for that scene was delayed when the donkey urinated. We had to have it cleaned up and sanitized. The audience found it very funny but the incident made for a very long night and several retakes." The episode's co-writer Michael Saltzman added, "This episode was a tricky one. It was very structurally driven, where you had to set up all these little things to put in motion that would culminate in utter chaos at the end — the marching band, the psychic, the FAA inspection, the 100-hour checkup. I recall it not working all that great early in the week, and it was Ken Levine (who was working as a part-time consultant), who convinced everyone on one of our punch-up nights that we weren't going big enough, that the ending had to be not just chaos, but an <u>insane</u> amount of chaos. I think this is when the marching band with the mule was written in. Bottom line, we just didn't have enough balls in the air initially. So we added some. It was also not a great studio audience and Steven was a little thrown in his performance because places that had been getting laughs and should be getting laughs were not getting laughs. And because so much of the episode was on his shoulders, it was difficult. He was great in it and pulled it off, but it was an effort to get there. That sometimes happens with studio audiences. Sometimes they're just electric and even straight lines get huge laughs. And other times you get an audience that seems to have come from a funeral, where, at best, you just get titters. Still, you'll talk to someone who came to the show afterward and they'll go on and on about how funny it was. It's weird. I'd love to see a scientific study sometime on what tipping point can make an audience into a poor or great audience. I recall David Angell once telling me as we went down to the stage for a show how much he hated show nights. I was surprised to hear that because I loved show nights. It's like you'd been rehearsing a play and this was opening night. We also had to all dress up in suits and ties or coats and ties, a tradition the guys carried on from *Cheers*, which, I believe harkened back to the days of *The Mary Tyler Moore Show* (and one I've continued when doing a multi-cam show). I asked Angell why he felt this way and he explained how the script was always perfect in his head, so now all that could happen was it would somehow fall short of that and never be as good."

"Plane Nine from Nantucket" (Season 2 Episode 16) Aired February 7, 1991

Written by Philip LaZebnik
Directed by Noam Pitlik

This episode's title is a takeoff on the 1959 Ed Wood horror film *Plan Nine from Outer Space*, universally considered among the worst motion pictures ever produced. The action begins at closing time in the terminal. Lowell thinks he's alone and begins singing "That Old Black Magic" on Fay's microphone, only to find that Joe is still lurking in his office. An embarrassed Lowell skulks out the door, and now it's Joe's turn on the mic, pretending he's a World Series play-by-play announcer.

Later, in mid-flight Joe and Brian are certain they've seen a UFO because nothing else could move that quickly. Unfortunately, on this flight they're transporting a load of mannequins and none of these passengers can back up the Hackett brothers' story. They merely "dummy up," as does Joe at first. For a second consecutive episode, humorless Inspector Hansen of the F. A. A. (Jonathan McMurtry) is a guest star as Joe and Brian hesitantly tell of their close encounter. It appears that the Hackett boys aren't the only ones who had this experience, and they agree to take a bunch of fellow UFO spotters on a flight. However, the attendees don foil hats on their heads and place lightbulbs in their mouths and a picture of the event makes the local newspaper called *The Nantucket Herald*, thanks to an aggressive reporter (Michael Eugene Fairman), and Brian and Joe's credibility disintegrates as a result.

In the meantime, Helen is trying to get Fay to pony up the $42.50 she owes her for lunches at the counter. Fay insists that she has paid in full. Lowell suggests they arm wrestle to decide it. In the end Fay was correct, the check for the full amount had slipped down below Helen's counter. Meanwhile Lowell is attempting to expand his vocabulary by listening to a series of tapes leading to his use of big, un-Lowellesque words and phrases such as bifurcated and torn asunder. Later when Lowell repairs the light on the tower, the Hackett boys think they're seeing yet another UFO. Executive Story Consultant Michael Saltzman recalled David Angell adding a line to the script, "As the two brothers look up at the stars, and Joe ponders about how vast and incomprehensible the universe is and doesn't that make you feel sort of small and insignificant, David's line for Brian was, 'Not when my shoes are shined.' It's a line that's not trying too hard, but feels so human, funny, and organic to the character. I always think of that joke when I remember David."

"Looking for Love in All the Wrong Places" (Season 2 Episode 17) Aired February 14, 1991

Written by Bill Diamond and Michael Saltzman
Directed by Noam Pitlik

The episode's title, "Looking or Love (in All the Wrong Places)" is the title of a huge country crossover hit by Johnny Lee from the *Urban Cowboy* soundtrack. Antonio Scarpacci (Tony Shalhoub) makes his first appearance in this episode as a waiter. We also get to meet his cousin Giacomo (Perry Anzilotti) as the busboy in this episode. Giacomo is mentioned numerous times in later episodes. This one was perfectly-timed to air on Valentine's Day 1991 and Roy has a blind date with a woman named Karen (Deborah May) he connected with from the back of a magazine. He lied about his looks, but she didn't. He also lied about having a Porsche. Deborah May said, "The most notable memory I have is that the gentleman who escorted us to our table and subsequently waited on us was also, like me, a guest star on the show – Tony Shalhoub, a great fellow and extremely successful, as we all know."

Meanwhile Brian has a date with a lingerie saleswoman named Stephanie (Claire Yarlett) he met in the terminal, and Joe is in the doghouse for buying the newly-slender Helen a big box of chocolates as a gift for the romantic holiday. She eschews them and gives them to Lowell who chews them. Co-writer Michael Saltzman recalled a funny Lowell scene, "When Roy's date tries to explain that she's not disappointed in what he really looks like and says to him, 'How do you know I don't like what I see?' Roy, unable to believe his luck says, 'Please tell me there's no one standing behind me.' And his date looks over his shoulder and says, 'Just some guy in overalls with chocolate all over his face' and the camera reveals

Lowell standing there with chocolate completely smeared in his teeth and all over his mouth. It's just so unexpected and never fails to make me laugh." After a dressing down from Fay about her angry response to Joe's thoughtful Valentine gift, Helen attempts to apologize with a present delivered by a courier to Joe with a note inside requesting that he meet her at "their special place." Wouldn't you know, they each have a totally different interpretation of that "special place" and Joe spends the evening awaiting Helen's arrival at the make out spot known as Indian Point, while Helen wastes the evening at Pontrelli's Restaurant. The name Pontrelli was inspired by Gina Pontrelli, an assistant to the producer. Co-writer Michael Saltzman recalled, "It was just one of those episodes where everything came together. Tony scored huge, and the episode ran like eight minutes long because of the laugh spread." A short time later, in Season Three Antonio joined the cast as a cab driver after losing the restaurant because of a lawsuit filed by a man who choked on a chicken bone.

"Love Means Never Having to Say Geronimo" (Season 2 Episode 18) Aired February 21, 1991
Written by Bruce Rasmussen
Directed by Noam Pitlik

The title of this episode is a play on "Love means never having to say you're sorry" - a famous line from the movie *Love Story*. This story begins with Fay recognizing a regular passenger as Mr. Smith, only this time he's using his real name Beekman (Robert Alan Browne) and is traveling with his real wife. Fay's words lead Mrs. Beekman (Laurel Lockhart) to seek a divorce lawyer.

Meanwhile, Joe and Helen think they finally have a night to themselves after getting rid of the third wheel, Brian, by hinting that he should go out for ice cream. Well, Brian doesn't take the hint, and quickly returns with the ice cream and a rented movie, putting the kibosh on the lovebirds' plans. Joe finally has to tell him that they are no longer the Three Musketeers, and Brian goes out on the town alone. He isn't alone very long, however – he meets the well-traveled and exciting Gwen Suzanne Holmes (Suzanne

Holmes is also the name of *Wings'* Associate Producer, by the way) played by Lisa Darr. Brian's so taken with this impetuous woman they opt to get married right away. Her gut tells her that the marriage should take place on the plane, followed by a skydive into their honeymoon. Helen and Joe toy with the idea of joining them and tying the knot, but when Gwen and Brian bail on the wedding and then bail from the plane via parachutes, Joe and Helen also say, "Never mind." After putting that misadventure behind them, Joe and Helen gladly welcome back their third wheel, the third Musketeer.

"All in the Family" (Season 2 Episode 19) Aired March 7, 1991
Written by Bryan Winter
Directed by Noam Pitlik

This episode borrows its title from the long-running Norman Lear CBS sitcom *All in the Family* and marks the fifth and final time young pilot Kenneth Margaret McElvey (Michael Manasseri) appears. Margaret? Yes, he was named for his great-grandmother who was an Indian fighter. Kenny and Brian are enjoying playing videogames on Fay's computer – a situation that delays Fay's ability to reserve seats on the plane for paying customers. Kenny is also moonlighting at the drive-thru window at Ahab's Fast Fish. His fun and carefree friendship with Brian comes to fisticuffs when Brian begins dating Kenny's mother, Melinda (Marie Marshall). Because of Brian's reputation with women, Kenny is certain that Brian will break his mother's heart. When he does exactly what Kenny envisioned, Brian attempts to make amends in Kenny's seafood drive thru and gets punched in the jaw as a result.

In other action Helen is suspicious of Joe when he refuses to let her look up a phone number in his address book. Conversely, he is suspicious of what she's hiding in her purse. Also Roy comes to the realization that it's time to look into getting a pair of glasses as his eyesight just isn't what it used to be – a situation exacerbated by Lowell who pokes Roy in both eyes, not realizing there was no glass in the frames Roy was trying on for size.

"Mother Wore Stripes" (Season 2 Episode 20) Aired March 14, 1991

Written by David Lloyd
Directed by Noam Pitlik

The episode begins with very little action as Roy and Lowell are involved in a very slow-paced chess game, and neither is certain whose turn it is. Elsewhere Fay's senior center is rehearsing for an upcoming performance of *West Side Story*. Fay is the leader of the Jets. The leader of the Sharks uses a walker.

In other action, while watching golf on the TV at Helen's lunch counter, a woman in the stands is hit by a golf ball served by former President

```
                         WINGS
                  "Mother Wore Stripes"
                      #40342-025



                        Written by
                       David Lloyd



                 Created and Developed by
                      David Angell
                      Peter Casey
                      David Lee


                       Directed by
                      Noam Pitlik
```

```
                                    FINAL DRAFT
                                  January 24, 1991
```

The cover of the script for the episode titled "Mother Wore Stripes" with guest star Barbara Babcock as long-lost deadbeat jailbird mom Mae Hackett..

Gerald R. Ford. She turns out to be Brian and Joe's deadbeat run-away wayward mother Mae Hackett (Barbara Babcock). Because of that TV sighting Brian tracks her down and lures her to Nantucket, excited about the reunion. Conversely, Joe wants absolutely nothing to do with her. Especially after finding out she's been working in the prison laundry at California State Penitentiary, while doing time for embezzlement. Brian invites her to stay at the house, to Joe's dismay. Bitter Joe later explains to her in the hangar that all these years he thought she had left because he broke her antique pitcher and gives her the one he made in school as a replacement. After many awkward moments, they share a drink and a hug before she has to return because her parole officer is waiting. When they finally embrace, they accidentally break his replacement pitcher. She is never seen again on the show.

"Murder She Roast" (Season 2 Episode 21) Aired March 21, 1991

Written by Dave Hackel
Directed by Noam Pitlik

The title of this episode is an obvious takeoff on *Murder She Wrote*. Executive Producer and writer Dave Hackel said, "Even when the focus was on one of the side characters [in this case, Fay], the network still wanted to see at least some of the principals involved and engaged. So, even though the focus is on Fay, we cleverly devised a way to have Brian temporarily stay over at her house. Brian and Joe's house was being fumigated. Joe stays at Helen's, and Brian stays with Fay." Joe claims that he never had a roach problem until Brian moved in. It's during this sleepover at Fay's that Brian, while watching one of his favorite TV shows, *Fugitives from Justice* sees a wanted woman, Florence Chambers (the Culinary Killer) featured on the program. When the last known photograph of her is computer aged, she bears an amazing resemblance to Fay. Florence poisoned several men and killed another with a frozen leg of lamb (and Fay just happens to have one of these on the top shelf of her freezer). The reality show on which Brian sees all of this is hosted by Maury Povich portraying himself. Hackel added, "Initially Povich was unsure he wanted to perform this role on our show – he was reluctant and envisioned it might cast his real TV series, *A Current Affair* in a bad light." The day after having watched the episode of the show with the Fay look-alike, Brian attempts to get Helen and Joe to follow him into Joe's office with no words, just a head gesture. One of the passengers in the terminal, a timid man from Providence named Carl Torley (Andrew Bilgore) follows them in, thinking he was also being summoned. About that guest shot, Bilgore said, "I loved playing Carl Torley and the writers actually wrote additional scenes throughout the rehearsal week which might have led to the character becoming more of a recurring oddball taken under the 'wing' of Steven Weber's character – but I think they ended up scaling it back due to the cast already having a 'lovable dumb guy' character, brilliantly played by Thomas Haden Church." Bilgore added, "Casting director Sheila Guthrie discovered me and brought me in to meet her colleague Jeff Greenberg. Initially I read for *Cheers*, but they felt I looked too young to be in a bar. Those producers went on to create *Bob* [Bob Newhart's 1990s sitcom on which he played a comic book illustrator]. I was told that they had shown my *Wings* performance to Bob while I was in the running for the pilot and that helped gain Newhart's support. A tiny bit of trivia – I ended up wearing the same glasses on *Bob* that I wore as Carl Torley. They were my personal glasses at the time, after all. I also loved working with director Noam Pitlik on the *Wings* episode. He was one of the nicest people I'd ever met. Loved him, and when I discovered that he had played Mr. Gianellli on *The Bob Newhart Show* I loved him even more. *Wings* was a great set. I remember Steven Weber making me feel welcomed and even offering the use of his dressing room phone if I needed it. This made a big impression and I always tried to live up to his example toward guest cast when I worked on *Bob*." Well, despite the uncanny resemblance, Joe and Helen poo-poo Brian's story about Fay. Even though the real Florence Chambers is apprehended quickly after the Povich episode airs, Fay does accidentally knock out Joe with that frozen leg of lamb.

In other action, Helen gets even with a surly customer (Christopher Michael Moore) at her lunch counter by serving him regular coffee (he demanded decaf). Because the customer is such a jerk Helen tells him that if indeed the coffee she served keeps him awake he can call her. She then proceeds to write down her phone number. Well, almost – she actually writes down Roy's number. This action pays dividends later when an exhausted Roy ingests countless cups of java at Helen's counter because some nut called him in the middle of the night and Roy simply could not get back to sleep afterwards.

Also, Lowell is helping his wife Bunny sell skillets door-to-door. Bunny is not a good salesperson, so it is suggested that Lowell peddle these appliances at the local swap meet. He does and trades them all in to become the sole east coast distributor of something called the Car-B-Cue which Roy reluctantly purchases and quickly grows to love (as does Fay).

"Duet for Cello and Plane" (Season 2 Episode 22) Aired March 28, 1991
Written by Philip LaZebnik
Directed by Noam Pitlik

Crystal Bernard as Helen Chappel packed her bags to try her luck in New York at the end of the episode titled "Duet for Cello and Plane."

The season two finale opens with a dancing Lowell. He is teaching himself the cha cha for an upcoming rotary club function. His wife Bunny loves dancing and Lowell wants to surprise her. Joe then enters the hangar, and Lowell asks him to be his dance partner, as doing it solo is rather difficult. Joe reluctantly acquiesces after seeing that no one else is around and is complimented by Lowell for being light on his feet.

In the terminal, Roy wants to oust a mysterious, foul-smelling, suitcase-carrying, babushka-wearing woman named

Mooshta (Ivonne Coll) who has been seated in the same chair all day long, searching and waiting for someone and scaring away some of the other passengers. She doesn't speak a word of English. Fay lets her stay at her house for the night. The next day Mooshta's relative shows up and both show gratitude to kindly Fay, and sneer at Roy calling him "patatata." We discover as they exit that patatata in their language means horse's ass.

Elsewhere in the terminal Joe wants to take Helen out for a night on the town, but she has a major audition for the Maine State Symphony coming up and practicing that very complex audition piece on her cello is the only thing on her mind. At the audition, Helen runs into one of her students, twelve-year-old Becky Wilder (Olivia Burnette) who is also trying out. Helen gets the job, but Becky admits she tanked her own audition on purpose to spend more time with her boyfriend. She was afraid she might stray and be unfaithful while on the road. When Joe overhears Becky's comments, he fears the same thing might happen to Helen. To allay his fears, Helen offers to turn down the job, but Joe wants it to be entirely her decision. Her nice gesture backfires and a huge argument ensues as does a huge mess in the hangar as a grease gun and a fire extinguisher are employed (sprayed on one another to excess). We then discover via a phone call that Helen isn't employed after all as the symphony has lost its funding. The next day Joe and Helen apologize to one another for the sloppy fight and the things they said to one another, but Helen is determined to achieve her musical goals. She takes a big impetuous leap and moves to New York, hopping on an Aeromass plane with cello case in hand as Joe says, "Don't go," and both say, "I love you." Season Two ends in a cliffhanger.

SEASON THREE

Andy Ackerman took over as the director. Tim Daly said, "Noam Pitlik was so wonderful for us as we were getting started on the series. Andy then became 'our guy' for such a long time and he was great." Tim also said, "Beginning with the first episode of Season Three I'm no longer credited as Timothy Daly, but rather Tim Daly. I used to get calls all the time about how I wanted to be credited – Tim or Timothy. I asked around and was told Timothy Daly sounded like an effete British actor, so I was Tim from then on." Ken Levine and David Isaacs began being credited as Creative Consultants. Levine added, "I was uncredited for several years, but I consulted all but maybe two seasons. I would go to the first run through on Tuesday, then come back to the writers' room and help rewrite the script. I provided fresh eyes and basically it was just nice to have another bat in the lineup for a night. I offered jokes, helped with story problems, and basically just pitched in with the rest of the writing staff. It was a great job because there were always terrific writers. We had lots of laughs and turned out quality work. We were on the second floor of the Billy Wilder Building that fronted Gower Avenue. It was not a great neighborhood. One day we came in and found a bullet hole in one of the windows. Every night about midnight an ice cream truck would stop across the street from us, and twenty people would converge on it. I don't think they were buying fudgesicles. We'd hear the calliope music as the truck approached and would say, "Cracky the Clown is here."

Tony Shalhoub was added to the regular cast as of Season Three's second episode, "Is That a Subpoena in Your Pocket" as cabdriver Antonio Scarpacci. Season Three consisted of 22 episodes with only the first eleven utilizing the opening credits with the Franz Schubert theme song. About that, David Lee and Peter Casey said, "We fought to keep it but the network wanted us to get right to the action. This was somewhat based upon what was learned about the show in one of those focus groups with those two-way mirrors.

We hated to lose those beautiful opening credits." The show ran on Thursday nights at 9:30, except for a very brief run on Wednesday nights at 9:30 during the late summer of 1992.

"The Naked Truth" (Season 3 Episode 1) Aired September 19, 1991

Written by Dave Hackel
Directed by Andy Ackerman

The episode begins with a recap of the Season Two finale. The action resumes months later. Out of the blue Helen calls Joe in the middle of the night from New York, waking both him and his new girlfriend Gail Scott (Gretchen German), a freelance writer from Washington, D.C. with a house on Nantucket Island. The problem is Joe didn't tell Helen about Gail, and this leads to his seeking advice from everyone in the terminal. The consensus is that Joe needs to tell Helen face to face, so he and Brian fly to New York the next day to track Helen down. The address she gave Joe leads to a seedy strip club in a less-than-desirable neighborhood. Helen is a waitress there - broke and extremely unhappy. Joe and Brian bring Helen back with them, but Joe has still failed to offer her the information about Gail. She finds out quickly when Gail drops into the terminal unexpectedly. Helen is furious, storms out of the hangar and returns to drive her Jeep through Joe's office. Upon leaving this time she says, "I don't know about you, but I feel better." About the scenes with the Jeep wrecking Joe's office, editor Darryl Bates recalled, "I remember that one well. It was literally the first thing I ever edited on *Wings*. I believe it was Andy Ackerman's first episode as a director for *Wings*. We *did* shoot that scene the day before the live audience shoot. As in all of those 'pre-shoot' scenes, I had very little time to actually edit. We didn't get the film processed and transferred until late the next morning, and we had to have the cut finished to show the audience that night. Only a few hours, really. So I was nervous, because it was the first thing I was doing for them, and because all pre-shoots are stressful. It ended up being organized and shot as a single camera scene with many different angles and setups and lots of little pieces. However, Andy did such a great job as a director and he shot the scene with such clarity, that I instantly understood what I needed to do as an editor, and the scene came together fairly easily. And interestingly, we didn't change it much for the final. And that's a testament to Andy's directing."

"Is that a Subpoena in Your Pocket?" (Season 3 Episode 2) Aired September 26, 1991

Written by Bill Diamond and Michael Saltzman
Directed by Andy Ackerman

Although not called "Part Two," this episode is a continuation of Season Three's debut episode. Joe's office is still in shambles because a hellbent Helen drove her Jeep through it. This lack of tidiness and order is driving Joe to distraction, but he's carrying on Sandpiper business as best he can under the circumstances. Lowell wants to rebuild the office for him, but Joe has another carpenter in mind by the name of John Livings. When that contractor abandons Joe for work on Carly Simon's beach house and Walter Cronkite's sundeck, Lowell becomes the only choice and Joe gives in. Joe is pleasantly surprised as Lowell's work is impeccable.

Tony Shalhoub
as
Antonio Scarpacci

Meanwhile, Helen is not too happy with Joe when he presents her with a bill for the damage to his office. He wants her to pay his $1,000 deductible. Helen adamantly refuses prompting new addition Antonio Scarpacci to suggest that Joe take her to court to get his money. This is the first time Tony Shalhoub appears as the airport's

Tony Shalhoub officially joined the cast as Antonio Scarpacci in this episode titled "Is that a Subpoena in Your Pocket?"

cabdriver. Creators David Lee and Peter Casey said, "When he auditioned for the role of the waiter the previous year, his character had a much more subtle and nuanced Italian accent than all the other applicants. He was so brilliant in the Valentine's Day episode in Season Two, we had to make room for him to come back and we had to create a reason for him to be there. It was determined that we would have him become a cabdriver at the airport." Writer/producer Christopher Lloyd added, "Tony Shalhoub is a very skilled comedic practitioner and everybody wanted to write for him. Such a wonderful combination of sweetness and quiet rage."

Joe follows through on the lawsuit against Helen, and the only person in the terminal brave enough to serve Helen with the subpoena is Roy. He once served his own mother with one. He serves Helen, and she in turn serves him – a face full of lemonade. Helen tries to finagle her way out of the subpoena and almost succeeds but Joe sees through her ploy. When she shows up to the courtroom on crutches Joe is certain she's up to her old tricks, but this time it isn't an act (which he discovers upon kicking one of the crutches out from under her causing her to collapse on the floor). She had fallen down her front steps and was injured earlier that day. Even with Joe's antics, the Judge (Phyllis Applegate) rules in his favor. Helen agrees to pay Joe $100 a month for the next ten months, and then drives through his newly reconstructed office a second time after Joe accuses her of not having a sense of humor. It may look as though the same footage was used for both of Helen's drives through Joe's office, but they are indeed different (and one would assume somewhat costly from a production standpoint).

"The Taming of the Shrew" (Season 3 Episode 3) Aired October 10, 1991

Written by Christopher Lloyd
Directed by Andy Ackerman

The episode begins with Lowell taking a few local orphans on a tour of the airport. Lowell says he is giving back because his brother was an orphan.

Elsewhere in the terminal, Joe and Gail (Gretchen German) are Maine-bound and attempt to escape the airport quickly to avoid Helen's wrath. Speaking of Helen's wrath, all of the airport staff notices her recent inability to control her ire and they force an intervention to have her attend anger management classes. The problem is they haven't fully planned this intervention well, and when Helen asks where she might seek help she is confronted with a room full of blank stares and crickets. After some careful thought they come up with a group called Transitions. Helen agrees to attend, and Brian goes along for moral support (and to meet women). Upon their arrival they realize there's been a bit of miscommunication as the group consists of only senior citizens. The meeting supervisor is named Sandy (Angela Paton). Helen is paired with a man named Harry (Charles Dugan) for a role-playing session with him portraying Joe. While they're role playing, the boom microphone is quite obvious in the shot in the upper right corner about 15 minutes into the episode. Brian who just came along to support Helen has a meltdown at the meeting over his estranged wife, Carol. The meeting helps both of them, and Helen, in a touching moment comes to the realization that her anger hasn't surfaced because she lost her boyfriend, but rather because she lost her *best* friend. Later, after she and Joe hug and make up, Joe offers to drive her Jeep out of the hangar just in case she still harbors some anger towards him, but Helen has forgotten to warn him of the frequent problem with shifting into reverse and Joe's office gets flattened yet a third time. Co-producer Michael Saltzman said, "I'm not sure whether or not when we shot the first episode if we even had landed on the idea of the office getting demolished a second or third time. I might be wrong, but I think it was David Lee who pitched it. Everyone immediately laughed at the idea of doing this outrageous and complicated stunt a second, then third time. There was a lot of discussion of, 'Should we really do it?' 'Has this ever been done before?' I think the fact that it had never been done before to anyone's recollection that made us all excited about it."

"I Ain't Got No Bunny" (Season 3 Episode 4) Aired October 17, 1991

Written by Ken Levine and David Isaacs
Directed by Andy Ackerman

The episode begins with Roy harassing a group of Hare Krishna men in the terminal. Roy thinks they're going to chant and beg for money, but they've just deplaned and are on vacation. In other action, Antonio has to rush himself to the hospital after ingesting a bowl of Helen's Quahog Chowder, not realizing that Quahog is the local name for clams and he's severely allergic. Roy is entering his chowder recipe into the Nantucket Clam Chowder Cookoff and is almost ensured victory – it's the recipe of last year's winner, Maggie Blankenship, who moved to Delaware (and sold Roy the recipe before moving). However, it's discovered that the savory recipe is a fraud – she used canned chowder.

In the hangar, Joe hears snoring coming from the plane, only to find a naked Lowell sleeping inside. Lowell is estranged from Bunny (Laura Innes) and has nowhere else to go. This comes about after he accused Bunny of sleeping around. His suspicions ring true when Bunny comes on to Brian in Joe's office. As much as he dreads doing it, Brian tells Lowell what transpired. Lowell took the news badly and perched himself on the steeple of the Unitarian Church to contemplate his situation, but the Hackett boys think Lowell's note about "ending it all" meant he was going to jump. What he meant was he was thinking of ending it all with Bunny. Brian, a pilot is oddly afraid of heights (go figure) so Joe climbs up to talk Lowell into coming back down. Lowell is still torn between leaving Bunny and staying with her, but when Joe points out that Bunny is directly below making out with Fred Haney in Haney's car, he comes to the realization that the marriage is indeed over.

"If Elected I Will Not Live" (Season 3 Episode 5) Aired October 31, 1991

Written by Larry Balmagia
Directed by Andy Ackerman

Helen gets a $54 parking ticket and is urged to pay it by Brian, of all people. If you recall from the "Hell Hath No Fury like a Police-woman Scorned" episode Brian had over 40 such violations (while using Joe's car). To pay for the ticket Helen puts an ad in the paper to sell her cello but calls off the deal when she discovers that the purchaser plans to use it in a novelty act - a chimpanzee will be playing the instrument with his feet and a banana.

Meanwhile Lowell is aiding Roy in his bid for town council by hanging posters in the terminal. Roy thinks he is running unop-posed after the shoe-in for reelection suffers a heart attack, but that quickly changes. First Joe throws his hat into the ring with Fay as his campaign manager. Fay inadvertently wows so many peo-ple with her work on Joe's campaign that *she* gets the newspaper's endorsement – not Joe or Roy. Roy vows to mop the floor with her at the debates even though she appears to be a sure thing. However, when Roy comes to her bemoaning his life as a loser and sharing the story of running for class president and being "pantsed" at the debate and then falling off the stage, she softens and deliberately throws the debate which is broadcast live on local WWEN-TV, and Roy wins the council seat (and finally gets the "loser monkey" off his back).

"My Brother's Keeper" (Season 3 Episode 6)
Aired November 7, 1991
Written by David Lloyd
Directed by Andy Ackerman

The episode opens with the Sandpiper plane full of passengers. Actor Kevin Brief portrayed one of the passengers and said, "We're all sitting there awaiting the pilot who is a few minutes late. I said something like, 'Where's the pilot?' None of us passengers realize that Brian is actually the pilot and all of us are in a state of pure panic as he gets up from his passenger seat, puts down his magazine and says, 'I gotta get to Boston. How hard can it be to fly one of these things?' Another memorable and fun episode 'teaser.' It's how I got the nickname of 'teaser man.' I was told they liked my char-

Siblings Tim and Tyne Daly Join Acting Forces -- Tony and four-time Emmy Award winner Tyne Daly ("Gypsy," "Cagney and Lacey") guest-stars as millionaire Mimsy Borogroves, who romances Joe's (Tim Daly) brother and showers their staff with gifts, in "My Brother's Keeper," on NBC's popular comedy series "Wings," Thursday, November 7 (9:30-10 PM EST). The episode marks the first time that siblings Tim and Tyne Daly perform together.

A family affair – Tim and guest star/sister Tyne Daly work their sibling magic in the episode titled "My Brother's Keeper."

acter and the way I said, 'Where's the pilot?' It was my first of four appearances on the show."

In the terminal Helen tries to broaden her horizons by becoming a realtor and attempts to sell a multi-million dollar property to a visiting billionaire. Tim Daly's real-life sister (four-time Emmy winner Tyne Daly) was nominated for an Emmy for her guest shot on this episode as Miriam "Mimsy" Borogroves, a very wealthy woman (old family money from textile mills) who takes an instant shine to Brian. She calls him "Brian with an I," but along with all the gifts she lavishes upon him she makes him her toady. The show's creators David Lee and Peter Casey said, "She was so good channeling Nora Desmond of *Sunset Boulevard* on this episode." Although most of her scenes were with Steven Weber, there is a very touching scene in Joe's office between the two Daly siblings. Tim Daly said, "It was so well written." Mimsy agrees to put her wealth to good use by funding Fay's new senior center, Roy's municipal building, and possibly taking advantage of Helen's real estate deal. The only person in the terminal who detests Mimsy is Joe Hackett (he hates the effect she has on the people around her), that is until she wants to give him a blank check for a new plane. However, when Brian tires of being her lacky he breaks it off with her, and there is a very negative chain reaction as she then reneges on the money she promised to Fay, Roy, Helen and Joe. Their anger at his decision leads Brian to try to patch things up with Mimsy (read: grovel), but to no avail. Just as Brian is about to leave her private jet which is about to take off, she demands he return the things she bought him – his pants and his underwear.

"Crate Expectations" (Season 3 Episode 7) Aired November 14, 1991

Written by Dave Hackel
Directed by Andy Ackerman

The episode opens with Joe attempting to eat a bowl of soup in his office while Brian and Lowell are playing catch. Fearing the ball landing in his lunch, Joe gets up to leave only to have the bowl spilled on him when Fay abruptly opens the office door just as he is about to exit. Elsewhere Brian fixes Helen up on a blind date with a man named Red Hastings and it's a disaster as Red is obsessed with everything red. He even dyed his cat red.

In other action it's Joe's birthday and he avers that now that he's firmly in his 30s he doesn't want a party, gifts or any fuss. His co-workers read between the lines and opt to throw him a last-minute surprise party. Joe overhears some of the plans being made but is unaware that Roy has forgotten an emergency town council meeting, and Helen and Fay forgot they are scheduled to be manning the suicide hotline that evening. They all move the party to the following night. Joe thinks the party is still on for that evening, however because he is told he needs to be in the hangar at 8pm for the delivery of a big crate – the new seats for the plane. He thinks it's all part of their plan for his birthday and boy is he disappointed when the only thing inside the crate Ed (F. William Parker) and Skip (Brian Donovan) from Ed's Crate and Delivery bring are airplane seats. Joe thought the airport employees would be inside the crate as a surprise. The gang attempts to make up for it by all gathering in another crate to be delivered the following night but a delivery mix-up takes them to Boston on a ship. The crate delivered to Joe on that second night contains only kitchen appliances.

"Ladies Who Lunch" (Season 3 Episode 8) Aired November 21, 1991

Written by Kathryn Baker
Directed by Andy Ackerman

The episode begins with Brian and a lone passenger who talks incessantly about insurance, leading Brian to feign narcolepsy. Once again, "teaser man" Kevin Brief was part of the opening action and remembered, "While I ramble on about insurance in the cockpit and Brian pretends to nod off from sheer boredom it's actually the camera that moves up and down, and not us in the plane, although our actions and reactions were very genuine – as if the plane really were in a nosedive about to crash land."

In the terminal a bit of panic has ensued because of the presence of Secret Service men. Air Force One will be landing in Nantucket on its way to Kennebunkport. Fay gets excited about the President George H. W. Bush visit as she has touched every first lady since Eleanor Roosevelt. Fay gets her wish, continues her streak and meets Laura Bush, but Roy gets arrested trying to get a photograph with President Bush and makes the TV news in a report by respected broadcaster Edwin Newman.

Elsewhere Joe has a problem with the refueling of the plane and leaves poor Gail alone in the terminal while he handles the situation. Gail (Gretchen German) and Helen have not gotten along well, and true to form when they run into one another at the lunch counter they begin to bicker and hurl insults. Joe has had enough of this scenario and recommends that they go out to lunch together to get to know one another better. They do, reluctantly. While eating, Gail and Helen bond a bit and begin comparing notes on Joe's faults, foibles, phobias, idiosyncrasies and shortcomings. The bonding is short-lived and unravels when Gail finds Joe and Helen passionately necking after having slapped one another in the face repeatedly with breaded veal (you had to be there). Producer Christopher Lloyd recalled that the meat used wasn't really veal, "They slapped each other with chicken cutlets." A heartbroken Gail leaves and is not ever seen again.

"Try to Remember the Night He Dismembered" (Season 3 Episode 9) Aired December 5, 1991

Written by Bill Diamond and Michael Saltzman
Directed by Andy Ackerman

Fog as thick as pea soup (according to Fay) is keeping passengers in a holding pattern in the terminal. With a lot of time to kill, Fay drags out her "Foggy Day Fun Box." Among the time-killing activities – paper airplanes launched from the second level. Co-writer Michael Saltzman recalled a game of Pictionary played in that episode, "I literally transcribed something that happened to me verbatim. Helen and Lowell are on a team playing Pictionary and Helen is desperately trying to get Lowell to understand what she's drawing. And he just keeps offering up one dumb answer after another. When the time's up, Helen explains what the clues were. She points to all the dots she was drawing and

This would have helped Lowell and Helen in their ill-fated Pictionary Game – a souvenir Wings Snowman pin from one of the cast and crew holiday parties. (Courtesy of Suzanne Holmes).

then to the stick figure 'See? Snow…Man. Snowman.' And it does sort of make sense. But then Lowell, who's just been so stupid and exasperating asks why she didn't just do this? He proceeds to draw the classic snowman – three balls of snow, a top hat, carrot nose, etc. while Helen is just standing there with egg on her face. That's exactly what transpired with me and my girlfriend when we played Pictionary one night in college."

To kill more of their downtime, Brian then shows his prowess with the art of hypnosis. He makes Joe cluck like a chicken every time the word tortilla is spoken, and he has Roy dance around the terminal singing "Buttons and Bows." Saltzman shared, "It's a song Paramount owned so we didn't have to pay for it [which is why it was also used in an episode of *Frasier* titled 'Look before You Leap']. We weren't really sure what to expect but when he came down for the first rehearsal, the song was accompanied with an elaborate and very physical dance performed by David that blew us away. It was so unexpected and so funny to see him do that, and everyone was delighted." Tim Daly said, "David Schramm was a brilliant comic actor. He was able to milk every last drop of comedy juice out of that scene. He was always dependable and able to find the funny." The scene continued with Roy admitting under hypnosis that he'd found a briefcase containing $250,000 and buried it in his backyard." His story is very believable, and they all show up later that night to dig in Roy's yard. When they dig a hole big enough to hide a truck Roy comes home and lets on that he tricked them into this because he's having a hot tub installed and this ploy saved him a fortune.

The back story of this episode is fascinating. Co-writer Michael Saltzman shared, "Peter Casey, David Lee, and David Angell had Bill Diamond and I come to their office to pitch us the rough idea for an episode they had picked us to write. As they described it the basic idea was that, under hypnosis, Lowell would remember a suppressed incident from his childhood, where he saw Roy kill someone in his house and then bury them in his backyard. After he'd convinced everyone to help him dig up the body in the dead of night to prove his case, he would remember that what he actually recalled was watching a show, like *Alfred Hitchcock Presents*, through the window of Roy's house. His memory was what happened on the TV show. So they had spent the whole night digging up Roy's house for nothing. Sounded great. We all broke the episode. Everyone was happy when we turned in the script. When it came time for the table read, things went spectacularly well. Huge laughs about the gang being stuck in the airport because of a dense fog. And more huge laughs when Brian put each character under hypnosis to reveal 'their deepest, darkest secret.' But then, the minute the word 'murder' was mentioned, the room went completely quiet. For the entire second half of the script, there was nothing but uncomfortable silence. The network notes weren't particularly helpful. All they could do was point out the obvious. The script was really funny, but then the minute Lowell mentioned watching a body being killed and dismembered... Yeah, yeah, we were there, too. We know. Now normally in this situation, a whole script might be tossed out. Maybe another script might be slotted into its place. But there was a problem. We had already dug an enormous hole in the floor of the soundstage. And built the back of Roy's house. It was a very, very expensive set to build. So we were stuck with it. And had to figure out how to come up with a story that would use it. We basically had half of a script that worked great... and then nothing. It was a somber return to the writers' room and Bill and I were especially quiet, because our names were on a script that was going to keep everyone there very, very late that night. But the mission was clear. Come up with a second half of the story that would use a giant hole in the set. A lot of time and pitches went by as the hours passed with no clear answer in sight. Finally, I had a thought. 'What if Roy had faked being under hypnosis, made up a story about burying a body in his backyard, and tricked everyone into digging a hole for a pool for him?' I sat there quietly, mulling whether I should pitch this idea or not. Finally, I decided I shouldn't. It was too broad and the guys would never go for it. I was already cowed by the fact that a script I'd co-written was the cause of our problems. I didn't want to pitch a big idea like that and get shot down. I'd keep thinking. Then, literally, about two minutes later, Steven Levitan tentatively spoke up and pitched, 'What if Roy had faked being under hypnosis, made up a story about burying a body in his backyard, and tricked everyone into digging a hole for a hot tub for him? I shook my head. It was the exact idea I had, except it was a hot tub instead of a pool. It was too broad. The guys wouldn't go for it. I then watched as Peter, David, and David exchanged looks. You could sense the excitement building in the room as they all came around to the idea. That was the fix. Roy would trick them into digging a hole for a hot tub. Steve instantly became the hero in the room, saving us hours upon hours of work. And I sat there, kicking myself for not having had the nerve to have spoken up in the moment. The episode turned out great." Steven Levitan added, "During my first season, I was learning the ropes. I was nervous, in awe of everyone around me and my scripts were fine at best. We had a giant and very expensive hole on a very expensive temporary set and we needed a story to utilize it. We sat around pitching for a while and I came up with the idea that Roy had conned everyone to dig up his backyard looking for something because he was too cheap to pay someone to dig for the hot tub he wanted. At first it was quickly dismissed as a weird idea, but then David Lee doubled back on it. We began pitching on it, that's what we eventually did and the episode turned out great. When I got picked up for my second season, Casey, Angell and Lee told me that pitch essentially saved my job. "

Of course, the dead body premise was totally scrapped and changed to $250,000 buried in the yard. However, the episode title was never changed – the dismembered part was left in.

"The Late Mrs. Biggins" (Season 3 Episode 10) Aired December 12, 1991

Written by Steven Levitan
Directed by Andy Ackerman

The episode begins with Fay embarrassing a rotund man into admitting his true weight for the safety of the other passengers (it takes a few tries to get him to reveal his true weight). After the admission, his conscience kicks in and he agrees to take a later flight.

Meanwhile, it's the off season on Nantucket and to pick up the financial slack Joe is flying in pizzas from the favorite eatery in Boston for a rich man with a beach house on Nantucket.

However, Roy is the main focus of this episode as he reluctantly agrees to date a friend of Fay's named Doris. Dating is hard for him as he really misses his ex-wife, Sylvia (Concetta Tomei) – the wife he told everyone has been dead for 16 years. She's actually been living in Boston with a wealthy plastic surgeon. Roy wants to win her back and flies to Boston with Brian to give it a whirl. She has a lovely, spacious home, a butler (Gene Knight) and a maid. She is happy, classy, very refined and confident. She wants nothing to do with him and rushes back to her dinner party after a brief reunion. The trip was a total waste, but Roy takes something away from the experience – Luciano Pavarotti's overcoat which was in the closet. This episode contains a funny Siegfried and Roy reference delivered by Brian. We get to see Sylvia one more time in the Season Five episode titled "Roy Crazy."

"The Bogey Men" (Season 3 Episode 11) Aired December 19, 1991
Written by Larry Balmagia
Directed by Andy Ackerman

The episode begins with a teaser showing Fay and Helen on the second level of the terminal watching and admiring the buns on the new baggage handler who is also a bodybuilder. The episode's title refers to a "Bogey" which in golf is one over par on a particular hole. True to form, Joe is hesitant about leaving the airline behind for a weekend golfing getaway with Brian at a resort named Turtle Shoals in South Carolina. Brian puts one over on Joe with his offer to pay for the mini-vacation, but Roy sees right through it. Brian is actually not paying a dime. He's receiving the getaway as a free promotion by a timeshare company. To get Roy to keep this on the QT, Brian must take him along. To make it a foursome Lowell goes, too. During the flight we discover that Lowell names his golf balls (Ed is his favorite) and he keeps them all in a Ziplock bag. The weekend doesn't go as planned as a four-hour sales presentation followed by endless hours of heavy rain and wind negate any chance of getting on the links. While cooped up in their small room waiting for the storm named Dwayne to pass the guys get on each other's nerves, and we never do find out the exact nature of that electronic device Roy used in the bathroom. Whatever it was, it made Lowell's eyelids flap like window shades.

Also, this is the episode in which Antonio with guitar in hand regales the occupants of the terminal with the song "Michael" by the Highwaymen over and over. He really only knows the one song, much to everyone's annoyance. He does however try out another tune titled "Antonio Comes to the USA." Unfortunately, it has the exact same melody as "Michael." When the boys return home from their dreadful weekend of golf they are unable to land because a man with a guitar is being chased down the runaway by a crazy woman (but it's unclear if the woman chasing Antonio is Fay or Helen).

"Marriage, Italian Style" (Season 3 Episode 12) Aired January 9, 1992

Written by Christopher Lloyd
Directed by Andy Ackerman

This is the first episode of the series that did not use the original opening credits with the Franz Schubert theme song. From here on in (until the series finale, that is), the opening credits roll over a teaser as it's known in the business.

In other sad news, the government will not be renewing Antonio's visa and this is forcing him to leave the country. He only has one month until his deportation. If he marries an American citizen, however, he can stay. Leave it to Brian to find a woman willing to marry Antonio sight unseen – loud, coarse, disgusting and unkempt Siasconset Sal, aka Sally McCabe (Susan Tyrell). She agrees to marry him if he'll pay to fix up her boat. Along with being Antonio's intended, she's Lowell's godmother. Just as the immigration officer George Fulham (Thomas Ryan) arrives on an Aeromass flight, Sal backs out of the arrangement because she had just won a bunch of loot in a crap game and can now fix up the boat herself. When a dejected Antonio begins to explain the situation to the immigration officer, Helen steps in and agrees to be his betrothed. Now they have to plan a big wedding in the hangar with just two days of notice. The wedding dress Antonio has shipped over from Italy is huge – it's the one his mother wore, and Helen has difficulty keeping it from slipping off of her shoulders. Despite many last-minute doubts about proceeding with the ceremony, Antonio and Helen are pronounced husband and wife by a Justice of the Peace (John Valentine). What Antonio has neglected to tell Helen is that they must remain married for three years before getting a "quickie divorce." This is part one of a two-parter.

"Divorce, American Style" (Season 3 Episode 13) Aired January 16, 1992

Written by Steven Levitan
Directed by Andy Ackerman

The episode begins with a recap of the previous week on *Wings*. Even though it bears a slightly different title, this is part two of "Marriage, Italian Style." At the reception, Helen has a hard time keeping a brave face, but does her level best. Lowell catches the garter and plans to use it to keep his pant leg from getting caught in his bicycle chain. The immigration officer (Thomas Ryan) reminds Helen that he will be stopping by frequently and unannounced. He got them a soup tureen as a gift because it symbolically "serves seven to ten," much like what happens to those who defraud the government. The arrangement keeps getting more bizarre as Helen finds out that Antonio has to move in with her to keep their sham marriage on the up and up. Helen discovers this while in the bathtub as Antonio enters the room unannounced. Brian then crashes their potty party with some great news – Antonio might be able to get his Visa through a new government lottery made available for some 40,000 immigrants. If he were one of the winners, they would not have to wait three years for a divorce. Helen quickly jumps on this opportunity and hires a crew to prepare some 10,000 entries. Helen finds out quite accidentally that Antonio is one of the lottery picks after he initially told her he wasn't selected. When confronted, Antonio admits that he would have told her eventually but wanted the marriage to last a while longer. The wedding of his parents, Angelo and Annamaria was an arranged marriage, but they grew to love one another. Antonio was hoping the same thing might happen with Helen.

In other developments, while at the wedding ceremony Joe found a matchbook in the pocket of his jacket with the phone number of a woman named Rachel (Lisa Howard) on it. Brian eggs him on to call her but later rues his actions – she is the owner of a car dented by Brian. Brian had borrowed Joe's jacket one night without letting him know, thus explaining how the matchbook got into the jacket pocket.

"Stew in a Stew" (Season 3 Episode 14) Aired January 23, 1992

Written by David Angell
Directed by Andy Ackerman

The episode begins with Brian in the cockpit experiencing a lot of turbulence yet remaining calm as he is transporting a plane full of nuns.

In the terminal, it's evaluation day. Lowell is not officially an employee of Sandpiper Air but wants to be evaluated anyway. Joe lavishes praise on him but makes one tiny criticism about tardy paperwork and Lowell takes umbrage with these comments and storms out of the office. Fay is called "the perfect employee," but is told that because of the economy she won't be receiving her annual raise this year. A disappointed Fay reminds Joe of how they first met six years earlier on Flight 211 from New York to Honolulu and how she encouraged him to open Sandpiper, but it is to no avail. But when expensive new flight jackets for the pilots arrive on the same day, she decides to find a new job. Brian comes to the rescue and hires a Bolivian woman named Teresa Melendro (Laura Fabian) to take Fay's place but what he fails to communicate is that she fails to communicate – she doesn't speak a word of English. Fay briefly goes

SO jealous – the souvenir Wings *leather jacket presented to cast and crew. (Courtesy of Jack E. Herman).*

to work for Roy, but Brian plays peacemaker and brings Fay back into the fray.

"This Old House" (Season 3 Episode 15) Aired January 30, 1992
Written by David Lloyd
Directed by Andy Ackerman

Borrowing the title from Bob Vila's long-running TV program, the episode begins with Antonio discouraging Roy from vacationing in Venice, Italy with a story he made up about mad turkeys attacking tourists there.

In other action a major storm has caused a blackout on the island and quite a bit of flooding damage. An uncredited Christopher Carroll is the news reporter assessing the flood damage during the

TV legend Captain Kangaroo, young Brian Hackett's hero. Brian wrote many letters to him that were never delivered, as discovered in this episode titled "This Old House."

opening credits. As a result of the storm the childhood home of Joe and Brian at 427 Madaket Way has been condemned and is about to fall into the sea. With nothing else to do the Hackett brothers visit the old place and reflect upon the past. The day before it is to be razed, they attempt to save the house as a landmark through Fay who's a member of the Historical Society, but to no avail. They plan one final night together in the house for old time's sake and Joe finds his old *Playboy Magazines* still in a secret compartment in the wall of the bedroom he and Brian shared as kids. Also located there were all the letters Brian had written to his hero Captain Kangaroo. Joe had intercepted each letter to avoid embarrassment and they were never delivered (explaining Brian's flipping Kangaroo the bird in a chance meeting years later). Much like David Lee and Peter Casey often did with the Crane boys on *Frasier,* this episode gave us glimpses of Brian and Joe as youngsters. As in other flashbacks, Valri Jackson portrays their mother, Mae Hackett, Adrian Arnold plays young Joe, and Spencer Vrooman is young Brian. After flashing back, Brian and Joe realize that the home harbors many bad memories and as long as it's condemned, they take out their frustrations with sledgehammers. After becoming human wrecking balls it's announced too late that the house will indeed be saved as a landmark. It seems that author Herman Melville may have stayed there, and possibly worked on *Moby Dick* during that time. There's a scene that harkens back to the old Road Runner cartoons with Lowell using a power saw to cut a circular hole on the second floor. Just like Wile E. Coyote he was standing in the middle while cutting and crashed through to the first floor. How was this scene produced? Assistant Director Leonard R. Garner, Jr. said, "I had to watch the episode again. I had forgotten about that one. It was a drop with a stunt double, plain and simple."

"Planes, Trains and Visiting Cranes" (Season 3 Episode 16) Aired February 13, 1992

Written by Ken Levine and David Isaacs
Directed by Andy Ackerman

The Crane Train is on Joe's plane heading for Nantucket. Dr. Frasier Crane (Kelsey Grammer) brings his mental well-being tour to the island, along with Lilith (Bebe Neuwirth), both of *Cheers*. *Frasier* was still more than a year away. Regarding bringing characters from another sitcom into the *Wings* realm, co-writer Ken Levine said, "The creators of *Wings* had been showrunners on *Cheers*, so the writing style was very similar. It never felt like a square peg in a round hole. Putting the Cranes in *Diff'rent Strokes* would have been a different story."

Lilith has little faith in the validity of this traveling tour technique and voices her doubts regularly. It becomes quite obvious when Crane's low self-esteem group arrives at the terminal. Look up the words timid and insecure in the dictionary and their pictures are surely there. They become even more ill-at-ease when Helen raises hell upon seeing Frasier in the terminal. She attended one of his

Advertisement for the "Planes, Trains and Visiting Cranes"
episode from 1992 with guest stars from Cheers *Bebe*
*Neuwirth and Kelsey Grammer (pre-*Frasier*).*

seminars while in New York and says it ruined her life because of his "If you can see it you can be it" mantra. It certainly didn't work with her musical pursuits. To keep Helen from derailing the Crane Train, Lilith recommends that Frasier invite her to his Nantucket seminar to try to smooth things over. Things go from bad to worse as Helen, Joe and Brian have a huge blowout on stage at the seminar and Frasier completely loses his cool and forgets that he is on camera. Embarrassed, Frasier agrees to a refund for every person in his audience. Co-producer Michael Saltzman shared, "For me, having Frasier and Lilith on the show was a big, big deal and I probably made a little bit of a fool of myself being so starstruck. *Cheers* was such an important and influential show in my life and I was just obsessed with it. In fact, Bill Diamond, my writing partner and I initially took less money and a lower title to work on *Wings* because we wanted to learn from the people who wrote on *Cheers*. So to have these two iconic characters appear on *Wings* meant A) Our show was part of the *Cheers* universe, which was very cool. Our characters existed in the same world as Sam and all the others, and B) We got to pitch lines and jokes for Frasier and Lilith. Having a front row seat to them doing what they do and maybe reading a line or joke that I pitched was sheer joy." Writer/producer Steven Levitan concurred saying, "It was a thrill to have Kelsey Grammer and Bebe Neuwirth on the show because I'm such a huge *Cheers* fan."

In other action, Brian has purchased a big screen TV for the upcoming Pickens/Pellateri fight. The guys plan to gather in the hangar to watch it, after which Brian will return the $3,000 set for a full refund. Fay's first husband was a Golden Gloves fighter and she knows a lot about the sport, more even than her male counterparts. The fight is a disaster, ending after only six seconds, but there is one even bigger disaster – the big screen TV is TKO'd while being moved around the hangar. Brian plans to blame it on vandals.

"Das Plane" (Season 3 Episode 17) Aired February 20, 1992
Written by Bill Diamond and Michael Saltzman
Directed by Andy Ackerman

Sheet music for the Raiders of the Lost Ark-*esque music played during Carlton Blanchard's journey to Las Cruces, Rock Springs, etc. in the memorable episode titled "Das Plane." (Courtesy of Bruce Miller).*

The title is an obvious play on the motion picture *Das Boot*. This episode marks the first of three guest appearances by William Hickey as the world's most annoying man, Carlton Blanchard. Fay is very proud of her charity work at an auction with proceeds for Nantucket Memorial Hospital. She helped raise some $15,000 intended for new equipment in the children's wing. One of the best donated items was a round trip ticket on Sandpiper Air. That's the good news. The bad news - the person who purchased the plane ticket was the aforementioned Carlton Blanchard, an old man who used to run the lumberyard. When Joe donated the ticket he tacked on the caveat, "Wherever Sandpiper flies," but Brian thought it was too wordy and left it off when the ticket info was given to the printer's office. This oversight led to quite an adventure to Las Cruces, New Mexico; Rock Springs, Wyoming; and beyond. Blanchard wants to go there to patch things up with his estranged brother. Brian and Joe see a little bit of their own strained relationship in this situation and begrudgingly agree. Antonio begs Joe to take him along so he can see the country. Co-writer of the episode Bill Diamond shared, "If Mike Saltzman and I ever had more fun writing for a character, I don't remember it. Carlton's first and last names came from people I knew from my hometown, for no apparent reason I can recall other than they sounded good together. Actually, his first name was that of perhaps the kindest, sweetest man I've ever met, an elderly Town Clerk who I'd struck up a close friendship with during the time I'd spent as a reporter on my weekly hometown newspaper after college. The character's disposition couldn't have been less like his real-life namesake, so it's perhaps not the most fitting honor to have bestowed on this fine and gentle man. But I guess the real-life Carlton always did seem to have a delightful, devilish twinkle in his eye, even at his advanced age, so maybe that was the inspiration." Michael Saltzman remembers the naming of William Hickey's character a wee bit differently, "My recollection was we were trying to think of an old-sounding name that was New England in nature. George Blanda had been one of the oldest players to play football. He retired when he was 48 and had grey hair. So I think it started with his name, but we didn't like the way Carlton Blanda sounded, so it mutated to Blanchard, this person Bill knew. And then Carlton, as I remember it, came from Carlton Fisk, the Boston Red Sox catcher. I didn't realize that was also the name of a friend of Bill's." Diamond resumed, "The fun part was just Mike and I trying to top one another with bizarre questions Carlton could ask. For instance, I remembered that someone I knew in graduate school had gotten bitten by a monkey while on vacation and had had to receive rabies shots for months and months. So it seemed like a perfectly reasonable question for Carlton to ask. I suspect the Grub Street guys probably had to cut the number of questions we had Carlton asking in the original draft of the script way, *way* down because we found the whole idea of this crotchety old man asking the most random and bizarrely specific questions to just be outrageously funny." Co-writer Michael Saltzman said, "It's always fun when you create a character that scores like that. Writing obnoxious lines is actually one of the most fun things you can do. Who doesn't like coming up with stuff you're not supposed to say in polite company? Hickey's performance was so weird and wonderful. Bill [Diamond] wrote the monkey line, but my line after that was Antonio tensely saying, 'I don't know. Maybe Joe knows,' redirecting Carlton in Joe's direction and away from him. My dad's name is also Joe, so that became something of a family catchphrase over the years." Not only are the questions Carlton asks bizarre, but his voice is extremely grating. That voice only exacerbates questions such as, "What do they do with the metal they punch out when making a flute?" and "How much does this building weigh?" He had a million of them, each more eyerolling than the last. Editor Darryl Bates shared, "Bill Hickey was a lot of fun, and a handful on the set. That bit about Las Cruces, New Mexico still makes me laugh when I think about it." Producer Christopher Lloyd added, "William Hickey had a rhythm and manner unlike anyone I've ever worked with. I remember Rebecca Schull standing offscreen and just watching him and marveling at his way of operating." Tim Daly shared, "Hickey was hilarious. A great character actor. We enjoyed having him on the set. Tony Shalhoub had difficulty getting through shared scenes without laughing hysterically. After we sent the audience home on the night of those shoots we'd have to recut a couple of scenes with Hickey and Shalhoub. Definitely the most annoying on-screen character ever – one you love to hate. Hickey was a bit frail and needed to be helped around the set on occasion but his comedic timing was sharp as a tack."

While on their cross-country journey, Saltzman recalled another hilarious line, "Lowell announces at one point in the small plane, 'You know they say it was flatulence that made the dinosaurs go extinct.' And someone else asks, 'What made you think of that?' And Lowell takes a beat and says, 'No reason.' But it's clear he just farted. It's a super classy, subtle fart joke and it always makes me laugh when I think of it." Speaking of that cross-country journey, composer Bruce Miller shared, "That score playing every time the map is shown on their journey was written to have a *Raiders of the Lost Ark* feel to it." While on the flight to New Mexico, the plane passes over Lancaster, Pennsylvania, and the topic of the Amish arises. Co-writer Michael Saltzman recalls one of the few times the show had a small issue with the censors, "When Antonio is reading from the guidebook as they fly over Pennsylvania, he comes across a passage of what not to say when meeting the Amish such as 'Yo Beardy,' 'Hey, Mr. No Buttons' and 'Excuse me, but I think your way of life is stupid.' Only the first two made it into the episode. I'm not certain if it was the censor, or the joke might have been cut down for time. But when the issue came up over whether it would offend the Amish, I offered that they didn't watch TV, so it wouldn't be an issue."

Halfway to their destination the plane malfunctions and Brian makes an emergency landing in a cornfield in the middle of nowhere. They get out of their predicament by promising the farmer (David Hayward) who owned said cornfield that they'd make some deliveries for him – chickens, grain, potatoes and a piglet (all, of course, in different states) if the farmer can get them a replacement part for the plane.

Well, Carlton finally meets his brother and, after coming to fisticuffs gets his old pocket watch back – only to later realize that the man he fought out on the tarmac wasn't his brother at all (and the pocket watch is different). Coincidentally or not, in a 1927 motion picture titled *Wings*, a different actor named William Hickey portrayed a character named Charlton Blanchard.

"Take My Life, Please" (Season 3 Episode 18) Aired February 27, 1992

Written by Christopher Lloyd
Directed by Andy Ackerman

The opening scene of this episode features guest star Oliver North (credited as Oliver L. North). Most people associated with the show think this was stunt casting by NBC. Steven Weber said, "Aside from the fact that he was a celebrity 'get' for the show, he was also infamous, a villain, you know? Whatever one's political sympathies, there was no denying the guy had lied to Congress. And now he was a guest star on the show? I think a bunch of us were upset and a little thrown by the idea that we were somehow normalizing this guy's criminality, even using his 'I cannot recall' line in a jokey exchange. I was more indifferent about it at the time and just shrugged it off. But I don't think I would be that way about it now. It was a weird moment and I have no idea how it came to be." Executive producer Dave Hackel added, "There was a change in that script. In rehearsals of that scene with Brian and Oliver on the plane, Brian asks 'Did Reagan know?' After a few rehearsals Oliver said he couldn't do it, he was uncomfortable with the line, so it was changed to 'Did it ever occur to you that what you did might be considered illegal?' It was all about the wording." Co-writer Bill Diamond added, "I can't say for sure if his appearance was because he was promoting a book but it does seem logical. I do remember that Mike and I weren't happy at all about him appearing on the show and I do seem to remember a rather ironically posed photo that was taken with him. Ironic for us; presumably not ironic for Colonel North."

In the terminal, Helen is very excited about having just made her first sale as a realtor for Bonnie Doone Real Estate and she is wearing the company's ugly plaid jacket proudly (while co-workers are sniggering). She sold the old Duffy place and is ecstatic. That is, until Mr. Liam McDougal (Eric Christmas) owner of the realty company enters and is none too pleased. It seems Helen has promised that the new owners of the Duffy house can keep the chandelier as part of the deal, not realizing that said fixture is valued at $50,000. She is promptly stripped of her gaudy multi-colored jacket and fired. Antonio suggests that she take a career placement test to see what else might lie ahead. The test results show that Helen should keep doing exactly what she is doing, but before telling her this Brian suggests they alter the results a bit to give Helen a ray of hope for the future by adding that she could be a lawyer or a stand-up comedian. Unfortunately she chooses the latter. She puts together an act which is painfully bad, but Brian's suggestion of using her cello as a prop seems to be the answer – until someone much funnier, Jim Tavare' (as himself) beats her to it on stage on the night of her debut performance at the Club Car, using his stringed bass as a prop. When it's her turn to go on stage, she hides under a table. The emcee for that comedy night at the Club Car was the *Wings* warmup man, Robert G. Lee (credited as Robert Gary Lee in this episode because of another Robert G. Lee in SAG). Robert elaborated, "I still did the warmup on the show, then when the time came I ran down on stage to film my intro to the comedy acts, and after I'd run back up into the bleachers. I believe I get about $1.50 a year in residuals for that episode, so my future is quite secure."

"Four Dates that Will Live in Infamy" (Season 3 Episode 19) Aired April 2, 1992

Written by Dave Hackel
Directed by Andy Ackerman

The episode begins with a familiar scenario – Brian being slapped by a female. Brian is not alone - the whole crew is having very little luck with the opposite sex of late. That is, except for Antonio who has joined a dating service called the Romance Connection. He's currently on a roll, consistently getting some. Because of his success

A postcard from the real Club Car on Nantucket Island, featured prominently in many episodes including "Four Dates that Will Live in Infamy."

with the service, the others in the terminal reluctantly give it the old college try. After their respective computer dates they all commiserate together in a friendly competition at the Club Car to determine which of them experienced the greater dating disaster. Helen, in fact is still on her date when they all meet up. Her date is Jeffrey (Cameron Watson) a waiter at the Club Car and he is still waiting tables as they all meet. In fact he even puts *her* to work because they are short staffed that night. Lowell's date with Sharon in the hangar (Laura Leigh Hughes) starts awkwardly but turns out to be the best of the four. Joe's date was really unusual. It was with a woman named Monica (Heather Lee) who only speaks through a lookalike blonde dummy named Trixie (voiced by Nancy Scher). Just as Joe is about to win the bet, Brian barges in, late as usual. And he's soaking wet. His date was named Barbara, a coarse, overbearing woman played by Peri Gilpin (who was originally up for the role of Helen on the show in 1990). Barbara mouths off to a biker (Eric Allan Kramer) who is hogging the use of a phone booth (she wants to answer the important call on her beeper) and tips over his hog in spite. To get even for the damage to his bike, the Neanderthal locks Brian in that phone booth and affixes a hose. While they're all so fixated on their own stories about their "dates from hell," none of them realize that their "misery dates" are also in the Club Car seeking out their next victims.

"The Bank Dick" (Season 3 Episode 20) Aired April 23, 1992
Written by David Lloyd
Directed by Andy Ackerman

The episode opens with a customer (Kevin Brief) getting his big breakfast at Helen's counter just as Roy announces the final boarding call for an Aeromass flight. The customer throws down the amount owed to Helen and leaves the untouched plate of food behind. Roy waits until the man has left the terminal and sneaks over, grabs the plate and, after doing a double take, leaves with the money the man left behind, too. Kevin Brief shared, "I earned the nickname 'Teaser Man' because out of the four episodes of the show on which I appeared, in three of them I'm in the opening

Steven Weber as Brian Hackett

*Brian Michael Hackett is dressed and ready for his vacation on
Barbuda after an I. R. S. windfall. (Courtesy of Suzanne Holmes).*

teaser." Brief added, "I had only recently moved out to California
and *Wings* was my first sitcom. What a way a start!! Everyone on
the show was so incredibly nice. To this day it's still one of my
favorite TV experiences."

The title of the episode is the same as an old W. C. Fields movie and
likely an intentional double entendre. Co-producer Bill Diamond
concurs saying, "I feel fairly certain that the episode was titled with
W.C. Fields in mind, and I feel fairly certain the double entrendre
was very much intentional, though neither Mike Saltzman nor I
were the writers of that episode." The Bank Dick here is Brian,
moonlighting to pay off the I. R. S. The large surprise refund he
received from the I. R. S. was in error. Joe had suggested that Brian

sock the money away for a rainy day, but in typical Brian fashion he lived for the moment and spent every penny on a vacation in Barbuda. About Barbuda, David Lloyd's son, Christopher Lloyd who also wrote and produced *Wings* said, "I went there during my *Wings* tenure as a guest on *Lifestyles of the Rich and Famous* – a regrettable decision." Well, now Brian has to scare up $5,000 pronto to repay the I. R. S. and so he gets a second job. Borrowing a title from Steven Weber's later sitcom, his life is *Cursed* as the bank is held up on his first day of work. Kevin Brief added, "It's interesting to note that Crystal's real-life father, Jerry Wayne Bernard plays a bank customer in the episode." The other bank customer was portrayed by actor Jim Hudson who said, "Tony Shalhoub is the first memory during those rehearsals that comes to mind. Tony's character was Italian-born and Tony had the perfect Italian accent. Often during the hothouse four days of rehearsals changes are made to the script. At the last rehearsal, Tony's character had a long paragraph. But this time the writers switched it to Italian. Tony had never studied the Italian language but gave his all. But he had trouble getting it perfect so the writers switched it back to English. Tony's Italian accent was so good it fooled everyone into thinking that he spoke Italian. Ironically it was an inadvertent tribute to Tony's brilliance as an actor."

The robber (Tony Maggio) wore a Richard Nixon mask, had two-toned wing tips and used the odd phrase, "We'll all be sitting in butter." That phrase and the wing tips come into play when it becomes obvious to Brian later in the day that his passenger on the plane is the same man who robbed the bank. The crook recognizes Brian and Antonio and holds a gun on them, but Brian puts the plane into a dive to try to get the robber to surrender that gun (and succeeds). Brian gets a cash reward for his heroics, which he once again squanders (on a motorcycle).

In other developments Antonio is returning to Italy for a few days to visit family and is taking photos of everyone and everything on the island to share with them, and Joe and Helen are at odds over Red Sox tickets she gave Joe as a gift while they were still dating. She thinks she should still be going along, but Joe has already invited another girl named Nancy. That point becomes moot because in taking their wallets at the bank, the thief also got the tickets. The police then give Brian those same tickets as part of his reward for capturing the bandit.

"Say It Ain't So, Joe" (Season 3 Episode 21) Aired April 20, 1992

Written by Steven Levitan
Directed by Andy Ackerman

The episode begins with Roy making one of those 1-900 phone sex calls on Sandpiper's phone and on Sandpiper's dime while Fay is away from her desk. In other action Lowell is doing Fay a favor by making a book on tape for her – Charles Dickens' *A Tale of Two Cities*. Lowell gets on Fay's bad side, however, when he forgets to turn off the recorder upon receiving a phone call and during play-back she hears how he really feels about the project.

In other goings-on, Joe Hackett's old strikeout record for Sias-conset High baseball is about to be broken by a young phenom named Ty Warner (Matthew Fox). Joe pretends it doesn't both-er him, but it does, and the gang needles him incessantly. Coach Snyder (Brian Doyle Murray) wants Joe to fly Ty and some pho-tographers to the game in Chatham. Upon arriving Joe opts not to land because of heavy fog, but the other passengers think he's overreacting and using the weather as an excuse to keep his old strikeout record intact. He turns the plane around and flies back to Nantucket. Aeromass then takes over, gets Ty there just in time to break the record and hit the game winning home run. About this particular episode, co-producer Bill Diamond said, "I believe this was Steven Levitan's first produced TV script. The story revolved around a star high school pitcher who was poised to break Joe's old record for most strikeouts recorded in a season. So I figured Steven should have the baseball that appeared in the episode as a memento to mark the event. As soon as we shot the final scene, I grabbed the ball off the prop cart and then went around asking the whole cast to sign it. But what I'd forgotten to take into account was, just because the audience was being let go, it didn't mean we were finished for the night. The director still had a bunch of pick-ups to shoot, which meant there was a pretty decent chance they'd need the baseball used in the previous scenes so that the footage would match what had already been shot. And there I was, holding the very baseball they'd used in the show, only now it was totally unusable, since I'd persuaded the entire cast to scribble their signatures on it in thick, black, indelible ink. As I ran around the set in a total panic, trying to figure out what scenes were going to be shot again and determine whether the ball was going to be needed in any of them, I became more and more convinced my entire career was about to go down the drain, and for such an outrageously stupid, self-inflicted reason. But of course, prop people are always prepared and *of course* it turns out they had a duplicate baseball. I'm not sure if they even needed to use it in the pick-ups. But rest assured, I've spent the rest of my career staying the hell away from the prop cart." Does Steven Levitan still have that signed souvenir baseball? "No I don't. I wish I did!"

"As Fate Would Have It" (Season 3 Episode 22) Aired May 7, 1992

Written by Larry Balmagia
Directed by Andy Ackerman

This is the Season Three finale. The gang is aboard the Cessna heading to a formal event in a major storm when the plane runs into engine trouble. Helen reflects upon how she got into this predicament. In her flashback, she collides with a man in the terminal and stains his very expensive silk Italian suit. He is furious and treats Helen like dirt, even after she offers to pay for the damage. She is surprised to discover that he is Peter Swinden (Ronald Guttman), the managing director of the Boston Philharmonic. She once sent him an audition tape and got no response. Because he will be in the terminal for a few minutes she gives him a piece of her mind, only to find out that he did indeed like her tape, but the label had fallen off of it and he had no way of contacting her. Coincidentally, his cellist for that evening has tendonitis, and he decides to use Helen to fill in. Helen wants the gang to be there to see her performance, but everyone already has plans. However, the episode is accurately titled "As Fate Would Have It," and one by one their plans for that night fall apart and suddenly all are available to go along for the ride which becomes a fateful ride into the sea. Production Assistant Tony Hicks recalled, "At the end of my first season on *Wings*, which was its Third Season, I had a Hollywood moment. The season finale called for a cliff hanger with our regulars flying to Boston for Helen's night with the symphony. They are all on the Sandpiper plane and flying through a storm when the engines fails. The plane was parked outside our soundstage and it (and the building next to it) had been covered in black tarps as a backdrop that would lend to the effect of the plane flying in the dark night. The night we shot the scene happened to be a stormy one with actual rain down pouring in L. A. All the cameras and equipment were outside under tents to protect them and crew from the rain. I got soaked running chairs and miscellaneous stuff around. It was either when they did a rehearsal with cameras or an actual first take, I remember someone yelling, 'We need more rain!'. The real downpour didn't read enough in-camera. So they turned on the special effects rain that was rigged. Rain on rain." The episode ends with the Cessna readying for a water landing. The story continues in the Season Four opener.

SEASON FOUR

This season consisted of 22 episodes and saw the addition of Farrah Forke as Alex Lambert – the helicopter pilot for whose affection the Hackett boys compete. She first appeared in the sixth episode of the season titled "Two Jerks and a Jill." Writer/Producer Adam Belanoff shared, "We often ate dinner in the *Wings* writers room and the tradition (by Season Four – and I'm assuming it continued after I left) was that the final writers room dinner was Dr. Hogly Wogly's Tyler Texas Barbecue, arguably the best barbecue in Southern California." Writer/director Ken Levine added to the Dr. Hogly Wogly story with, "I remember rookies had to eat a Texas hotlink and writer/producer Bruce Rasmussen's face turned beet red." The show ran on Thursday nights at 9:30 until February of 1993 when it was moved to an earlier timeslot – Thursday nights at 8:30.

"Lifeboat" (Season 4 Episode 1) Aired September 24, 1992
Written by Christopher Lloyd
Directed by Andy Ackerman

The episode begins with a recap of the Season Three cliffhanging finale. Everybody's OK but all have been in the middle of nowhere in the lifeboat for eight hours, the end result of crashing the plane. Lowell was briefly unconscious and remembers nothing. Strange as it seems, it was Roy who rescued him. Assistant Director Leonard R. Garner, Jr. said, "We used Paramount's big water tank for that difficult scene. The entire cast was in a lifeboat for most of the episode. Numerous takes were needed to get everything just right. There was one great blooper taken from this episode. It's on the blooper reels on You Tube. Helen is supposed to shoot up a flare, but she aimed too high and hit the boom microphone, probably hurting the sound engineer's ears for a few moments. She was supposed to be aiming at her cello that surfaces after the plane sinks to the bottom. The cast was waterlogged but we eventually got

Timothy Daly as Joe Hackett

Joe Hackett with his real true love, his Cessna, which survived the crash that closed out Season Three. (Courtesy of Suzanne Holmes).

through it." Writer/producer Steven Levitan added, "Done where some of the greatest water scenes in cinema were shot. We did the whole episode before it became clear that you could hear the hum of air conditioners in the background. The entire episode had to be dubbed." Adam Belanoff concurred saying, "An outdoor parking lot at Paramount was filled with water. Unfortunately there was this sound from a circulating fan coming from a nearby building that couldn't be easily removed from the dialogue track and the entire 'out at sea' sequence had to be looped." Post production sound was done at Larson Sound in Burbank.

The episode is titled "Lifeboat," and Roy references the Alfred Hitchcock thriller of same name, saying he feels as though he's in the film. When the raft begins to take on water, the guys take turns jumping into the water to lessen the weight in the boat. Just as the lifeboat begins to deflate, the Coast Guard comes to the rescue. The next day Antonio returns from visiting family in Italy, and everyone is happy they made it through the ordeal unscathed, but now Joe has to try to put the pieces of his business back together. He decides that it's just not worth it and folds the business, opting to move to the South Pacific. It took a lot of convincing but Helen agrees to go along. That is, until they become aware the plane has been returned to the hangar. Lowell's friend who owns a salvage company found it intact. It landed on a sandbar and Lowell had it towed back to the hangar. Joe kisses the plane, his baby, and suddenly the South Pacific adventure with Helen is history. Sandpiper Air lives!

"The Fortune Cookie" (Season 4 Episode 2) Aired October 1, 1992

Written by David Lloyd
Directed by Andy Ackerman

The title of this episode harkens back to a wonderful Jack Lemmon and Walter Matthau film of the same name also involving an insurance scam. Lowell diligently tries to return the plane to working order after the crash, but it takes money and it seems the insurance company, Unified General has only sent a check for $262 because of a high deductible and plane depreciation. Brian suggests that Joe feign injuries to squeeze a lot more money out of the insurance people. Joe sees it as fraud while Brian sees it as justice. With no other way out of the financial mess, Joe agrees and is seen by shady Dr. Lenny (James Handy), who also sometimes poses as a lawyer and an ordained minister. Joe gets cold feet at the last minute and Brian takes to the wheelchair instead, claiming to be incapacitated. Helen plays a trick on the boys by having her gorgeous friend Susan (Barbara Lee Alexander, aka Barbara Niven) portray the insurance adjuster. When Susan lures Brian out of the wheelchair with her feminine wiles, the Hackett boys fear they will go to prison for insurance fraud. Helen and Susan eventually let on that it was a prank and the boys find that they have been taught a very valuable lesson.

"Noses Off" (Season 4 Episode 3) Aired October 8, 1992
Written by Ken Levine and David Isaacs
Directed by Andy Ackerman

This episode's title is a play on a play titled *Noises Off.* Joe and Fay are very excited about the first Sandpiper flight since the accident.

In other action Roy has a new toady – a kid named Marty (Scott Grimes) who is doing all of Roy's chores and running all of his errands. Suddenly a man enters the terminal, asks Joe if his name is Hackett. When Joe says yes, the man proceeds to punch him squarely in the nose. Playboy Brian should have been the Hackett getting coldcocked because the man delivering the sweet juicy Hawaiian Punch was a jealous boyfriend seeking retaliation for the Hackett who was dating his girl, Lucy Chase. She spent the night with Brian. Joe then visits Dr. Lasker (Peter Brown) and gets his proboscis packed with cotton and covered in a huge bandage. Lasker is a plastic surgeon and almost talks both Hackett boys into having more work done. Lasker urges Brian to fix the unsightly bump on his nose. Later, a passenger in the terminal played by Kevin Brief (in his fourth and final appearance on the sitcom) lets everyone know that Lasker does that with every one of his patients. The doctor's a quack who coaxes patients into getting more work done needlessly. About the experience, Brief said, "It was David Angell, Peter Casey and David Lee, who had just returned from a vacation in Barcelona to see the 1992 Olympics who urged the writers of the episode, Ken Levine and David Isaacs to use me. Originally my speech was to be a lot longer, but a lot of what was in the original script was surgically cut. Maybe Lasker did it." Lasker's nurse Janine was played by the late Lana Clarkson (allegedly shot a few years later by music producer Phil Spector). Brian is extremely self-conscious about the bump on his nose and makes an appointment for the vanity surgery. Joe is finally able to talk Brian out of the surgery while still in the doctor's office. As he is about to take the heavily sedated Brian back home Joe re-injures his own nose when he walks into a door abruptly opened by Helen.

This episode contains one of Tim Daly's favorite scenes in which the men in the terminal have a discussion about who the handsomest man in the world is. Daly said, "I love the 'Men of *Wings*' scene. My choice for handsomest man was Peter Jennings, Antonio says Sylvester Stallone, Roy says John Forsythe, Brian says Kevin Costner, but Lowell's was the best – Tom Petty. That was hilarious." Did Petty have any reaction to that scene? Did he take offense? Daly replied, "I don't think he responded at all. If he did I never heard about it." Regarding the scene, co-writer Ken Levine said, "Tony Shalhoub in particular was hilarious. I love stories where you could stop for a few moments and just let your characters relate to one another."

About Roy's John Forsythe comment, the *Wings* warmup man, Robert G. Lee said, "My biggest honor working for *Wings* was that after a few years they agreed to let me work in the writers room as a punch up writer. Let me say right now I was mediocre at best and was intimidated out of my mind. After several frustrating weeks of whiffing on nearly every pitch, I finally got a gag in. Somehow the guys got into an argument about which male TV actors they found attractive. Roy Biggins thought the whole discussion was beneath him, so he left in a huff. But just before he stormed out, he turned around and said 'Fine! John Forsythe!' It made the guys in the room laugh, and it made the show." Kevin Brief added, "Even though this was my last episode of *Wings,* I did get to work on another Grub Street show a while later – an episode of *Frasier* [titled "RDWRER"]. Coincidentally, it's the episode with guest star Rebecca Schull."

"Blackout Biggins" (Season 4 Episode 4) Aired October 22, 1992
Written by Steven Levitan
Directed by Andy Ackerman

The episode begins with Antonio attempting to win a local tourism contest for best poem. His is called "Waiting for a Fare," and it's quite dark and angry. A bit later Fay is called on the carpet by Joe for not filing paperwork on time, an oversight which led to his being fined $500. She doesn't take criticism well at all and the tears begin to flow uncontrollably. To pay Joe back the $500 Fay begins raiding the terminal trash bins for recyclables.

Meanwhile everyone else is gathered around the TV set at Helen's lunch counter ready to watch the Red Sox game. Roy dislikes the rap version of "The Star-Spangled Banner" he witnesses before the game and professes that he can perform it much better. The gang calls his bluff and the opportunity comes to fruition. Brian's old college roommate is the public relations director for the Red Sox and he gets everything set up. Suddenly Roy has second thoughts about going through with it, while everyone around him clucks like a chicken until he gives in. This is nothing new because behind the scenes, Thomas Haden Church and Steven Weber provided animal sounds between takes on a regular basis to lighten the mood. When the big night comes, Roy is so nervous he passes out on camera before singing even one note. Adding to his embarrassment, the video of him fainting is used incessantly for the next week by WWEN-TV sports broadcaster Dave Barr (Keith Sellon-Wright). Roy gets an opportunity to redeem himself, but before that happens he asks for Helen's assistance to be able to reach that one really high note in the song. This time the gang attends the game to see the event in person, but Roy's performance doesn't suck. He does a good job, until the end when his microphone cuts out. Determined to prove he can hit that high note he attempts to sing the entire song again, but gets dragged off the field, much to the delight of Joe, Brian, Helen, Fay, Antonio and Lowell. This embarrassing moment made the whole trip worthwhile.

"Mathers of the Heart" (Season 4 Episode 5) Aired October 29, 1992

Written by Adam Belanoff
Directed by Andy Ackerman

The episode begins with Lowell fixing Helen's lunch counter stove – a job from which he emerges with a smoking baseball cap caused by an errant wall of blue flame. This leads Roy to call him Backdraft. Lowell misinterprets Helen's thank you kiss on the cheek for sexual attraction and decides to seize the moment and ask her out on a date, but not before asking Joe if it would be OK. When he does muster the courage to ask her out it takes Helen by surprise and she laughs in his face. She later apologizes and agrees to go out on one date. That one date turns into several. Ironically, she enjoys his company calling it "refreshing," but he is bored out of his mind and is the one who breaks it off. The breakup happens at an art gallery, although one of the artists (played by Erick Avari) is quite impressed with Lowell's interpretation of his paintings. About the experience Avari said, "It was a quick shoot for me and though I spent a minimal amount of time on set I established friendships that I maintain today. It was one of the most respectful sets I have been on. The guest cast were all treated like guests and were made to feel at home. What a novel idea huh?" About Avari, writer Adam Belanoff said, "He took this short-scripted interchange as an effete artist who compliments Lowell for Lowell's astute take on his work and turned it into something truly memorable."

Later in the episode, Joe consoles a despondent Helen, and they ponder whether their own breakup was a hasty decision. Belanoff added, "The episode idea came from David Angell, David Lee and Peter Casey. They had already worked out the broad strokes when they called me down to their office to pitch what they had and I went off from there to write the outline and first draft. It was supposed to be filmed somewhat later in the season, but the morning we were prepared to read and begin production on 'The Houseguest,' a crew member went to pick up Bill Hickey and discovered that he'd had a heart attack. Hickey was rushed to the hospital and with that episode indefinitely on hold, the guys asked me what kind of shape my script was in. I showed them a rough draft and they were pleased enough to put it into production the following day after we did a polish that afternoon." About Thomas Haden Church's prolonged "ThursDAYYY" and "SaturDAYYY" answers to Helen's invitations, Belanoff shared, "That was all scripted but Church played it so well. There was also his line, 'That's another reason I wish I was Jewish' that was pitched on the floor as a last-minute alternative. It caught Rebecca Schull (who happens to be Jewish) by surprise and she burst out laughing so we had to take it again." By the way, that outtake is available for viewing on You Tube.

"Two Jerks and a Jill" (Season 4 Episode 6) Aired November 5, 1992

Written by Dave Hackel
Directed by David Lee and Andy Ackerman

The action begins in the terminal with Fay on the microphone sending the passengers off with a greeting from the native Algonquin Indians. Then Lowell's buddy Tucker (Tracey Walter) visits the airport to confirm plans to go to the dump and shoot rats that evening. They firm up their plans within earshot of Antonio, and then have to invite him along, much to Tuck's dismay. Lowell rues the decision to bring Antonio along when Antonio bags more rats than any of the others. Antonio instantly bonds with Lowell's buddies, and Lowell is envious of all the attention they're paying him.

In other action Brian and Joe are peeved about a new helicopter pilot who has cut them off a couple of times on the runway. That is, until they get to meet her in person and fall immediately in lust. This episode marks the first appearance of Alex Lambert played by the lovely Farrah Forke who shared, "Alex is story editor Adam Belanoff's creation. The reason the episode is titled 'Two Jerks and a Jill' is that Belanoff's girlfriend was named Jill and he patterned the character after her. He and I have been friends for many years." About the character portrayed by Farrah Forke writer/producer Christopher Lloyd shared, "The character was easy to integrate because she was a natural foil for Crystal, and a natural magnet for the horny Hackett brothers."

Now with fresh meat in the terminal, the Hackett boys compete for Alex's affection, but she wants none of it. She immediately nicknames Brian as Slick and Joe as Ace. In fact, "Slick" is used in her very first encounter with the boys, and Ace comes very soon after. Forke added, "On screen, Brian wanted to date me but initially I nixed all of his advances. In real life the situation was reversed. I had a real crush on Steven, but the attraction was not reciprocated. We were the best of friends but never more than that." Alex has a lot of chopper experience, having flown an Apache in Desert Storm. She started her chopper business in Florida but thought it might be a bit more successful in New England. When the brothers find out she's joined a gym on the island they also sign up for memberships, only to embarrass themselves attempting to use the unfamiliar equipment.

"It's So Nice to Have a Mother around the House" (Season 4 Episode 7) Aired November 12, 1992

Written by Ken Levine and David Isaacs
Directed by Andy Ackerman

The episode begins with impatient Helen leaving a nasty telephone message for a man named Michael (Scott Thompson Baker) who has obviously stood her up...or not. An out of breath Michael then enters the terminal with flowers and a totally believable story about his tardiness. Helen was only halfway through her phone message at the time and attempts to cover it up with a wild story about terrorists forcing her to leave the vitriolic message.

In other action, everyone admires Antonio's new gloves. They are genuine calfskin and cost only ten bucks a pair. His uncle makes them in Italy. Everybody ponies up the money to get their own pair, and Antonio has them trace their hands on a piece of paper for accurate measurements, but then unwittingly faxes enlarged hand pictures to his relative and every pair of gloves that arrives from overseas is far too big.

Elsewhere Brian asks Alex if she'd like to accompany him to a party on his boat to watch the tall ships. Surprisingly Alex says yes. Brian then scrambles to get Lowell to lend him the houseboat for the night. Tragedy strikes when Brian and Alex accidentally sink Lowell's boat which contained everything Lowell owned. A heartbroken Lowell then moves in with Brian and Joe and surprisingly proves to be a great roommate, cook and housekeeper. When Lowell's insurance check comes, the boys keep it a secret as long as they can to avoid losing their new roomie who makes them such delicious meals every day. Lowell accidentally finds the check when looking for the keys to the airplane but likes the feeling of being needed and decides to stay at the Hackett house. He also promises to lighten up on the strict rules and regulations he imposes upon them.

About the character of Lowell, co-writer Ken Levine said, "One of the great things about Lowell was that he could always surprise you. You think he's just this simpleton with limited skills and it turns out he has all sorts of unexpected talents. We were looking for a way to use Lowell out of the airport setting and came up with the idea that he has to be Brian and Joe's housemate because Brian crashed his boat. But the spin was making him Felix Unger with all the pros and cons that went with that. Once we had that in place the writing was very easy. This is why I always preach that the real hard work and attention needs to be spent on breaking the story."

Having Lowell as a housemate proved to be fertile ground and he remained with the Hackett Brothers for an entire year.

"Just Say No" (Season 4 Episode 8) Aired November 19, 1992

Written by Adam Belanoff
Directed by Andy Ackerman

The title of this episode was inspired by Nancy Reagan's "War on Drugs" mantra, "Just Say No." The action begins on a flight experiencing a bit of turbulence as a passenger and Joe share stories of having survived a plane crash.

Meanwhile Lowell is reading down the passenger list so Roy can re-enter the names into his computer, Joe hears the name Shannon Moss (Teri Austin). Shannon is now a hot-shot lawyer, and is the one woman around whom Brian is powerless. He is completely whipped in her presence. He claims that this time will be different because he's older and wiser, and she's living with a guy named Mark whom she's mad about. But true to form Brian lets his guard down and "Moss grows on him" when he finds out that Mark has broken it off with her. As per usual Shannon leads Brian on and reels him in saying, "I want you back in my life," only to quickly toss him aside like an old shoe. The episode's writer, Adam Belanoff said, "The story was heavily inspired by an ex-girlfriend, the notion being that we all have someone in our lives who, no matter how many times they break our hearts, we'll always take back only to have our hearts broken again."

"It May Have Happened One Night" (Season 4 Episode 9) Aired December 3, 1992

Written by Christopher Lloyd
Directed by Andy Ackerman

The title is a takeoff on the Clark Gable and Claudette Colbert film from 1934 titled *It Happened One Night*. The episode begins with Fay in Joe's office reading a letter from a disgruntled customer. It's a scathing recount of his experience with the pilot and the plane. The one saving grace in the letter is the glowing report about the lovely woman behind the ticket counter - Fay.

Elsewhere in the terminal Roy is frantically trying to find an annoying cricket in his private office to no avail. Lowell is eventually called upon for assistance. Back in Joe's office after hours Alex pops in and asks Joe if he would like to share a whiskey. He is pleasantly stunned at this, but of course says yes. About the "whiskey" she and Joe shared, Farrah Forke said, "It was flat Coca Cola. I'm sure the props department had planned on it. Dark and flat and not-so-pleasant to sip." Alex is there in Joe's office because she needs to bend someone's ear. Her old live-in boyfriend from Florida is engaged and she is not handling the news well. She's in no condition to drive and invites Joe over to her place. Later that evening, Antonio sees Joe's Jeep outside of Alex's building and spills the beans to the others. Much to everyone's chagrin, neither Joe nor Alex will divulge what, if anything happened that night. Alex doesn't remember, and Joe won't tell her anything about that night because for once, he's in the driver's seat. Alex has been in control up until now but briefly he has the upper hand. Joe finally admits to her that he was a gentleman, and she kisses him passionately, thus wresting control once again.

"The Customer Is Usually Right" (Season 4 Episode 10) Aired December 17, 1992

Written by Janet Leahy
Directed by Leonard R. Garner, Jr.

Leonard R. Garner, Jr. directs his first episode of Wings, *"The Customer Is Usually Right." (Courtesy of Jack E. Herman).*

He had been assistant director since the show began, but with Andy Ackerman having ongoing back issues after falling off a horse, this was Lenny Garner's big break as director. He shared, "Apparently they liked what I did because I got to do three more the next season which turned into seven, and finally ten more while totally surrendering my A.D.[assistant director] job to devote my full attention to directing. I was also an actor. At the time I used the name Lenny Garner for my acting work and Leonard R. Garner, Jr. for my directing gigs. I eventually dropped the Lenny and used the full name, but most people still call me Lenny." This is the show's second of six Christmas episodes. It opens with two customers fighting over one last Aeromass seat on the final flight on Christmas Eve. The woman in the fight is a plant, making the male passenger bid $100 over face value to secure the seat. Once he's left the terminal, Roy and the woman split the profit.

Elsewhere Lowell has purchased a drum set for his son as a Christmas present and drives everyone mad when he sets it up in the hangar. Lowell learns "In a Gadda da Vida" by Iron Butterfly, much to everyone's dismay. Fay puts him to shame with what she learned while in the USO All-Girl Band in Korea 1952.

In other action Antonio was Boston-bound to have Christmas eel with family but when his cousin Giacomo came down with the mumps all plans were off. Antonio felt bad enough already, but then gets invited to spend the holiday with Roy and his mother. Fay is going to the Berkshires with her seniors' group. Joe, Brian and Helen are going to spend Christmas Eve together. Helen has made her usual gingerbread house, and Brian can't wait to eat her out of house and home. Joe goes to rent a video, but all that is left is *Psycho*. Upon looking at his receipt from the video store his OCD kicks in when he notices a fifty-cent rewind fee for the video he returned. He is certain the tape was already rewound and just can't let it go. He returns to the video store and confronts a young long-haired punk named Carter (played by Phil Buckman) behind the counter who gives him a lot of flak and attitude. Joe raises a big stink about the stinking fifty cents, Carter then fires the elderly woman named Debbie Murphy who works in the rewind department. In this case the customer was not right – it appears that Lowell watched *Sea of Love* the night before Joe returned it. Lowell wasn't kind and didn't rewind. Joe finds out that Debbie was so upset about being terminated she collapsed, and he then spends the evening in the hospital at her bedside along with her family under the alias Jed. He makes certain to leave as Debbie begins regaining consciousness. It's interesting to note that the woman who portrayed Debbie, Ellen Albertini Dow lived to be 101.

"Exit Laughing" (Season 4 Episode 11) Aired January 7, 1993

Written by Larry Balmagia
Directed by Andy Ackerman

This was the first *Wings* episode to air in 1993. It opens with Brian piloting with a very smart young man in the cockpit. The youngster corrects Brian when he says that the plane is just like

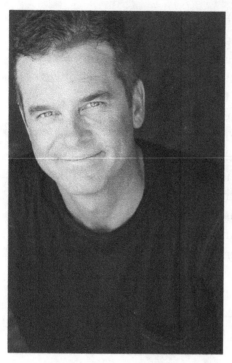

Actor Steven Eckholdt, who played "Laffy Guy" Connor McDevitt in the episode "Exit Laughing" laughs all the way to the bank. (Courtesy of Steven Eckholdt).

a big bird, citing the fact that birds and planes have vastly different methods of achieving lift.

Meanwhile Antonio is getting very little sleep because of an inconsiderate neighbor with a loud high-powered leaf blower. His big mistake is in telling Roy about it. Roy then takes the matter into his own hands and only makes things worse for Antonio (who ends up with a black eye).

In other action, an old fraternity brother of Joe's, Connor McDevitt (Steven Eckholdt) stops by the airport and wants to see his old friend. Connor and Helen are immediately attracted to one another. She thinks he might be a pilot, but he's an oceanographer who has worked with Jacques Cousteau. Connor's in town to study the whale feeding grounds off Stellwagen Bay. About that Eckholdt said, "There's some truth to that. I studied both oceanography and medicine in school." Helen is instantly smitten with the guy, only to discover while on a date with him at the movies that he has the most hideous and annoying laugh she's ever heard. And she hears it a lot as they go to a Jerry Lewis film festival. About securing the role of Connor, Eckholdt shared, "I auditioned with an annoying laugh. I went in with the attitude, 'If I get the role great, if not it's not the end of the world.' They liked me and they liked the laugh, but strangely the laugh was tweaked all week. It ended up being quite a bit different from the one I auditioned with. They wanted it to be more nasal-sounding. The more nasal the more annoying. The audience nearly crapped itself on the first take. We did it a few more times on shoot night, but the audience was always there with the laughter." Producer Adam Belanoff shared, "David Lee told the writers room about a friend who had shared a story about a blind date that was going perfectly until the date's laugh became so off putting that there was never going to be a second date. Building off that notion, Larry Balmagia wrote 'Exit Laughing,' which turned out quite well. Sometime later David went back to his friend and told him, 'We used that great date story of yours on *Wings*.' David's friend responded, 'That wasn't my story. That was an episode I saw of *The Golden Girls*."

Eckholdt added, "There's a great and funny plot twist in this episode. Helen wants to break off the relationship with me because of my laugh, but I'm oblivious to that. Before she breaks it off *I do it* because I can't stand her Southern accent." Andy Ackerman directed the episode and Eckholdt recalled, "He is great. I worked with him several times on *It's Like...You Know*. He knows what he wants, what the audience wants, and what the producers and network want. He delivers it while making it appear as if it's the actor's choice." Did he ever cross paths with the cast of *Wings* again? Eckholdt said, "Yes. I saw Steven Weber years later at an audition and he remembered me and called me 'Laffy Guy.' I also did a celebrity skiing event with Tim Daly in Deer Valley." About the cast he added, "I didn't see any egos. It was a great cohesive unit, which is why the show worked so well for eight seasons. They couldn't have been nicer or more welcoming. There was great chemistry on and off camera."

"What the Cabbie Saw" (Season 4 Episode 12) Aired January 14, 1993

Written by Steven Levitan
Directed by Judy Askins

The episode begins with Alex chastising Joe and Brian for staring at her butt as she walked by (she saw their faces in the glass door). They apologize for their boorish behavior and walk away while Alex turns and watches their butts as they go. About that scene, Farrah Forke shared, "I thought that scene was PERFECT! It turned the

L-R: Rebecca Schull, Tim Daly, Farrah Forke, Steven Weber, Crystal Bernard, Thomas Haden Church, David Schramm, Tony Shalhoub

Smiling faces galore (well, except for Lowell). Left to right Rebecca Schull, Tim Daly, Farrah Forke, Steven Weber, Crystal Bernard, Thomas Haden Church, David Schramm and Tony Shalhoub. (Courtesy of Suzanne Holmes).

tables. Alex was a woman that had no qualms with being sexual. She just wanted it on her terms. Not unlike me. Don't mess with a strong woman."

Later that day Antonio is certain the man sitting at Helen's lunch counter is the same man he saw robbing a jewelry store a day earlier. To keep the alleged thief in the terminal until the police arrive, both Sandpiper and Aeromass announce that flights have been delayed. After the man is apprehended, Antonio is thoroughly grilled by a detective named Howard "where's your hall pass" Crawley (Robert Fieldsteel) whom the Hackett boys remember being shoved into the girls' locker room wearing only a shower cap back in their school days. After Crawley leaves, Roy tries to talk Antonio out of going to the arraignment scheduled for the following day as it may put him in grave danger. For once it appears that Roy is right.

Because of a technicality, the alleged robber Frederick Watts (Beau Starr) gets released and Antonio is in a state of panic. Antonio is certain he is being followed and that Watts is out to get him and wakes up the Hacketts and Lowell in the wee hours of the morning seeking safe harbor. When Lowell's pizza arrives the guys scare the bejeebers out of the delivery guy (Gabe Dell, Jr.) thinking he might be Watts. After getting almost no sleep, the boys go to work the next day and Watts is once again in the terminal. Antonio is tired of hiding and confronts the man only to discover that the guy isn't after him. He has the hots for Helen ever since she gave him a free piece of pie earlier in the week. He strongarms Antonio into introducing him to her.

"Labor Pains" (Season 4 Episode 13) Aired January 28, 1993

Written by Dave Hackel
Directed by Andy Ackerman

The episode begins with Brian paying Helen for his tuna melt sandwich and accidentally exposing the swatch of his childhood blue blanket he still carries around in his pocket. It's his good luck charm and Helen wants to hold on to it for a while so maybe it'll bring her luck. Brian continually attempts to get his "blanky" back as his luck is in a downward spiral without it.

Meanwhile Lowell discovers that his friend Dewey at Logan Airport makes more money than he. Dewey invites Lowell to join him at his place of employment. With a little coaxing Lowell decides to ask Joe and Roy for a raise now that he has some leverage. Roy believes they can schmooze Lowell into staying on in Nantucket without giving him a dime more. The "schmoozola," as Roy calls it, begins at La Maison, the most expensive restaurant in town (a tax write off for both Roy and Joe). The deal even comes with a hooker named Marcia Peebles (Lisa Edelstein), but no raise is offered. Antonio encourages Lowell to call their bluff and take the Boston job thinking they'll back down at the last moment. While awaiting his flight to Beantown, Lowell encounters his replacement – an African American mechanic named Gil Cooper (Phil LaMarr). Lowell says his goodbyes and everyone thinks it's the last they'll see of him. However, the following day all are surprised to see Lowell back at work in the hangar. He's in the process of taking two sealed drums out to the ferry to be transported. When Joe and Brian hear banging coming from inside each container, they find Gil in one, Antonio in the other.

"I've Got a Secret" (Season 4 Episode 14) Aired February 4, 1993
Written by Adam Belanoff
Directed by Andy Ackerman

This episode has the same title as a long-running Mark Goodson/Bill Todman panel game show. Writer Adam Belanoff shared, "My recollection is that it came out of the writers' room and I honestly don't recall if the initial idea was mine or someone else's though the script undoubtedly owed a lot to everyone in the group, particularly David Isaacs and Christopher Lloyd who added some tremendous jokes along the way." It opens with a discussion about Lowell's Jewish girlfriend Melissa. Her family is very religious and Fay wonders how they came to accept that she is dating Lowell. Lowell says it's not a problem as long as he gets a bris (but he has no idea what that is). When Roy explains it as delicately as he can, Lowell decides to break it off (break off the relationship, that is).

In other action Brian wants Joe to be spontaneous and go with him to Atlantic City to see the fights. Fay is a huge boxing fan and wants to tag along. However, Brian already had plans to accompany Helen to a dull party that her friends were throwing. Luckily Alex offers to take his place. That night, Antonio shows up at Helen's house to return a Cindy Crawford workout tape, and Helen and Alex invite him to stay and he fits right in. Antonio gets a facial while there and also divulges an embarrassing secret from his past about the day he tried on his sister's wedding dress and while admiring himself in the mirror realized that his entire soccer team could see him through the window. For years afterwards he was called "the boy in the dress." About Antonio, writer Adam Belanoff shared, "Tony Shalhoub not only delivered everything you might have imagined but always imbued it with something beyond what you'd envisioned. Sitting at a table read, you couldn't wait to discover what Tony was going to do with a line or a bit because you knew his delivery was going to be both unexpected and likely funnier than it read on the page." After Antonio's admission, Alex lets on that she posed for *Playboy Magazine.* Everyone promises not to tell. But everyone finds out and then they locate a copy of the magazine in Roy's office collection. It's the April 1986 edition. Alex thinks it was Antonio who spilled the beans, but it was Helen. After many cross words in the ladies' room between Alex and Helen, Fay (really needing to use the restroom) orders them to apologize to one another, make up, and leave.

"The Gift Part One" (Season 4 Episode 15) Aired February 11, 1993
Written by David Angell
Directed by Andy Ackerman

The episode opens with a couple of very astute observations about the plane's engine (including the word astute) by Brian and Joe, much to the annoyance of Antonio. Then Fay finds a column in the newspaper about Winston Catlow of the Nantucket String Quartet leaving his position over creative differences. He used to be Helen's cello teacher. Everybody in the terminal is suggesting that Helen pursue the opening. They've forgotten that her cello went down with Joe's airplane and a new one costs about $15,000. Brian suggests she get a second job and she does just that – gutting fish at Siasconset Seafood Company. Her boss, Gus (Ken Magee) flirts with her and offers a better job as a come on, but she stops him dead in his tracks with a long string of insulting comebacks that win her the approval of her co-workers. A short time after taking the job she gets laid off and is back to square one. Brian calls a family meeting and suggests to Joe that they take out a second mortgage on the house to buy Helen that new cello.

At this same time there are open auditions for a local musical production titled *Phantom of the Oprah.* It's about a deranged former producer of Winfrey's TV program. Fay, Lowell, Roy and Antonio hope to get cast. Lowell gets the part of a stagehand, Roy is cast as a producer, Fay is the understudy of the woman playing Oprah and Antonio plays a man who is only attracted to women who used to be men. Part one closes with Brian and Joe presenting the gift cello to Helen. Her reaction is not quite what they expected as she hurries out of Joe's office saying, "How could you guys do this to me?"

"The Gift Part Two" (Season 4 Episode 16) Aired February 18, 1993
Written by David Angell
Directed by Andy Ackerman

After a recap of Part One, the action continues with Brian and Joe following Helen into the kitchen. She says she can't accept the gift cello out of pity. The guys say it was just an act of friendship. She's truly in awe that they got her a $12,000 hand-crafted cello. Brian could have gotten it much cheaper had he shopped around (he paid $15,000). Helen finally accepts the gift and goes for the audition in front of the creepy Karl Spengler (Robert Martin Robinson), his sullen cohort Lydia (Mary Woronov) and the lecherous Johnny Toshiba (Derek Basco) who verbally expresses his immediate attraction to Helen. About the job, Derek Basco shared, "It was super fun working on *Wings*. I remember all the guys playing hacky sack on set. Tim Daly and Steven Weber welcomed me and were very kind. It was a good way to bond with everyone. Andy Ackerman is a genius at directing comedy. Crystal Bernard (Helen) seemed very glamorous to a young actor like me. And so it was not hard to say those lines. 'I mean it Carl. I really really want her!' But looking back, it seems quite ridiculous. Thomas Haden Church and Tony Shalhoub are great character actors. I was fortunate to see their genius up close since I am a character actor, too. I had a lot of fun filming it in front of a live studio audience. The three-camera half-hour sitcom is my favorite. And *Wings* will always be my first love."

Helen gets the quartet job, but the conductor lets her know that she was their third choice (the first two declined the position). Helen soon begins to understand why the others turned the job down as those in charge make the Addams Family appear normal. Helen wants to quit the string quartet (which includes a 50-city tour) but doesn't want to disappoint Joe and Brian – especially after they also buy her a dress for opening night. Luckily for her, the quartet's former cello player, Winston Catlow (Basil Langton) crashes the performance and the quartet disbands. After everyone else leaves the auditorium, Helen decides to give a private performance for Joe and Brian. They are confident it's dark enough in the audience that they can pretend to be enjoying her work while listening to their Walkmans.

In other action, Fay, Roy, Antonio and Lowell are rehearsing for *Phantom of the Oprah* with the play's director Ed Snow played by Jim Brochu who recalled, "David Lee was an old friend of mine and though the part was not written for me he thought about me when they were casting it. When I came in for the audition, I told him about a crazy director I had in summer stock and I was basing my characterization on him. One of the favorite things this old director used to say was. 'Theater is not down there; theater is up here!' (with appropriate gesture). Well they put it right into the script. The shoot was an absolute delight. Andy Ackerman is a director I had worked with before, a charming man who knows exactly what he's doing. We did that scene in one take. All of the actors were genuinely very sweet except for David Schramm who was rather standoffish. People ask me if the leg warmers were my idea…nope, written right in the script. And yes, the sweet Thomas Haden Church did his own rope swinging. His voice was dubbed in later, however." Jane Childerhose who portrayed one of the panel members in the play recalled, "It was my first SAG job and a really good experience. Thomas Haden Church was hysterical as he was swinging across the stage on set as the Phantom. Both Tony Shalhoub and Rebecca Schull were very nice to us day players. I still remember David Angell at the audition had us all sing a silly ditty he composed for the show. I also remember having a lovely conversation with Angell's wife Lynn on shoot night." Childerhose added, "We had a larger-than-normal amount of guest cast and extras for this episode so we spilled over onto the next soundstage for dressing rooms. Along with Derek Basco, I recall Steven Weber and Tim Daly playing hacky sack on set."

Well, all (except Roy) were understandably crushed when *Phantom of the Oprah* lost its sponsor Leo's Sludge and Septic who saw their rehearsal and then said they wanted nothing to do with such trash. That news was delivered by Antonio, and cast members said Tony Shalhoub found it difficult to deliver the line without laughing out loud.

"I Love Brian" (Season 4 Episode 17) Aired February 25, 1993

Written by Ian Gurvitz
Directed by Andy Ackerman

The episode begins with Antonio sharing his first experience watching an *I Love Lucy* marathon and telling how much he loved it. Everyone else at the lunch counter concurs except for Brian who thought the whole show was rather ridiculous.

In the meantime Alex is upset because she doesn't have tickets to see the upcoming Clint Black concert as she's a huge fan. When asked about that, Farrah Forke said, "I had no idea who Clint Black was, but I was a huge fan of his wife, Lisa Hartman. She was TV's *Tabitha,* and I always wanted to be Tabitha." About "stunt casting" as it's called, executive producer Dave Hackel said, "We'd often get presented with an opportunity. Casting would say something like, 'So and so is available, let's utilize them.' Then we would have to figure a way to plug them into an episode of *Wings* and have it make sense for the show and the characters." The writer of this episode, Ian Gurvitz said, "It was the first episode I wrote after coming on the show. The title 'I Love Brian' came from *I Love Lucy,* though it wasn't exactly a loving tribute. One of the *Wings* creators was not a fan of the hijinks in Lucy and, truthfully, neither was I. It was the '50s, you can't blame them for not being ahead of their time. Then again, *The Honeymooners* was often smarter and less slapstick. I guess it's a matter of taste. Still, the episode was supposed to be sort of a knock on those 'Lucy tells a big lie then has to sneak into a famous star's hotel room' type episodes. I don't know if it really came off that way. I thought a better title would have been 'Black and Blues,' but titles don't really matter. I remember Clint Black being very gracious and surprisingly good. Very natural. The set was also very well done. Tribute to Roy Christopher, the set designer. Kirstie Alley was great in her small cameo as Rebecca Howe - a crazed Clint Black fan. She just came over from the *Cheers* set and nailed it, not just with the lines that were written, but she riffed a bunch of ad libs and then went back to work. Very professional. Great energy. And funny. Years later I ran into Clint Black at a local store and re-introduced myself as the guy who wrote the episode. He was extremely nice and said he'd enjoyed it." Producer Christopher Lloyd recalled, "Clint Black had a special hair attendant who spent an hour getting his part just right. And the final step in his beautification was someone directing a blow dryer at his cowboy boots to give them a special shine."

In the episode, Brian attempts to win Alex's favor by telling a bald-faced lie about his being very close friends with Clint. Alex thinks it is total B.S. – that is, until he lands tickets to the sold-out show. He lucks into the tickets by asking just the right person – Lowell who has four of them. Lowell often goes to concerts with his rat-shooting buddies just to find unusual items (such as glass eyes and retainers) under the bleachers. Brian's offer of $300 secures the four tickets. Once again Brian succeeds by the seat of his pants. Well, almost. With four tickets Helen and Lowell go along, and after the concert the girls expect Brian to introduce them to Clint. Laughter ensues when Brian and Lowell pretend to be waiters at the after party, clumsy ones at that, and get ousted from the premises by a large bodyguard (Andy Garrison) after spilling a tray with filled champagne glasses on the singer. The girls, however, have no difficulty finagling their way into the party, and Helen saves Brian's boney butt by convincing Clint to pretend to be a longtime friend of his.

"The Key to Alex" (Season 4 Episode 18) Aired April 8, 1993
Written by David Lloyd
Directed by Andy Ackerman

The episode opens with Lowell wanting a cool nickname like his friend Scab O'Neill. Roy calls him Slackass and Lowell likes it, considers it, but comes up with three better ones – "Turbo," "El Conquistador d'amour," or "Jerry." Decisions, decisions.

At the same time Brian is attempting to find "The Key to Alex." She's very aloof and cold to the Hackett brothers. Brian tries the sympathy ploy (involving an old football injury) to no avail. An idea

Writing credits for David Lloyd – the only writer who disliked the double propeller graphic behind the names and requested that his name appear in typeface with no background as seen here in the opening credits for the episode titled "The Key to Alex."

springs from Helen's date with a new guy named Stan (Gregory Balaban). Helen likes his sensitivity. He shed a tear when she told him the story of her lost kitten. Both Brian and Joe give sensitivity a whirl to woo Alex. Joe exaggerates his love of dogs in front of Alex and it lands him a babysitting job with her huge, angry canine named "Chopper." Unlike in the movie *It's a Wonderful Life*, every time a bell rings Chopper attacks. Brian goes in another direction and uses jealousy. He tells Alex that he wants to make his girlfriend jealous. She works at the Club Car (Cherie Lyn Michan) but she's not really his girlfriend. In fact, she doesn't know him from Adam. Alex agrees to go along with the plan if Brian promises to leave her alone afterwards. Smart Alex sees through his scheme, however, and gives Brian a taste of his own medicine. She has a huge, tough guy named Otto (Robert Shafer) show up to pretend to be an old boyfriend in a jealous rage after seeing Alex out with Brian. About that week on *Wings*, Robert Shafer shared, "*Wings* was cast by Sheila Guthrie. She had taken a liking to me on a couple of previous auditions, and when I came to 'The Key to Alex,' I remember there was some serious competition, including some pro football play-ers. I thought they were going for BIG on this role, but in the end I booked it. And that week literally changed my life. The cast was very kind and welcoming and the process that week was new and interesting. I had mostly been making indie films and so network TV was very different, especially because it was filmed in front of a live audience. The whole week was geared towards the Friday shoot date. Every day after lunch, the writers would gather on the stage in their directors' chairs and each scene would be rehearsed and camera blocked. The next morning, the changes to the script would be wait-ing in your trailer. Otto's scene didn't change much, so by Friday, I was raring to go. I had several friends in the audience, and I liked having an audience because of my theater background. I remember thinking, 'Whatever you do, don't be the one to blow this take.' It was surreal, because the warmup comic that worked the crowd had just led them through a chorus of the theme song from *Gilligan's Island*, which kind of relaxed me, because it was so incredibly silly. We nailed the scene in one take, and they moved on. What made the week even better was Cherie Michan, the woman playing the waitress. I was in hot pursuit and I bought her a dozen red roses and a *Wings* tee shirt as good luck gifts before the show. That night, at the wrap party, both Steven Weber and I were after her, but I 'won' the day and ended up living with her for four years. Steven told me over drinks that he wanted to do the kind of acting that I was doing. I was a method actor, and he was very interested in that process. I, of course, wanted his job, as a network TV star. The grass is always greener... And so it goes. Cherie and I ran into one of the producers, David Angell, a couple of years after we shot the show, and he loved that the show had brought us together."

After striking out repeatedly with Alex, Joe and Brian then attempted something new – honesty. They met with Alex at the Club Car and for a while there she is impressed with their sincerity and candor. But when she tells Joe she likes that he's responsible and hard-working, and likes that Brian is spontaneous and unpre-dictable it fans the flames of sibling rivalry once again and Alex rolls her eyes and walks out while the brothers continue their one-upmanship at the table.

"The Houseguest" (Season 4 Episode 19) Aired April 15, 1993

Written by Bill Diamond and Michael Saltzman
Directed by Andy Ackerman

The episode begins with Joe, Brian and Lowell heading to Boston to see Bruce Springsteen in concert. Lowell has a knack for snagging tickets to sold-out shows. However, on their way Lowell realizes that he left the tickets on Helen's lunch counter – much to the pleasure of Helen, Antonio and Fay who quickly jump on an Aeromass flight to Beantown with those tickets to see "the Boss."

Much later, the Hackett brothers espy the world's most annoying man, Carlton Blanchard (William Hickey) seated at Helen's lunch counter. They try to avoid him and his inane questions, but to no avail. Carlton says he is in the terminal to meet his son, coming in via Aeromass. Allegedly, Carlton, Jr. backed out at the last moment, leaving Carlton, Sr. alone on his 70th birthday (truth be told, he has no son – it is a ruse for attention, and hopefully a birthday party). Dejected, he leaves the airport with his head down. Helen feels sorry for him and offers to throw a party, against everyone else's wishes. As the old saying goes, no good deed goes unpunished. When Blanchard takes a spill in Helen's house during the party, he becomes her houseguest while he convalesces. He milks the injury for all it's worth while dangling the threat of a lawsuit in front of Helen. Later, when she catches him dancing in the living room, Helen kicks the old man and his eight cats to the curb, only to see him fall again on the way out. About the episode, co-writer Michael Saltzman said, "Bill and I actually wrote 'The Houseguest' after we'd left the show. The creators asked us if we'd like to do a guest episode that brought Carlton back. We were working on another show at the time but we jumped at the chance. I went to attend the table read, which was super late in starting because William Hickey hadn't shown up. As it turned out, he'd had a heart attack that morning and the episode was postponed until he could do it. When they finally shot it later in the season he didn't seem quite himself, but was still very funny."

"Goodbye, Old Friend" (Season 4 Episode 20) Aired April 29, 1993

Written by Christopher Lloyd
Directed by Andy Ackerman

The episode opens with Brian and Joe throwing around numbers such as 36-24-36, 37-24-34. Alex overhears them and confronts them about it, thinking they're talking about her measurements. Quick-thinking Brian uses the combination lock on his gym bag to try to prove her wrong. An embarrassed Alex sees the error of her ways, apologizes and walks away while Joe gives Brian a thumbs up for being fast on his feet.

In other goings on Roy has a miserable cold and Antonio marvels at Roy's tiny, baby-like sneezes. Also Helen has a squirrel problem in her attic keeping her awake nights. She hasn't slept well in days, but when she gets concussed by the door to the kitchen of her lunch counter her doctor (Ted Sorel) adamantly states that she must remain awake for the next 18 hours and that is no easy feat given her lack of sleep. Also, Lowell's old friend and inspiration Weeb Gilroy has died at the age of 90. Weeb taught Lowell how to be a mechanic. Lowell's attempts to write an appropriate eulogy fall short, but he goes one better by adding the finishing touches to the old plane on which he and Weeb worked. Joe and Lowell take her for a spin. It's interesting to note that Brian's joke about a priest, a rabbi and a guy wearing lederhosen all taking a trip together isn't a joke at all as all three such men stroll through the terminal after he mentions the setup to the joke. Rebecca Schull's late husband, Gene Schull is the uncredited man in lederhosen in that scene.

"Another Wedding" (Season 4 Episode 21) Aired May 6, 1993

Written by Larry Balmagia
Directed by Andy Ackerman

The episode begins with a present for Fay's birthday - Joe lets her take the controls of the plane while he co-pilots. Of course, all of this occurs in the hangar on the ground with Lowell shaking the plane to create the feeling of turbulence while making fake engine sounds.

In the next scene all of the guys are ingesting massive amounts of coffee at Helen's counter. They're all hungover from the air traffic controller/tower guy Walter's (Ralph Bruneau) bachelor party the night before. Walter had as much to drink as the other guys but he's fit as a fiddle. He's very excited about his upcoming nuptials. Helen plans to go to the reception with a guy named Henry Applegate (Timothy D. Smith) who works in air freight. He is a bit of a dweeb but a great dancer. Brian is going to attempt to bring Alex. Bunny Mather (Laura Innes) shows up unexpectedly to the ceremony and Lowell is hopeful they can get back together. However, she is there with a new guy named Phil (Lee Brooks). Roy's seat is at the children's table, much to his annoyance. Antonio is very proud of his new suit (purchased especially for the wedding), that is until Helen's date, Henry shows up wearing the exact same one. Antonio's new suit quickly bears a large gravy stain causing Antonio to be hesitant about asking a sad-eyed lonely girl across the room for a dance. He later finds out that she's a perfect match because she is also sporting a big stain. Elsewhere at the reception Joe can't seem to avoid a guy named Al (Bill Gratton) whose lone interest is whales. Alex shows up late to the party and the episode closes with a nice moment in which she poses as Lowell's new love, Yvette who drives a Vette in an attempt to make Bunny jealous. Alex and Lowell then dance to his favorite tune, "Isn't It Romantic?" About that final scene and the dance with Lowell, Farrah Forke remembered, "The scene with me and Tommy Church was forced. I was still new on set and Tommy and I had not had really, any scenes together. I was wearing a lovely dress. I do remember Tommy looking at me. He hadn't seen Alex in anything other than jeans. No one had. Not the producers or audience. Tommy was so sweet. I could feel his empathy for me. He just took my hand, as he was supposed to, and led me to the dance floor. It was almost like he was my big brother that night. On screen and off. You know how I feel about him. He was the dancer that he was supposed to be."

It's interesting to note that actor Ralph Bruneau who also portrayed Walter the tower guy in the earlier episode titled "Airport 90" (along with being alluded to in other episodes) was named International Mister Leather 2017.

"Date Package Number Seven" (Season 4 Episode 22) Aired May 13, 1993

Written by Steven Levitan
Directed by Andy Ackerman

This episode begins with a brilliant scene in Joe's office. Joe is strumming a few chords on his guitar, Antonio is tapping on a coffee cup, Lowell is sanding Joe's door. Sounding very much like a jazz ensemble (think "The Girl from Ipanema"). Brian then begins to perform a bit of scat. An inspired moment.

In the terminal, Lowell and Roy simply can't put down a fun video game someone left behind on a flight, much to Fay's annoyance. Fay gets hold of it and keeps it behind her counter for safe keeping. Roy and Lowell then pay a young kid to go up to Fay's counter and ask for his videogame back, saying he accidentally left it on the plane. The young man gets paid after completing the mission, and then Roy and Lowell fire up the game and pick up where they left off.

In the hangar, Brian is taking a few shots at the basketball hoop mounted there as Alex strolls in looking for Joe. She sinks a shot on the first try. Producer Adam Belanoff shared, "Farrah Forke was required to sink a basketball from a good distance which she managed to do on the very first try to huge audience applause (later removed in post production). Unfortunately, when they went in for pick-ups it took her many attempts to make the shot again." One thing leads to another after the free throws and totally spur of the moment Brian and Alex head off to Maine for a lobster dinner. At least Alex thinks it's all totally spontaneous but discovers the next day that she's fallen victim to Brian's "Date Package Number Seven." Brian is unaware that she now knows that he calls ahead to plan all the things in "Date Package Number Seven" such as the tandem bike found lying against a tree, and the elderly couple hired to say they met on that very spot exactly 50 years ago. Brian then gets invited to Alex's place the following night for a taste of his own medicine with an ice bucket lap bath. About that scene, Farrah Forke shared, "If I remember correctly, they were real ice cubes. More than one take. Weber and I and the whole crew couldn't stop laughing. Most of the crew were men. Yep, there were a few of us women that have always wanted to dump cold ice on a man's —-ya know—I felt like I was living some girl's dream. Not mine, but some girl that wanted to do that. I do believe that 'Alex' was a character that did that—that put those actions into motion and she was always stronger than me. Talk to the writers about that. A bunch of men that wrote an incredible woman. They —the writers —are why she existed. Adam Belanoff, Steven Levitan and Chris Lloyd." Joe sees the ice incident as a clear path for him to pursue Alex's affections, but instead his conscience leads him to tell Alex how much his brother Brian likes her. She softens and agrees to go out with Brian again, giving him a second chance.

SEASON FIVE

*David Angell and Peter Casey seen from the back outside Tom
Nevers Field in a frequently used transition between scenes. At
this time they and David Lee moved on to work on* Frasier *which
debuted in September of 1993. (Courtesy of Suzanne Holmes).*

This season consisted of 24 episodes. Davis Lynch (Mark Harelik) became a semi-regular character in the fourth episode of the
season, "Business or Pleasure." As of Episode Eight, "Joe Blows
Part Two," Sandpiper Airlines became a partnership between Joe
and Brian. Fay's hair was now more white than blonde. The show
still aired on Thursday nights at 8:30 until summer reruns on Tuesday nights at 9:30.

"Stop in the Name of Love" (Season 5 Episode 1) Aired September 16, 1993

Written by Dave Hackel
Directed by Andy Ackerman

This episode borrows its title from one of Diana Ross and the Supremes' biggest hits. Fay starts her day like every other day – with a big scream in the terminal. This time, however, she's totally unaware that others are already at work and they are quite taken aback. When Roy walks in, back from vacation asking if anyone wants to see his tan lines, they all then scream in the terminal in tandem.

The next day, Brian rudely awakens Joe (whose hair is noticeably shorter than the previous season) to tell him that he is happy. He and Alex are hitting it off and his life is good. Knowing Brian's usual pattern with women Joe tells Brian to take it slowly this time. Brian promises that he will but breaks that promise very quickly. That is until his conscience gets the better of him (in the form of visions of Joe, Helen, Fay, Antonio and Roy while romancing Alex in her bedroom). Brian explains to Alex that this time it's different and maybe they ought to wait. After careful consideration she concurs. At the terminal Helen gives the details of the horrible date she had the previous day with Larry, the insurance salesman (he tried to sell her a policy) while Fay is ecstatic about having gotten her registration card for the community college. She's taking classes in psychology.

"Terminal Jealousy" (Season 5 Episode 2)
Aired September 23, 1993

Written by Mark Reisman
Directed by Leonard R. Garner, Jr.

Helen is concerned about a tough new health inspector making the rounds. In other action, Brian takes up jogging to keep up with Alex, but in the process falls down and injures his tail bone. Director Leonard R. Garner, Jr. said, "Steven Weber was always a gamer and went along with whatever we wanted him to do, but he had very little faith in people finding his injured tail bone funny in this episode. He saw during the shoot, however, that the audience was in hysterics and his full confidence in the episode returned." Unable to sit for the time being, Brian can't take any flights and Joe is almost maxed out on hours already. Alex offers to help, but Joe is ill-at-ease with anyone new taking the reins. Roy plants and sows

Sneaky Roy Biggins plots many an evil scheme in this episode
titled "Terminal Jealousy."

the seeds of "Terminal Jealousy" when he suggests that Joe take Alex
up in the plane for a test flight while he drives Brian to the doctor.
Roy then feeds Brian's jealous tendencies with visions of what could
happen between Joe and Alex alone together in the cockpit.

Instigator Roy strikes again when the health inspector Helen
has been dreading enters the terminal. Helen has no idea that the
inspector and Pam Chase (Holly Gagnier) an old schoolmate who
used to torment Helen in her chubby youth are one and the same.
Roy suggests that Helen go over and tell Pam off for what she did in

the past. Helen follows Roy's advice and then after finding out why Pam is there receives numerous health violations.

Speaking of Roy, he's attempting to get the Boston Celtics to name Aeromass as their official airline, but not having much luck in that arena. After finding out that all of their problems that week were incited by Roy, the gang gets him back through phony phone calls pretending to be Red Auerbach to finalize the Celtics deal, and Jack Nicholson to purchase the oceanfront property he's been trying to unload. The playing field is leveled when they hear that Roy has made a sizeable down payment on a new 727, thinking that he had made those two big scores.

"Bye Bye Bunny" (Season 5 Episode 3) Aired September 30, 1993

Written by Ian Gurvitz
Directed by Leonard R. Garner, Jr.

The episode begins with Antonio attempting to find the owner of a cell phone left in his cab. When that phone rings, the woman on the other end is looking for her husband, Phil (Gordon Clapp). The caller's name is Betty and during the conversation it becomes obvious that the woman Phil was with the other night wasn't Betty. When Phil returns to retrieve his phone, Antonio makes certain that Phil calls Betty to apologize.

At the same time we discover that Lowell has stood up a lovely young lady named Lisa (Linda Larkin). Obviously he is still experiencing great difficulty getting over Bunny. It's suggested that he get a divorce, but he has trouble letting go. When he finds that Bunny favors getting a divorce he has to go along. Lowell finds his divorce lawyer, Warren T. Banks (Peter Van Norden) on the back of a matchbook and Helen and Joe tag along to the lawyer's office for moral support. When Bunny runs late, the lawyer thinks that Joe and Lowell are the couple getting divorced saying, "I've never done one of these before." The divorce leads to what Joe and Brian perceive as a very rough night for Lowell who keeps his roommates awake most of the night while crying Bunny's name. They discover at breakfast that he was crying her name because she slept over and they were carrying on like newlyweds. Lowell and Bunny are suddenly getting along so well Lowell begins looking for an apartment for the two of them, but the plot thickens as Joe discovers that Bunny has a fiancé in Boston, and Fay gets duped into breaking the news to Lowell. Bunny comes clean and the couple decides to part ways for good this time. About the actress who portrayed Bunny, the writer of the episode Ian Gurvitz said, "Laura Innes was remarkably funny - a really solid actress. She went on to star on *ER* and did a great job directing an episode of the show where a crazed patient stabs Noah Wylie's character, John Carter." For those curious to see Innes' work as a director, the *ER* episode is titled "Be Still My Heart" from 2000.

"Business or Pleasure" (Season 5 Episode 4) Aired October 7, 1993

Written by Steven Levitan
Directed by Leonard R. Garner, Jr.

The episode begins with Lowell trying to remember a phone number for a hardware store while everyone around him is announcing flight and gate numbers as he searches for a quarter for the pay phone. When he finally gets through to Larsen's Hardware he has forgotten why he called.

Lowell also has problems with Joe's airplane – the oil pump is leaking like a sieve and because of finances there isn't a spare available and Joe has to cancel a flight to Boston. Joe might even have to take on investors to stay afloat. One possible investor, Davis Lynch (Mark Harelik) becomes somewhat of a recurring character. Lynch is not the stuffed shirt they expect. He is casually dressed and even gets airsick. Joe makes the mistake of bringing him over to Helen's counter for something to settle his stomach and this meeting cooks up a romance. Helen reluctantly does Joe a favor by playing "tour guide" to Lynch, but quickly falls for the wealthy investor. They share a crab dinner where the deadpan/slow-talking/wide-eyed waiter, Mark (John Hawkes) steals the scene. After all is said and done, Lynch declines the offer to invest in Sandpiper, but does offer a similar investment deal to Aeromass.

"An Affair to Forget" (Season 5 Episode 5) Aired October 14, 1993

Written by Dave Hackel
Directed by Andy Ackerman

The title of this episode is a play on the 1957 classic *An Affair to Remember* starring Cary Grant and Deborah Kerr. Brian and Alex make plans to finally lift their abstinence rule with a special getaway to Connecticut for the upcoming weekend. Joe flies them there on a foggy night, and his next stop should be to drop Helen off in New York City to see Davis. However, the fog is so dense they are grounded and ruin Brian and Alex's first sexual adventure.

In other action Roy's dream girl named Barbara Farkachevs-ki (Stacey Pickren) is in the terminal often on business, but he's too chicken to ask her out on a date. Antonio and Fay suggest a complete makeover for Roy. As much as they're disgusted by the thought of doing it, they do want to help him. The new look is an improvement, and Roy finally gets the courage to strike up a conversation with the woman. After a good start he panics, stammers and frightens her away.

"A Black Eye Affair" (Season 5 Episode 6) Aired October 28, 1993

Written by Steven Levitan
Directed by Andy Ackerman

The island is celebrating the yearly Cranberry Festival in this chapter. The title of the episode is a play on the term for a formal gathering, "A Black Tie Affair." It begins with a competition for worst drivers' license photos in the terminal. If pictures were taken that same day Helen would win the competition hands down. She hasn't been sleeping well while awaiting a call from Davis, who has cancelled the last five dates at the last minute. When he calls at the lunch counter an unkempt Helen has four hours to get herself together in time for what will only be their second date. The Cranberry Festival in town means there are no restaurant reservations to be had. So Helen then hires Lowell, a surprisingly great cook to make a gourmet dinner for Davis and her. To complicate things, Helen's old friend Stella (Cynthia K. Ambuehl) needs a shoulder to cry on after a breakup. Roy recognizes Stella as the "Slick and Speedy Motor Oil Girl" from a calendar in his office. Helen pawns Stella off on Joe who then takes Stella out for the evening. Helen then goes to the gym with Alex to sweat off a few pounds before Davis' arrival. While on the racquetball court she gets a black eye, thus the episode's title. Makeup only partially covers up the injury. After a long series of spills, allergies, mishaps and chaos Davis actually does show up at Helen's door at the moment when she absolutely looks her worst.

"Joe Blows Part One" (Season 5 Episode 7) Aired November 4, 1993

Written by Steven Levitan
Directed by David Lee

This episode is a rarity in that it begins with a slow and sexy instrumental piece of music – not the usual short, upbeat ten second instrumental *Wings* piece. The title, "Joe Blows" has special meaning, as creators David Lee and Peter Casey recalled, "Joe Hackett was almost called Joe Blow of Blow Air, but thoughts of actress Joan Hackett led to the Hackett name."

The episode begins with Joe lying motionless, face down in a swimming pool, followed by an explanation of how and why he got there through a series of flashbacks. The first flashback is of a disgruntled and very petty customer (Tom O'Rourke) whose briefcase bearing the initials P. M. S. disappeared from the plane's baggage area. He threatens a lawsuit if it isn't returned by 4:30 that day. Fay isn't working that day. She's taking part in a protest because her second husband George's cemetery is being turned into a golf course and she brings that problem to Joe. Joe is annoyed that Fay forgot to tell him about an upcoming newspaper interview, Helen's boyfriend Davis is a no show again and she needs to vent in Joe's office. In fact everyone brings their problems to Joe and piles on - Antonio needs a co-signer for his new taxicab and Brian laments that even though he and Alex finally had sex, it wasn't very good, while Roy is taunting Joe with his expensive new Aeromass radio commercial. To top it all off Lowell is raising a din in the hangar with the old motorcycle he's restoring. When it all finally becomes too much to handle, the episode title comes into play, "Joe Blows." His cool is blown, he has a meltdown in the terminal and his escape is Lowell's motorcycle.

Joe finds a crowded pool party to crash and we're suddenly back to where the episode started with Joe floating in the pool fully clothed attempting to break an underwater record while being cheered on by a very youthful crowd. One member of the crowd played by actor Keith Rosary yells, "A minute 47, that's a record." Rosary recalled, "My first TV job ever was on *Cagney and Lacey* with Tim Daly's sister Tyne, and without realizing it at the time I was about to audition for Tim's show. Even though they were looking for a surfer dude I went for the audition. Everyone who auditioned was white, except for me. I was told I did a great job and that they wanted me to then meet the producers. I read my lines and David Angell asked me if I'd seen the show because he knew that I lived on Cape Cod. I hadn't, but he liked me and I got the part. Our scene by the pool was done prior to show night at the Hollywood Roosevelt Hotel on Hollywood Boulevard. Because I was a principal player they gave me a nice suite for a couple of days at the hotel. It was a great and fun experience." However, there's much more to Rosary's story – "I still live here near Nantucket and a friend of mine who was a builder was working on a house for David Angell in Chatham after the shoot. My friend reconnected me with Angell and there was interest in me being used for an upcoming TV project. Angell, in fact purchased plane tickets for my girlfriend and me so that I could have time to discuss this with him on the flight. Well, my girlfriend at the time was notoriously late and with traffic we missed the plane out of Logan Airport on September 11, 2001, arriving just as it began taxiing away. I was so upset – here was my chance to discuss my future with David Angell and we missed the plane. Sadly, everyone knows the rest of the story – that plane was the first one to hit the World Trade Center later that day."

The episode ends with the words, "To Be Continued."

Joe Blows Part Two (Season 5 Episode 8) Aired November 11, 1993

Written by Ian Gurvitz
Directed by Leonard R. Garner, Jr.

Part Two of Joe's big meltdown has Helen calling in a missing person report, and Lowell calling in a missing Harley Davidson report. Hard as it is to believe, Brian steps up to the plate and hits a home run in his attempt to run the company in Joe's absence. He's never behaved this responsibly before. Joe's credit card bill arrives and it shows that he's been up and down the east coast spending like a sailor. Now he's in Mustique, Brian's old stamping ground, so Brian jumps in the Cessna and goes there to fetch his wayward sibling. Joe wants to stay in Mustique, so for now a newly mature Brian is left to run the business. The plane gets re-possessed but Brian finagles a strange but effective chain reaction to get it back – actions which include holding a children's birthday party on the Cessna while dressed as a clown. The writer of the episode, Ian

As of this episode Sandpiper Air is a partnership between Joe Hackett and his "wingman" Brian. Simon Says hands on hips.

Gurvitz said, "The clown suit was part of the rewrite. It added humor to a long, poignant, dramatic scene involving a reconciliation. I got to tell a story about writing the episode in a podcast called *Storyworthy* a few years ago while I was promoting a book." After a few weeks, a well-rested Joe returns and is welcomed by all. He had run out of money and had to come back. Neither Hackett brother wants to run the airline alone, the onus is too great, so from this point on they are partners. As an aside, this is the episode in which Lowell says that he thinks Ernest Borgnine is sexy.

"2 Good 2 Be 4 Gotten" (Season 5 Episode 9) Aired November 18 ,1993

Written by Rick Copp and David A. Goodman
Directed by Leonard R. Garner, Jr.

The episode begins with Antonio setting up a table in the terminal to sell some of his possessions. It seems he's had to make many unexpected repairs to his cab and badly needs the money. He also has to send part of his paycheck home to Italy every month to help out the family. Meanwhile Roy's overbearing mother is holed up in his office and she is running him ragged.

Over at the lunch counter, Alex passes along a message to Joe from Brian about flying in an old friend of his named Sandy Cooper. Everyone is excited except Joe whose immediate response is, "Oh, no." This is truly one of the most memorable and most popular episodes of the series. One of co-writers of "2 Good 2 Be 4 Gotten," Rick Copp shared, "My writing partner David A. Goodman and I were just coming off five straight years of sitcom staff writing and were not actively seeking out another one. I was busy at the time writing *The Brady Bunch Movie* and David was working on his own projects, but Mark Reisman who we had worked with on *Flying Blind* on Fox the previous year had recently started working on *Wings* as Executive Producer. He called us and asked if we would be interested in a freelance assignment. We thought it would be fun so we brainstormed some episodes and went over to Paramount to pitch to the writing staff. The one they liked the best was about an old high school friend of Joe's who turns up and is so sweet to

```
                              WINGS

                        "2 Good 2 B 4 Gotten"

                           #40345-081




                           Written by

                            Rick Copp

                               &

                         David A. Goodman




                     Created and Developed by

                          David Angell
                          Peter Casey
                          David Lee


                          Directed by

                     Leonard R. Garner, Jr.


           This script is not for publication or reproduction.
           No one is authorized to dispose of same.  If lost or
           destroyed, please notify Script Department.

           THE WRITING CREDITS MAY NOT BE FINAL AND SHOULD NOT
           BE USED FOR PUBLICITY OR ADVERTISING PURPOSES WITHOUT
           FIRST CHECKING WITH TELEVISION LEGAL DEPARTMENT.

           Copyright 1993 Paramount Pictures Corporation
           All Rights Reserved


     Return to Script Department
     PARAMOUNT PICTURES CORPORATION          REVISED FINAL DRAFT
     5555 Melrose Avenue
     Hollywood, California 90038             October 22, 1993
```

*The cover page for the "2 Good 2 Be 4 Gotten" script by Rick Copp
and David A. Goodman – the first of three memorable Sandy
Cooper episodes. (Courtesy of Rick Copp).*

everyone, so nobody believes him when he tries to tell them about
her crazy side. They all think Joe is overreacting. But in the end
Sandy traps Joe in the basement and forces him to recreate their
senior prom – her dream date that never happened, proving she is,
in fact, totally bonkers. We went off to write it, they liked our draft,
and within a couple of weeks they filmed it. It was one of the easi-
est jobs I ever had. The episode proved so popular with viewers, the
following season they asked us to come back to do another Sandy
Cooper show and we were happy to do it." When asked if he still
had a copy of the script Copp said, "Believe it or not, yes. I didn't
think I did but then I found it."

In the episode Sandy calls Joe "Joey Bear." When asked if anyone ever refers to him as Joey Bear Tim Daly said, "It hasn't happened yet. I hope it never does. But those episodes with Valerie Mahaffey as Sandy were hilarious, so much fun, and she was brilliant with the way she went from crazy to seemingly normal and back again so seamlessly." Once again after finally being released from Sandy's "Little Cellar of Horrors," Joe has no proof and the gang thinks he is exaggerating. On her way out, Sandy whispers to Joe, "Next year, homecoming."

"Come Fly with Me" (Season 5 Episode 10)
Aired December 2, 1993

Written by Howard Gewirtz
Directed by Leonard R. Garner, Jr.

The episode begins with Roy, Fay and Antonio in the terminal attempting to win a radio trivia contest. The radio voice is a legendary late great named "the Real Don Steele," and the piece of music that plays while the contestant thinks of the answer is the same one used on the vintage game show *The $64,000 Question* hosted by Hal March (a huge part of the TV Quiz Show Scandals of the 1950s). When they finally get through on the phone and are the correct numbered caller, Roy blows $12,000 with a really dumb wrong answer – Rich Little.

Also hanging out at the terminal on this lonely and cold Saturday night with nothing to do – Lowell, Brian and Joe. Helen is expecting Davis. but true to form he cancels last minute. Lowell was supposed to go out on a rat shoot with friend Tucker but backs out of that last minute to keep lonely Joe company. Joe suggests they take the plane to Boston. After some coaxing Lowell, Brian and Helen tag along. While there, the foursome visits a few boring bars. But then they are all invited to a wild party. It's packed with good-looking people and Joe, Brian and Lowell seem to be having unusually good luck with the ladies. It appears to be a very positive turn of events for all four of them as Helen is also very popular with the guys there. Then she finds out why - they think she's a hooker as all of the other women at this particular party are. One guy named Ted

(Christopher Fuller) offers Helen $500 to dress up like Little Bo Beep, tie him to the bedpost and spank him. For a brief moment, she actually considers it. Five hundred dollars is five hundred dollars. Upon returning to Nantucket, disappointment looms as it's discovered that Davis felt so guilty he canceled his business meeting and came to Nantucket to see Helen, and Tucker went out on the rat shoot without Lowell.

"Happy Holidays" (Season 5 Episode 11) Aired December 16, 1993
Written by Mark Reisman
Directed by Andy Ackerman

This is the series' third of six Christmas episodes. Helen has tentative plans to spend the holiday with chronic date-canceller Davis in Manhattan, Antonio will be watching *A Very Snoopy Christmas* and playing Santa's elf, and Brian is planning to share a cottage with Alex in Vermont, but instead she wants him to go with her to Florida to meet her four brothers who very rarely get holiday leave from Fort Benning at the same time. She wins. Fay is being a real taskmaster regarding the party she and Helen are throwing for the local children. Joe had tree duty and picked out a nice one for the terminal (at least it starts out looking nice but quickly becomes a poor tree - a Charlie Brown tree), and Lowell is rehearsing to play Santa Claus for the holiday event but he can't seem to get his "ho ho hos" just right.

While on the clock as a cabbie, Antonio's fare is Lowell's ex-wife Bunny (Laura Innes) who is returning from being a guest at a wedding. In typical Bunny fashion she makes a pass at Antonio and he completes the pass. Afterwards he feels so guilty he goes to confession but it doesn't allay his unease – especially while playing Santa's elf with Lowell as Santa. He is riddled with guilt. Fay goes postal when her party is a flop and the only children who show up are snarky teenagers, and arguments breakout between Helen and Fay, Brian and Alex, Joe and Roy, and of course (after admitting to making merry with Bunny) Antonio and Lowell.

"Ready Teddy Go" (Season 5 Episode 12) Aired January 6, 1994

Written by Jeffrey Richman and Joyce Gittlin
Directed by Andy Ackerman

This was the first episode aired in 1994. It's also the first episode co-written by Jeffrey Richman and Joyce Gittlin. About working on *Wings*, Gittlin shared, "I worked on the show as a creative consultant. This was the first episode for Wings that Jeff and I were credited as writers. The entire experience was extremely positive. There was humor, encouragement, and generosity on a daily basis. I was the first female writer in the writer's room and David Angell, Peter Casey, David Lee, and Dave Hackel ran the room with respect for all writers. All of them were gentlemen with a sense of humor and working with them was a delight."

The action begins as Fay's psychology studies at the community college are starting to come in handy with some of the Sandpiper customers at her ticket counter. Speaking of psychology, Fay kidnaps a rat from the school's lab to keep it from being shocked in an experiment (she hides it in Joe's office). When Professor Lawson (Stephen Rowe) comes to the terminal demanding his rodent back and threatening her arrest. Fay refuses to give her back and Lawson suddenly changes his tune and congratulates her as being the only caring student in his entire class behavior experiment. There is a snag in Fay's plan to return the rat, however – Roy has grown very attached to her (he calls her Cupcake) and tells the professor he set her free outside the hangar. We know he is lying when we hear "the Itsy Bitsy Spider" being played on a phone keypad in his office (it's a trick the professor had taught the animal).

Elsewhere, the terminal is filled with doubting Thomases who are certain that Davis (Mark Harelik) will cancel plans with Helen yet again. Helen has total faith in Davis this time and he does arrive punctually for once. He offers to take everyone to lunch, but Joe insists on paying. Before Lynch lunching, they follow Davis to his hotel room. Davis wants to drop off his luggage and take a quick shower before going out. While he's in the bathroom, Helen goes through his luggage and finds a sheer and very sexy teddy she thinks is intended for her. She has mixed emotions about it – should she be flattered or offended? Such a gift is rather inappropriate this early in their relationship. Helen treats Davis icily in their cozy dinner in his hotel room later that night. When he presents her with a gift box, she thinks the teddy is inside but it's a collection of scented soaps. She can't leave well enough alone and confronts him about the teddy. He did indeed buy it for her in Paris but realized it was too soon to give it to her, waiting until at least date number ten. Then comes the uncomfortable question about how she knew it was in his suitcase.

"Oh, Give Me a Home Where the Mathers Don't Roam" (Season 5 Episode 13) Aired January 20, 1994

Written by Shelly Landau
Directed by Peter Bonerz

The first mention of "the Big-Faced Girl" (here known as Denise) is made in this episode. It all begins with a discussion about a newspaper survey that shows that 75 percent of co-workers become romantically involved.

At Joe and Brian's house, Lowell's nagging about tidiness and promptness has become unbearable. It's been over a year since they took Lowell in (after the sinking of his houseboat) and the decision is made to ask him to move out. Lowell doesn't handle the news very well and for the time being lives in the terminal. Antonio follows the tradition started in Italy of always welcoming friends to move in, but quickly rues his generosity toward abrasive Lowell. With Fay's help Lowell finally gets a place of his own – but he is very skittish as he has never lived alone before. In the terminal Helen buys Alex a gift for no reason (a helicopter pin) – a decision she soon regrets when Alex feels she has to reciprocate. Helen's nice gesture soon snowballs into a big fight.

"The Faygitive" (Season 5 Episode 14) Aired January 27, 1994

Written by Shelly Landau
Directed by Peter Bonerz

The title is an obvious play on the movie and TV show title *The Fugitive,* and the episode begins with Joe complimenting Brian on being a surprisingly good business partner. Joe leaves for a date trusting that Brian will complete all the important paperwork. As soon as Joe leaves Brian pays Fay to come in to take over, and in turn she has a deal with Lowell for a free pepperoni pizza as he steps in to balance the books.

The next day in the terminal, Fay says that she has been getting a series of phone calls from people asking her many suspicious questions. It's in this episode we discover Fay's many unusual surnames – Schlob, Dumbly, and best of all DeVay (as in "old soldiers never die, they just Fay DeVay"). The mystery has a very sweet ending when the gentleman who hired the private investigator to find Fay turns out to be a Korean War veteran named Pete Nash (Roy Dotrice) who once danced with Fay in her days with the U. S. O. (and broke one of her toes). At the time she said that she owed him another dance. All these many years later (since his wife died) he decided to do some of the things he never got around to doing in his life, one of which was collecting on that dance she owed him. Not much has changed – he's still a very bad dancer.

In other action, Roy recommends a guy to repair Antonio's cable and, in true Roy fashion, the shady repairman gets Antonio his cable illegally. Antonio gets caught and has to pay a fine (but for a while, he enjoyed getting an abundance of channels and became a cable TV addict).

"Say Uncle, Carlton" (Season 5 Episode 15) Aired February 3, 1994

Written by Steven Levitan
Directed by Peter Bonerz

The episode begins with all of the terminal employees complaining about the inconvenience of the parking lot being resurfaced and having to take a shuttle to the terminal. All of this is small potatoes compared to the return of the world's most annoying man, Carlton Blanchard (William Hickey). Supervising Producer Ian Gurvitz said, "I remember him holding a long, thin unlit cigarette at the table read the whole time. He spoke slowly and his read seemed like ten minutes, but he was so funny on film." Gilbert Gottfried who played Carlton's nephew and only heir added, "He was rather weak and frail and sometimes had trouble moving about the set, but as soon as those lights went up and the cameras were rolling he was spry and a totally different person. I've heard that about many actors during my life and got to see it happen before my eyes." Because he can no longer drive, Carlton wants to hire Antonio to be his chauffeur for a week. Carlton is being honored as the Retired Businessman of the Year, and his opportunistic nephew Lewis, a Manhattan stereo salesman and the heir to the lumberyard fortune is flying in to be part of the ceremony. About Gottfried, Tim Daly said, "He was really nice, funny, and loud – a natural. We loved working with him." About this episode, Gottfried shared, "I was already pretty established by this time and didn't have to audition for the role of Lewis. They asked me to do it. I do have a great memory about director Peter Bonerz on this episode. After one of the takes, he told me to 'Act Better.' I wasn't quite sure what that meant, but a while after shooting the episode I ran into Marcia Wallace who worked with Bonerz on *The Bob Newhart Show*, and I told her I worked with Bonerz on *Wings*, and she laughed and said, 'Did he ask you to act better.?' We shared a laugh over that. Apparently he used that term often."

Gottfried shared a sweet moment about being backstage with Crystal Bernard – "Right before our cue, Crystal hugged me offstage. Her Helen character insulted me a lot on camera and she was so sweet and kind – she apologized for having to say all those nasty things about me. It's something I'll never forget."

About William Hickey, Gottfried shared, "He told me he was Irish but grew up in a Jewish neighborhood, had mostly Jewish friends and classmates. One day he asked his dad if their family was Jewish or Irish, to which Bill's dad replied, 'We're not Jewish and we're not Irish. We're Hickeys."

On the way to drop Carlton off at his banquet, Antonio, Alex, Roy, Lowell and the old man get trapped in the taxicab. Antonio has parked too close to the wall, and a van has parked too close on the other side. When Antonio tries to back up it's discovered that the battery is dead and all are stuck in the vehicle for hours because even the windows fall victim to the lack of power. About that scene, writer/producer Steven Levitan said, "Getting the cast stuck in a car with William Hickey was certainly fun and memorable." Supervising Producer Ian Gurvitz said, "We shot the scene in the car right after the 1994 Northridge earthquake and everyone's nerves were on edge from the aftershocks. Actors packed in a car on a soundstage with everyone looking up at the ceiling, dreading falling lights."

"Hey, Nineteen" (Season 5 Episode 16) Aired February 10, 1994

Written by Howard Gewirtz
Directed by Peter Bonerz

A fuzzy lost dog named Max has been following Antonio around the airport. Max melts the heart of every woman in the terminal, leading the guys to use the canine to get dates. Antonio is allergic to pet dander but puts up with it as it helps him get lucky. He and Roy share the pooch for that very purpose. All good things come to

She was just about 19 in this episode titled "Hey, Nineteen" – actress Liz Vassey as Courtney, Joe Hackett's young love interest. (Courtesy of Liz Vassey).

an end, however as the owner eventually comes by to pick up his lost pet (and they discover that he uses the dog to meet women as well).

In other action, Fay's classmate and study partner at the community college, Courtney Blake (Liz Vassey) visits the terminal. Helen used to babysit for Courtney. Despite the age difference, Courtney and Joe hit it off really well. Obviously the episode's title is inspired by the Steely Dan classic of same name, and about that Vassey said, "I'm not really a Steely Dan fan. But wait! Before I get attacked by Dan Fans I do have a solid reason: I had a friend who played them constantly, so I suffer from overexposure. I recognize that

Back row: Liz Vassey as Tess Galaway, Matt Borlenghi as Johnny Barzano, Timothy Fall as PJ Morris. Middle row: David Arnott as Cal Evans, Brian McNamara as Randy Fitzgerald, Sean O'Bryan as Joe "Iowa" Dantley. Front: Luke as "Jimmy".

PIG STY

Actors Tim Fall and Liz Vassey guest star in the "Hey Nineteen" episode, and later co-starred in this sitcom titled Pig Sty *on Fox. Vassey and Fall are both in the back row.*

they're a great band, I have friends who love them, but I also never need to hear them again because I've already heard them about 47 times more than the general population. In the episode, Joe and I are going to a Pearl Jam concert, and I do love Pearl Jam." When asked if her romantic scenes with Tim Daly were awkward Vassey said, "Are you kidding? I got to kiss Tim Daly and get paid for it. I don't recall many retakes, but with multi-cam comedies, you rehearse all week up until the day you shoot the episode. I couldn't believe kissing him repeatedly was my job." Don't you also roller blade in the episode? She said, "Yes, but you didn't ask if I did it well. The answer is a solid no. I was always very good at starting and then going very fast. Stopping was a whole other story. I'm very athletic, but I'm better when my feet are on solid ground."

Later that evening Courtney is reading poetry at a place called "the Cup." She invites Joe's co-workers to come by for moral support. At the college coffee house, the deadpan host on the microphone is named Trevor and played by Tim Fall. About the episode Fall said, "'Hey, Nineteen' was a good title for the episode because Liz Vassey was very close to 19 when she did it. How interesting and wonderful that we got to co-star on the Fox series *Pig Sty* a short time later. The 'Hey Nineteen' song was still relatively new at the time. Liz is so charming and funny, much younger than I but so good and so seasoned. She got an early start to acting and was very mature for her age and a total pro." Fall added, "I vividly remember the cup on the wall in the coffee house. I play Trevor and first introduce the poetry of Lowell. I'd never worked with Thomas Haden Church before but our paths had crossed on the Paramount lot. Years later I got to do an episode of his *Ned and Stacey* sitcom on Fox after he left *Wings*. I didn't audition for the role of Trevor, but I had auditioned for another role a while back. I didn't get that part, but they had me in mind for this deadpan, pony-tailed coffee house open mic announcer role. I remember the cast being so warm and inviting. No jerks on that set. You know, there's a lot of down time during the week of working on an episode and we all sat around together and talked. They were extremely nice to the guest stars. It was a fun and memorable week." Courtney's poem is titled "My Lover," and Joe thinks it's about him. The poem was actually written for her 45-year-old English professor, Michael. The episode is directed by Peter Bonerz, about whom Vassey said, "Was very kind and easy to work with. Such a pleasant week." Tim Fall elaborated, "That week I got to chat with Bonerz between scenes and told him I'd been on Newhart's 90s sitcom *Bob* and he shared a bunch of wonderful stories about his days on the old *Bob Newhart Show*. I saw him most recently on an episode of *Parks and Recreation*." The action ends with Joe reading a poem titled "Dumped" at the Cup.

"Exclusively Yours" (Season 5 Episode 17) Aired February 14, 1994

Written by David Lloyd
Directed by Peter Bonerz

The episode begins with creature of habit Fay announcing Flight 20. There are no ticketholders in the empty terminal, but she follows through nonetheless to Joe's bewilderment. Producer Adam

Belanoff pointed out something in the credits I'd never noticed before, "Writer David Lloyd didn't like that 'double propeller' graphic that appeared under names in the opening credits so his 'Written By' credit (and only his) appears in typeface with no background. Watch for that on every episode he wrote beginning in Season Four."

In other developments, Helen is reworking the menu using names of people around the airport. There's Helen's hash browns, Sloppy Joe Hackett, Antonio's spaghetti and meatballs, the Alex and Brian soup and sandwich combo, Roy's jumbo turkey leg (which changes to the Roy salad), and Fay's bran muffin. Lowell wants to be on the menu, too. Helen hasn't planned anything but leaves it up to him to decide what food item he will be. He likes the Lowell melt, Lowell kabobs, and the favorite "Lowell Slaw." Antonio and Fay are a bit peeved about the choices with their names attached and Helen eventually has to scrap the whole idea.

In other action when a man named Gus (Michael Danek) asks Alex out on a date, she says no. Brian gets wind of this, and as a result, she and Brian decide to make their relationship an exclusive one. However, when Joe lines up five dates in a row, each night with a different girl, Brian has second thoughts. Those second thoughts really get tested when Joe charters a plane full of models for a photo shoot in the hangar and then invites them all over for a party at his house afterwards. Just Brian's luck, Alex is out of town visiting an old roommate. He makes a valiant effort at being a good boy but gets locked in one of the rooms in his house with one of the models. Roy shows up at the party even though he wasn't invited. Joe fixes him up with the models' rough, tough and crude manager Vi (Lee Garlington) and he's extremely grateful.

"Moonlighting" (Season 5 Episode 18) Aired February 17, 1994

Written by Ian Gurvitz
Directed by Peter Bonerz

This episode is not to be confused with the popular series starring Cybill Shepherd and Bruce Willis. It begins with Roy tricking

Lowell into becoming a junior executive trainee for Aeromass (it's a ruse to get Lowell to do Roy's chores).

It's the off-season for tourism on Nantucket Island and the gang shares details of their absolute worst moonlighting experiences. At the moment Alex is a serving wench at King Arthur's Bar and Grill. Joe recalls his worst moonlighting job – flying around a famous chimpanzee named Mr. Bongo (Eddie). About that scene, Tim Daly recalled, "That was memorable. Quite a few takes were necessary. The chimp kept putting his hands through the non-existent windshield glass. He also kept grabbing for my hat. You just didn't know what to expect." The writer of the episode Ian Gurvitz added, "Oh, the monkey. I remember watching it in the mockup plane wondering if it could go apeshit at any time. But the handlers always seemed to be right on it." Fay once worked as "Lucy the lobster" in a full lobster costume handing out flyers for the Lobster Bucket with coupons for a free oyster shooter. Antonio was a cemetery plot salesman for Whispering Pines Mortuary and got excited because his client George Wexler (Dan Castellanetta) was buying all top of the line items, spending a fortune, thus guaranteeing that Antonio will get a bonus. As soon as Antonio leaves Wexler's office, Wexler fetches a noose from one of his desk drawers and strings it up with intentions of hanging himself. About a minute later, Antonio returns to the office as he's forgotten his pen, only to find Wexler about to end it all. It seems Wexler's wife is fooling around with his brother, his daughter's a hooker, his son's in a cult, and his partner is an embezzler who ran off with their secretary. Wexler says he has nothing to live for. He was going to let the insurance money pay for the exorbitant arrangements not realizing that insurance companies don't pay for suicides. Antonio's large commission went right down the tubes. About that scene, Gurvitz shared, "Dan Castellanetta was a total pro. I was impressed that he was doing our show given his day job. He was so understated and he and Tony were great together. Would've loved more." Brian and Helen did some disastrous moonlighting together in a magic act at Roy's Whale Lodge. The magician's props arrived but he didn't, so Brian improvised with Helen as his assistant (the lovely Helena). The magic act bombs. It's a stag party and the guys in the audience are expecting a stripper, so the lovely Helena improvises from inside the box into which knives are thrust in the magic act. All of these stories made Alex feel better about her waitressing job but it's short-lived as the gang decides to head over to King Arthur's to razz her while at work.

"Sleepless in Nantucket" (Season 5 Episode 19) Aired March 10, 1994

Written by Jeffrey Richman and Joyce Gittlin
Directed by Peter Bonerz

The title of this episode is a play on the popular Tom Hanks motion picture *Sleepless in Seattle*. The episode begins with Fay on the microphone attempting to explain Sandpiper's new three-digit flight numbering system (they used to be two digits) but failing miserably.

Meanwhile Lowell has to come up with a good name for his soon-to-be godchild. His sister is having a baby and it's a Mather tradition that the godfather supplies the name. Lowell is partial to either Kelbo, Maurice or Felix. Meanwhile, Brian is spending more and more time at Alex's place, prompting Joe to suggest they finally officially move in together. The couple thinks it's a great idea at first, until they quickly get on each other's nerves with their idiosyncrasies. Brain hates her retainer that fixes her underbite and her constant sniffing, and she hates his throat clearing, his basketball hoop hamper, and large eardrum-piercing speakers. Joe is enjoying having the house to himself and will do anything to keep Brian at Alex's place. Joe even helps Brian move those behemoth speakers of his over and over again just to get him out of the house.

"Boys Will Be Girls" (Season 5 Episode 20) Aired April 7, 1994

Written by David Lloyd
Directed by Peter Bonerz

The episode begins with Fay lying to a passenger about the in-flight movie and meal. This passenger is rather eccentric and daft, believing he's on his way to Washington to meet with President Roosevelt.

Elsewhere Brian and Joe are dreading the return of their old caustic football coach Dan Mattay (Jack Ging) for a dedication of the new school gym. It seems Mattay often gave both of the Hackett brothers a really hard time, referring to them as girls. Recalling what a sound sleeper the coach is (often with the help of hooch), the boys plan to sneak into the coach's room that night and dress him up like a girl with a wig and makeup. Being such a sound sleeper, the Hackett brothers don't realize that the coach is actually dead in his bed when they play their prank and they even take a photo while each is kissing the coach on the cheek. The next day when the news comes out about how the coach was dressed when he was found deceased the guys dread how the coach's son Bud (the late Brian Turk) will handle the news. Their worry was all in vain as the news about dad dying in a dress opens the door for the son to admit that he's a cross dresser, too. It's no coincidence that Lowell picks up a bunch of Hackett photos that have just been developed at the local equivalent of a Fotomat, including the one involving the kiss on Mattay's cheeks, then suddenly demands a raise.

"Roy Crazy" (Season 5 Episode 21) Aired April 14, 1994
Written by Mark Reisman
Directed by Peter Bonerz

The episode begins with Brian and Alex deciding what kind of message they should leave on their answering machine now that they're cohabitating. At Helen's lunch counter there is a visitor from a previous episode – Mark, the deadpan, slow-talking/wide-eyed waiter at the Crab House (John Hawkes). He is infatuated with Helen.

Meanwhile over at Roy's Aeromass counter it's Sylvia (Concetta Tomei), Roy's ex-wife. Roy's hesitant about going over to talk to her as last time her rottweiler attacked him. Except for Brian it's the first time any of the gang has gotten to see Sylvia. She seems to want Roy back for some reason that no one can figure and a night in her hotel room is planned. It all makes sense when Lowell intercepts a phone call at the Aeromass counter divulging that the ex-wife is coming to sleep with him because she caught her man in bed with his secretary.

Lowell thinks the call is about Bunny, but Brian realizes that the message is about Sylvia, who is using Roy to spite her significant other. Even though they're not friends, per se, Brian shows up at Roy's hotel room to warn him. At first Roy is skeptical but that changes rather quickly when Sylvia is seen in bed wearing a mask. Roy has a rare moment of human dignity and walks out on her. But fear not, the old Roy quickly returns when he lies about the goings on at the hotel to Antonio and Joe the next day.

"Long Distance Lament" (Season 5 Episode 22) Aired April 28, 1994

Written by Shelly Landau
Directed by Peter Bonerz

The episode opens with a visibly upset Antonio. It seems he nearly had a head-on collision in his cab. Roy takes advantage of him, asks for change for a twenty repeatedly. The very distracted Antonio ends up forking out almost $100 without realizing.

In other action, lies and their consequences take center stage in this episode. Brian and Alex are attempting to avoid their Elvis Presley-obsessed friends Bob and Sally Crandall, and Fay is seeking someone to take over the job of Safety Warden. Nobody wants the position so Fay talks Lowell into the job and he is ecstatic. Meanwhile Helen has a hot new outfit for her weekend in New York with Davis who again cancels on her last minute. After Helen leaves Davis a nasty message he shows up last minute with flowers, but she's already out on a date with Roy's newest employee Jeff (John Putch) who's been asking her out unsuccessfully for weeks. Joe discovers he has two dates that same night (he forgot all about one of them). He really wants to see Joy but doesn't want to hurt Sandra (Julia Paige). When Joy cancels after Joe backs out on Sandra with a flimsy excuse, he and Davis go out for a night on the town. Their destination - the Club Car, the same place as Helen and Jeff. When Sandra, whom Joe canceled on (to go out with Joy) walks in, Joe hides under tables to avoid being seen. Helen is under the same table avoiding Davis. There's still more trouble brewing when the Crandalls show up at the

Club Car – Alex and Brian lied to them about their plans for the night and wind up under the tables as well.

"Call of the Wild" (Season 5 Episode 23) Aired May 5, 1994

Written by Howard Gewirtz and Steven Levitan
Directed by Leonard R. Garner, Jr.

This episode shares a title with a classic Jack London novel. It opens with Lucky Vanous who had his 15 minutes of fame in a Diet Coke commercial in which he portrayed a construction worker who took off his shirt at the same time every day, much to the enjoyment of the ladies in the office building next door. He's about to board an Aeromass flight and Helen, Fay and Alex ask him to take his shirt off. He says yes but has trouble with the zipper. Helen and Alex try to help, but time is of the essence because of the final boarding call for his flight, Fay steps in and gets the job done by ripping the shirt off his back. About that, Farrah Forke recalled, "He was shirtless most of the week. The costume designers were trying to make sure his shirt would come off in one take. They had it 'teched.' It wasn't Velcro. They made sure it would look real. Those girls were really on top of it – really talented costume designers." Speaking of shirts, a more mature Brian is becoming more conservative and businesslike (as are his ties) of late.

A short time later Brian's old buddy Danny Quinn (the late Charles Rocket) comes to town and even Danny comments about Brian's new, more reserved attire. Their exploits together with the opposite sex are so off the wall and memorable Danny wrote a book about them (*Tequila Nights*). These include the time Danny got Brian thrown in jail. Joe invites himself out with the two of them and Brian tries to be good because he's going steady with Alex. Initially Alex is OK with Brian going out with the boys, but when it happens four nights in a row Alex begins to change her tune. She really raises a stink when he wants to go out for a fifth night and questions their relationship. Brian realizes he made a big mistake when Danny tells Brian that he envies the fact that Brian has someone at home waiting for him. Danny can't party as he did in the old days and has the hangover from hell. Brian tries to get back with Alex but she's changed the locks and doesn't accept his apology.

Elsewhere, one of Lowell's childhood TV heroes, "Big Strong Man" (Robert Ridgely) has fallen on hard times. Lowell takes him in. Big Strong Man then takes advantage of Lowell's good nature, idol worship, liquor cabinet, credit card and ATM pin number. Eventually Lowell gets wise to Big Strong Man's scheme after being taken to the cleaners.

"A Decent Proposal" (Season 5 Episode 24) Aired May 12, 1994
Written by Mark Reisman and Ian Gurvitz
Directed by Peter Bonerz

Alex Lambert's favorite song, "I Can't Stop Loving You" by Ray Charles from the episode titled "A Decent Proposal."]

The title of this episode is a play on *An Indecent Proposal,* a film starring Robert Redford and Demi Moore. This Season Five ender begins with a guest appearance by "the Genius of Soul" Ray Charles. In the opening scene he is seated at one of the tables near Helen's lunch counter. It seems that Alex's favorite song is "I Can't Stop Loving You," and Brian asks Ray if he would mind singing a few bars of the song to her to help the estranged couple get back together. Ray smiles and says, "No." About having Ray as a guest star, Farrah Forke said, "I loved him. He was awesome. When I met him he took my hand and felt my arm all the way up and let out a sexy growl. I discovered years later in the film *Ray* with Jamie Foxx that he did that to all women and could tell by their arms if they were pretty or not. I got so excited when I saw that scene because that's exactly what he did to me. That was one of my all-time favorite experiences on *Wings*." The co-writer of the episode, Ian Gurvitz said about Ray, "I would guess it started with his being available for a cameo so we worked backwards to the bit. I think he got $10K for saying one word. 'No.' I remember him walking on stage with his guy and all I could think was holy shit. That's Ray Charles. He sat down and did the scene, basically a long Steven Weber set up which he did great. But it was the shocked look on Brian's face afterwards and the embarrassed slinking away that made it. Can't remember if we even did more than one take. Was cool to have him in the show."

Brian then tries anything to get Alex back in his life including taking the microphone from Fay and singing a made up song called "Nothing Rhymes with Alex." One might notice that in the magazine rack by Helen's counter is a periodical titled *Wings*.

Meanwhile in Joe's office, a meeting with Mr. Elias (Timothy Stack) for a bank loan goes poorly when everyone who enters is taken aback by the man's unsightly new hair plugs. At the same time Antonio takes a message that Davis was coming to the island to see Helen. She fears it's to break up with her. She couldn't have been more off course as instead of ending the relationship he proposes. She says yes. The bank also says yes to Joe's loan. Even after all those yeses, Alex still says no to a reconciliation with Brian. The season closes with Brian lamenting the loss of Alex in the wee hours of the morning in Joe's bedroom saying that once you break up you just can't get back together, only to then coincidentally find Joe and Helen in bed together post-proposal to close the episode and the season.

SEASON SIX

The Season Six cast is ready for takeoff. Left to right Amy Yasbeck, David Schramm, Rebecca Schull, Steven Weber, Tim Daly, Crystal Bernard, Thomas Haden Church and Tony Shalhoub.

Alex and Brian had broken up near the end of Season Five. Just ahead of Season Six, Farrah Forke said, "Thomas Haden Church, Christopher Lloyd and I did a press junket of Nantucket. It was so much fun. Afterwards I was ready to go home, but they talked me into staying a few extra days to hang out with them in New York. It was so memorable. It's odd that a short time after this junket I was called and told I wouldn't be used for Season Six. I never really understood this as I was told just a short time earlier that I was one of the main reasons the show had shot up in the ratings. It was painful then and it still hurts today. Especially since I was then asked back for one more episode, one of the famous Mary Pat

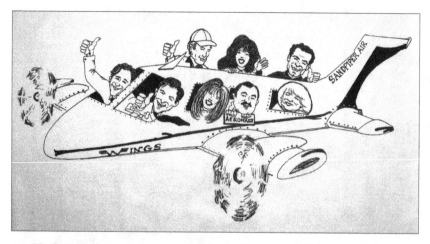

The Season Six caricature tee shirt logo. (Courtesy of Suzanne Holmes).

Lee episodes. I thought I might be asked to return as a regular, but it didn't happen. My hair was darker by that time in preparation for a role in Robert DeNiro's *Heat*. *Wings* wanted me to lighten it for the episode but I said no, the movie was too important." This season brought about a new team at the helm, Howard Gewirtz and Mark Reisman. A record 26 episodes were produced. Many episodes from here on in consisted of another short scene with dialogue as the end credits roll. About those extra scenes, writer and producer Lissa Kapstrom said, "It was part of our push to be quirkier. Those extra scenes over the closing credits from the Sixth Season on allowed us to make the series edgier and weirder." However, as Associate Producer Suzanne Holmes recalled, "On some episodes we were instructed not to do one of those scenes over the credits because NBC planned to run promo material there." Amy Yasbeck joined the cast as Helen's formerly wealthy sister, Cassandra (nicknamed Casey) in the second episode of the season titled "Twisted Sister." This was Thomas Haden Church's final season as a regular cast member. The program now aired on Tuesday nights at 8:00.

"Whose Wife Is It Anyway?" (Season 6 Episode 1) Aired September 20, 1994

Written by Ian Gurvitz
Directed by Leonard R. Garner, Jr.

TV Guide *reminds us that in September of 1994* Wings *moves to Tuesday nights at 8. Set your VCR now.*

The title is a play on both *Whose Life Is It Anyway?* and *Whose Line Is It Anyway?* The episode begins with a recap of the Season Five finale cliffhanger. After spending the night together, Joe makes breakfast for Helen, but she says she can't stay. She still goes to meet Davis, her fiancé in New York.

In the terminal, Lowell reads Brian a letter of farewell from Alex and embellishes it a lot to ease Brian's pain. Brian and Joe commiserate about losing the loves of their lives but decide to soldier on because they're the Hackett Brothers and they vow to continue chasing women until they're old because they're the Hackett Brothers. That mantra doesn't last long and Joe chases after Helen and tries to talk her out of marrying Lynch. Joe finds her in New York just as she's about to board the elevator to meet Davis. About that elevator scene Tim Daly said, "That is one of my favorite scenes. Watching it was kind of an out-of-body experience. I remember watching and saying to myself, 'These young actors are really funny.'" After asking Helen to marry him twice, Helen says yes and she and Joe kiss, accompanied by some wild audience applause and cheers.

The credits roll over Lowell and the oft-mentioned cousin Beevo (with his back to the camera) discussing cross stitching and the special gift pillow they both made for Helen and Davis (later altered to read the names of Helen and Joe).

"Twisted Sister" (Season 6 Episode 2) Aired September 27, 1994
Written by Steven Levitan
Directed by David Lee

The title of this episode shares its name with a rock band headed by Dee Snyder - most famous for "We're Not Gonna Take It." In the opening scene it's obvious that Steven Weber has had a considerable amount of his hair cut off. It's noticeably shorter. He is conversing with Roy about the difficulty of getting over Alex.

Elsewhere Joe shows off the ring he bought for Helen with his "ring fund." He started the fund in seventh grade and is then razzed about it. There's one problem, however – the ring's inscription says "Melen" instead of Helen. He's going to give it to her that night – the anniversary of their first kiss (oddly he recalls that date and she does not). Lowell promises to take care of getting the inscription fixed so Joe can present the ring to Helen that evening as planned.

Speaking of Helen, her formerly-wealthy sister Cassandra (aka Casey) played by Amy Yasbeck makes her first appearance in this episode and Antonio falls head-over-heels. Despite losing everything, snobby Casey still constantly puts down Helen and Joe's lifestyle and life choices. Joe was hoping for dinner alone with Helen to give her the ring, but Casey comes along and complicates things. Joe brings Brian along to help get rid of Casey early enough (the cue being when the band plays "Isn't It Romantic?") to salvage his evening plans. Upon being seated, the waiter played by Layne Beamer confronts Brian and feigns concern over the breakup with Alex. About playing a waiter, Layne Beamer said, "Although I have worked as a room service waiter, the fact that I never actually waited tables made me feel like a bit of a poser as a professional actor. I had to audition, but I don't remember who the other actors were who auditioned." Lowell and Antonio drop by the fancy Lexington's Restaurant with the re-inscribed ring under the guise that the package they present to Joe contains a fuel pump for the airplane. Casey beats Joe to the punch and gives Helen a big old gaudy diamond ring that she no longer wants (she calls it a "starter ring"), and when Joe demands that Helen give it back a fight ensues. When Casey and Helen storm out of the restaurant, the waiter confronts Joe about the argument and tells Joe that if he needs to talk about it, he's there for him (much to Joe and Brian's annoyance).

Was Amy Yasbeck nervous on this, her first episode? Beamer said, "She certainly seemed nervous and I believe felt a bit insecure. My part got a little smaller and I lost a good laugh between the original table read and the final version. Sorry, I can't remember what the changes were but the writing 'didn't work for her character' somehow. It's always interesting to watch as producers, writers and fellow cast members dance around what are clearly 'power moves' as someone tries to establish themself as an equal on set."

About the other cast members Beamer shared, "While I didn't actually 'work with' Tony Shaloub and Tom Haden Church (my recollection is that they stepped into the scene while I was off camera) they were very welcoming, as were Tim Daly and Steven Weber. It has been my experience that day players or weekly co-stars can be pretty much ignored or treated as functionaries by series regulars, but the real pros (especially those with theater backgrounds) go out of their way to welcome and make comfortable those performers who are short-term guests on their set. It was great fun to watch the cast, especially Tony Shalhoub and Thomas Haden Church working on the other scenes all week." Did Beamer get to work with any of the cast again later in his career? He said, "No, but I certainly enjoyed watching them in all of their subsequent work and I was saddened by the death of David Schramm."

Once Joe gets to explain why he was so upset about Casey's ring, Helen sets things straight. What Helen doesn't know at the time is that Casey's husband Stuart invested everything the couple had amassed together in a yacht, leaving her high and dry (standing alone on the dock as he sailed away). Casey is penniless and even her credit cards have been canceled. Helen offers to let her stay at her place until she gets back on her feet, much to Joe's dismay.

The episode was directed by series co-creator David Lee, about whom Layne Beamer said, "I remember that he was gracious and helpful as a director and that the set seemed to run smoothly with him at the helm. I certainly would not have guessed that he had not directed many more episodes."

The credits roll over a scene in which Antonio practices speaking to Casey by using Fay as a stand in. All goes well until the real Casey arrives in the terminal and Antonio, as per usual, stammers uncontrollably in her presence.

"The Shrink" (Season 6 Episode 3) Aired October 4, 1994
Written by Mark Reisman
Directed by Leonard R. Garner, Jr.

The episode opens with Lowell being angry with Antonio. It seems during a ride in Antonio's cab, the windows were rolled down and Lowell's treasured orange baseball cap flew off to parts unknown. The cap held a lot of personal memories for Lowell, including the first time Lowell, Jr. threw up (it was in that hat).

At Helen's lunch counter, Joe and Helen are selecting a date for their wedding. Joe wants a June wedding and consults *The Farmer's Almanac* to determine that June 12th should be the day. Egged on by Casey, Helen doesn't want to wait that long – she likes November 15th. They get distracted from their planning when Brian has a panic attack while flying a full load of passengers. He wants Alex back and doesn't want to go on without her, threatening to down the plane. Once he lands it's recommended that he see a psychiatrist. Joe goes to Dr. Grayson's (George Plimpton) office with Brian for moral support and winds up getting some help himself. However, the advice Grayson gave Joe in the office almost gets the Hackett wedding called off for good. Luckily, Grayson comes through the terminal on his way to a month's vacation in France, and while there he gets the engaged couple back together. As Grayson exits, he places an orange cap on his head – just like the one Lowell lost. Over the closing credits, Brian and Grayson are in the cockpit, with Lowell in the periphery planning how to stealthily get back his hat.

"The Spark and How to Get It" (Season 6 Episode 4)
Aired October 11, 1994

Wings *100th Episode Celebration Invitation. (Courtesy of Suzanne Holmes).*

Wings *100th Episode Salute proudly made the cover of* Hollywood Reporter *Magazine. (Courtesy Suzanne Holmes).*

Written by Howard Gewirtz
Directed by Leonard R. Garner, Jr.

The episode opens with Lowell trying out his speech for the graduating class at M. I. T. (Murray's Institute of Tools). Lowell graduated Murray Cum Laude.

In other action Casey wants to borrow $200 from Helen to get her hair done but Helen and Joe send her to the much less pricey local haircuttery known as Yankee Doodle Scissors. Casey's been borrowing way too much money from Helen with no means of ever paying any of it back. On the way to Yankee Doodle she instead stops at a new place called Beevo's. They do a real number of her hair. Turns

This would have looked nice on Joe's desk – the souvenir Wings *100th episode clock. (Courtesy of Suzanne Holmes).*

"The Spark and How to Get It" – with commemorative Wings *wine. (Courtesy of Suzanne Holmes).*

Amy Yasbeck and Writers Assistant Wendy Ellison share a moment at the 100th Episode Party. (Courtesy of Suzanne Holmes).

out, it's owned by Lowell's cousin Beevo who previously had shaved animals for surgery.

Meanwhile Dr. Grayson tells Brian he's finally totally over Alex and ready to date again. Brian has a great girl named Joan (Dedee Pfeiffer) right under his nose, but he says there's no spark there. An attempt is made to ignite it, but to no avail. Instead Brian chooses to tomcat around again at the Club Car for "Chicks Drink Free Night." While there, Brian envisions himself as a man in his 60s still using the same corny lines to pick up women. Poor Antonio gets kicked out of the Club Car twice for following Brian's advice to use the "good cop/bad cop" routine. Neither Antonio's good cop nor his bad cop was welcome inside.

We see more of the aforementioned elderly, smarmy and paunchy Brian over the closing credits.

"The Waxman Cometh" (Season 6 Episode 5) Aired October 18, 1994

Written by Shelly Landau
Directed by Leonard R. Garner, Jr.

The episode begins with Antonio reading the obituaries. Joe thinks it's morose until Antonio explains that the people going to and from funerals need cab rides – it's good for business. Joe is enlightened and adds a couple of flights to his schedule as a result.

Meanwhile Lowell is about to turn 31 ½. It's a family tradition that Mathers receive part of the inheritance of Snooky Mather when they reach that age. Snooky got his fortune in the Crash of 1929 (not the stock market crash, but rather the one in which Joe Kennedy crashed his Duesenberg into Snooky's ice truck). Lowell is about to earn $25,000. Instead of socking it away for his retirement, he decides to pursue his dream of owning and refurbishing the old Wax Museum on the island. In a way, he "waxes nostalgic" with statues of George Washington, Abraham Lincoln, Barney Fife, Stan Laurel and Granny Moses from *The Beverly Hillbillies*. The Colonel Sanders lookalike however is a real person – the tour guide Gilbert (Bill Wiley). On opening night, Helen and Joe get it on in the *Bonanza* display (and Roy sees the whole thing), and Lowell borrows a tuxedo from the wax Fred Astaire for the event. There is one ongoing problem in the museum – the wiring keeps blowing fuses and eventually causes a huge fire that ends Lowell's business. Executive Producer Howard Gewirtz said, "Most of the wax statues used in the episode came from the local Hollywood Wax Museum. This episode is based upon a true story. My oldest friend from childhood at one point in his checkered career actually created a wax museum in Vermont with his artist wife. He was an investment banker and had money, but this was a sizable investment and he wanted me to invest in it, too. Well, I may be stupid but I'm not dumb and a wax museum just sounded like the worst possible idea. While at a story pitch meeting for *Wings* they were trying to think of an investment that Lowell could blow his money on. I knew exactly what it should be, but how could I shit on my childhood friend and his investment that way? It brings up the question: What will a writer do if he has a great idea but it can hurt someone? The answer is: The writer will fuck over his friend. I went ahead and pitched the wax museum idea in the room and how can you not love it? It's the perfect insane investment. Of course, that's the joke of the show. I called my friend to at least give him a heads up. He thought it was a great idea – good publicity for the museum. To throw my friend a bone we agreed to rent three wax figures from his museum in Vermont. That way he'd be getting a few grand. However, when the episode aired and Lowell's museum catches fire from faulty wiring and is destroyed, at first Lowell is crushed. But then thinking of the insurance money he yells, 'I'm out clean, I'm out clean.' I think you can imagine the telephone conversation with my friend after he saw the episode. It was not pretty." The credits roll over a cute final scene with Roy Biggins as Oliver Hardy seated on a bench in the museum next to the wax Stan Laurel.

"Is that a Ten-Foot Sandwich or Are You Just Glad to See Me?" (Season 6 Episode 6) Aired November 1, 1994

Written by Ellen Byron and Lissa Kapstrom
Directed by Jeff Melman

The episode opens with a new very slick-looking Antonio. Fay knows that the look is intended to impress Casey but tells Antonio he looks like a tango instructor on a cruise ship. Antonio, with lit cigarette in hand tells Fay that Casey wouldn't notice him if he were on fire, so he was attempting to change that. Well, the cigarette in his hand does lead to his being on fire, and sure enough Casey walks right past him without even a glance.

We are introduced in this episode to "the big sandwich" which becomes a recurring item of interest in subsequent episodes. No party was complete without "the big sandwich," and size did matter. The co-writer of the episode, Lissa Kapstrom recalls, "It was the first *Wings* episode Ellen Byron and I wrote and marked the beginning of a weird new direction the show was taking. We felt accepted right from the start with this episode. We were young writers and this was probably our third job, so it was very reassuring. We even received fan mail about it. *Wings* was unique in that about 50-60 percent of what we wrote actually wound up in the episode. Yes, there was certainly some rewriting and constant punching up of the jokes, but there was a trust element and a good chunk of what we put on the page ended up in the show."

In other action, Joe and Helen are getting sick and tired of needy and inconsiderate Brian and Casey constantly interrupting their romantic interludes at home and at work. To make amends, Brian and Casey decide to throw a surprise engagement party for Joe and Helen, and Brian orders "the big sandwich" while Casey's more refined tastes suggest otherwise. While planning the party at the Harbor House in room 412, Antonio, Helen and Joe get the idea that Casey and Brian are having an affair. But when they arrive at the hotel room they see the banner that says, "Joe and Helen Forever" and see champagne and think the room was the surprise for a romantic evening. They couldn't have been more wrong when everyone barges into the room with the "big sandwich" on their shoulders only to find Joe and Helen in bed getting it on. The credits roll over Joe and Helen in bed after the party. Joe says he's ready for more, Helen says he's insatiable and after a couple of beats hands over another section of "the big sandwich."

"All's Fare" (Season 6 Episode 7) Aired November 8, 1994
Written by Steven Levitan
Directed by Leonard R. Garner, Jr.

The episode opens with Brian having a very vivid and weird dream while taking a nap behind Joe's desk. In the dream, Roy and Antonio are playing dueling white grand pianos. On top of the piano is Casey singing "Call Me Irresponsible." In the dream, Lowell is a surgeon about to operate on a clown, and Fay is his nurse. Also in that dream Helen comes on to Brian. The director of the episode, Leonard R Garner, Jr. shared, "After directing a few episodes I got creative. In that dream sequence Helen and Brian are making out on her lunch counter. Suddenly she pushes Brian off the counter and then pounces off the counter on top of him. There was a mat down below so that once Brian rolled off of it, Helen had room to pounce. It was very effective." When Brian wakes up, he's just in time to keep Joe from drawing a big handlebar mustache on his face. Brian describes the dream to Joe who laughs about all of it – except the part about making it with Helen. From that point on, the conversation turns ugly.

Elsewhere, in non-dream action, Lowell has begun wearing a suit and tie to work to garner more respect. It works on Fay but not on Roy who sends him out to clean the throw up from a cub scout troop on one of his Aeromass planes. Meanwhile Casey is think-ing of signing up for a class or two to broaden her horizons, and Antonio is on the horns of a dilemma. He's been hired by a wealthy businessman named Gavin Rutledge (Jonathan Frakes) to drive him around and run errands for him all week. But here's the rub, Rutledge falls head-over-heels in lust with Casey. Casey recipro-cates very quickly as Antonio's frustration grows – especially when Antonio discovers that Rutledge is married with kids. Despite badly needing the money to settle a debt with the I. R. S., Antonio spills the beans about Rutledge's marital status (and abruptly gets fired) and Casey is grateful. Admittedly she is not yet ready to date so soon after being dumped by Stuart. Casey says thank you by giving Antonio the diamond bracelet given to her as a gift from Rutledge.

The closing credits again show the white grand pianos, only this time it's Lowell on top of them in his dirty, oil-stained suit sexily singing "Call Me Irresponsible." Once again it was a dream of Bri-an's, and this time Joe *was* able to paint a big handlebar mustache on him while he slept.

"Miss Jenkins" (Season 6 Episode 8) Aired November 15, 1994
Written by Michael Sardo
Directed by Leonard R. Garner, Jr.

The episode opens with guest star Soupy Sales as Fred Gardner approaching Roy's ticket counter. Gardner is a Simon Says instruc-tor and also has designs on marrying Roy's mother, Eleanor Bluto Biggins (it's said she's four-feet ten inches tall, dons a blonde wig,

Associate Producer Suzanne Holmes with special guest star Soupy Sales between takes for the "Miss Jenkins" episode. (Courtesy of Suzanne Holmes).

Author Bob Leszczak with Soupy Sales and friend Bob Marsicano. I suddenly have a craving for pie.

and has a pack of Lucky Strikes tucked into her support hose). Fred could soon be Roy's new stepdad. Before Fred leaves the terminal, Lowell challenges him to a round of Simon Says. The Simon Says "flap your wings like a hummingbird" bit

Because of her short hair on the "Miss Jenkins" episode, few realized she was portrayed by Peggy Lipton, formerly known as Julie on The Mod Squad.

was very memorable, and it was something Thomas Haden Church had done behind the scenes before. A member of the crew recalled Church's hummingbird impression fondly and thus it was inserted into the Simon Says challenge scene with Soupy. Roy finds out that Gardner has been known to trick elderly women out of their savings and tries to put a stop to the wedding to his mom. But Roy gets off easy when Gardner drops dead in the middle of a Simon Says round. Director Leonard R. Garner, Jr. recalled, "When I got to work with Soupy, he was Soupy! I had watched that show as a kid and he was very happy to make a fan happy. Unfortunately, I had an episode to direct because I could have sat and talked with him for hours."

Elsewhere, a Miss Laura Jenkins (Peggy Lipton) is on Brian's passenger list for his next flight to Boston. She was Brian and Joe's ninth grade English teacher and a real hottie. She left the island to get married on Monday, August 17, 1974 (as Brian recalls). She's just as beautiful as ever, and Joe and Brian agree to discuss being pilots in her classroom for career day. Before Brian can leave the classroom after the career day speech, "Laura" asks him out on a date for dinner that same night. They also spend the night together, to the amazement of all of her former students, Casey, Helen, Lowell and Joe. Joe demands all the intimate details, but Brian is embarrassed to admit that Miss Jenkins gave him an "incomplete." When it comes to the "F" word, he gets an F. An embarrassed Brian confronts her the next day and she comes to the realization that he can never see her as anything but "Miss Jenkins, the teacher" and they decide to keep it that way. Megan McGinnis who played a student named Susie in this episode later snagged a semi-recurring role on *The Marvelous Mrs. Maisel* on which Tony Shalhoub is a regular. The credits roll over the traditional Schubert theme.

"If It's Not One Thing It's Your Mother" (Season 6 Episode 9) Aired November 22, 1994

Written by Joyce Gittlin and Jeffrey Richman
Directed by Jeff Melman

The episode opens with Fay seeking a loan to purchase a ticket to a special Barbra Streisand concert. When Roy overhears this he wants in – he's an even bigger fan than Fay. There's only one seat available so they decide to split the seat so each will at least see part of the concert. Lowell overhears their excitement and thinks they're dating. In true Roy fashion, he hogs the seat for both halves of the concert and when Fay attempts to enter the venue she is carted off and locked in a little room under the stadium. When they return to the terminal after the concert, Fay is livid and bogarts all of Roy's Streisand souvenirs. Their characters didn't often get along well on camera, but Rebecca and David were good friends in real life.

Elsewhere in the terminal Casey brings the news that Mrs. Deedee Chappel (Debbie Reynolds), Casey and Helen's mom is coming in for a visit. The wrinkle is Casey hasn't yet told her mother that she and Stuart are estranged. *Wings* First Assistant Director Barbara Bruno shared, "My absolute favorite guest star was Debbie Reynolds. She was just incredible. I ended up picking her up at the airport myself because for some reason the limo didn't show up." Just like old times, Casey is the center of mom's attention. Often it's as though Helen isn't even there. Joe and Helen are hoping for a $10,000 check from Deedee (she gave Casey that amount for her wedding). Deedee left home with the intention of giving Helen and Joe that amount but had a connecting flight in Las Vegas and she gambled away most of it, and Helen and Joe are both crushed and somewhat angry. While on Nantucket, Deedee cooks her usual overabundance of fattening and filling foods, and everyone overindulges. Antonio becomes Deedee's annoying shadow, and she just can't seem to shake him. Later, as Deedee gets ready to board her return flight, she finds Helen waiting for her at the gate. There they have an emotional and somewhat tearful reconciliation. The credits roll over Roy escaping the terminal after he sees that the very angry Streisand devotee Fay has finally left and the coast is clear. Lowell and Brian who ate an excess of Deedee's food the day before are still too full to move from the terminal's lunch table area and park themselves there indefinitely.

"The Wrong Stuff" (Season 6 Episode 10) Aired November 29, 1994

Written by David Lloyd
Directed by Leonard R. Garner, Jr.

The Aeromass pilot played by Jim Bock wore this nametag, a tribute to late line producer Roz Doyle on every episode on which he worked (Courtesy of Jim Bock).

The episode title is a takeoff on the motion picture *The Right Stuff* (a 1983 film about the Mercury astronauts) and begins with Joe's news about leasing a second plane, causing competitive Roy to announce a $39.95 special fare rate. Brian then gets on the Sandpiper microphone and announces $29.95. The back and forth continues until Brian agrees to fly everyone for free. Jim Bock was the background actor who portrayed Aeromass' pilot in over 100 episodes and shared, "I started out on the show as a terminal passenger extra. We had a great second assistant director Sam Epstein – the ultimate in no-stress directing. Sam asked me to try on the pilot uniform. It fit, and he said that I was the new Aeromass pilot [1993-1997]." Background actors are rarely listed in the credits, but Bock recalled "The red-haired woman behind the Aeromass counter in many episodes was a really sweet background actor named Katie Wilde." Bock added, "My name tag on the show read R. Doyle – a tribute to *Wings* line producer Roz Doyle, later immortalized on *Frasier*. She lost her life to cancer. I never got to meet her, but I wore her name and her memory on every show."

Try as they might, Sandpiper simply cannot keep up with Aeromass. Roy is giving away free Waterpiks, free "point and shoot" cameras and other freebies with his flights. Joe's suggestion that Sandpiper should "get back to basics" is obviously not the right answer to the problem. Brian has a better answer – a celebrity spokesperson who has a connection to flight, astronaut Lt. Col. Charles "Ace" Galvin (Robert Culp) who is readily available for endorsements. About Culp guest starring on the show, Tim Daly said, "Among my all-time favorite guest stars. He had been a childhood hero of mine ever since *I Spy*. It was such a treat having him on *Wings*." It seems the legend that is Ace Galvin and the real Ace Galvin are mutually exclusive. Galvin is crude, reckless, and without a pilot's license since landing a Tomcat at Dollywood. Joe begins to have his doubts about Galvin being Sandpiper's spokesperson, but when he sees the man hold court with the passengers and kids in the terminal his faith in the man is restored, at least temporarily. However, when Joe sees him act like a maniac later that day at a party in the hotel room (which has been completely wrecked as if rock stars were staying there) he and Brian have a change of heart. The Hackett boys worried for nothing because Roy steals Galvin away for twice the money and a used Lexus. All ends well for Sandpiper, however, when Galvin is taken into custody after peeing on the Clinton's pet cat named Socks at a White House ceremony and Roy's big, expensive promotion is canceled. Over the credits we are treated to a cheesy and awkward Sandpiper Air TV commercial made by the Hackett Brothers.

"Insanity Claus" (Season 6 Episode 11) Aired December 13, 1994

Written by Ian Gurvitz
Directed by Leonard R. Garner, Jr.

The show's fourth of six Christmas episodes opens with a crowded holiday terminal and three uncouth passengers dressed as the wise men (more like wise guys) at Roy's counter. They need to get to LaGuardia Airport quickly, but that Aeromass flight is booked solid – that is until the wise men get much wiser and offer Roy an extra $80.

Behind the scenes with (left to right) Second A. D. Sheila Stewart, First A. D. Barbara Bruno, and director Leonard R. Garner, Jr. (Courtesy of Jack E. Herman).

Meanwhile Joe and Helen are excited about spending their first holiday together as an engaged couple. They can't wait to get started, but Fay makes them stay around for the terminal Christmas party (and her disgusting lemon bars). Roy is taking his mom to the Bowling Hall of Fame in St. Louis this yule. And for once Antonio has a girlfriend with whom to spend Christmas. Her name is Phoebe (Cathy Silvers) and this year it looks as though Brian will be the only one alone on the holiday. But wait, Bob played by Dann Florek enters the scene. Bob is the air traffic controller (filling in for Walter who's having eye surgery) and every day Bob has a jelly donut. It's routine. Helen happens to be out of jelly donuts on this particular day and Bob goes absolutely dough-NUTS. Bob goes back to the control tower while Helen seeks out a jelly donut. She finds a chocolate one and sends it up with Antonio but it's not good enough. Bob comes back brandishing a weapon ruining everyone's Christmas. Lowell Mather decides to take matters into his own hands with a blueprint of the airport and a grappling hook. Antonio perspires a lot in the control tower what with Bob aiming his gun at him. Things get worse for Antonio when Bob's wife is called about the standoff and it's discovered that she is Phoebe, Antonio's new girlfriend. To get Bob's gun away from him, Joe describes the miserable lives of the people who work in the airport. He finally gets the gun away just as the police walk in. Because they and their lives were all just insulted by Joe, no one will admit to the police that Joe, who's now holding the gun is not the bad guy. Over the credits, there's a cleaning man in the control tower and Lowell with suction cups on the window is trying to get his attention, but eventually topples over.

"She's...Baaack" (Season 6 Episode 12) Aired January 3, 1995
Written by Rick Copp and David A. Goodman
Directed by Rick Beren

This is the first episode aired in 1995. It opens as Lowell chastises Roy for eating a cheeseburger at Helen's counter. It seems over the weekend he saw a calf being born and it changed him. He's now a vegetarian and screams, "Murderer" at people eating meat or wearing fur and/or leather.

In other action, Fay has parted with some of the clothing of her ex-husbands (all named George) and given them to Antonio because he is the same size, height and build. The problem is, most of the outfits are gaudy 1970s leisure suits, bell bottoms and disco wear. So as not to hurt Fay's feelings, Antonio wears the outdated garb, at least temporarily.

In other news, Casey lets everyone know that Sandy Cooper (Valerie Mahaffey) is making a return visit. Everyone is happy about that, except for Joe, of course. Sandy has an insane infatuation with Joe, but she doesn't let any of the crazy be seen except in his presence. Co-writer of the first Sandy Cooper episode, Rick Copp said, "The first one proved so popular with viewers they asked us to come back and do another and we were happy to do it. This one involved Sandy trapping Joe all over again for an elaborate wedding. By the next year, David A. Goodman and I were at Universal developing a *Knight Rider* series and couldn't do the third Sandy Cooper episode which was about a baby. I did see it, though, when it aired."

This time Sandy's in town to pick up some of her things as her parents have sold their old house on Nantucket. Sandy's a circuit court judge now. Helen lets her stay at her house instead of a hotel and Joe fears the Joey Bear madness will soon rear its ugly head. Brian says he is not 100 percent certain that Joe is making up all of the elaborate Joey Bear stories and suggests he use a tape recorder in Sandy's presence. Joe gets the admission of guilt on tape but Sandy, Helen and Brian were all in on this plot and Joe is made to look like a fool. When Joe gets to Helen's house, however, Sandy is there in a wedding dress in the midst of another elaborate and bizarre "Joey Bear" scene involving a wedding, a wedding cake, and a quick, imaginary honeymoon in Europe. Once again, no one believes Joe when he tells them about the surreal experience. As Sandy exits she says, "Next year, Joe, Jr."

The credits roll over orgasmic sounds coming from Helen's kitchen. It's Lowell, no longer a vegetarian succumbing to Helen's delicious pot roast. The director, Rick Beren said, "I had been the technical coordinator on the early episodes of *Wings*. I was also working on *Cheers*. When both shows started shooting on the same night I was no longer able to do both so I left *Wings* to stay with *Cheers*. However, I did ask executive producer Dave Hackel if I could direct *Wings*. He said yes, and even after Hackel left the show after season five in 1994 he made certain that his promise was fulfilled. I got to direct four episodes of *Wings*, and this was the first."

"Have I Got a Couple for You" (Season 6 Episode 13) Aired January 10, 1995

Written by Mark Reisman
Directed by Jeff Melman

The episode opens with Antonio apologizing to Lowell whose hands are bandaged. It seems Lowell was kind enough to help Antonio change the spark plugs on his cab, but the bar that holds up the hood failed to do its job and slammed on his hands. Antonio wants to be by Lowell's side to "be his hands" while he heals. Things get really "out of hand" when Lowell needs help eating ("potato, potato, pea"), dressing, bathing, and even using the men's room ("pee").

Elsewhere Brian is trying out a new "singles laundromat" in Boston called the Laundromate. And Casey wants to tag along. Fay

Have I got a couple for you. A couple of unredeemed studio audience tickets, that is – one from 1990 and the other from 1995. Somebody missed out on a lot of laughs. (Courtesy of Joel Tator and Mike Armijo).

is making plans to attend a seniors' dance. She tries to help Joe and Helen (who are in a rut looking for a new and exciting experience) by fixing them up with a "fun couple" named Scott (Tony Carreiro) and Gwen Tucker (Amy Van Nostrand, Tim Daly's real-life wife at the time) from New York. Fay plays cribbage with Gwen's Aunt Mimi. Scott is a cardiologist and he and Gwen have been married for two years. All four of them plan a getaway to Vermont. Joe and Helen love hanging with the Tuckers, but the Tuckers

quickly tucker out on Joe and Helen and start seeing other couples. They found Joe and Helen to be too clingy and needy. The dejected Hacketts then try to glom onto another couple.

The credits roll over Antonio cleaning Joe's plane as the still incapacitated Lowell tells him where the dirty spots are, yelling, "Spot...spot...spot." At this point, Lowell is faking it to get Antonio to do all his work.

"Fools Russian" (Season 6 Episode 14) Aired January 31, 1995

Written by Howard Gewirtz
Directed by Jeff Melman

The title is a play on the classic Johnny Mercer/Rube Bloom song "Fools Rush In" – a big hit in the rock and roll years by both Brook Benton and Rick Nelson. The episode opens with Lowell agreeing to go with Fay to her reunion. She wants to be accompanied by a young, buff stud to make the other ladies jealous. Lowell takes his role in this too seriously and persistently attempts to get the story straight regarding how they met, how many times a week they have sex, etc. The overzealous Lowell leads Fay to cancel the arrangement.

Meanwhile Roy is planning to get married. She's a mail-order bride from a Russian catalog. Her name is Anya Volkova (Natasha Pavlova) and Roy's about to meet her face to face for the first time. The writer of the episode, Howard Gewirtz shared, "That was an episode I first wrote for a sitcom called *Sibs* which was a Gracie Films Production starring Alex Rocco, Marsha Mason and Jami Gertz. We tried to redo that as a new pilot called *Related by Birth* – both shows created by Heide Perlman, sister of Rhea of *Cheers*. The original episode title was 'Fools Russian.' The title was retained for *Wings*. It was a terrific vehicle for David Schramm and he got to show his range and vulnerability. The woman who played the Russian mail order bride was very beautiful and quite a character. She was actually Serbian." Because the art loving Anya doesn't know anyone in the U. S. Helen has her stay at her place. Anya is beautiful, but she says she is bound to Roy, her fiancé. That is until she meets another art lover at Helen's counter named Evan Daniels (Perry Stephens) and there's quite a spark there. Helen finally brings Roy to his senses when everyone sees how unhappy Anya is to be marrying him. In a very rare Roy moment of human kindness he calls off the nuptials. As a reward Helen treats him to dinner at Casa Kielbasa. The credits roll over Antonio writing a letter to a possible Russian mail order bride of his own.

"Let's Call the Whole Thing Off" (Season 6 Episode 15) Aired February 7, 1995

Written by Ellen Byron and Lissa Kapstrom
Directed by Jeff Melman

The episode's title refers to a classic tune written by the Gershwins, George and Ira for the Fred Astaire and Ginger Rogers film *Shall We Dance*. The song has the memorable line, "I like po-TAY-to and you like po-TAH-to." This episode opens with Lowell in summer jogging attire on one of the coldest days of the year. He's in training for the annual February 11th Polar Bear Competition. Antonio joins him but sprains a groin muscle getting into his

The hilarious and notorious nude run across the stage by Thomas Haden Church and Tony Shalhoub between takes in the "Let's Call the Whole Thing Off" episode in Season Six. Needless to say, the audience roared. (Courtesy of Suzanne Holmes).

Speedo. Lowell wins the competition, but he's frozen and has to be wheeled into the terminal afterwards until fully thawed.

This next anecdote has been confirmed by multiple members of the cast and crew and even one member of the studio audience that night named Robert O'Brien. A few scenes required several retakes and thus the studio audience that night was beginning to get a bit restless so Thomas Haden Church and Tony Shalhoub lightened the mood and entered Helen's kitchen area, undressed completely and then ran around the stage covered only in pots and pans (they were already scantily clad for the jogging scenes – there wasn't much to remove). The studio audience roared with laughter and a 15-minute break was taken for everyone to regain composure. Sadly, this outtake doesn't appear to have been saved or used on any of the *Wings* blooper reels available on You Tube, but luckily a photo of the event has survived.

In other action at the airport, Joe and Helen have finally decided that May 27th will be their wedding date. Joe wants a nice practical and frugal wedding, while Helen wants a big extravagant one. Joe has always been very anal retentive when it comes to planning, and he has compiled a large binder with every imaginable option covered. Fay calls him "Binder Boy." Joe wants to have the wedding at his house with a D. J. It all turns into a heated negotiation with Brian acting as Joe's counsel and Casey as Helen's. The guys don't want to give in on having mini hot dogs and "the big sandwich." To see how others do it Joe and Helen opt to crash a wedding and take notes. The wedding they crash is an expensive one and they snag the unused invitation for Jorge and Juanita Rodriguez and stay for the dinner. Joe and Helen's bickering about having their own wedding there leads the married couple to bicker and split up. Coincidentally said married couple arrives at the airport the next day and are planning separate honeymoons. Joe and Helen apologize and try to get the couple back together, but instead the two newlyweds realize they're wrong for one another and head downtown to get the marriage annulled. The bandleader for the wedding Joe and Helen crashed was played by Steve Susskind who had recorded the hit doo wop songs "Please Love Me Forever" and "Glory of Love" with the Roommates in the early 1960s. Over the credits Joe and Helen crash another wedding, this time as Dr. and Mrs. Yashahara.

"Remembrance of Flings Past Part One" (Season 6 Episode 16) Aired February 9, 1995

Written by Ian Gurvitz
Directed by Jeff Melman

Helen is going to her reunion and is proud of a slinky new size four dress she will be wearing, as opposed to the size 20 dress she wore to the senior prom. Normally she would be so proud to have handsome Joe on her arm, but just two days before the event an enormous zit erupts on his nose. Antonio calls it a volcano. Brian names it Jerry. An old girlfriend of Brian's named Sara (Sheila Kelley) is coming to the reunion. Brian apologizes to Sara for how they left things when they last saw one another. Brian invites her to dinner, not realizing that she now has a young son, Jason (Zachary B. Charles) who came with her. Brian and the young man really hit it off.

In other action Lowell reunites with his favorite old shop teacher, Mr. Conley (Tom Hatten) who inspired Lowell to become a mechanic. However, Lowell quickly discovers Conley is a "freakin' psycho." About this particular episode, the writer's assistant, Wendy Allen-Belleville recalled, "One of the other classmates, first name of Wendy [played by Lesley Boone] – a former cheerleader who made Helen's life miserable during high school was in attendance at the reunion. Helen, who had been an insecure overweight gal in high school was nervous about seeing Wendy again. In the script, in telling Antonio and Fay about how awful Wendy was to her, Helen was to call out Wendy's first and last name one time as she described her old nemesis. However, during the first run through Crystal stumbled when she said Wendy's last name. Later that day in the writers' room they decided to change Wendy's surname. Several of them pitched a myriad of new ones, when one of the writers, Steven Levitan looked over to me and said 'ELLISON,' my maiden name and last name at the time. Fortunately, all the writers concurred, and that scene was updated and when Helen recalled Wendy Ellison, my full name was stated not once, but three times!" It seems the two schoolmates, Helen and Wendy have traded places because now the old classmate named Wendy Ellison is morbidly obese and can no longer tease Helen about her weight. However, now she's ribbing Helen about her dark roots showing through the blonde. Antonio, who went to school in Italy, came along to the reunion and surprisingly fit in nicely, pretending to know all of the alumni.

Elsewhere Brian asks Sara if she and Jason would like to move in with him as they've all been getting along so well. Sara has another issue on her mind that needs to be addressed first. When Sara finally gets to talk to Joe in private, she admits that Jason may be Joe's son. If this is true, both Brian and Helen will be devastated. Part one ends there, except for a short scene as the credits roll with Antonio being invited by the loony Mr. Conley to go on a field trip with him to Pluto. Bob Moore who portrays the bandleader in the reunion scene was part of the show's Wrong Brothers – the regular warm-up entertainers for the studio audience on show night.

"Remembrance of Flings Past Part Two" (Season 6 Episode 17) Aired February 14, 1995

Written by Howard Gewirtz and Steven Levitan
Directed by Jeff Melman

It's Valentine's Day and the episode begins with a recap of Part One. Then Joe and Sara have a long conversation in the terminal to make certain that Helen and Brian don't find out that Jason may be Joe's son. Little do they realize that Roy is still in the building at the time. The next day Roy actually gives Joe the sound advice not to say anything to Brian or Helen until the blood test results are in (to see if Joe is indeed Jason's father). However, when Brian intercepts a call about the blood test Joe has to spill the beans and Brian's reaction is not a positive one. Later that evening Joe goes over Helen's house for a romantic Valentine's Day dinner and Helen takes the news surprisingly well. The phone call finally comes in and Joe finds out he is not the father. Sara then knows who the father definitely is and says she owes it to her kid, Jason to take him to see that man in San Francisco. Sara and Brian tentatively agree to see one another again in a few months, but realize it's just not meant to be.

Speaking of Valentine's Day, writer's assistant Wendy Allen-Belleville recalled, "A light-hearted moment off-camera with the late David Schramm. It was 'show night' – filming Tuesdays in front of a live audience on Stage 19 at Paramount Pictures. The crew was getting set up for the next scene and David Schramm and I were sitting on the main set, chatting. Somehow we got on the topic of my birthday, which is Valentine's Day. He pulled me up to standing and proceeded to dance with me, singing 'My Funny Valentine,' and even dipped me. It was a lovely moment with a kind-hearted man." The credits roll with the traditional Schubert theme.

"Gone but Not Faygotten" (Season 6 Episode 18) Aired February 21, 1995

Written by Shelly Landau and Michael Sardo
Directed by Leonard R. Garner, Jr.

The episode begins with Lowell singing "Moon River" (with all the wrong lyrics) while repairing some equipment in Joe's office. In other action Fay bursts in asking for the afternoon off so she can attend the circus. When Joe says no Fay quits. The airport workers throw her a retirement party with "the big sandwich." For Fay they get the biggest big sandwich, the "Cordoba." The cake for the party was supposed to say "Good Luck Fay," but instead it's one of those Magic Eye 3D cakes. If one relaxes one's eyes one will see the image of Fay. Antonio is able to see it and gasps – "she's naked."

The applicants to replace Fay at the ticket counter balk at the salary available. Julia Sanford portrayed the woman who, upon seeing the salary on a slip of paper laughs hysterically and walks out of the terminal. About that experience Sanford shared, "Thanks for reaching out to me. *Wings* was the first sitcom that I ever worked on and I was so excited that I was going to be on a wonderful and popular prime time TV show! I almost couldn't believe it and it will always be one of the highlights of my career. From the moment the script was delivered to my front door by messenger (no email in those days), I had the time of my life!! I still remember the feeling of pride as I drove onto the Paramount Lot and was told where to park. I can honestly say that everyone I met on that set was kind and friendly. That includes the director, Lenny Garner, who was so nice and made me feel welcomed and important. He definitely made me feel at ease and appreciated. I was in a short scene with Tim Daly, Steven Weber and Rebecca Schull but worked most directly with Tim Daly, who was very focused and easy to work with. The other people in the cast that I will always remember with warmth and appreciation are Tony Shalhoub and Amy Yasbeck. Even though I didn't have a scene with him, Tony went out of his way to come over and introduce himself to me and welcome me to the show. I will never forget that! Not only is he extremely talented, he is an incredible human being! Years later, I worked on *Monk* with him and he was still just as warm and friendly as he had been when I met him on *Wings*. I didn't work directly with Amy Yasbeck either but from the time I met her in the makeup room and for the rest of my time on set, she was very friendly and treated me like a friend. I will never forget her either! As I said, working on *Wings* was one of the joys of my career. On top of being one of the best shows on the air with an incredible cast and crew, of course, we got to shoot in front of a live audience and experience the laughter and energy that can only come from an audience in the moment. If I hadn't already been hooked on acting, I would have been after that night!!"

Helen then suggests that Sandpiper hire Casey to replace Fay. Hesitantly Joe and Brian ask Casey and, to their chagrin, Casey says yes. All are pleasantly surprised when she does a great job. In fact one of the happy passengers gives Casey two tickets to the Celtics game for that evening and she in turn gives them to the Hackett boys. It seems the only way Joe and Brian can get to Boston in time is to take the ferry. The two brothers who run the ferry are very much like older versions of Joe and Brian and are named Benny (Michael J. Pollard) and Earl (Jack Kehler). Brian notices the similarity immediately. And who do they run into there at the ferry terminal? Fay is on the microphone announcing departures – and frequently has to be dangled over the side of the ferry while wearing a wetsuit to remove a dead squid from the engine. Retirement wasn't all it was cracked up to be and she got lonely, so she took the ferry job, but she really wants her old job back. With Casey doing such a wonderful job as her replacement, that feat will not be easy. At first the Hackett brothers keep both of them on, but it's not financially prudent, and the two ticket agents fight like cats and dogs. Casey gives Joe and Brian an ultimatum and gets fired. She then takes Fay's old job at the ferry, and as the credits roll she gives Benny and Earl the same ultimatum.

"Ex Lies and Videotape" (Season 6 Episode 19)
Aired February 28, 1995

Written by Ellen Byron and Lissa Kapstrom
Directed by Jeff Melman

The episode's title is a takeoff on the Steven Soderbergh film *Sex, Lies and Videotape* from 1989. In the opening scene, Helen tries on her wedding dress at work to see what the gang thinks of it and runs through the terminal quickly because she doesn't want Joe to see her – it's bad luck for the groom to see it before the nuptials.

Caroline Aaron as Shirley on the set of The Marvelous Mrs. Maisel. *Aaron played Mary Pat Lee in two beloved episodes of* Wings. *In the doorway, wearing the vest is your author and SAG/Aftra background actor Bob Leszczak.*

But as luck would have it, he does get a glimpse. While Helen seeks a new dress for the ceremony, she does have some good news – the reverend she wants to use to marry them is available.

Brian also has some good news. He's been invited to be a guest on *The Mary Pat Lee Show* for their "Smart, Sexy and Single" segment. Mary Pat's daytime talk show is very popular and Brian gets enough audience tickets for everyone (except Fay who has to stay and take reservations) to join him at the broadcast. The person who is most excited is Antonio who worships the ground on which Mary Pat walks. When asked who she thought Mary Pat Lee was inspired by actress Caroline Aaron said, "Probably Sally Jessy Raphael. And Mary Pat was way ahead of her time. She was very much a feminist, very much about women's empowerment. She was one tough cookie." Did she have to audition for the role? Aaron said, "No. I was good friends with David Schramm, my daughter's godfather. Plus I had auditioned in L. A. for *Frasier* for the role of Roz Doyle. Lisa Kudrow had also auditioned for it but it went to Peri Gilpin. *Wings* and *Frasier* were created by the same guys, so they knew what I could do and they wanted me for the part."

Joe and Helen will likely arrive late for the Mary Pat broadcast as they are scheduled to meet with the aforementioned Reverend Powell (Richard McGonagle) that same day. In fact, they are likely to arrive extremely late because the reverend is the slowest talker on the planet. Caroline Aaron added, "I've forgotten his name but the actor who originally was to play the reverend was fired because he was speaking too quickly. He just couldn't slow it down enough for their liking. They wanted someone who could speak painfully slow and they got him." About this first of two Mary Pat Lee episodes co-writer Lissa Kapstrom said, "I love our Mary Pat episode, which was kind of a takeoff on Oprah and the daytime talk show craze. The episode was so popular that Mary Pat Lee was invited back for another in a later season." Caroline Aaron recalled, "The set they built for Mary Pat's show was huge. It split the audience in half. It was ideal for this four camera show." When the talk show begins, Brian realizes that he's been duped. The show's topic is actually, "Men who can't commit – what the hell is their problem?" Waiting in the wings to tell all is Brian's ex, Alex Lambert (Farrah Forke). Forke said, "After being told I wouldn't be used in Season Six I was asked back for this one more episode – a Mary Pat Lee episode. I thought it might be to return as a regular, but it didn't happen." Caroline Aaron added, "Farrah Forke was very close to David Schramm, as was I. Even though Forke came back for that episode after not being asked back for the season there was no tension in the air. Theirs was such a welcoming atmosphere and a well-oiled machine. On some shows one feels like a transfer student, but not this one. You were welcomed with open arms." Lowell is afraid he left his iron on and while in the audience gives out his address on the air (213 Church Lane – an inside joke as Church is the actor's last name) and says that the key is under the mat. Of course, he later got home to find he'd been robbed (all they left was the iron and it was off). Needless to say Brian is humiliated on live TV.

Afterwards Alex comes to the terminal and half apologizes to Brian for how vicious things got on the talk show. While each of them professes utter disgust for one another, they kiss passionately, they yell a bit more, and then sleep together. Joe thinks they're getting back together, but Brian wants to dump her. That is until she dumps him, and then in true Brian fashion he wants her back. Over the credits we hear Alex taking off and Brian at the gate calling her back, only to change his mind yet again with Joe's help.

"Portrait of the Con Artist as a Young Man" (Season 6 Episode 20) Aired March 21, 1995

Written by Joyce Gittlin and Jeffrey Richman
Directed by Ken Levine

The title is a play on the James Joyce novel, *The Portrait of the Artist as a Young Man*. The episode opens with Antonio rehearsing a song in the hangar he wrote for Casey (with Casey rhymes such as *Cagney and Lacey,* Donald and Daisy). Despite the strange lyrics, Fay tells him it's lovely so as not to hurt his feelings.

Meanwhile Joe has film in his camera he wants to use up, but every time he goes to take a snapshot of his brother, Brian makes a funny face or gets into a weird pose. Joe gives up and leaves the camera on his desk. For a gag, Brian then takes a picture of his privates not knowing that when the film is developed the photos will be sent to Helen's parents. This might just be TV's first "dick pic."

In other goings on it's Casey's birthday. About the birthday scene, director Ken Levine shared, "Crystal dropped an entire birthday cake [but the props department was well prepared with a replacement cake]. That blooper was included in Dick Clark's blooper show, and I got a nice residual check every time it ran. So thank you, Crystal." Brian's birthday gift for Casey was a used book about pleasuring women, Fay gave her salt and pepper shakers, Antonio gifted her $200 earrings, and Lowell made her a weird metal shoe rack. When Casey shows the rack to a friend with an art gallery, the curator flips and wants him to make more items possibly for his own gallery show. Lowell could possibly be launched as an artist with Casey as his representative. At first Lowell isn't interested but when he hears about the money he can make he's all ears. Casey then brings in Maya Wolverton (Christie Mellor) of the Wolverton Gallery. Mellor shared, "I happen to be an artist, but at the time I was mainly acting, so it wasn't ever asked about, nor was it a prerequisite for playing the part, as far as I know. The audition was the most memorable thing about the part, to tell you the truth. The original Maya Wolverton was pretty wild and interesting, she carried a ferret in her purse. So I had so much fun at the audition, just doing a lot of business with the 'ferret' in my purse and she was a little more over the top. The room seemed to enjoy it. No idea who else might have auditioned for the role. The part got chipped away more every day (my impression at the time was that Thomas Haden Church didn't think it was funny, or for some reason didn't like it) so by the time the week was out, I wished they had just given the role to a tall, slender art gallery owner. I felt like I was playing dress-up in someone else's clothes and there was nothing funny left of the part. I barely remember what I ended up doing. The fun was excised, along with most of my lines, and everything seemed problematic, I felt like I'd been cast in one role I was right for, and now I was in a role I wasn't right for. I just basically wanted the job to be over! Except that Steven Weber and Tim Daly were so nice and really seemed to go out of their way to make me feel comfortable and at home. I had worked with Tim Daly on an episode of a very cool show he did with Eve Gordon called *Almost Grown* a few years before, and we'd had fun. It was a 1950s flashback episode where we stole a saint from an Italian mobster's lawn, and Eve and I are interrogated by the mobster. It's not listed on my IMDb for some reason. It was a fun show. Amy Yasbeck was also very warm. She introduced me to the joy of a chopped egg and mayo sandwich for breakfast, which I still enjoy. It was all a fine experience, enjoyable hanging out with the cast members and I was happy to have the work, even if it didn't end up as hoped. I think I still get a few foreign residuals."

Maya then wants to see Lowell's other works such as "Towel Rack." She likes what she sees and wants Lowell to have 20 other pieces done in a week. Lowell gives it the old college try, all hopped up on diet cola for energy, but the pressure is simply overwhelming. Casey eventually has to face the fact that Lowell isn't cut out to be an artist and she cancels the show at the gallery. The credits roll over Antonio attempting to cheer up Casey with his bizarre Lacey/Daisy dedication song.

"The Love Life and Times of Joe and Helen" (Season 6 Episode 21) Aired April 4, 1995

Written by Steven Levitan
Directed by Jeff Melman

For all intents and purposes this is a flashback episode or a clip show. With the Joe and Helen wedding only weeks away, it was a way to clarify previous happenings on the show for those who came to the party late, possibly because of the popular *Wings* reruns on the USA Network. The episode opens with Brian showing off his new camcorder. He bought it with petty cash but justifies doing so by saying that it's to make a special wedding gift for Joe and Helen. After Joe leaves the room excited about that, Brian admits he was especially quick on his feet coming up with the excuse (although now he's committed to making the stupid video). He then goes around to every member of the gang and asks them separately about Joe and Helen. A studio audience was not present for these short personal videos, each of which leads to a flashback of a previous episode. Likely the opening sequence with Brian showing off his new camcorder was filmed in tandem with another episode when an audience was present, and the rest was shot at another time sans audience.

In Brian's video, Fay recalls how Joe and Helen first got together (the clip is when they first kissed). Then Brian asks Joe and Helen to recall their first date. They were in Joe's car not realizing that Brian was in the backseat the whole time. Antonio gets his turn next and shares that Valentine's Day memory when he was still a waiter at Pontrelli's and Joe showed up to the date very late. Roy then shares his thoughts, "I give it a year, tops. Those two sure could fight" leading into the messy one-take flashback scene in the hangar in which Helen squirts Joe with a grease gun and he covers her in foam from the fire extinguisher. This leads to the clip in which Helen leaves for New York to try to make it as a cellist, along with her return to the island several months later. The consensus is that Helen went psycho over Gail, the woman Joe was dating while she was in New York and that led to (another clip) her driving her Jeep through his office - twice. Then Brian and Lowell (who wants to be in the shot with Brian) recall the famous veal/chicken slapping scene between Joe and Helen that caused the breakup with Gail. Antonio then shares that he is Helen's first husband. Theirs was a marriage of convenience to keep him from being deported and the clip with Helen stepping up to be Antonio's bride to appease the immigration officer follows. Fay then tells how Joe and Helen saw other people for over a year after that initial breakup, and many of the dates were really bad ones, as seen in still more clips (Joe and the puppet lady, Helen and the weird laugher, Helen mistaken for a hooker at a party, and Joe with that 19-year-old for whom Helen used to babysit). Then Fay brings up Davis Lynch (and more clips are seen). Roy picks up the story of Helen and Davis and how it drove Joe nuts. Lowell then remembers the day Davis proposed to Helen (more clips). Brian recalls the night after Davis proposed and Helen said yes but wound up sleeping with Joe (clips). Antonio then shares how Joe followed Helen to New York to keep her from marrying Lynch, proposing to her in an elevator. Then one by one they each send a special message to the soon-to-be-hitched couple ending in a big sloppy kiss by the happy couple.

The episode ends with a peek into the future as Joe and Helen's grandkids watch the video, not believing their grandparents were ever that young. The credits then roll over some amazing and hilarious slapstick moments from other past episodes, including more of the meat-slapping scene synchronized to music.

"A House to Die For" (Season 6 Episode 22) Aired May 2, 1995

Written by David Lloyd
Directed by Jeff Melman

The episode opens with Helen's stress over her dress. It seems her wedding dress has a zipper instead of buttons, and the sleeves are not what she ordered. The wedding is only three weeks away and she's freaking out. Casey tells her to go to her happy place. For Casey, it's lying on a tropical island. For Helen it's – being Marcia, Marcia, Marcia on *The Brady Bunch*. This leads to a funny dream sequence with Helen in 70s garb surrounded by the other Brady kids with Joe as the captain of the football team asking her to the prom. The young actors who portray the Brady kids all also appeared in two Brady Bunch motion pictures. The young man who portrayed Bobby Brady, Jesse Lee Soffer later found success in *As the World Turns* and had a long run in *Chicago P. D.*

A vintage comic book of The Brady Bunch *to go along with the wonderful Brady-infused episode titled "A House to Die For" in which Helen finds her "happy place."*

In his office, Joe breaks the news to Casey and Brian that Helen and he are moving in together so they can get fully settled in time for the wedding, and can then come back after the honeymoon all ready to start their life together. Because Casey lives with Helen, she will now have to move in with Brian at Joe's old house. Or should they move into Joe's old house and let Casey and Brian live at Helen's place? No, neither of those options will work – Joe thinks Helen's house is too feminine, and she thinks Joe's place is too frat house masculine (and stinky). After coming to that realization they decide to find a new place that will make both of them happy. One place they're considering is the home of that annoying old man Carlton Blanchard who is said to be gravely ill (but never seen in this episode). His nephew, Lewis (Gilbert Gottfried) can't wait for the old man to kick the bucket as he is the sole heir to the lumberyard fortune (which includes a 1968 Barracuda). He begins selling off items "at prices so low he's practically giving it all away." Gottfried said, "I'm not sure but possibly Hickey was too weak to appear in this episode and so we merely mentioned that he was upstairs in bed, not unlike those Suzanne Somers scenes on the phone as she was exiting *Three's Company* – not really part of the show but still included." Gottfried recalled, "I say one of my favorite lines in this episode. Casey says, 'Lewis, from head to toe you are the most repulsive man I've ever met, to which I reply, 'Oh, so you've been checking me out."

Brian wants Carlton's car, Roy wants the furniture, and Joe and Helen want the house. After knocking at death's door, stubborn old Carlton makes it through the health crisis and survives (much to Lewis' disappointment) and the scene ends with Lewis climbing the stairs with a pillow in his hands, intending to smother the old coot. About the doctor (Richard Voigts) in this episode, Gilbert Gottfried said, "He was an actor with one of those amazing stage voices." The credits roll over Lewis returning to the terminal to meet a hooker he hired for Uncle Carlton saying, "If this doesn't kill him, nothing will."

"Nuptials Off" (Season 6 Episode 23) Aired May 9, 1995
Written by Michael Sardo
Directed by Jeff Melman

The episode begins with Antonio entering the terminal in a nice suit. He's been to the christening of his cousin Vincenzo's new baby, and it's one ugly baby (confirmed by Helen's scream when Antonio shows her a photograph). Antonio is the godfather. Because of the godchild, Antonio wants to become more religious.

Meanwhile Lowell is unwell – a fever, body aches, the shakes. Fay suggests he should go home and rest, but he feels he must carry on the Mather tradition of never missing a day of work. Elsewhere Joe the perfectionist is getting antsy because Helen hasn't yet ordered the special cocktail napkins for the wedding. She apologizes and to make up for it offers to go downtown for the marriage license. There is a snag, however. The paperwork for her divorce from Antonio was never filed. She had spilled champagne on the papers while celebrating and placed them under her cash register to flatten them out and then forgot all about them. They are still there and it takes 120 days to finalize divorces and the wedding is only a few weeks away. This problem is so big, Helen swallows her pride…and goes to Roy. He suggests sending Joe away for a weekend of fly-fishing while Antonio, Brian and she secretly go to Tampico, Mexico to get a quickie divorce through an acquaintance named Pepe. Ah, but there's still another wrinkle. Antonio being Catholic must first get an annulment and that has to be granted by the pope. Joe's plane to his fly-fishing excursion is delayed and he almost catches Brian, Helen and Antonio taking off to Mexico. Lowell almost spills the beans but Joe sees that he's had too much cold medicine and isn't thinking straight and blows off everything Lowell has said about Helen and Antonio. The credits roll over Helen just making it back to her lunch counter after the quickie divorce in time for Joe's return to the terminal. She and Joe embrace as she attempts to obscure his periphery because Brian and Antonio are wearing oversized souvenir sombreros.

"Et Tu, Antonio?" (Season 6 Episode 24) Aired May 16, 1995

Written by Ian Gurvitz and Mark Reisman
Directed by Leonard R. Garner, Jr.

The episode begins with Helen and Joe's first wedding gifts arriving in the mail. A nice crystal vase (from her side of the family)… and a sneaker phone (from his).

Elsewhere Antonio is awaiting the arrival of his cousin Dominic (Maurice Godin) and Dominic's girlfriend Teresa (Fabiana Udeno). Dominic owns a chain of leather goods stores and he has changed quite a bit from the humble shoe repairman Antonio used to know (he's now very cocky). The episode's co-writer, Ian Gurvitz said, "I think his wardrobe was meant to show that he was kind of gaudy and over-the-top. Sort of benign Eurotrashy clothes. The opposite of Antonio. Made him feel like the guy was better than a humble cab driver. I remember Tony playing the hell out of being a good guy with conflicting emotions. I think he liked having an episode with some depth. Everyone knew then what a great actor he was and is, so the success he's had and is having is hardly surprising." Dominic's main squeeze, Teresa, however, has grown into an amazingly beautiful woman – so lovely in fact that Antonio can't help having impure thoughts in her presence. He expresses guilt over these feelings, and yet can't control them. It doesn't get any easier when Dominic has business in New Jersey and leaves Teresa in Antonio's capable hands. Antonio fears that she may also be attracted to him, but Brian puts the kibosh on that notion by reminding Antonio that he is the all-time strikeout king.

That placates him, at least temporarily. Antonio cooks dinner for Teresa and there is indeed a mutual attraction – Brian was wrong. And to make matters worse, Antonio's murphy bed keeps coming down at inappropriate times. At first Antonio dreams of sweeping Teresa away from Dominic, but then his conscience takes hold and he makes certain that the couple gets back together. As the credits roll, Antonio tries to pry himself into one of Dominic's leather suits but has a great amount of difficulty.

"Boys Just Want to Have Fun" (Season 6 Episode 25) Aired May 23, 1995

Written by Michael Sardo and Shelly Landau
Directed by Rick Beren

The title is a play on the Cyndi Lauper hit "Girls Just Wanna Have Fun." The episode opens with Brian showing off the nicks he received during his morning shave. He had just gotten out of the shower and was shaving naked when Casey walked in, let out a blood-curdling scream, and Brian got a much closer shave than he had intended. Despite recommendations to cover up, because he owns the house he has designated it as "Nakedland" – a realm of which he is president. Speaking of being naked, director Rick Beren shared, "There's a scene in which Brian is changing in Joe's office. He's changing behind Joe's open filing cabinet when Casey barges in and sees him naked for a second time that day. We were going to have him wear a little something, but we couldn't get the right shot to make it look real. Steven Weber chose to go all in and took it all off for that scene in front of the studio audience. He was a gamer and he really made that scene work."

A short time later, after the wedding rehearsal, Joe, Brian and the guys get very excited about what comes next – the bachelor party. However, their night of ogling busts turns out to be a real bust when Brian books the hotel for the wrong night, the pizza delivery guy gets lost, the hotel's video player is for Betamax tapes and the only available video is *Terms of Endearment*, and the stripper shows up sick with a high fever.

Over at Helen's house she's looking forward to a nice hot relaxing bath, a mud mask and a good night sleep but Casey throws her an intense bachelorette party instead – a vastly more exciting party than Joe's including a more-than-half naked male stripper (Blaine Gray). The character of Joanne at Helen's party was played by Sara T. Ballantine, daughter of actor and comedian Carl Ballantine. Over at Nakedland, Casey accidentally crawls into Brian's bed with him. She was confused because both rooms look alike in the dark. Their usual disdain for one another quickly morphs into passion and against their better judgment they have sex – several times. The credits roll over the traditional Schubert theme.

"Here It Is, the Big Wedding" (Season 6 Episode 26) Aired May 23, 1995

Written by Ellen Byron and Lissa Kapstrom
Directed by Jeff Melman

The bachelor/bachelorette party episode ("Boys Just Want to Have Fun") aired back-to-back with this one. It opens with Joe serving breakfast to a hungover Helen. Initially she feared HE would be the one with the hangover from his bachelor party, but her party was indeed the only wild one. She's still wearing the handcuffs placed on her by the male stripper from the night before. The very OCD Joe has a wedding schedule (which he padded by half an hour). All is going according to Hoyle, except for Brian picking up the tuxedos – he's still in bed with Casey. That also means Casey is late doing Helen's makeup and hair. Antonio is an usher and hopes to impress Casey with his tuxedo. Little does he realize that he's just a bit late to have that happen (Brian's been there and done that). Brian finally arrives with the tuxes and they don't fit – one is way too small and the other too big. There is an inside joke in the name on the tuxes. Instead of Hackett, Brian picked up the tuxes for the Hackel bar mitzvah. This was a tribute to the show's former executive producer, Dave Hackel who said, "Now that you mention it I vaguely recall that. I had already left *Wings* by that time but we often use names of real people. It's hard to think up names. I often use ones from my kindergarten class and it's great that some of the real people have gotten to hear their names in shows on which I've worked. For them it's a little bit of immortality." When Brian and Casey meet in the hallway at the Century House before the wedding ceremony they immediately find themselves once again in the throes of passion and find an open and roomy closet. When Antonio overhears that Brian slept with Casey he goes postal and scuffles with Brian into the hotel bathroom and as a result Helen's ring lands in the toilet. Joe is still in his boxers because Brian has lost the correct Hackett tuxes he misplaced while experiencing the heat of passion. Joe attempts to retrieve the ring, getting his hand lodged in the loo. Antonio is so upset about Brian making it with Casey he begins drinking and is "in his cups" by the time the big event takes place. The episode's co-writer Lissa Kapstrom said, "One of the favorite episodes on which I worked. Joe's hand is stuck in the toilet for the entire ceremony. A very funny chain of events and chaos." Rebecca Schull added, "I recently watched a few episodes on that Antenna TV 30th Anniversary *Wings* Marathon special. I hadn't seen the show in a while and I laughed at that wedding episode where Helen and Joe say their vows in the bathroom with Joe's hand caught in the toilet. The episodes have held up well." Things didn't go well for Helen, either. She has indelible marker above her upper lip making her look like Adolph Hitler, and her eyes are very red from the hangover and the accidental use of Binaca as eyedrops. Despite the absurd circumstances the wedding takes place in the john and when Helen sheds a tear Joe has the toilet paper roll handy to dry her eyes. As the credits roll everyone but Joe and Antonio leave the bathroom, all following Helen and throwing rice. Antonio passes out drunk on the floor in front of Joe, still seated next to the bowl, waiting to have his hand freed.

SEASON SEVEN

The plane looks so much bigger on TV. Rear left to right Amy Yasbeck, David Schramm, Tony Shalhoub. Middle left to right Rebecca Schull, Crystal Bernard. Front left to right Steven Weber, Tim Daly.

Joe and Helen are married and begin the season on their honeymoon. Lowell left Nantucket (moving on to a starring role as Ned in the Fox sitcom *Ned and Stacey*) but did return for one final episode for closure. He ended his long run on *Wings* with the need to join the Witness Protection Program after seeing a mob hit being committed. His brief replacement was a former Marine named Budd Bronski played by actor/comedian Brian Haley. There were 26 episodes produced again this season and the show still aired Tuesday nights at 8:00. Summer reruns briefly aired Wednesday nights at 8:00 in 1996.

"Burnin' Down the House Part One" (Season 7 Episode 1) Aired September 19, 1995

Written by Ian Gurvitz
Directed by Jeff Melman

The title is inspired by a famous song by the Talking Heads. The episode begins with a recap of the wedding and Season Six finale. Joe and Helen are on their honeymoon in Jamaica, registering at the hotel as Mr. and Mrs. Hackett for the first time. They stay in room 52. Writer Ian Gurvitz remembered, "Those alleged Jamaican scenes were done at the Loew's Santa Monica Beach Hotel if I recall correctly. We rarely went on location but it must have been worth it because we were always very cost conscious." Like many newlyweds Joe and Helen spend most of their time in the hotel room. Oh, they had plans to play tennis, go snorkeling and parasailing but "other stuff" prevailed. That "other stuff" involved a lot of time in bed. About those scenes Tim Daly said, "They were always uncomfortable. Nothing is less sexy than getting romantic in front of a room filled with strangers. And you're constantly contorting yourself so you're not exposing parts that you don't want to expose. It's never great."

Meanwhile, Antonio is a wreck. Ever since the wedding he's been on a bender. He took up smoking, he's not shaving, and he was arrested for peeing off the Nantucket lighthouse. No one knew what became of Antonio but they all took bets, and getting arrested for peeing off the lighthouse was Lowell's choice (although he doesn't appear in this episode) and he won the kitty. Brian is at wit's end because the entire business is on his shoulders – Joe is on his honeymoon, Fay and Lowell are both on vacation. Brian hasn't slept in 28 hours. There is not a lot of joy in the terminal, except maybe for Roy who just sits back, watches and laughs.

Antonio thinks he's totally blown any chance of dating Casey, but then out of the blue she asks him to help her move into Brian's place before Helen and Joe come back from their honeymoon. She offers to buy him lunch the next day as a thank you. Brian then shows up just after Antonio leaves with the rest of Joe's belongings. Because Casey and Brian can't keep their hands off one another they immediately get intimate in Helen's home, undress in the living room, and Casey's bra unknowingly lands on the fireplace screen and starts a blaze that levels Helen's home. Oh, what a welcome home this will be for the newlyweds. This is even worse than when Brian had to tell Lowell he sank his houseboat. This careless act involves family - his brother and new sister-in-law. Even after all of this occurs and all the yelling and finger pointing between them continues, Brian and Casey still have an uncontrollable and unquenchable sexual attraction. Joe and Helen return full of glee from their honeymoon, but it will be short-lived. Brian and Casey try to tell them at the terminal, but they simply can't do it. Later that day Joe and Helen are devastated when they find out their house has been leveled, but they still don't know that Brian and Casey were to blame until Casey lets the cat out of the bag. Helen is heavily sedated clutching the only item she was able to salvage – a charred fern in a flowerpot. About this scene, Tim Daly shared, "One of my favorite scenes. Brian and Casey have burned my house down and I start laughing hysterically. Once I stop laughing I tell Brian I no longer want him in my life. It's not a funny scene by an account but it's so well written." Joe says he will buy Brian out of his share of the house and the business. Joe has a wife now and someday will have kids. Having Brian around is too risky. They're done. Part One ends with the credits rolling over the traditional Schubert theme.

"Burning Down the House Part Two" (Season 7 Episode 2) Aired September 26, 1995

Written by Howard Gewirtz
Directed by Jeff Melman

The episode begins with a recap of Part One. Brian and Casey are trying to salvage something, anything from the charred remains of Helen's house. Brian finds the unscathed suitcase his dad left the Hackett Brothers in the series' debut episode ("Legacy") in 1990. It has a picture of Brian and Joe as boys – a photo that reunited them after six years of estrangement. Brian hopes it might work its magic yet again. In the meantime Brian is staying at Roy's place and not loving it. Helen seems to be adjusting well, even making jokes at her lunch counter – that is until she sees a man smoking and turns the fire extinguisher on him. When Casey enters the building we discover that Helen is wearing one of Casey's expensive designer dresses because all of her own clothing was lost in the fire. Helen chooses that day to refill the ketchup bottles, making sure to wear most of the condiment on Casey's irreplaceable Valentino frock.

In other action Joe has hired Al Skoog (Stephen Wesley Bridgewater), a lawyer with a really bad combover to be his mouthpiece in the dissolution of the Sandpiper partnership with Brian. This time the photo in the suitcase is ineffective – Joe really meant it when he said that he wanted Brian out of his life. In fact he's already replaced Brian with a new pilot named Scott Summers (Peter McDonald). Fay returns from a vacation cruise to Iceland just in time to meet Scott the pilot. Fay mentions a man named Lyle whom she met on the cruise and he appears in a later episode titled "Bye George." Well, just as Brian is about to leave the island for good, Joe's conscience makes him see a vision of his loony dad Donald (Don Murray) and guilt leads to a change of heart. The episode ends with Joe saying, "Don't go" to Brian.

About stunts, such as the scenes involving the house being burned down, editor Darryl Bates shared, "Almost anything like that, be it stunts or fires or animals, even significant wardrobe issues, is almost always shot the day before. It's just easier than taking the risk of boring an audience when things bog down, which they inevitably do on more complicated scenes. Once in a while, if it's feasible, they will shoot the entire thing the day before and then run it again live for the audience to get their live reaction (which can be priceless). If the live take of the bit doesn't go as planned, they know that they have the prior day's shooting as a backup, and they don't have to spend any more time in front of the audience while getting it to work. I would say that we pre-shot a little something the day before on most of our episodes." The credits roll over the traditional Schubert theme.

"Death Becomes Him" (Season 7 Episode 3) Aired October 10, 1995

Written by Mark Reisman and Ian Gurvitz
Directed by Leonard R. Garner, Jr.

The title is a play on *Death Becomes Her*, a popular Meryl Streep/Goldie Hawn film. The episode begins with Eleanor Kingsbury (Marian Seldes) cutting in line for a Sandpiper Air ticket. She's one of the richest women on the island and wants to charter a flight to bring her late father's body back from Miami. When Fay nervously leads Kingsbury into Joe's office both Joe and Brian are hanging upside down. The bar from which they're hanging is something they bought after seeing an informercial on TV hosted by Harvey Korman. It's the second time we see Brian in this position (the first being the early episode titled "Hell Hath No Fury like a Policewoman Scorned"). Kingsbury needs them to leave for Miami immediately, but they already have scheduled flights that day. However, when they see the generous amount on the check she gives them for their services, all other Sandpiper flights are axed for the day.

While fetching Harrison Kingsbury's body the boys party a bit too much in Miami (Eleanor paid for their overnight accommodations). Trouble ensues when in the middle of the return flight the boys notice that they've picked up the wrong body. In fact, it's a woman named Pearl Nadelman. Kingsbury's body ended up in Brooklyn. A quick exchange of the two bodies will remedy the situation, but Brian and Joe have a hard time making Eleanor wait for the swap. There's no way the bodies can be switched in time for the viewing so Joe dresses up as Harrison Kingsbury (makeup, gray whiskers, etc.). Steven Weber said, "My favorite episodes of the show are the crazier ones. This one was so memorable. Having Tim play the old dead guy lying in the open casket was so great." The outtakes with Weber and Daly laughing in this scene are priceless (and available on You Tube). Joe does enjoy it, however, when Harrison's scantily-clad, sexy, grieving young gold-digger widow leans over the coffin. When Eleanor is alone with the casket, she calls the dead guy a horrible little man. She is angry that he left most of his estate to his buxom young bride and then Eleanor admits that she poisoned his cognac, leading to his death. Joe then sits up and alerts the family just as the body swap is about to take place. The credits roll over the traditional Schubert theme.

"The Person Formerly Known as Lowell" (Season 7 Episode 4) Aired October 31, 1995

Written by Mark Reisman
Directed by Jeff Melman

Author Bob Leszczak's souvenir Sandpiper mug – quite different from the mug Lowell brings back from Dollywood in the episode titled "The Person Formerly Known as Lowell."

The episode's title was inspired by the name "The Artist Formerly Known as Prince" and begins with Lowell Mather returning from a vacation in Dollywood with a souvenir cup for Roy. Actually, one might call it souvenir "cups" because it features a pair of very large breasts.

Lowell has been missing from the first three episodes of Season Seven. Actor Thomas Haden Church announced that he wouldn't return to the show for Season Seven and that it wasn't a ploy to get a raise, but few believed him. That is, until a pilot he made for the Fox network titled *Ned and Stacey* sold thus finalizing the Lowell role. Well, almost. Church agreed to come back for one final appearance on *Wings* for the sake of closure and continuity.

Author Bob Leszczak's own Brother P-Touch label maker, purchased as a result of watching the 1995 episode titled "The Person Formerly Known as Lowell" from Season Seven.

Elsewhere, with Helen's house burned to the ground Helen, Joe, Brian and Casey are all living together in Brian and Joe's house and getting on one another's nerves. Joe's solution to the problem – a Brother P-Touch label maker to denote ownership of items such as shavers and toothbrushes. This episode led to the sale of at least one Brother P-Touch (I, your author bought one as a result of watching this episode and I still have it and use it). This label maker will now keep Casey from using Brian's razor and tossing out Joe's weird-looking citrus (tangelos) – everything in the house will get a label. In the meantime Roy needs Lowell to go to Logan Airport to repair one of his planes. Antonio strongarms Roy into letting him go along (he really needs to get off the island for a while and really wants some hot wings). Roy gives in. When Antonio and Lowell return late, Roy is livid until Lowell explains his tardiness. He witnessed a murder in Antonio's favorite hot wing joint. Antonio had gone to the men's room, and Lowell witnessed the slaying while Antonio was away, dealing with the extra hot "gangway sauce" and its side effects. The police showed up and Lowell was taken in for questioning and then picked the murderer out of a lineup. The guy he fingered was a mobster. Things heat up when mob man Bobby Lasko's lawyer (Andrew Robinson) shows up and threatens Lowell. Producer Christopher Vane admitted, "Bobby Lasko was the name of a grammar school classmate of mine."

Two agents of the FBI (Tucker Smallwood as Agent Stark and Danny Goldring as Agent Douglas) show up a short time later urging Lowell to enter the Witness Protection Program and testify against Lasko. If he opts not to testify the Witness Protection is unnecessary. Lowell now has a huge decision to make in his life. He does the right thing as per his conscience and testifies (to keep Lasko from killing again) and leaves Nantucket for parts unknown. Lowell hugs Joe's plane before leaving and tosses Joe his baseball cap to be remembered by. As the credits roll, Brian nails the hat to the wall outside Joe's office, and cleverly Joe uses the label maker to create two strips that say "Lowell's hat. Do not remove." However, behind the scenes Church's departure from *Wings* was considered, and I quote, "The end of an earache."

"Hooker, Line and Sinker" (Season 7 Episode 5) Aired November 7, 1995

Written by Christopher Vane
Directed by Rick Beren

When asked about his favorite episode of *Wings*, producer Christopher Vane said, "Probably 'Hooker, Line and Sinker' because it was the first one I wrote. I absolutely love how Tony reacts when he finds out the woman he's fallen for is a prostitute. He's such a great actor, he made everything work. In fact, if we wrote a bit for Tony that didn't work, we knew it was our fault and we'd rewrite it."

The episode opens with Roy admiring Casey's pencil sketches. In turn, Roy shows her his manuscript for a book to be called *My Big Buddy*. It's a children's book, a semi-autobiographical one and he wants Casey to draw the illustrations for it. At first she says yes, until she reads the entire manuscript which turns really dark in later chapters.

In other action Antonio has a hangdog expression because Edna, the big-faced girl has dumped him. To make him feel better, Joe and Brian take him out for a night at the Club Car. The Hackett Brothers fix Antonio up with a woman at the bar named Heather James (Susan Diol) not realizing she's a call girl and wants $300. Antonio sees her again and starts getting serious enough to ask for her hand in marriage. Luckily the Hackett boys don't have to explain the situation, she does the job very effectively and lets Antonio down gently. However the brief romance has given new

PARAMOUNT **MULTI - CAMERA FILM** **TELEVISION CALL SHEET**				

Production No.: 40340-128 W.A. No.: B6574 — Date: TUESDAY SEPTEMBER 26, 1995

Production Name: WINGS — Day 4 Of 4 Days

Producer: ROBIN CHAMBERLIN — Crew Call: 930A/1030A/11:18A/1130A

Executive Producer: ANGELL/CASEY/LEE/GEWIRTZ/REISMAN — Shooting Call: 7 Pm

Director: RICK BEREN — Rehearsal: CAMERA BLOCKING

Episode: HOOKER LINE AND SINKER — Location: STAGE 19

SCHEDULE

SET	SCENES	TIME	CAST	D/N	PAGES	LOCATION
CAMERA BLOCK-REH	B-C-L-N-A-J- E-H-TBK-D-K-P	1130-230				STAGE 19 X3919
SAFETY MEET						
CAMERA RUN W/NOTES		app 230p				
MU/WARD		5-430p				
AUDIENCE IN		6 P				
LINE THRU		635P				
WARM UP		645P				
INTRO AND SHOOT		7 P				

NOTES — Total pages:

K = Minors under 18

TALENT

CAST AND DAY PLAYERS	ROLE	MAKE-UP/LEAVE	SET CALL	REMARKS
1 TIMOTHY DALY	JOE HACKETT		1130A	STAGE 19
2 STEVEN WEBER	BRIAN HACKETT		1130A	X 3919
3 CRYSTAL BERNARD	HELEN CHAPPEL		1240P	
4 REBECCA SCHULL	FAY EVELYN COCHRAN		115P	
5 DAVID SCHRAMM	ROY BIGGINS		130P	
6 TONY SHALHOUB	ANTONIO SCARPACCI		1130A	
7 AMY YASBECK	CASEY DAVENPORT		130P	
8 SUSAN DIOL	HEATHER		1130A	

ATMOSPHERE AND STANDINS	SPECIAL INSTRUCTIONS
7 SI w/N (KAREN- KIRK- CHERYL- (LARRY- RICHARD- ANGELA (KEITH)	
4 counter persons 1 Baggage man	
1 Lg person 4 waitpersons	
8 Termin/Rest pat w/4 chgs	
15 Termin. w/3 chgs	
20 Rest pat w/2 chgs	
ADVANCE SHOOTING SCHEDULE	

The call sheet for the "Hooker, Line and Sinker" episode filmed in 1995.

confidence to Antonio who says, "I'm back." The episode's director, Rick Beren said of *Wings*, "A real gem of a show and a great and welcoming cast and crew. I directed four episodes and it was so much big fun – a joy each time." The credits roll over the traditional Schubert theme.

"She's Gotta Have It" (Season 7 Episode 6)
Aired November 14, 1995

Written by Ellen Byron and Lissa Kapstrom
Directed by Jeff Melman

About writing for this sitcom, Lissa Kapstrom said, "I shared an office with my writing partner Ellen Byron. This show was unique in that 50-60 percent, sometimes more of what we wrote actually wound up in the episode." The title is inspired by the Spike Lee motion picture (and subsequent TV series) *She's Gotta Have It*. The episode begins with Joe, after the big fire, reprimanding Helen for not keeping copious notes, photos and receipts for all of her belongings. His are in a strongbox able to withstand heat, as one would expect of OCD Joe. Roy suggests a few items from his forged receipt collection for them to present to the insurance company. Things are looking up, however, when the insurance adjuster is an old friend named Phil (Tom Parks). Even with no receipts for Helen's items, the settlement is quite good.

Back at Helen's lunch counter, Antonio is distraught. He has a dead-end job, no money and no romance. He decides to get back with Edna, the big-faced girl. In other action Casey wants more out of her relationship with Brian than just meaningless, frequent and destructive sex. She wants to try "dating." They try it, but it doesn't work out – they're only compatible in bed. They have nothing else in common.

Meanwhile, Helen decides to do some shopping in New York to replace a few items she lost in the fire and goes way overboard. Joe intercepts Helen's visit to a Rock and Roll Memorabilia Auction where she purchases items such as Elton John's silver lame platform shoes. The auctioneer is played by actor Craig Richard Nelson, not to be confused with *Coach* star Craig T. Nelson. About that, Craig Richard Nelson said, "The name I use is my real name. It's also Craig T. Nelson's real name, but I was using it first so he had to change his." About the role Nelson said, "Luckily I didn't have to audition first. Most of the *early* auditions consisted of loud/fast talking. When they got to me I discovered they were seeking a more deadpan delivery. The director, Jeff Melman was very happy with

Actor Craig Richard Nelson who portrayed the deadpan auctioneer with a string of Monkees puns in the episode titled "She's Gotta Have It." (Courtesy of Craig Richard Nelson).

my deadpan approach. I had some great lines in that episode, many of which incorporated the titles of songs by the Monkees." Speaking of the Monkees, Peter Tork is a guest star trying to buy the old Monkee-mobile from the TV series, but he's bidding against Helen who's scooping up everything in sight. Nelson added, "Tork played music for everyone during our breaks. Unlike his frenetic character on the *Monkees* TV show here he's playing a more subdued more real version of himself." When asked about one-time guest shots on established TV shows, Nelson shared, "They can be tough because the rhythms of the regulars are set and you're trying to fit in, treading on their territory. This show was very welcoming, however, and I already knew Tim Daly from having done an episode of a CBS series titled *Almost Grown* with him." Nelson added, "But I did discover that freedom wasn't appreciated. They were seeking a line with the name of a very expensive restaurant for Steven Weber and didn't appreciate my suggestion of 'Café de la Paix through the Nose.'" They wound up using 'Chez Pay up the Wazoo.'" Eventually Joe talks Helen out of blowing the money they need to build a new house and she lets Tork have the Monkee-mobile for $24,000. As Joe is escorting her out of the auction, a Rolling Stones leather jacket from the "Sticky Fingers Tour" goes up for auction and Joe goes running back in with the auction paddle in hand. The episode ends with everyone being startled by Edna, the big-faced girl. We never get to see her, the camera shot is from her perspective, but we see the disturbing reactions as Roy, Helen, Brian, Casey and Fay eye her as the closing credits roll.

"So Long, Frank Lloyd Wrong" (Season 7 Episode 7) Aired November 21, 1995

Written by Howard Gewirtz
Directed by Rick Beren

The episode's title is a takeoff on the name of architect Frank Lloyd Wright and begins with the mechanic replacing Lowell, former Marine Budd Bronski (Brian Haley). Roy and Joe think he is a no-show, but he's already been diligently working in the hangar for hours. He calls everyone "sir," has a crew cut, apologizes often, stands at attention and is very loud. About that, Brian Haley said, "Loud? I don't think he's loud. He's hyper insecure. He's my self-doubt on steroids." About snagging the part of Budd, Haley said, "I did not audition for the show. I was hot at the time and they just offered it to me." About the character, producer Lissa Kapstrom said, "It was a difficult character to write for. It was hard to replace Lowell who was such a great side character. While not critical to the show, Lowell made for some wonderfully funny window dressing." Frequent director Leonard R. Garner, Jr. added, "The man who portrayed Budd was a very fine actor. I always tried to help new people rather than be part of any problems." Co-Executive producer Ian Gurvitz added, "Characters like Lowell are unique. When they work, they work great, and it's usually some combination of the part and the actor. Lowell wasn't just 'the dumb guy.' Everything about him was unique. He was written well, and Tommy delivered on stage. Personally, he had other ambitions, so no one was surprised when he moved on. At that point, you scour the town looking to replace that energy in the ensemble. Sometimes you luck out. Brian had that manic persona. A little crazed. A bit simple. But it always felt like he was just replacing Lowell in the story and maybe we never figured out what to do with him. He did a great job with what we gave him." Budd double and triple checks everything he does as he once had "an incident" in his last job (a loose bolt which led to the downing of a plane in Iowa, with no casualties). He never wants that to happen again, so he overcompensates. Budd's excuse for the incident was caring for his cat, Sergeant Whiskers who couldn't pee. When asked whether he was a "cat person" in real life, Haley said, "I love all God's creatures, great and small, but no I am a dog person. I love doggies and they love me."

Elsewhere Casey is excited to see a world-famous architect named Y. M. Berg (Edward Hermann) in the terminal. While he's on the island, Joe and Helen ask him to design their new home. Actually, Berg overhears them discussing buying a house from a kit while at Helen's lunch counter and offers to design their new place but Joe and Helen are initially unaware of his credentials. The results are less than satisfactory as the plans Berg draws up are of a house shaped like a number seven. At first Joe is willing to go along with the weird abode, but Helen has her heart set on a traditional "Cape Cod" design with a picket fence. Helen bravely enters Berg's office alone to say she didn't like the seven. Well neither did the Nantucket Architecture Board - the plans were not approved, so Berg has new plans for a more traditional home that Helen loves, but Joe feels the need to confront Berg himself and storms into his office without knowing of the new, more traditional blueprints. Berg is very offended by Joe's insults and the deal is nullified. It looks as though it's back to a pre-fab house for the Hacketts.

The credits roll over Antonio trying to fill the void in his life since Lowell left, and he attempts to make Thanksgiving plans (and many more) with Budd. It's interesting to note that Amy Yasbeck's sister named Patricia Yasbeck is an uncredited extra in this and two Christmas episodes.

"When a Man Loves a Donut" (Season 7 Episode 8) Aired November 28, 1995

Written by Jeffrey Richman and Joyce Gittlin
Directed by Leonard R. Garner, Jr.

The title is a takeoff on the number one Percy Sledge and Michael Bolton song "When a Man Loves a Woman." The episode begins with Brian watching the Three Stooges on a TV in Joe's office.

Casey wanders in, obviously not a Stooges fan (proving once again that the only thing those two have in common is sex).

In the terminal, Joe and Helen begin providing picnic baskets as in-flight meals. Also Brian and Joe have plans to go to the Mud Bowl but Helen nips that in the bud with plans for Joe and her to spend the weekend with a wonderful couple of locksmiths, Wayne and Lois, whom they met on their honeymoon. This news upsets Brian considerably. Speaking of Brian, everyone is starting to notice that he's putting on weight and eating everything in sight, including stacks of pizzas and shakes delivered discreetly by Budd. Helen, who knows about weight issues urges him to attend Eat-a-holics. She goes with him to a meeting for moral support. Brian gets up in front of the group and pretty well sums up why he's overeating. It seems that since Joe got married, the Hackett Brothers don't do all the fun things together they used to do, and he's compensating for that void with food. Joe and Brian talk things out and Brian realizes his life isn't all that bad and that Joe is still there for him. However, when Joe realizes that he will be with "just Helen" every single day for the rest of his life while Brian tomcats around with a vast array of women, *he* becomes an Eat-a-holic, too.

In other goings on, Antonio splurged on very expensive leather shoes that hurt his feet (they just don't fit properly but he insists on continually wearing them thinking they will stretch), and Casey shows up at a job interview while the interviewer is watching the Three Stooges on a small TV in his office (the same exact brand and model of TV I, your author once owned). Mr. Douglas (Gregg Burger) is a huge fan of the Stooges, and what Casey learned from Brian about the comedy trio comes in quite handy for the interview. As the credits roll, Casey is offered the job, and when asked if she will be there Monday at 8 sharp she says, "Soitenly."

"The Big Sleep" (Season 7 Episode 9) Aired December 12, 1995

Written by Michael Sardo
Directed by Jeff Melman

The episode opens with Antonio listening to self-improvement tapes. They cost him $495 and afterwards Antonio insists he's a

Casey Chappel's verbose Nantucket tourism slogan. (Courtesy of Suzanne Holmes/The Wings *Yearbook)*

changed man. Casey has news as well. She is the new Assistant Director of Tourism for Nantucket Island. Her first duty was coming up with the not-so-catchy slogan, "Welcome to Nantucket. Approximately 56 square miles of smiles, which you'll enjoy especially in summer."

Meanwhile Joe and Helen are very excited – the plans are ready for their new home, designed for them by the day manager of a local Baskin Robbins. Helen loves the walk-in closet in the blueprint, but Joe wants to eliminate it to have room for a 60-inch TV. An argument ensues. Joe gets very little sleep as a result, but with what little sleep he does get he has a bizarre dream. Most of the dream is sexual in nature, but it ends with Joe dying in a plane crash. After hearing about the death dream Brian won't let Joe fly, but Joe insists he has to. Brian gets especially panicky when each element of Joe's dream comes to fruition including the appearance of a clown, then a group of Tigers, Antonio forcing his way onto the plane, Budd's crush on Joe, and Roy undressing/doing a belly dance in the terminal. Joe starts believing their flight to finalize the blueprint for the house is indeed jinxed and tries to talk Helen out of it, but to no avail. Sure enough, during the flight there is engine trouble. All of that however was a dream within a dream within a dream. The credits roll over Brian and Joe discussing the dream. In other action, in the background Roy's belly dance in the terminal happens for real this time.

"'Twas the Heist before Christmas" (Season 7 Episode 10) Aired December 19, 1995

Written by Ellen Byron and Lissa Kapstrom
Directed by Jeff Melman

This is the show's fifth of six Christmas episodes. It opens with Antonio at Helen's lunch counter noticing that Carlton Blanchard's nephew, Lewis (Gilbert Gottfried) has entered the terminal. His frail uncle could die with the slightest exertion, so Lewis bought him a home gym for a present.

Meanwhile Joe and Helen have a free cabin in Vermont for the weekend because Joe's friend broke his leg in three places and can't use it. There is one snag, however – Helen's Christmas party is that same night. The party is very important to her - she wants their house to be known as "the Christmas House." She and Joe compromise. They'll have the party and then zoom up to Vermont to take advantage of the free lodging and skiing. Fay has other plans, but Antonio comes to the party with a nice gift for Joe and Helen - a music box that plays "Isn't It Romantic?" He is crestfallen when he finds out they didn't get him anything. Because Brian said he was coming to the party with a date named Erica (Suanne Braun), Casey scrambles to find one and as a last resort invites Lewis Blanchard to the holiday party as her date. About that scene, Gottfried shared, "Tim Daly's character calls me a homunculus in the party scene. Homunculus. I had to look it up." About Amy Yasbeck Gottfried added, "I got to work with her again and with her husband John Ritter in both of the *Problem Child* movies. There's a story I've heard about Amy and John riding in a car while having a big argument about which one of them worked with me more. I don't know why that was so important, but it was to them for some reason." Amy was also a guest in 2020 on *Gilbert Gottfried's Amazing Colossal Podcast* on iTunes and Sirius XM (as was Steven Weber). Speaking of Weber, Gottfried said, "He considered me the crazy uncle who was always dropping by. My first day on set I was wearing shorts, a tee shirt and sunglasses and Weber made fun of my New York attire, but that didn't stop me from wearing it the next day."

Brian's date has the worst breath on the planet (prior to this she and Brian had only spoken at her drive-thru window at the bank). Her halitosis is a running joke that keeps on giving. Budd shows up, reluctantly because he feels like he is a crashing bore at parties. In a funny solo scene he bolsters his confidence in front of the bedroom mirror. About the episode Brian Haley recalled, "Working with Gilbert Gottfried is always a treat. He's one of my favorite comedians and a really great guy. I worked with him again on *The Weird Al Show*. It's always nice to work with a fellow stand up."

Joe can't wait to get rid of all of his guests so as to begin his weekend of skiing, but he hears on a weather report that the storm may close all airports. Just as everyone is about to leave they all notice things are missing from their coats. While they were all listening to the carolers at the door, someone was robbing them blind. They were all in the bedroom at one time or another and a Rashomon recollection confirms that, but who stole all of their money and traveler's cheques? The carolers did it. They were running a scam in the neighborhood. While everyone was listening to their singing at the door, one of their cohorts shimmied up the side of the house to the bedroom, broke in and purloined their wallets. There is a happy ending as everyone gets their possessions back. Gottfried remembered one memorable outtake – "As I exit one of the scenes, Tim Daly is supposed to say, 'Goodbye, Lewis,' but he inadvertently said, 'Goodbye, Gilbert.' We had to do another take. I got to work with him again on *Superman: The Animated Series* when I voiced Mr. Mxzyptik. *Wings* was a very fun and welcoming group of people." Gottfried described his character as, "My typical obnoxious self. And how appropriate that Carlton and I had really annoying voices on the show. It proves we were related."

The credits roll over the traditional Schubert theme.

"Honey, We Broke the Kid" (Season 7 Episode 11) Aired January 2, 1996

Written by Lori Kirkland
Directed by Jeff Melman

Tall TV star Clint Carmichael portrayed Austin Houston, P. I. *in this episode titled "Honey, We Broke the Kid." (Courtesy of Clint Carmichael).*

This is the first episode aired in 1996. The title is obviously inspired by the film *Honey, I Shrunk the Kids.* This chapter opens with Helen in Joe's office asking if it would be OK to babysit for friends Bob (Robert Curtis Brown) and Linda's (Carolyn Pemberton) daughter Emily (Chelsea Lynn) over the weekend. Joe is hesitant because they know so little about taking care of children. But then Joe remembers that he practically raised Brian, so he does have some training under his belt. When Emily is dropped off Joe and Helen realize they really are asea in handling children. While trying to feed her all healthy foods they gave her a bigtime tummy ache.

In other action Casey is gleeful about getting a celebrity named Deke Hathaway (Clint Carmichael) who plays a character named *Austin Houston, P. I.* on TV to do her Nantucket tourism commercials. About his character, Clint Carmichael said, "It didn't hurt that I had *Magnum, P. I.* credits. This was one of the times being a six foot four, 235-pound actor paid off. It was both flattering and fun to play a comedic take on the macho TV image. The opening scene where Helen goes a bit crazy at Deke's first appearance was so much fun at taping. The audience was on board from the get-go." Antonio is Deke's biggest fan and can't wait to meet him, and Helen has a bigtime crush on him. Brian, however, has heard that Deke is openly gay. Antonio is not aware of this and he and Deke become close buddies. Casey is also not aware of Deke's sexual preference and tries to get his attention, but of course to no avail. Carmichael said, "Amy was a doll. So much fun to work with and just as nice off the set and hanging out. Beautiful, incredibly talented and generous. An absolute sweetheart." About Tony Shalhoub Carmichael said, "He is as nice as they come – humble, warm and charming. We had great fun with our characters on this one. Gay characters in 1996 weren't exactly groundbreaking but it was still something that was dealt with cautiously. As an example, in the original draft of the script at our table read, Deke kisses Antonio on the mouth. Tony and I both wondered if that would make it to the taping as we thought it'd bring down the house, but on tape day it became a kiss on the nose. And it still got a huge reaction, owing in no small part to Tony's reaction before he says, 'You Hollywood people.' We did two takes as I recall and the first had a massive reaction. Just before we did the first take Tony warned me about holding for the laugh. He knew it could be huge. I was grateful for the tip as it seemed I had to hold forever for the laughs to die down enough to continue." Carmichael added, "Playing Deke wasn't uncomfortable. It felt kinda cool taking a little risk. Boy did things change quickly as just two years later it seemed every show had a similar storyline or were creating series regular roles for gay characters. I also had a small role as a gay character in a groundbreaking Showtime series called *Brothers*. It was important because it was one of the first TV episodes to deal with AIDS." Did Carmichael get to work with any of the cast and crew again? "Yes, I had the pleasure of working with Amy again in a show called *Alright Already* which starred the very funny Carol Leifer, I used to cross paths with Robert Curtis Brown who portrayed Bob in this episode and still do on occasion at auditions. Robert's a great guy and an always working actor who went on to play Ashley Tisdale's dad in *High School Musical*. I'd also previously worked with director Jeff Melman on *My Two Dads*. Jeff has a very prolific TV directing career and was a sure hand at the helm." The credits roll over the traditional Schubert theme.

"B. S. I Love You" (Season 7 Episode 12) Aired January 9, 1996

Written by Christopher Vane
Directed by Leonard R. Garner, Jr.

A Wings *envelope that just might have contained a chain letter from Roy Biggins in the episode titled "B. S. I Love You." (Courtesy of Suzanne Holmes).*

The episode opens with Antonio and Fay receiving a chain letter in the mail from Roy. Fay sends the letter to 20 other people but Antonio tears his copy up. Bad luck instantly follows him as his cab gets hit by a truck driver in the airport parking lot and then somehow ends up in the ocean (it will take a month for repairs). Actor/comedian Gregory Behrendt played the truck driver and shared, "*Wings* was my first TV experience and it was a blast. I did have to audition for the part, but I don't really have any specific memories other than I got it." About the experience on set, Behrendt said, "I screwed up my line on my first take – I reversed the line, but I nailed it on the next take. The director, Lenny Garner was very cool about it. In fact everyone was very nice, especially Steven Weber who made a point of making me feel welcome. Years later I got to be on *The View* with Tim Daly. He didn't remember me, but why would he? He was super nice."

Because of the broken chain letter, Antonio's bad luck continued and he crashed his rental car and injured his nose while trying to avoid hitting a squirrel. He later got chased by a pack of wild dogs and singed off an eyebrow. Conversely Roy has a hot new girlfriend and Fay wins $50 with a scratch-off lottery ticket.

In other action, over at Helen's lunch counter was an elderly man named Jack (Pat Hingle) who claimed to be Joe and Brian's long-lost grandfather. They haven't seen him in almost 30 years. Brian is very demonstrative with his affection for the old man, but Joe is rather hesitant at first, but he eventually comes around. Grandpa Jack has presents for the boys and a bunch of exciting adventure stories, but when Helen and Casey stay up late watching old movies and see one of his stories on the screen verbatim they smell a rat. While looking through old photos, Helen proves that Jack is an imposter. He looks totally different in the photos and has tattoos. When confronted they discover that the imposter's real name is Leonard Stanwyck and he was in the "loony bin" as he calls it with Brian and Joe's dad and learned all about the boys because their dad talked about them constantly. Leonard was released from the facility because he's "much better now" and plans to see the world and have some of those adventures he lied about. The credits roll over the traditional Schubert theme.

"Sons and Lovers" (Season 7 Episode 13) Aired January 16, 1996

Written by Jeffrey Richman and Joyce Gittlin
Directed by Jeff Melman

The episode opens with invitations arriving for Roy's birthday party, much to everyone's dread. He is a Leap Day baby. One adhering to that calendar only has a birthday every four years. Roy likes to think that he is only twelve. Joe equates receiving the invitation with jury duty – you get the notice, you go and wind up surrounded by angry people. The party is held in a place similar to a Chuck E. Cheese and Roy expects gifts for a twelve-year-old, and makes it known that he doesn't want any gifts of clothing or school supplies.

In other action, at Helen's lunch counter (make certain to notice the loaves of bread behind Helen's lunch counter in this episode – the brand is "Weber's White Bread") Antonio is reminding Brian about all the favors he's done for him in the past. *He* needs the favor this time – his license expired and he needs Brian to drive his cab this coming weekend. But Antonio has rules for Brian – no religion talk, no politics. Just respond with "uh huh," "you don't

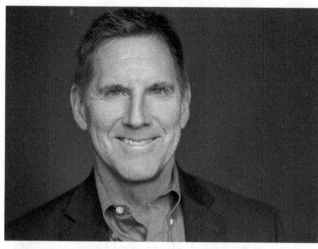

Roy is lukewarm to R. J.'s boyfriend Luke, played by Tim Bagley in "Sons and Lovers." (Courtesy of Tim Bagley).

say," and "sounds great." Brian agrees only because it gets him out of going to Roy's party.

Speaking of Roy's party, someone Roy didn't invite is coming – Roy's gay son, R. J. (Abraham Benrubi). Helen ran into him on a flight and invited him. In the terminal father and son have a strained-but-warm exchange. Things change, however, when R. J. introduces his boyfriend, Luke (Tim Bagley). About the episode Bagley recalled, "My agent didn't want me to take the role. Abraham Benrubi is straight in real life, but I'm gay. I figured who better than a gay man to play this gay character? This was 1996 – a time in our history when it was still risky to one's career to be 'out.' Ellen DeGeneres came out in 1997, and that changed everything for us. A few years later almost every show had gay characters, but television wasn't there yet in 1996. Despite being warned not to, I went for the audition and got the part. I wasn't going to let fear stop me. The script was extremely well written and lent a normalcy to our being a couple. I was very proud to represent. A very sweet moment happened with my fellow actor, Abraham Benrubi in the scene in the back of Antonio's cab. You can't see it on camera but Benrubi held my hand in the scene. It was unexpected and a very sweet gesture that connected us immediately, and it made me feel so proud." Bagley added, "The day after the episode aired I was at the gym taking a shower, and a guy kept looking at me. I was trying to send him the message, 'No pal, it ain't going to be that kind of party,' and finally he walked up to me and asked me if I was on *Wings* the night before. He told me how much he and his girlfriend had enjoyed my performance and the show as a whole. After that I never ever took a shower at the gym again." As R. J. and Luke prepare to leave the island early because of Roy's displeasure about their being a couple, Roy does come around a bit and tries to understand his son and his lifestyle – even getting on the terminal microphone to profess his acceptance.

Did Tim Bagley get to work with any of the cast again after *Wings?* He said, "Yes. I had always obsessed over how good Tony Shalhoub was and I was thrilled I got to be on *Monk*. They were actually looking for someone in his 70s to play his nemesis in one episode. I was the youngest one in the audition but got the part. Tony is truly one of the nicest people in the business, and an amazing actor – it was a joy to be asked back to do several episodes. And I later met Steven Weber at a restaurant and he came over to my table and said, 'Aren't you going to say hello?' I didn't think he'd remember me from my one guest shot on *Wings* and I didn't want to disturb him at his table, but along with Shalhoub he's unbelievable nice. The cast of *Wings* was a nice group of people – a family."

The credits roll over Brian still driving the cab, but now he's suddenly discussing politics, religion and sports. A moment later we see why – Antonio is in the backseat gagged and bound.

"Bye George" (Season 7 Episode 14) Aired January 30, 1996
Written by Jim McCoulf
Directed by Jeff Melman

The episode opens as Helen warns Joe to wear a jacket while outside tossing around a football with Brian, but he refuses – and then comes down with a bad cold, and Brian later comes down with the same ailment. There's a good reason Joe winds up in bed with a cold in this episode, as writer Jim McCoulf explains, "Because of scheduling issues, they needed an episode written in one week. And it had to be done while the staff was on break for Christmas/ New Year. No pressure. Oh—and Tim Daly wouldn't be able to shoot his scenes live. He would be out of town doing a movie with

Whoopi Goldberg so we would have to pre-shoot any scenes he was in and obviously limit his participation. We've all seen the typical clunky way of handling that—a character does several pre-shot scenes where he is telephoning one of the other characters on the show. We all wanted to avoid that. I believe it may have been Howard Gewirtz who came up with the idea of having Joe sick in bed, and other characters having to come upstairs to see him. So that problem was solved. Although there was an audible moan from the studio audience on show night when it was announced that Tim Daly wouldn't be performing live."

In the terminal, Fay is skittish about having invited a man she hardly knows by the name of Lyle Bartlett (Norman Lloyd) a retired maître d' to spend a week with her. They met on a cruise and he was first mentioned in the episode titled "Burnin' Down the House Part Two." At first she asks for Brian's help to get out of the invitation but quickly has a change of heart. The elderly couple hits it off nicely and quickly plans to be married. Everyone thinks it's all happening too fast. About the setup, writer McCoulf elaborates, "The idea of having Fay getting married, but having to call it off to save George/Lyle's life was a little tricky to handle. Rebecca Schull was so sweet and well-liked, we couldn't do anything too mean or horrible to her or the audience would lynch us. But we still wanted to be funny, so it was a fine line that was always difficult for the writing staff. At one time, I believe Dick Van Dyke was being considered for the part of George/Lyle. I don't know if it was ever offered to him. But I have to say, Norman Lloyd did an incredible job. I'm in awe of the man. He's what, 106 now? And living through his *second* pandemic." All goes well until the wedding vows are read and Fay discovers that Lyle's real first name is George (Lyle is his middle name). Having lost three Georges already she doesn't wish to continue with the ceremony. She feels the George curse will claim another victim. She asks Joe for advice. He's still fighting off his cold and still groggy from the antihistamines but when he asks, "Do you love this George enough to buy him a headstone" she says no. She now has her answer. McCoulf added, "It was a terrific show. It was huge fun and the producing/writing staff were great to work with." The credits roll over the traditional Schubert theme.

"The Team Player" (Season 7 Episode 15) Aired February 6, 1996

Written by Howard Gewirtz
Directed by Leonard R. Garner, Jr.

Fred Stoller, who played masochist Mr. Lundy in the "Team Player" episode shares a moment with Tony Shalhoub. (Courtesy of Fred Stoller).

The episode opens with Casey bragging about the 15 percent increase in winter tourism on Nantucket island since she got her job as Assistant Director. One of her tour groups is on its way into the terminal – the I. S. M. – the International Society of Masochists. Nobody wants to be uncomfortable, miserable and bored more than they. The group is headed by a hangdog, deadpan masochist named Mr. Lutz (Fred Stoller) who is having the time of his life being so miserable. The first actor chosen to play Mr. Lutz that week was let go after two days because his SAG union dues were not paid up. Fred Stoller then got the call and said, "I just had three days on that episode. My agent got the call. I think they may have been familiar with my recent guest spot on *Seinfeld* – a fairly substantial role. The agent did send the video of that episode for the producers to review." Many of Stoller's scenes were with Amy Yasbeck, about whom Stoller said, "Was the sweetest. The first thing she said to me was, 'My boyfriend thinks you're wonderful,' and as she walked away, her stand-in told me that the boyfriend was John Ritter." Stoller added, "I did interact off set a lot with Steven Weber, Tony Shalhoub and Amy. They gave me a lot of behind-the-scenes gossip. Weber had just seen me on *Seinfeld*. He loved my part and

Actor David Gianopoulos who portrayed Bruins goalie Danny "Dead End" Connelly in the "Team Player" episode. (Courtesy of David Gianopoulos).

recited the lines back to me. He's a big comedy fan, very humble and self-deprecating. And Tony Shalhoub was the nicest person I have to this day worked with. He'd sit with the extras at lunch, interacted with everyone. At the time, his film *Big Night* was due to come out. I said, 'I'm sure that'll be good for you and you'll go on to big things.' He said, 'Time will tell.' Again, a very humble man. Years later I got called to audition for *Monk* because of his recommendation. It led to a fun week of work and he was just as amazing and kind on that show."

In other action, Joe already has plans with Helen for the evening, but Brian is trying to sway Joe to go with him as he just scored two center ice tickets to the Bruins/Rangers game. He got them from one of the masochists who really wanted to go badly, but being a masochist surrendered them. Oh, but with Fay away today, who will watch the counter if they go? Antonio steps in and he's really excited about the opportunity (he even practiced at home in case such an opportunity ever came about). One of the passengers arrives late but Antonio has already given that guy's seat to a standby passenger. However, the tardy passenger being bumped from the flight is the goalie for the Bruins, Danny "Dead End" Connelly (David Gianopoulos). About his character, Gianopoulos said, "Danny was an intimidating guy, used to getting the puck he wanted and the stick he wanted. He was the star of that team. Much like a Tom Brady wanting less air in the footballs used." After missing the game and a 10-0 loss

"Team Player" guest star Jay Leno with author Bob Leszczak on the set of The Tonight Show.

as a result, Connelly holds a press conference and mentions Sandpiper and Antonio in his tirade. As an angry mob surrounds the airport. Antonio begins disguising as a woman to keep from being recognized and beaten up. About that, Gianopoulos said, "Tony Shalhoub in heels was a brilliant comedic moment. So funny." The mob even follows Helen and Joe to their home. While they are in bed watching late night TV, Jay Leno on *The Tonight Show* (making a cameo appearance) tells a Sandpiper Air joke. Casey sees all this as a golden opportunity saying there is no such thing as bad publicity. She wants Connelly to come back to Nantucket to get an apology from Sandpiper and Antonio at a press conference. Reluctantly Antonio goes through with the apology, but Connelly is so insulting and arrogant, Joe and Brian step in and kick him out of the building. Gianopoulos shared, "Those insults I hurled at Antonio at that press conference were all scripted – Antonio Sockpuppet, Antonio Scarpukey and Antwerpio. I've worked on many sitcoms, but this experience was truly memorable. The cast was amazing. I had to run fast and jump on their merry-go-round that week to keep up." To keep from being recognized and then mobbed Antonio, Brian and Joe disguise themselves in Hasidic Jewish attire. About that scene, Fred Stoller said, "It was a HUGE crowd pleaser." However, Antonio was seemingly off the hook when Danny Connelly accepted an offer to play for the Rangers. Now *he* was the enemy of Bostonians as announced by sportscaster Fred Roggin, and Connelly then gets pelted with oranges. About that scene Gianopoulos remembered, "That was done in about five minutes outside the studio door. Luckily the oranges hurled at me missed my head. What a fun scene." He added, "Years later, at a newsstand in Larchmont Village, California a young 15-year-old kid started yelling, 'Hey, Danny Connelly!' I'd forgotten that was the name of my character on *Wings*. He remembered me from the episode and started reciting dialogue from it, saying it was his favorite episode."

The credits roll over Roy describing his favorite TV dinners to Mr. Lutz, boring him to tears (and masochist that Lutz is, he loves it).

"Love at First Flight" (Season 7 Episode 16) Aired February 13, 1996

Written by Michael Sardo
Directed by Darryl Bates

Writer's Assistant Wendy Allen-Belleville is dipped and twirled for her Valentine's Day birthday by the affable David Schramm between takes. (Courtesy of Wendy Allen-Belleville).

Director Darryl Bates recalls, "This *was* my first ever episode as a director. I'll always be grateful to David [Angell], Peter [Casey] and David [Lee] for giving me that chance. And it was incredibly scary. As it should be. There's a lot of responsibility there and a lot of money on the line. However, three things helped. One, the cast had a tradition of taking it easy on first-time directors, especially one of their own. They give you a special slate with your name on it to take home, and during the week they are very generous in tolerating your lack of experience and your mistakes. I can't overstate that. Secondly, because I was homegrown, I had the tolerance and support of all the writers and producers, who genuinely wanted me to succeed. Being an insider had other advantages. I knew that I could edit the episodes that I'd directed, so I had the chance to save myself from many of the myriad of mistakes that I'd made. Also as an insider, I'd been able to spend years watching Andy Ackerman direct our show. I watched him solve many a stage challenge, and I knew intimately how he liked to film our set. That gave me an advantage when it came to directing my episodes. Thirdly, I was very lucky to have as my guest star Ally Walker, who's as good an actor as you'll find, and was an absolute joy to work with. A difficult actor could have crucified me, and she was the polar opposite of that. I'll be forever grateful."

On screen Roy tells Antonio that he ran into his old flame, Edna the big-faced girl. Roy is thinking of asking her out, and requests Antonio's permission. Meanwhile, Antonio will be going to dinner with Budd at Lexington's, but Roy dating Edna doesn't really sit well with him. Antonio has second thoughts about the situation and eventually Roy gives her back.

In other happenings, Helen wants to know what Joe has planned for their first Valentine's Day as a married couple, but he's keeping it a secret until the last minute. However, he does give in and divulges his plans early. He will be going to New York with Helen for dinner, a Broadway show and a stay at a nice hotel. Brian calls Valentine's Day the stupidest holiday manufactured by florists and greeting card companies (because he doesn't have a date). Casey has drawn many wine lovers to the island for Valentine's Day, helping the area rake in some off-season bucks. While Joe and Helen await Brian's return, Brian and his passenger Melissa Williams played by Ally Walker (along with the large bottle of Nebuchadnezzar wine in tow for the wine lovers, aka oenophiles), Brian and Melissa really hit it off while in flight. They make out on the plane and Brian asks her to dinner, but he discovers too late that she's getting married in a few hours. She has cold feet and her intended, David Barnes (Matthew Porretta) is at Helen's lunch counter back at the terminal. Melissa almost throws away ten years with David after being with Brian for just an hour, but wisely she goes ahead with the wedding. The credits roll over the traditional Schubert theme.

"Lynch Party" (Season 7 Episode 17) Aired February 20, 1996
Written by Ian Gurvitz and Mark Reisman
Directed by Jeff Melman

Who are these people? The answer is blowing in the wind. Clockwise Crystal Bernard, Tim Daly, Steven Weber, Amy Yasbeck.

Joe returns from a flight and has forgotten to pick up Helen's monogrammed towels while in Boston. It's a slow day at the lunch counter so Joe and Helen plan a "matinee" in Joe's office. That is, until Casey enters with a newspaper article about Helen's ex-fiance - financier Davis Lynch (Mark Harelik). About Harelik, co-writer Ian Gurvitz said, "We did a big search for Helen's love interest. Read a lot of actors. Maybe even went after some names. I remember we met with a guy named John Fugelsang, a comic. He now has a big political show on Sirius. I did an episode of that show promoting one of my books a few years back. Harelik was a solid actor. Very professional. And he always wore two different color socks." It seems Davis was in Rangoon for 16 months under house arrest and just got released. He had been there on emergency business before things went awry. He's now on his way to Nantucket probably expecting to marry Helen. She never got to tell him that she married Joe. While dealing with Davis, Helen attempts to get Joe temporarily out of the way by getting him to fly back to Boston to get her monogrammed towels. This will buy her some time to iron things out with Davis because she neverrrrr. She neverrrrr. She neverrrr told him about her wedding. However, during the coup in Rangoon Davis fell in love with someone else – a woman named Caroline who risked her life to get him released from captivity. Davis (Dear Davis) wants the ring back (a family heirloom) but it is stuck on Helen's finger (but removed thanks to a dab of Roy's hair oil). Conveniently Helen invents a syndrome called Faulkner's that causes fainting (a syndrome she also feigned on the night Davis gave her the ring), and it gets her out of a jam (and out of explaining things) when Joe returns from Boston early because the towels weren't ready, and he comes face to face with Davis in the terminal. The credits roll over the traditional Schubert theme.

"One Flew over the Cooper's Nest" (Season 7 Episode 18) Aired February 27, 1996

Written by Ellen Byron and Lissa Kapstrom
Directed by Jeff Melman

An unredeemed Wings *meal ticket. Helen suggests you stay away from the tuna fish. (Courtesy of Jack E. Herman).*

Inspired by the Jack Nicholson movie titled *One Flew over the Cuckoo's Nest,* this episode begins with Helen running up to the counter to get Roy, Antonio, Casey and Fay to quickly stop eating their tuna sandwiches. It seems the board of health has called to let her know that the last shipment of tuna may have been contaminated. Symptoms, if any, will arise within 72 hours. With the possibility of death looming, Antonio and Roy share truths about the way they've tricked one another over the years (things they later regret telling). They aren't the only ones in a panic – Joe has sighted Sandy Cooper (Valerie Mahaffey) on the tarmac coming towards the terminal. Joe thinks she's there for him, but she's actually there for Brian – they're dating! Joe's attempt to trap Sandy into having one of her psycho moments within earshot of Helen backfires and he looks like a total buffoon. Executive Producer Howard Gewirtz said, "We did three episodes with that wonderful actress Valerie Mahaffey. She played a bright, sophisticated woman whom Joe claimed was psycho for him and everyone thinks he's just full of himself. That psycho scene in the first episode is pretty golden as she recreated a scary prom with Joe locked in her basement. We actually did the same stunt the next year and got away with it but first had to write it so that the audience actually believed that she had gotten help and was truly sorry. Then of course she goes psycho again with a mock marriage to Joe. We pulled it off, but when we tried it a third time we didn't get away with it." Writer Rick Copp who had penned the first two Sandy Cooper episodes with writing partner David A. Goodman said about the third one, "David and I were at Universal developing a *Knight Rider* series and couldn't do that third Sandy Cooper episode which was about a baby. I saw it, though when it aired." After Joe has a meltdown in front of Sandy, Helen goes along with him to see a psychologist, Dr. Grayson (Robert Joy) – the son of the other Dr. Grayson whom Brian saw after the breakup with Alex. Grayson puts Joe on a prescription that makes him act much goofier than normal. When Joe goes in for his next appointment with Dr. Grayson, only Sandy is there. This time a teddy bear is the counselor and we find that she and her Joey Bear are having a baby. Sandy fakes giving birth to a stuffed bear on Grayson's couch and leaves the office just in the nick of time as Grayson enters having missed all of the wacky goings on. Once again – no witnesses. And as she departs she once again calls him Joey Bear and says next year she's bringing mother (but that threat is never realized – it's Sandy Cooper's final visit). The credits roll over the good news that no one is in danger from the contaminated tuna fish – it was a different batch.

"Driving Mr. DeCarlo" (Season 7 Episode 19) Aired March 12, 1996
Written by Christopher Vane
Directed by Jeff Melman

Inspired by the title of the Jessica Tandy classic *Driving Miss Daisy*, this episode begins with the gang attempting to fight off the boredom of the off season on Nantucket by showing off what David Letterman used to call "Stupid Human Tricks." Casey can turn her tongue upside down, Brian can make his pecs jiggle independently of one another, and Roy can play "Yankee Doodle" by making fart noises with the palms of his hands. When asked, Budd does a trick with a lit cigarette in his closed mouth flipped over onto his tongue without burning himself. About that Brian Haley shared, "It's a simple parlor trick I learned in my 20s. Hint: practice with an unlit cigarette."

Meanwhile Antonio's latest fare is a wealthy, nicely-dressed, middle-aged man named Don DeCarlo (J. J. Johnston). Being of Italian descent, DeCarlo takes an instant shine to Antonio and offers him $500 a day to work for him. DeCarlo is from Sicily and is in the "import/export" business. Everyone, including Antonio thinks DeCarlo is a mobster and that Antonio should get out of working for him immediately. Joe and Brian assist by telling DeCarlo that they've made Antonio a better offer. DeCarlo is no mobster but rather a diamond broker, and without that job Antonio will now be much "broker" and will have to return his $2,500 suits bought with the DeCarlo salary. Writer Christopher Vane shared, "I was raised in a very heavily Italian neighborhood and there was always speculation about who might be 'connected.' Oddly enough, after all these years I'm now friends with a man who, like DeCarlo, is a diamond broker and does indeed carry around equally large amounts of jewels. He's not a mob guy either. I think."

In the terminal, Helen spots her old English teacher Claire Bennett (Jane Carr). Helen is ashamed that she never read *Don Quixote* in Bennett's class and got a D-minus on the final exam. She feels she let down this teacher who saw such promise in Helen. When Claire comes to Helen's house, Claire purposely spills red wine on Helen's silk blouse. She's hawking stain remover, sprays a little on and the stain is soon gone. The same with the snack tray full of snacks intended for Claire – she dumps the contents of the snack tray on the rug and then uses the carpet cleaner she's selling and that stain is now also history. She's a representative for the Real Way company (a takeoff on Amway). The credits roll as a weeping and once again impoverished Antonio is back working in his cab while wearing his expensive suit bought with his DeCarlo salary. His fare is Helen's teacher Claire who proceeds to pour a drink on him as soon as she gets in the vehicle, trying to sell more stain remover.

"A Tale of Two Sister Cities" (Season 7 Episode 20) Aired March 26, 1996

Written by Jeffrey Richman
Directed by Leonard R. Garner, Jr.

The title is a play on Charles Dickens' *A Tale of Two Cities* and it was the best of times and it was the worst of times as Clete (Keith Neubert), a handsome and muscular young stud makes Helen's water jug delivery. A jealous Joe tries to show off and takes the two large water jugs from Clete's broad shoulders onto his own, only to drop them causing a large spill in the terminal's kitchen area.

Speaking of kitchen areas, Roy tries to lure Brian into an investment opportunity – Rob's Kabobs. Other talk in the terminal – Casey's job is being terminated. She got her two-week notice from the Tourism Board. But just as her position was about to end Casey's boss calls and says one of her ideas has been picked up after all. Nantucket will now have a "Sister City." The lucky city is Khirinan from which one-third of the world's talcum powder comes. Brian will be Casey's escort to the big Sister City event. Fay attempts to impress those visiting from Khirinan by dressing in their native attire, in purple. Their Prince Restivon (Raye Birk) arrives without his Princess Fala (Jocelyn Seagrave). She arrived separately on a Sandpiper flight a day earlier, and spent the night with her pilot, Brian. Brian was unaware she was a princess and tries to get out of going to the Sister City event that night as a result, but a special request is made by the princess for him to sit next to her at the head table, and her large bodyguard Jaffra (Michael Bailey Smith) won't take no for an answer. About his experience on *Wings* Smith shared, "The audition was the typical process. I went in and read, they put me on tape, and then a few days later my manager called to tell me I got the role. I was pretty excited about getting this gig because it was a top-rated show. My career kind of went in spurts. I would book a lot of movies in a row, then a bunch of TV dramas, then a bunch of commercials, then a bunch of sitcoms. So, that year, I booked *Family Matters*, *The Drew Carey Show*, and then I booked *Wings*. It's always fun to work on a show that you watch. You find yourself on the set and with the series regulars and it's so cool to turn something that you see on TV into reality. The one thing that I noticed that was different from *Wings* compared to other sitcoms is their shooting schedule. Most shows shoot for five days. You block and rehearse the first few days, then do dry runs the next few days, and then on Friday, you do the live show. *Wings* was different. They had their schedule down so well, they only shot for four days. I can't remember if we went from Monday to Thursday or Tuesday to Friday but either way, they had their schedule fine-tuned. I also noticed a difference in the atmosphere on the set of *Wings*. It was fun and relaxed. I think a big reason is because of the two stars, Tim Daly and Steven Weber. They both made the set fun and easy. Plus, it's good when you have a show that has been successful for many years. I also remember the entire cast was very welcoming. I've been on TV shows where the cast was not welcoming at all and that's disappointing and I never understood that. Working with Tim Daly and Steven Weber was really great. Both guys were super nice, fun, and helpful. During the party scene, I remember having some additional dialogue but the director wanted to cut it due to time constraints. When you're co-starring on a sitcom as an actor, every bit of dialogue is like gold and you want to keep it. Tim went to bat for me, trying to convince the director to keep it. We ended up not doing the dialogue but it was really cool to see Tim fight for me. I will never forget that. Playing Jaffra was great. He was a fun character, had a cool accent and I had a goatee with slicked-back hair. It was a cool look. During that time, I worked out at Gold's Gym in Venice Beach and I remember during the filming Tony Shalhoub had asked me where I worked out and if I knew of a good trainer. I said I did and got him introduced. The next thing you know I would see Tony working out at Gold's Gym. That was pretty cool."

At the event Helen tries to distract the prince from seeing the princess flirting with and kissing Brian. In doing so she leads Joe to think the prince is coming on to her. To top it all off Antonio has lost the princess' dogs on the way to the dinner that were his ward. Needless to say Casey loses her job and soon becomes the new water jug delivery person at Helen's lunch counter (Clete's replacement) and Nantucket begins to search for a different Sister City. The credits roll over the traditional Schubert theme.

"What about Larry?" (Season 7 Episode 21) Aired April 9, 1996

Written by Mark Reisman and Michael Sardo
Directed by Jeff Melman

The episode opens with Brian recognizing George Kennedy wearing a Members Only jacket in the terminal and then fawning over him and his role in the *Airport* movies, attempting to get him to do some scenes with him. Unfortunately for Kennedy, his flight is delayed 30 minutes and he must grin and bear it. Kennedy came to Nantucket so that he wouldn't be bothered by fans, but it's just not working out.

At the lunch counter, Helen is excited because the contractor search for the new house is beginning. After meeting with a parade of losers, Larry Mohr (Mark Blum) shows up and the Hacketts are immediately impressed. That is, until Larry has something of a breakdown when his wife kicks him out and he's so depressed he can't work. He stays with Helen and Joe, sleeps on the sofa, and is extremely needy. Joe wants to fire him but Helen feels sorry for the guy. To get him feeling better so he can go back to work Helen throws him a 40th birthday party. The biggest surprise at the birthday party (to which none of Larry's friends showed up) is the arrival of George Kennedy to tell Brian to stop calling him. Joe promises to get Brian off George's back if he'll give an inspirational speech to Larry to get him back to work. Then Cathy (Joanna Daniels), Larry's wife stops by to give Larry some of his things. She says she'll only take him back if they can move to Miami and open a little restaurant and get the hell off Nantucket Island. He agrees and Joe and Helen are back to square one trying to find a contractor. Actor Mark Blum who portrayed Larry Mohr in this episode died on March 26, 2020 of Coronavirus. The credits roll over the traditional Schubert theme.

"The Lady Vanishes" (Season 7 Episode 22) Aired April 23, 1996

Written by Ian Gurvitz and Michael Sardo
Directed by Jeff Melman

Inspired by the Alfred Hitchcock film of same name, the episode titled "The Lady Vanishes" begins with a crowded terminal. A lovely young woman enters and since few seats are available asks Antonio if she may share his table. They instantly hit it off talking about Dylan Thomas only to be interrupted by Joe needing help moving a filing cabinet in his office. An angry Antonio obliges and then returns to the table to find the lady has vanished and in her place is an overweight bald man. Antonio then trashes Joe's

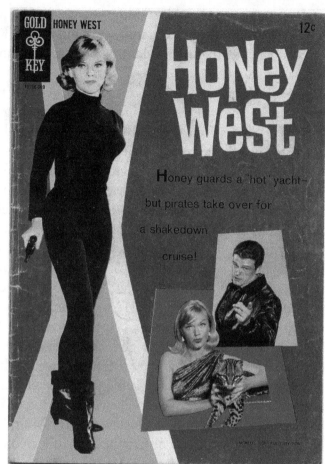

A Honey West *comic book. The star of that show, Anne Francis guest starred as Vera, the tough noir-speaking informant in the episode titled "The Lady Vanishes."*

office…and Joe. Next Antonio pays off Roy for his passenger list so he can hunt down the mystery woman, but to no avail. A desperate Antonio then places an ad in the newspaper but the wrong female answers it – a chatty nasal-sounding woman by the name of Rita (Ellen Ratner). The whole gang then gets involved. Antonio has a caricature of the woman drawn, and also recalls the shoes she wore - shoes only available in Boston. This leads to finding out her name, Ariel Reed (Michelle Nicastro). About Nicastro, the episode's co-writer Ian Gurvitz said, "The real story about that episode was the actress who played the girl who got away. Her name was Michelle Nicastro. She was a great singer who was in *The Swan Princess*. She was married to Steve Stark, who was a development guy at Paramount and went on to run Kelsey Grammer's company. They had two daughters. Beautiful family. Like one of those frame pictures you'd buy. The thing is Michelle got cancer and fought it for years. We all knew Steve during that time. I cast her again on *The Tony Danza Show* and she was great and seemingly in remission. All seemed good. She passed away in 2010, which was sad for everyone who knew her and Steve."

Then a tough, streetwise woman named Vera (Anne Francis), TV's *Honey West* comes in with info about how to find Ariel. Vera has a manner of speaking right out of *Dragnet*. Gurvitz added, "We were stoked to have her on the show and to tap that vein of noir speak." Antonio finally finds Ariel and so do the police. The caricatures he's posted all over town led the cops right to her. Her real name is Gretchen Tyler and she's wanted for embezzlement.

Elsewhere Helen is amazed that Brian can tell so much about a woman just by looking. Just one example – one shoulder of a blouse slightly faded and no jewelry, single mother. He's accurate every time and teaches the skill to Helen. As the credits roll, Antonio is again talking to the whiny woman who mistakenly answered his ad, and this time he's glad to have an escape when Joe asks him for a favor in his office.

"Life Could Be a Dream" (Season 7 Episode 23)
Aired April 30, 1996

Written by Lori Kirkland
Directed by Jeff Melman

The origin of the title of this episode likely comes from the lyrics of the old song "Sh-Boom (Life Could Be a Dream)" by the Chords (as well as the Crew Cuts). The episode opens with Joe the Builder (in a scuffed yellow hardhat). He dug up their time capsule buried years ago with his own items sealed inside, as well as those from Brian, Helen and Casey. The first canister Joe digs up is actually the wrong one. It contains "Jingles," Helen's pet they buried decades earlier. When he gets the correct canister with the burial date of July 15, 1973 on it he finds his own Little League trophy, Casey's pet rock, Helen's Three Musketeers bar, and Brian's *Playboy Magazine* (the "women of James Bond" issue, the only issue Roy needs

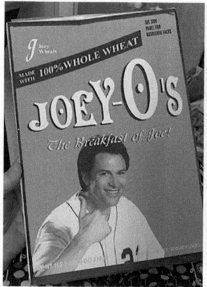

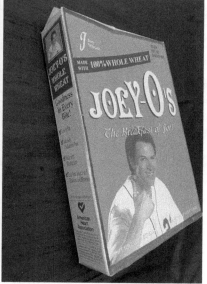

Fortified with eight essential vitamins and iron — Joey O's are a great way to start your day, from the episode titled "Life Could Be a Dream." (Courtesy of Suzanne Holmes).

Even more than Red Bull, Joey O's give you "wings." Side view of the Joey O's box. (Courtesy of Suzanne Holmes).

for his collection). At the bottom of the canister is a pile of letters. Each of them wrote about what they thought they'd be doing in 20 years. Joe envisioned he would be a famous and beloved Boston Red Sox player (number 22) celebrating "Joey Hackett Day," nicknamed "The Hack" with his own "Joey Os" cereal. He would be married to Casey and the island would be renamed "Nanhackett" in his honor. He also put his hand on a man on crutches played by actor Van Epperson and healed him. About that episode, Epperson recalled, "Yes, that was me. I was young in my camera work after many years of live stage work. I was aware that I was working with some of the finest professionals in the business and I had my eyes and ears peeled for everything I could learn from being around them and working with them."

Brian envisioned himself as a secret agent, a la James Bond, fighting off a constant barrage of perps while carrying on a conversation about bowling with Helen and Joe. Casey's vision was to be a super-model with her own line of perfume called "Casey" (with Joe and

Joe and Helen are dressed in bowling shirts in one of the segments of this episode. Cast and crew got souvenir bowling shirts with "On a Wing and a Spare" written on them. (Courtesy of Suzanne Holmes).

Brian as her sassy/flamboyant hair and makeup guys). Helen's dream (or so she says) was becoming the world's all-time greatest rock cellist with millions of adoring fans clamoring to meet her. Helen greatly embellished her letter. She's the only one who actually had her real dream come true because her letter simply stated, "In my future, I, Helen Chappel hope to marry Joe Hackett." It's in this episode that we discover that Helen's surname, Chappel is spelled with two Ps. Her name is on the dressing room door after her rock cello performance and on the letter in the canister. Because of all the costume changes in this episode, parts of it were recorded the night before the audience was present. The credits roll over the traditional Schubert theme.

"The Lyin' King" (Season 7 Episode 24) Aired May 7, 1996

Written by Christopher Vane
Directed by Jeff Melman

A very obvious takeoff on the title of *The Lion King*, this episode begins with Fay composing her own eulogy. She got the idea from a magazine article which stated that if one writes one's own eulogy, one can plan one's life around how one wants to be remembered and thus become a better person. She inspires Antonio to write his (his goal is a lofty one - billionaire married to Claudia Schiffer).

In other action the sexiest girl in high school, Tracy Hayes (Carol Alt) is still as sexy as ever. The writer of the episode, Christopher Vane shared, "Tracy Hayes was named after a real person – the hottest girl at Stamford Catholic High School. It was only appropriate that the lovely character in this episode share the name." When Tracy visits the terminal the Hackett boys attempt to act cool but fail miserably. She's currently a nude dancer who has finally earned enough money to go to law school to fulfill her own dream. She invites the Hackett brothers to see her final nude show in Boston. Joe then needs to concoct a way to make Helen let him go to see her show. As luck would have it Helen is going out to the movies with Casey that night so he's free to fly to Boston with Brian. All goes swimmingly until Casey tries to back out because she's too tired, but Joe embarrasses her into keeping her plans for the evening. Joe makes up a story about spending time at an "old folks' home" (as an excuse for not going to the movies with Helen and Casey). He then feels very guilty for lying and actually spends some time at a local retirement home before heading over the Boston to see Tracy's nude show. While at the home he plays checkers with an elderly man named Lou (Phil Leeds), and then Lou begs Joe to bring him along to Boston. Steven Weber said, "My all-time favorite guest star on the show was Leeds. In the scene he shouted, 'He screwed me, he screwed me blue' and Tim nor I could keep from laughing. He was an old-time comic and character actor and I just loved him." Writer Christopher Vane concurred and said, "Leeds' reaction and stammering on the camera shot through Carol Alt's legs is priceless and hilarious." The outtakes with Leeds, by the way, are on You Tube and are not to be missed. The credits roll with Brian and Lou still at the table in the Shangri-La strip club, discussing the coleslaw at the buffet as Lou berates Brian for looking like a hippie.

"Love Overboard" (Season 7 Episode 25) Aired May 14, 1996

Written by Ellen Byron and Lissa Kapstrom
Directed by Leonard R. Garner, Jr.

The episode begins with the Hackett boys watching Mo Vaughn hit a grand slam for the Boston Red Sox on TV. While watching, Casey sees a guy getting beaned in the bleachers with a foul ball. It's her ex-husband Stuart (John Ritter) who left with every dime she had two years earlier. She strongarms Brian into flying her to Boston so she can clobber Stuart. About Ritter, co-writer Lissa Kapstrom said, "Amy Yasbeck was dating Ritter at the time and she brought him on. He was such a pro and a joy, and he and Amy had such amazing chemistry." Brian and Casey find Stuart and get close enough to grab some of the hair from his hair plugs but he gets away. Casey thinks she'll never see him again, but he surprisingly shows up at Tom Nevers Field. Their reunion is not a friendly one, but he tells Casey he has no money – the corn pad business was now wearing a toe tag. Podiatry has been using laser technology and his product is no longer necessary. Casey decides to give him another chance.

In the terminal Roy suggests that Antonio and he check out a cruise ship docked on the island for the next few days. It promises to be filled with (or, in *Wings*-speak will be "silly with") elderly women, divorcees and widows wanting someone to talk to and someone to dance with. Antonio fears he doesn't know how to dance. He never learned because his father didn't think dancing was macho. Reluctantly Antonio gets late night dancing lessons from Roy at the terminal after everybody leaves. Antonio is very clumsy at first but he comes around quickly. The studio audience goes wild during a long and inspired dance sequence between the two including dips. In fact they later win a blue ribbon on the ship. While on that cruise ship, Antonio spots Stuart's yacht (*The Princess Casey*) and Stuart is in fact still on it enjoying margaritas. Brian and Casey then find the yacht, climb aboard, and see that Stuart has been lying to Casey – he still has a lot of money. After Casey tosses some of his money overboard he comes clean – he wanted a divorce and wanted her to think he was broke so he could keep the yacht. Plus he hasn't paid taxes in five years. An angry Casey then throws him overboard. About that scene director Leonard R. Garner, Jr. said, "Ritter was an incredible physical comedian, so funny. There was a big mat waiting for him over the side when he was pushed off the yacht." Antonio and Roy dance some more as the credits roll.

"Grouses, Houses and Bickering Spouses" (Season 7 Episode 26) Aired May 21, 1996

Written by Jeffrey Richman and Lori Kirkland
Directed by Jeff Melman

Kirby Tepper played Felix, the wonderful, wonderful contractor in the episode titled "Grouses, Houses and Bickering Spouses." (Courtesy of Kirby Tepper).

The episode opens with Joe and Brian waiting to get into the bathroom. The house only has one bathroom for four people and that's why orderly Joe has made up a schedule. The only problem is the girls aren't following the schedule. It seems Casey and Helen swapped times and now Joe has to adjust his schedule board.

At the terminal Antonio is briefly ecstatic over a refund from the government for $1,002. His enthusiasm is short-lived as he breaks a tooth on a piece of candy and has to spend some of the money from that check to get it fixed. Speaking of getting things fixed, Felix the contractor (Kirby Tepper) stops by with bad news for Helen and Joe. Not only is there a sinkhole where the foundation for their new home is being built, but now the special wood is on back order and it'll take a bit longer to build the home. About the audition for the part of Felix, Kirby Tepper said, "The casting director, Jeff Greenberg brought me in to the second or third round of casting, called 'going to producers.' It meant you avoided the first rounds of auditions and were being brought in as one of the casting director's choices. Jeff was a longtime acquaintance who at one time had also been an actor. He also cast me in a *Cheers* episode titled 'Rebecca's Lover, Not.'" When asked to describe his Felix character, Tepper said, "A timid contractor is a great way to describe it. I thought it was a cool way to portray a contractor, rather than writing him as a stereotypical blue collar guy." Behind the scenes Tepper shared, "After the dress rehearsal one of the writers handed me a script change, and it was changing 'that' to 'which' in one of the lines. Those kinds of things are indicative of how TV works and how each writer on a staff of writers has to make sure they have a hand in the script in order to justify their huge salary." Well, the building of Joe and Helen's new house is now on hold, but Joe thinks he has the answer. He finds a wonderful home with a "For Sale" sign in front of it on the way home from the airport. This will solve their bathroom use problems instantly. It's impulsive but Joe and Helen buy it the same day. There's one problem – unloading the old plot of land with the sinkhole is a must to be able to afford the new house. They get lucky and Felix, the wonderful wonderful contractor opts to buy the plot of land. He's always liked that area and he and his wife can build a nice place there. About the cast, Tepper shared, "I can't say enough about them, especially Crystal and Tim. I was, at the time, very close friends with Tim's cousin, so I spent a lot of time with him during the week. Crystal Bernard could not have been kinder and more generous. I didn't have much to do with Tony Shalhoub or Thomas Haden Church but I remember they were both so professional and approachable, though we had no reason to talk much other than when on stage." Finally, with a new house it'll be just be Joe and Helen with no more bathroom schedules. To celebrate, Joe lights up a cigar while still in the old house, and Helen and he get romantic, not realizing the cigar has fallen onto some old newspapers used for packing and – they burn the old house down. The episode was directed by Jeff Melman, about whom Tepper said, "Was supportive and very easy to work with. He had an excellent reputation for being good at what he did." This cliffhanger is resolved in the first episode of Season Eight. The credits roll over the traditional Schubert theme.

SEASON EIGHT

The vast crew for Season Eight. Two trees would have to die to list them all. (Courtesy of David Lee and Peter Casey).

THANKS FOR
FLYING WITH US.

David, Peter and David

A gift receipt for the Wings *Yearbook for cast and crew. (Courtesy of Jack E. Herman).*

This is the final season, of which there were 24 episodes produced. Even though the Series Finale titled "The Final Approach Part One and Part Two" aired seamlessly back to back, they are counted as two separate episodes. Joe and Helen, Brian and Casey all now lived in the new house on the beach (beach people). Joe's hair was noticeably shorter this season. Budd (Brian Haley) was no longer a member of the cast. For the first time, Brian wore mostly short-sleeved shirts and Casey's hair was much less red and had more of a brownish hue. The program now aired on NBC Wednesday nights at 8 PM. Reruns in the summer of 1997 briefly aired on Monday nights at 9:30.

"Porno for Pyros" (Season 8 Episode 1) Aired September 18, 1996

Written by Ian Gurvitz
Directed by Jeff Melman

Extras Talent Coordinator Jack E. Herman and First Assistant Cameraman Echol Marshall in front of Helen's counter, one of the many dollies used on the show, and a Panavision camera. (Courtesy of Jack E. Herman).

This episode title shares a name with an alternative rock band of the 1990s. It opens with a recap of the cliffhanger that ended Season Seven. Joe and Helen have burned Brian's house down in a bizarre accidental reciprocal move for when Brian and Casey burned down Helen's house. Brian's expecting a big fat check to cover the loss, but then the insurance company's Claire Barnett (Roma Maffia) investigates because it's just too coincidental that there have been two Hackett fires because of sexual activity within a year. There are possible arson and fraud charges looming, sending Joe and Helen into panic mode. Also, Antonio immediately develops the "hots" for Claire the investigator. When he drives her to her hotel room, the sexual tension between them flares up and so does a fire when Claire's cigarette burns down the hotel. Yes, another fire caused by sex. Needless to say, after Claire and Antonio have incendiary sex, Brian is promised that he will get his big fat check by the now very sheepish Claire. The credits roll over a scene with Antonio, to whom the Hacketts now owe their lives, playing volleyball outside Joe and Helen's new house, demanding more daiquiris.

"...Like a Neighbor Scorned" (Season 8 Episode 2)
Aired September 25, 1996

Written by Howard Gewirtz
Directed by Jeff Melman

This episode, number 150 begins with Antonio opening a large package containing items left behind from his late Uncle Bernardo. Among the items are numerous scented love letters from G. Lollobrigida. Everyone thinks they're from Gina Lollobrigida but we later discover that the significant other was named Gino Lollobrigida (about which a dejected Antonio says is not as good). Also, Antonio is dating a beautiful woman named Alicia whom he

The 150th episode of Wings *titled "...Like a Neighbor Scorned" is celebrated with a big cake (but no "Big Sandwich"). Left to right Rebecca Schull, David Schramm, Tim Daly, Steven Weber, Crystal Bernard, Amy Yasbeck and Tony Shalhoub.*

We discover in this episode, "… Like a Neighbor Scorned" that Peaches and Herb are one of Joe Hackett's favorite musical acts.

met in his taxicab and the two of them quickly become an item. Antonio kisses her hand as she leaves the terminal. Alicia is played by actress Ana Auther who shared, "What an interesting project. Writing about one of the best shows with the best casts ever sounds like a good idea to me. I had the pleasure of playing an improbable love interest of Antonio's, the great Tony Shalhoub. Thinking back on it all, as a young actress, I was in awe of the talent that surrounded me. Tim Daly, Steven Weber, Amy Yasbeck, Rebecca Schull. I took for granted that every subsequent set I would work on would be like that one. It would not be the case. Not only was the chemistry undeniable, but there was such a cohesive and welcoming spirit on set that made for an easeful working environment. And as the $1.27 residual checks continue to arrive, I still muse fondly about the experience and am reminded that this wonderful show lives on in all corners of the world."

In other action, much to the chagrin of Joe, Helen invites the neighbors Steve and Babs (Chris Elliott and Kelly Coffield) over for dinner. This was a huge mistake as this seemingly charming couple is even loonier than Sandy Cooper. In a reciprocal move, the Hacketts are then invited over their house the next day. Before that occurs, Steve shows up at the terminal in a panic. He needs $5,000 by Tuesday and asks Joe if he can borrow it to pay back gambling debts or risk getting his legs broken. At home, Babs accuses Helen of boinking Steve. After this display, Joe and Helen no longer want to go over to the neighbors' house for dinner and make up a story about going out of town for a dying Aunt Sophie only to then sneak back into their own house. This plan backfires when Steve and Babs burst in brandishing shotguns thinking they're burglars. Joe and Helen try to play nice and Joe gives Steve the money for his gambling debts (trying to keep these neighbors from hell from going off the deep end even more) only to find that Steve and Babs were only renting the house for a month and were leaving the next day. The credits roll over another set of new neighbors knocking at the door and Helen slamming the door in their faces. After pondering the situation, she then opens the door again, grabs the bottle of wine they brought as a gift and slams the door one final time.

"Maybe It's You" (Season 8 Episode 3) Aired October 2, 1996
Written by Mark Reisman
Directed by Leonard R. Garner, Jr.

The episode begins with Antonio telling Helen what he saw yesterday – Fay stealing lipstick at Town Pharmacy. The gang begins to fear she's a kleptomaniac. Elsewhere Brian's last single friend, David Thornton Patrick McCall (Mark Arnold) is getting married – he received an invitation. Joe is upset that he didn't get invited because, after all he was friends with Dave even before Brian. Turns out it slipped under the seat of Dave's car and Dave shows up personally to deliver the invite – immediately after Joe has left a scathing and embarrassing message on Dave's voicemail.

Also, there's a new Brian afoot. New Brian emerges as a result of having no date, and he swears that he will now seek out women who have a kind heart instead of hot bodies. He meets a girl on the plane with whom he connects instantly. Her name is Dani (Jenny McCarthy) and Brian thinks of taking her to the upcoming McCall wedding at which he's an usher. It should be noted that, even though she is nothing like the character portrayed in this episode, the character of Dani was named for a crew member named Dani Morris. On their first dinner date, Dani proves to have frequent and embarrassing manic episodes over little things such as breadsticks and the song "Up Where We Belong." While Brian is seeking stability in his life, she's a temp and loves jumping from job to job. And her nickname for him, "Bry Bry" doesn't sit well. It takes a great amount of intestinal fortitude, but Brian is finally able to break it off with this annoying woman. The credits roll over Fay swearing never to steal anything again, and Antonio entering the scene in an orange jumpsuit picking up trash, hating himself for stealing one pair of tweezers.

Supervising Producer Christopher Vane recalled, "Because of this episode, Jenny McCarthy became a really hot commodity. She was beautiful and funny – a rare combination. All of the networks were clamoring for her. We even had a meeting at Fox for which Peter Roth rolled out a red carpet covered with rose petals, and people were chanting, 'We want Jenny.' Well, Fox didn't get to sign her, NBC did, and numerous writers, directors and crew from *Wings* later worked on the series she did eventually get simply called *Jenny*, but we discovered that she was a much better second banana than a lead, and the show was sadly short-lived."

"Single and Hating it" (Season 8 Episode 4) Aired October 9, 1996
Written by Ellen Byron and Lissa Kapstrom
Directed by Leonard R. Garner, Jr.

The episode opens with Fay and Roy both getting flyers on their windshield for an upcoming singles mingle. Meanwhile in Joe's office, Joe and Helen are making plans for their anniversary – plans that don't include Casey and Brian for a change. Because they now wind up being free that night as a result, Casey and Brian are going to the singles mixer. The only one really excited about the mixer is

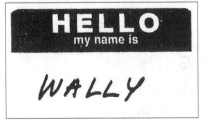

Brian's name tag alias from the episode titled "Single and Hating It." (Courtesy of Suzanne Holmes/The Wings Yearbook).

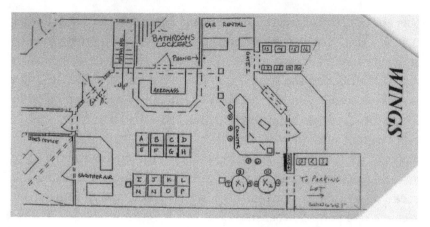

A luggage tag imprinted with a Wings *set blocking map, created by the background actors as a gift. (Courtesy of Jack E. Herman).*

Antonio who thinks he is an elite and important resident of Nantucket because of the invitation. Brian uses the alias of Wally at the mixer and everyone in attendance that night has some huge flaw. Mike (Tony Carlin) makes a weird throat noise after each sentence. A man named Edwin (Brian Drillinger) thinks Casey's a hooker and constantly talks about his vacations with his mother. A tall woman Brian meets (Judy Gold) only discusses cheese. Then Brian meets the female bartender (played by Allison Dunbar – Dunbar being the perfect surname for a bartender, by the way) and she seems almost human but wants nothing to do with him.

Meanwhile, a huge rainstorm causes flooded, washed-out roads and bridges, trapping everyone at the mixer – including Joe and Helen who only stopped by to bring Brian, er, Wally his wallet. It's not the first anniversary celebration they'd wished for but when Joe and Helen pretend to be a couple who met that night and planned to be wed, the nightmarish evening improves. Sitcom veteran Stephanie Faracy plays Carol, the pushy woman running the event. The credits roll over the traditional Schubert theme.

"Too Beautiful for You" (Season 8 Episode 5) Aired October 23, 1996

Written by Lori Kirkland
Directed by Joyce Gittlin

Extras Talent Coordinator Jack E. Herman rushes by Amy Yasbeck, Steven Weber, David Schramm and Rebecca Schull between takes in front of the Cart Blanche lunch wagon in the episode titled "Too Beautiful for You." (Courtesy of Jack E. Herman).

Creative consultant Joyce Gittlin, along with her regular duties of breaking stories and punching up scripts also co-wrote numerous episodes of this sitcom with her former partner Jeff Richman. However, Gittlin added, "There was a lot of encouragement and kindness when one sought advancement. I wanted to direct. Along with my regular work on the show, involving a few days each week I made an offer to observe the floor on the other three days. Not only did they allow me to do this, but I was mentored by Jeff Melman, Lenny Garner, Marcia Gould and David Lee. In fact, Lee invited me to his house to teach me the ins and outs of blocking. It was such a welcoming environment – all of us rowing the same boat together." She added, "I love them all. Their kindness led to great advances in my career. I'm still friends with Peter Casey and his wife Rosie, and Dave Hackel and his wife Sally. I looked forward to going to work each and every day."

The episode opens with the appearance of competition for Helen's lunch counter – a mobile lunch cart called "Carte Blanche" with savory, high quality food. To get her regular customers back, Helen tries a 1950s "doo wop diner" motif with her donning roller skates (on which she's quite proficient). Even Joe has strayed and gone to ordering from the cart. Helen attempts other motifs, too – Japanese and Mexican, to no avail. But they all come running back to Helen when the "cart lady" (K. T. Vogt) moves her business to Boston for more volume.

In other goings on, Antonio is a new volunteer at the suicide hotline. On his first night on the job he helps a woman named Elise (Tracy Scoggins), hits it off with her and gets a date. Everyone at Sandpiper tells him not to go out with this troubled woman – that is, until they see how drop dead gorgeous she is. Antonio dates her and she actually really likes him. When Elise's old beau Eric (Philip Casnoff) comes over to try to win her back Antonio thinks he's about to be dumped, but she sends Eric away instead. They both know it won't last, but for now she's with Antonio and he's living for the moment. The credits roll over the traditional Schubert theme.

"The Gift of Life" (Season 8 Episode 6) Aired October 30, 1996

Written by Michael Sardo
Directed by Leonard R. Garner, Jr.

The episode begins with most of the gang in their Halloween costumes at the airport. Joe is Pinocchio, Fay is the bride of Frankenstein, Roy is a pirate, Casey is a cheerleader, Brian is half man/half woman, and Antonio is a tornado (a costume so unusual that it needed explanation).

Meanwhile, a medical courier named Dave Gardner (Josh Mostel) at Helen's lunch counter says he has "the gift of life" in the cooler he's bringing on the plane. Everyone thinks it's a heart. But when the courier's estranged wife says she wants him back, he backs out of the flight and is so excited he accidentally leaves the cooler behind when he exits the airport. It then becomes Joe and Brian's duty to make the delivery to the hospital in Boston – while still dressed in their costumes. Steven Weber recalled, "I loved these crazier episodes. I loved when Joe and I have to deliver a human

Script supervisor Marcia Gould and Extras Talent Coordinator Jack E. Herman hug as the Cessna watches with envy. (Courtesy of Jack E. Herman).

organ while I was in Halloween drag." They finally find out where the heart is supposed to go, Boston University Medical Center, but someone with an identical cooler in the airport grabbed the wrong one. The heart has traveled instead to a teen Halloween party and time is of the essence to get it back. The absence makes the heart grow fonder. Joe (aka "Old Dude") and Brian find the party and the cooler. They deliver it to the hospital just in time – a United States Senator was waiting for that heart. But what they think is a heart (it says "Nelson's Heart" on the container) is really semen from a prized racehorse named "Nelson's Heart" intended for a mare. The credits roll over the traditional Schubert theme.

"Olive or Twist" (Season 8 Episode 7) Aired November 6, 1996

Written by Jeffrey Richman
Directed by Jeff Melman

The title is a play on Charles Dickens' *Oliver Twist*. The episode begins with Antonio reading an article about an organization known as the Society for Inter Solar System Teamwork (SISST) claiming that aliens will make contact on Nantucket on the 18th of the month. He dismisses it as a bunch of hooey, but Roy and Fay are intrigued by the possibility. The landing is alleged to be at Siasconset Point in three nights.

The Wings *Season Eight Softball Team "strikes" a pose. Back row left to right Stephen Welke - Director of Post Production for Paramount Studios; Michael Waynes - Owner, Executive Mobile Car Care Service; Jackie O'Keefe - Dave Hackel's assistant; Extras Talent Coodinator Jack E. Herman; Peter Holmes - Production Assistant; Darryl Bates – Editor; Christopher Porterfield - Production Supervisor; Ian Gurvitz - Executive Producer. Bottom Row left to right Suzanne Holmes - Associate Producer; Jennifer Carroll - Production Assistant; Ricardo - Paramount Studio Operations. (Courtesy of Jack E. Herman).*

Elsewhere in the terminal, Brian is in a good mood – the insurance check for his burned-down house finally came through. Helen and Joe can't wait to get rid of him so they aid in his search for a house. While searching, Brian finds a vintage diner in which he wants to invest at Casey's behest. Casey talks him into buying it as it will give her a job, too (she's had great difficulty finding work of late). They're going to call it Brian's Martini Bar. Joe and Helen help with the martini menu – the Martini Navratilova, the Idi Amini Martini, and the Itsy Bitsy Teenie Weenie Yellow Polka Dot Martini. The first customer through the door on opening night slips and falls. That's when Brian discovers the place isn't insured. To keep from losing every last dime, Casey and Brian visit the injured man, Albert "Albie" Moorehead (Stuttering John Melendez) to settle out of court. Albie still lives with his very loud and obnoxious mom (the late Diana Bellamy – heard but never seen). Before long the sign that used to say "Brian's" changes to "Albie's." The credits roll over Fay and Roy who, after seeing the aliens land have half a red face, although they vow to tell no one what they did or saw.

"Wingless Part One" (Season 8 Episode 8) Aired November 13, 1996

Written by Christopher Vane
Directed by Darryl Bates

Actor Jonathan Slavin as the overwhelmed Cord Clayton in the three-part episode titled "Wingless." (Courtesy of Jonathan Slavin).

"Wingless" is a three-part episode that used two different directors. Addressing that, Darryl Bates said, "The reality of directing in series television is that much of it is determined by schedule. Unlike me, who directed and edited the same show and was there full time, freelance directors work on lots of different shows during a television season, and have their schedules booked months in advance. Shows usually don't have the luxury of booking directors together with their multi-part episodes. They might, however, book a beloved director for a season-ending episode or a series-ending episode. Secondly, it is really the responsibility of the producers and writers to maintain the tone of the series and the style of those multi-part episodes, both in the actual writing and by overseeing run-throughs during those episodes. Television directors have a hand in this, but it's a smaller role. Finally, if there were any special stylistic touches that I might have made in the first part of a three-parter (in this case, there really weren't), I certainly would have discussed them with Jeff [Melman] before he started directing his episodes."

The episode opens with Helen writing a speech on running a successful business for the upcoming annual Chamber of Commerce Luncheon. Antonio gave a speech there a year ago – "The American Dream, Don't Hold Your Breath." In her speech, Helen also speaks of her husband's thriving business (while he happens to be on the phone pleading with the bank to give him another week to pay up). The plane has been repossessed. Joe needs to find an investor quickly. He finds one named Jonathan Clayton (Mitchell Ryan). Problem is, Clayton's not looking to invest, he's looking to buy the business. It's the only option as Joe has been dipping into savings to keep the company somewhat afloat. So, they sign the papers, get the plane out of hock, and Clayton names his son Cord (Jonathan Slavin) as their new boss. Cord's just out of school. About the role, Slavin said, "Up until that point this was the biggest TV job I had. It was a long audition process. Many heavyweights tried out. I had previously worked on a couple of *Caroline in the City* episodes for NBC and so they were kind of in my corner. My future husband and I were just living together at the time and he was more savvy on the computer. He found a chat room where I found out lots of *Wings* trivia before the audition. Now this was a three-episode arc, but I was booked one episode at a time – just in case they had to make a change along the way. I wasn't committed to all three." About the man who played his father, Mitchell Ryan, Slavin shared, "My real first name is Jonathan and his character's name on the three episodes of the show was Jonathan. Like me, he was mostly a stage actor and kind of a fish out of water in this medium. He was so nice and we had a great time working together. In fact, we got to work together again a while later on *Dharma and Greg* and had a nice reunion" Turns out the kid, Cord is a real screw up. He failed out of six colleges, has a terrible hangover, and has no experience. The episode ends with him reassuring Joe and Brian that he has respect for the eight-year-old company and will not make huge, sweeping changes. But in the same breath wants to change the Sandpiper name. The credits roll over the traditional Schubert theme.

"Wingless Part Two" (Season 8 Episode 9)
Aired November 20, 1996

Written by Ian Gurvitz
Directed by Jeff Melman

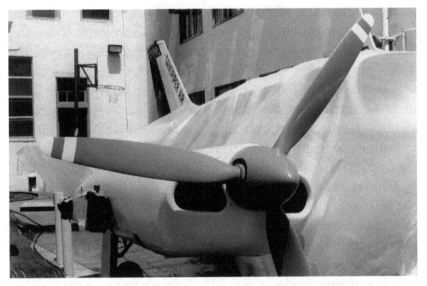

Wingless, indeed. The wings had to be removed to get it through the doors into the Stage 19 hangar. (Courtesy of Suzanne Holmes).

The episode begins with a recap of part one. Then Joe has to cancel a flight because he can't find Cord to sign off on refueling the plane for takeoff. Cord (Jonathan Slavin) strolls into work at 2pm and Joe is furious. Fay, however, kisses up with a muffin basket for the new boss and the promise of a pedicure. About working with the cast, Slavin said, "Tim Daly and Steven Weber were wonderful to work with. In fact, Weber said that my character reminded him of his character when the show was just starting. I didn't get to see much of Tony Shalhoub during that period as he was focused on the film *Big Night* and wasn't around as much but in the short time we were around one another I could see that he was a great guy. Crystal Bernard entertained the crowd during the warmup with her music. She sang and a friend brought a guitar. That was quite a treat. David Schramm was funny and snarky – what a talent. Rebecca Schull has marvelous comic timing and being a stage performer we bonded instantly, and Amy Yasbeck and I have mutual friends. She is a really cool chick. Our paths have crossed several times." Cord says that Sandpiper needs a "Really Big Idea," but he has no idea what that should be. The idea, however, falls right in his lap and he makes Sandpiper an exclusive private charter service. He then leases the plane out as a crop duster, and Sandpiper is also booked for a three-month tour for the musical group, the Todds (Nina and Tammy). About that, guest star Jonathan Slavin as Cord said, "The Todds were an obvious play on the Judds. And the two actresses who portrayed the Todds were so good and so funny." Casey is the flight attendant for this venture. Joe has all of the Todds' albums, and this is a much larger plane than we've seen Joe pilot before. In fact this is the first time Joe and Brian are seen wearing headsets in the cockpit. Unfortunately a short time into the tour Nina (Cynthia Sikes) and Tammy (Karen Kilgariff) Todd have a huge falling out and cancel the tour. Upon hearing about the Todds canceling their tour, Cord gets ready to skip town. Joe follows him to beg him to stay but it's to no avail. Cord boards an Aeromass flight with a connection to London. The credits roll over the traditional Schubert theme. In the credits Mr. Clayton's first name is listed as Jonathan, but in the scene between Roy and Antonio he's called Edgar Clayton for some reason. It should be noted that a boom microphone can be clearly seen for a couple of seconds over Amy Yasbeck's head 15 minutes into the episode in one of her scenes with the Todds on the plane.

"Wingless Part Three" (Season 8 Episode 10) Aired December 11, 1996

Written by Lori Kirkland
Directed by Jeff Melman

The episode begins with a recap of the previous two parts of this three-part arc. Cord is gone but Joe is attempting to hide that information from the elder Mr. Clayton lest he shut down the airline. Brian, Joe and Helen follow Cord to New York and find him in a rest room at the airport but he slips out again. But Cord's conscience gets the better of him and he returns to help Sandpiper.

Getting ready for "the Big Ugly" in the board room in "Wingless Part Three." Seated left to right Steven Weber, Tim Daly, John Ducey and Jonathan Slavin. (Courtesy of John Ducey).

But how does one put a positive spin on having lost $30,000 in the past few weeks on a tour gone sour? Joe and Brian then tutor young Cord on the use of corporate speak and political spin. When they all arrive at the intimidating corporate conference room in Chicago for an important company meeting all are nervous. Cord panics while conducting a slide presentation and bails again leaving Joe and Brian to take over the presentation.

One of the board members is portrayed by actor John Ducey. About working on the show, Ducey said, "*Wings* is a hit show that basically slipped under my radar. It premiered when I was in college and then when I moved to L. A. I didn't own a TV set for the first 18 months. This was my first sitcom, which over the years provided most of my work. My major scenes were with both Tim Daly and Steven Weber. They were very laid back. What struck me most was how fantastically funny both of them were. Not just during the scenes but in between as well. I was blown away. When I finally sat down to watch the show I realized how difficult it was to translate that on-set magic to the small screen. And the people who can do it are amazing talents. My memories are all positive, for sure. I did not interact with the other cast members outside of the board room scene. I was a pretty shy kid. I have crossed paths with Tim Daly and Jonathan Slavin again over the years." Before the meeting takes place, Helen overhears some of the board saying that Sandpiper was set up to fail with Cord in charge. It was supposed to be a tax write off. Joe doesn't want the airline to merely be a tax write off, and finally convinces Mr. Clayton to be a silent partner.

This three-part episode had two different directors, Darryl Bates and Jeff Melman. About the directors, Jonathan Slavin recalled, "Both were great, and that was helpful to this wide-eyed kid. Both were very kind." John Ducey shared, "This was my first job with Melman, but far from my last. We crossed sitcom paths many times after that week." The credits roll over the traditional Schubert theme.

"All about Christmas Eve" (Season 8 Episode 11) Aired December 18, 1996

Written by Michael Sardo
Directed by Joyce Gittlin

The title is an obvious takeoff on the Bette Davis film *All about Eve*. This is the show's sixth and final Christmas episode, and it opens with Roy in a great mood, singing "Deck the Halls." Antonio is also happy because he has a girlfriend to spend the holiday with - Elise. Tony Shalhoub's real life wife Brooke Adams portrays a nun named Sister Mary McKenna of Little Sisters of Hope, and she needs a ride. She becomes Antonio's fare. She's not dressed in her habit and Antonio has no idea that she's a nun and thinks she might have a hot date. When he finds out her line of work he drives her free of charge. Her destination? Unknown. She says she had a vision that someone on Nantucket Island needed to be saved, and so they drive around until it's found.

In other action, the package that was supposed to contain Joe's new flight jacket gift (Helen's Christmas gift for Joe) has a little girl's dress inside in an apparent mix-up. Luckily the store in which Casey works has flight jackets in stock. When they go shopping after hours, Casey, Fay and Helen get locked in the store. Here's

Mr. DeMille, it's time for our closeup! Left to right Extras Talent Coordinator Jack E. Herman, Assistant Director Barbara Bruno, and Second A. D. Sheila Stewart. (Courtesy of Jack E. Herman).

David Schramm and Amy Yasbeck make things merry at the Wings *Christmas party. (Courtesy of Suzanne Holmes).*

where the nun's vision comes into play – she's the one who rescues Casey, Fay and Helen from their predicament.

Meanwhile, Joe and Brian are at home waiting and waiting for Helen's return home to a beautiful holiday-decorated house. The waiting really annoys Brian, who has a date with a girl named Yolanda that evening. Joe has a couple of surprise Christmas Eve visitors – Lou (Phil Leeds) with whom Joe played checkers in a previous episode at "the home," and his brother Harry (Abe Vigoda). Lou and Harry haven't spoken in 30 years. Phil Leeds utters the same line that made Steven Weber laugh uncontrollably in his previous appearance in the episode titled "The Lyin' King" - "You screwed me blue." There is a happy, Christmassy ending as Lou and Harry make amends, and Helen makes it home in time to enjoy the holiday with Joe. The credits roll over the traditional Schubert theme.

"Let's Talk about Sex" (Season 8 Episode 12) Aired January 8, 1997

Written by Ellen Byron and Lissa Kapstrom
Directed by Leonard R. Garner, Jr.

This is the first episode of 1997. It begins with Joe and Helen in bed. They're becoming an old married couple because she's reading the new edition of *People Magazine,* and he's playing a video game on his new laptop. Sex has become secondary in their lives and they unwittingly go on *The Mary Pat Lee Show* to discuss that. They think they're on there to discuss a happy first year of marriage. Much like when Brian was a guest on Mary Pat's show, the topic promised is not the topic delivered. Caroline Aaron reprises her role as the brash Sally Jessy Raphael-esque daytime talk show hostess. Antonio is her biggest fan and he is ecstatic when he sees her in the airport. She's there to meet Roy – they're dating. They met at a Food-a-Holics meeting a few weeks back and hit it off. Their meeting in the episode "Ex Lies and Videotape," however was not as pleasant. She ridicules Roy on the air in that episode and he says, "She's mean." But things are different here and Caroline Aaron shared a funny anecdote about her second appearance, "The bed scene with Roy and me on the telephone is memorable. First of all, the bed was up really high to get the right camera angle. It was so high it was hard to get into and out of, so there was an apple box there to climb on. It was not part of the script but when David Schramm climbed onto it, the bed broke and collapsed on the floor. I told David, with whom I was great friends for many years, that this was why we never had an affair. Of course, this led to a long break in shooting so that they could fix the bed."

Elsewhere Brian is a mess – his shoe is falling apart (requiring masking tape to hold it together) and he ran out of shampoo and used dishwashing liquid on his hair (and it shows). What he needs is someone to run all of his errands for him. What he needs is Casey, and he hires her to do all the things that his schedule will not allow. Basically, she's a wife without a ring and a marriage license. But his demanding ways eventually lead her to quit.

In Boston on *The Mary Pat Lee Show,* things get combative when it's discovered that something Joe said to Roy in confidence about the importance of sex in a marriage dwindling over time is broadcast live on air. Roy is very upset that Mary Pat betrayed his confidence as well as that of his so-called "friends." Although he is very much in love with Mary Pat, he breaks off the relationship when he realizes she can't be trusted and that her show is the most important thing in her life with him coming in a distant second. About the experience, Caroline Aaron said, "What a remarkable ensemble. Everyone was so welcoming, so talented all around. They are all brilliant, funny people and highly underappreciated." Compared to the Shirley Maisel character she portrays on *The Marvelous Mrs. Maisel,* Aaron said, "Mary Pat Lee was much tougher than Shirley. Shirley is mushier." Speaking of *The Marvelous Mrs. Maisel,* I, your author, am a regular tailor in the Maisel and Roth garment factory on the show, and Caroline and I cross paths regularly. The credits roll over a disheveled Joe and Helen who emerge from backstage on Mary Pat's show after finally having sex after weeks of putting it off.

Caroline Aaron shared, "I had a huge Mary Pat Lee poster used on the show hanging in my garage for the longest time. I used it as a threat to get my real kids to behave, telling them that if they were bad the poster would be moved into a prominent place in our living room. They behaved – it worked."

"Hosed" (Season 8 Episode 13) Aired January 15, 1997

Written by Christopher Vane, Art Baer and Ben Joelson
Directed by Leonard R. Garner, Jr.

Beginning with this episode, notice the board behind Fay – from now until the Series Finale in the left column, Martha's Vineyard is spelled Martha's VineyRAD.

Art Baer and Ben Joelson were writing for sitcoms in TV's infancy. Coincidentally, they had worked with Rebecca Schull in New York some 40 years earlier. Supervising producer and co-writer of this episode Christopher Vane recalled, "Art Baer gave me my first job on *The Love Boat*, and I played softball with him. He and his writing partner Ben Joelson were two of the nicest guys in the business. Art had told me a story about an unscrupulous salesman, not a vacuum cleaner salesman but still I thought it would make for a great episode of *Wings*. I made sure that Art and Ben got 'story credit' for the episode, even though they had no real involvement. Sadly Ben passed away shortly before the broadcast, so when the episode did air we created a nice tribute to him at the end. That ending was only seen the one time and is not available in syndication nor on the DVD set."

The action begins with Joe watching a football game on TV when a door-to-door vacuum cleaner salesman named Dennis Lundy (Sam McMurray) rings the bell. This high-tech and very expensive vacuum has a patented whisper drive. This intrigues Joe and he gets "sucked in" and buys one. He's so pumped about this new acquisition he throws a Hosemaster party. When Helen accidentally breaks the expensive new vacuum, she discovers that the lifetime warranty was a farce. Then comes the dirty work – breaking the news to Joe. Joe is very upset about the vacuum, but even more upset by Mr. Lundy's way of doing business, denying he ever said the vacuum had a lifetime warranty (and blaming his non-existent twin). Joe even attempts to call Mike Wallace to do a piece about this corrupt company on *60 Minutes*. Joe and Helen resort to trickery to get the vacuum back. Initially it's to no avail because the vacuum store has a security camera. However, that same security camera holds a video of Lundy and a female customer having sex in the back room. A disgruntled employee named Teddy Kolb (Leslie Jordan) sells Joe that sex tape, and Joe gets his vacuum back in an expensive trade for that tell-tale video.

In the terminal, Roy's niece is visiting, and Brian expects her to resemble Roy, but Lydia (Kimberly Oja) is quite comely. Brian invites himself to Lydia and Roy's night of Polish cuisine and even offers to pay. Roy is fine with Brian dating Lydia as long as Roy is always part of their plans. Despite the fact that she's a Biggins, Brian really grows fond of Lydia. Unfortunately, Lydia and Roy meet someone else – someone better and more generous, and break it off with Brian. The credits roll over Antonio using Joe's repaired vacuum, accidentally breaking it a second time, and then quickly fleeing.

"Just Call Me Angel" (Season 8 Episode 14) Aired February 5, 1997

Written by Christopher Vane and Lori Kirkland
Directed by Jeff Melman

The episode title is a line borrowed from a classic song titled "Angel of the Morning" by Merilee Rush, and later Juice Newton. The episode begins with the Hackett Brothers on a return flight from Las Vegas where they celebrated Brian's birthday. While in Vegas Brian got drunk, chased women and gambled. Joe used the hotel gym, bought himself a man's travel case (which Brian calls a makeup case because it has a lighted mirror), and utilized a full book of cost-cutting coupons. One of those coupons was for a buffet from which Joe gets food poisoning – along with the pilot and co-pilot who were also present at said buffet. Brian then becomes a hero when he volunteers to fly the plane and is later called "The Angel of Flight 28." San Francisco 49ers quarterback Steve Young was on the same flight and recognizes Brian as the man

Extras Talent Coordinator Jack E. Herman and Associate Producer Suzanne Holmes share a moment in front of Helen's lunch counter on a dark Paramount Stage 19. (Courtesy of Jack E. Herman).

Supervising Producer/Writer Christopher Vane showing off his souvenir Steven Weber "The Angel Made Me Do It" tee shirt, and Impastor hat. (Courtesy of Christopher Vane).

who was passed out in his hotel's hallway earlier that same day.

Carolyn Hennesy played a flight attendant on that episode and recalled, "49'ers star quarterback Steve Young was guesting, playing a passenger on the plane; he and I had a very brief but funny scripted interaction. When Steve was on set, everyone...grips, electric, camera operators, execs, crafty...*everyone* was in this boiling pot of frenzy, the lid only being kept on by sheer will and professionalism. You could tell it was a struggle for grown men not to fan-boy. However, everyone wanted Steve to sign their scripts, so the word went out at some point that everyone's script would be put into a box, they'd be taken to Steve's dressing room, he'd sign them and they'd be returned. Now, I didn't particularly care, truth be told, about having a Steve Young signed script; he was a very nice fellow, but I wasn't a football fan. In addition, it was difficult to really talk to him any place but on the airplane set as his fiancé was in a constant state of 'hover,' and when Steve wasn't on stage, she'd whisk him back to his dressing room and there they'd stay. So tape day arrives, the audience is loaded and we're almost at go time. Steve and I are in our places when out of the blue he turns to me and says something along the lines of 'Do you ever get nervous? How am I doing? Am I okay? Tell me I'm gonna be okay.' All of this, naturally, endeared me to the handsome fellow and I said 'Steve, you're fabulous. You're funny, charming, natural...,' etc. And then I said, 'But if you really want my support when we're filming..,' pausing for only the coyest of smiles, 'please sign my script.' (Look, I may not have cared greatly, but when the dude's in front of you... right?) He got this big grin on his face, whipped out a pen and signed it right then and there. Filming progressed and he really WAS terrific with what they gave him. At the end of the night, after the episode was in the can, the crew was clearing out and Steve, his intended and their entourage had gone, the signed scripts were handed back to all who'd turned them in. And that's when the word went out that someone...no idea who...had knocked on Steve's dressing room door earlier in the evening, opened it and had seen *not* Steve Young but someone associated with him signing all of the scripts. To this day, I have no idea whether or not this is true, (although I remember at the time a pall settling over the soundstage...I think everyone did believe it) but if it is, it means the one person who didn't care half as much as anyone else on that show walked away with the only script actually signed by Steve Young."

As a result of his heroic act as surrogate pilot, Brian suddenly gets endorsements galore, and raises the ire of the more responsible Hackett, Joe who is envious of the attention Brian is receiving. The hero worship starts to go to Brian's head and he tells Joe to start looking for a new pilot. But, as they say, fame is fleeting and soon a new hero emerges – a firecat named Lulu who saves an entire family from an inferno. Brian Hackett soon becomes "Brian who?" As the endorsements fall like dominoes, the Angel comes crawling back with his halo between his legs. The episode's co-writer and supervising producer Christopher Vane recalled, "We had some tee shirts made up with Weber's picture on them with the phrase, 'The Angel Made Me Do It.' Years later I wore the shirt on the set of another show on which Weber was guest starring and made it appear as thought it were a total coincidence – as if I wore the tee shirt all the time. I still have the shirt, by the way."

The credits roll over Helen and Joe leaving for a getaway to a cabin in Vermont, and Joe bringing his "man's travel case" much to Helen's chagrin and embarrassment.

"Fay There, Georgy Girl" (Season 8 Episode 15)
Aired February 12, 1997

Written by Ken Keeler
Directed by Jeff Melman

Actor Taylor Nichols who was "Taylor-made" for the lovesick Russell Greaney role in the Season Eight episode titled "Fay There, Georgy Girl." (Courtesy of Taylor Nichols).

The title borrows the opening line from the old Seekers' classic tune "Georgy Girl." The song is part of the soundtrack of the Lynn Redgrave film of the same name. The episode opens with Roy and Antonio comparing notes on the worst Valentine's Day ever. Poor Antonio is declared the winner.

Fay then enters with news she is finally getting rid of all of the items of her three late husbands, all named George. She's selling them at a flea market and soon cleans up with hundreds of dollars in her purse. She makes so much money she wonders why she didn't sell the junk earlier. But later that night, Fay has a Dickensian moment when she's visited by three ghosts – all three of her Georges, all disturbed that she sold their possessions. She is so rattled by the apparitions that she makes a concerted effort to get back every item she sold, even placing an ad in the paper. Fay finally comes to her senses and is able to "let go."

Meanwhile Brian and Casey will each be alone on Valentine's Day this year, so Casey comes up with a plan for them to use one another as bait. If they look like a couple, they'll appear more desirable to others when they're out and about. The other Hackett brother and his bride Helen aren't doing anything special. Well, at least Helen said she didn't want to do anything special for Valentines Day, but Joe misread that as the truth and now has to scramble to salvage the day (and his marriage). They take a flight together with a man named Russell Greaney (Taylor Nichols) who wants to propose to the woman he loves with a banner. The woman named Nancy (voiced by Lynn Dee Smith) has no idea who he is – he's been admiring her from afar at the diner at which she works. When those plans with Nancy go South, he hits on Helen. When that doesn't pan out either, he moves on to Casey. About earning the role of Russell, Taylor Nichols said, "The casting director, Jeff Greenberg was a fan of my work and when he liked you, he would attempt to push your boundaries. I did have to read for the role but apparently Jeff thought I could play this fanatic named Russell. I loved the character – somewhat of a Romeo. When things didn't work out with Nancy, he moved on to Helen and then at the end of the episode clicked with Casey." About being a guest star, Nichols added, "It's great but sometimes you feel almost like an intruder. This cast was extremely welcoming – there were no big egos there, but they were such a well-oiled machine and you had to fit into their party. I think directors, like the wonderful Jeff Melman who directed this episode (and several other shows on which I've worked) feel almost like guest stars as they're not there each and every week." Did Nichols get to work with any of the cast again? "Yes, I was on *Monk* with the great Tony Shalhoub who was very effusive about being happy to have me on the show. And I worked with Crystal Bernard in a film titled *Gideon* on which she played my love interest. I didn't get to be her love interest on *Wings* but I did in this wonderful film which was loaded with big names such as Shelley Winters, Charleton Heston and Carroll O'Connor, to name a few. It was very memorable." The credits roll over the traditional Schubert theme.

"Escape from New York" (Season 8 Episode 16)
Written by Jeffrey Richman
Directed by Jeff Melman

Antonio enters the terminal with a newly concocted bucket list of items. He orders a Fresca because he's never had one before and checks it off the list. The bucket list is a result of Antonio almost

From the episode "Escape from New York," Extras Talent Coordinator Jack E. Herman (with headset) is outside the trailer surrounded by Calvert DeForest (aka Larry "Bud" Melman front center), an unnamed Teamster (far left) and numerous drag queens used in the episode. (Courtesy of Jack E. Herman).

Behind the scenes of the "Escape from New York" episode (a recreation of Manhattan on the Paramount lot) – Associate Producer Suzanne Holmes and Extras Talent Coordinator Jack E. Herman. (Courtesy of Jack E. Herman).

being hit by a car. Had he not gone into the video store to see if the new Jackie Chan film was in yet he would've been a goner because a car careened into the very spot Antonio had been standing only moments earlier. Also on Antonio's bucket list – getting closer to Joe Hackett. Joe is convalescing at home from dizzy spells and a bad back, and Antonio keeps him company and plays nursemaid in a sick 'Kathy Bates in *Misery*' kind of way.

Some parts of this episode were pre-shot on Paramount's back lot on a set that resembles New York City streets. Speaking of New York City, Helen is ecstatic because she was just gifted tickets to *Rent* on Broadway. Joe can't go because he is too dizzy to fly. Roy begs Helen to take him, but she goes to New York with Brian instead. However, they never get into the theater – the tickets are held under the credit card holder's name, not Helen's. and the woman in the ticket booth simply won't surrender the tickets without seeing the card. So, Brian and Helen decide to just go to dinner. Those plans go awry when Brian rescues a woman in distress in an apartment window only to be led into a macabre Hitchcock-like scene when he enters her apartment, and Helen is taken in by a game of Three Card Monte on the streets of New York and loses a Benjamin. About playing the dealer, actor Eric Howell Sharp said, "I got an audition for a role and went to producers - I think it was 1995. Might have been later. I don't recall. It was a co-star bit. One or two lines. I was nervous. There were many producers and writers in the room. I did not get it but a few months later they called me in to audition for the Three Card Monte dealer in the 'Escape From New York Episode'. I remember that card magician Joe Monti was up for the part and so was Israel Juarbe - both of whom were far more established than I was so I didn't have high hopes of landing the part. On the day of the audition I stopped in a souvenir shop on Hollywood Boulevard and got a shark tooth necklace to wear for the audition. I felt the accessory helped me find the character. I did get the role and was over the moon. I still wear a shark tooth necklace for luck when I audition for roles because of this. On the day of the shoot, I didn't know how to do Three-Card Monte (now it is a huge part of my magic show) so I marked the back of the cards with a Sharpie so I would find the queen when I wanted to while the cameras were rolling. The line was 'Keep your eye on the red queen. Just follow the red queen. Follow the honey and double your money' - Crystal Bernard then steps up to try her hand at the game. I 'Let' her win and gave her change for a real bill with counterfeit money and that is the scene. We shot on the Paramount New York City Street set. No live audience for this one. In between shots I forgot I was wearing a mic and so everyone heard me talking to a crewmember saying something along the lines of

'The secret of the overwhelming success of this show - being on the air for eight seasons - is that everyone loves working with each other. You can feel the respect and camaraderie among the cast and crew. It is palpable.' I also remember gushing about Crystal Bernard who I adore. I think word got back to her that I was very complimentary of her on the set because when we came back from lunch to shoot the scene, she was incredibly nice to me. She is a real star. Side note: I sat down to eat lunch at the same table with Tony Shahloub who I didn't have scenes with but he was very nice and pleasant. Everyone was. The director was Jeff Melman. Another kind and generous soul. He shot this scene nine ways from Sunday and I think the end result is a memorable moment in TV history. I am proud I could be there. Being on the famous Paramount lot and working with such stellar talents remains one of my fondest memories in my three decades as a professional entertainer. I cherish and relish that opportunity."

As a result of the card shark's trickery, Helen and Brian are left in New York City almost penniless and without credit cards to get home. They attempt to hit people up for handouts (including Calvert DeForest/Larry Bud Melman in a cameo) to no avail. When it begins to pour outside, they duck into a nightclub. The bouncer there, played by Ray Laska tells Brian and Helen that there's a cover charge, that is unless they're entering the contest – a drag contest. Brian attempts to pass Helen off as a drag queen to win $250 to get them back home. She dances on stage in what could pass for an early episode of *Pose* to the song "I Will Survive" by Gloria Gaynor but loses to Miss Ginger Vitus. However, there is a consolation prize of tickets to see *Rent*. Ray Laska shared, "I was the bouncer at the club that was having the female impersonator contest. Anyway, there were about 30 actual female impersonators on the sound stage while we were shooting. After a while it apparently slipped my mind because I caught myself really admiring the legs on this one girl and suddenly realized, 'THAT AIN'T A GIRL!!' The legs were pretty nice, though." The credits roll over the traditional Schubert theme.

"House of Blues" (Season 8 Episode 17) Aired March 5, 1997

Written by Jeffrey Richman
Directed by Jeff Melman

An original 45 rpm copy of "Cherish" by the Association – a big part of the episode titled "House of Blues."

The episode begins with Joe and Helen's realization that they don't ever get enough time alone to take photos of just the two of them – Brian and Casey are always there. The time has come to set their seemingly eternal houseguests free. It finally happens and now Joe and Helen can stroll around nude if they want to. The problem is a couple of teenage boys from the neighborhood (Justin Burnette and Lance Robinson) take photos of them naked and threaten to post them all over the neighborhood and on the internet if Joe doesn't let them use his house for a teen party. The two young neighbors sound very much like the animated dolts named Beavis and Butthead. Joe says no – a decision that comes back to haunt him.

Meanwhile Brian and Casey find a place to live, but it's out of their price range. That is, unless they can talk Antonio into moving in with them. He does, and for a while he's never around – always staying over at his girlfriend Elise's place. Antonio and Elise's song is "Cherish" by the Association. About getting to use a famous song such as this, freelance composer Bruce Miller said, "A call would go out to the publisher. There would be a licensing fee paid to the publisher of the work for a specified term, and each time the episode airs the publisher and songwriters get paid. Every licensing deal is different and not always infinite." Fay and Roy sing the song as an impromptu duet in the terminal.

When Elise dumps him, Antonio is constantly in Brian and Casey's way and both of them begin to rue their decision to ask him to move in. When Antonio ruins both of their dates on the same night they kick him to the curb. In the interim, Casey and Brian are now seeking a new roommate and not finding anyone suitable until the perfect tenant, Matthew Evans (Todd Waring) comes by and wants to pay six months in advance, $100 more each month to get out of where he's staying (the Just Washed Inn at the wharf), and offers use of his Boston Celtics season tickets. About the experience, Waring shared, "It was a fun part in a fun and highly successful show, with top-notch comic actors. Prior to rehearsing and shooting, there was the usual table read, where the cast, director and writers sit around some tables, and the actors read the script aloud. By the time I had gotten onto the lot, parked, and found the room it was already chock full, and I had to snake my way around to find my chair. Because *Wings* had become such a hit, the room where they were having the table-read was crammed with some NBC execs as well. In this case, they included Joel Thrum, Head of Talent, and Brandon Tartikoff, President of the network. Joel Thurm had always been in my corner at NBC and brought me in to read on several shows, so when I saw him, we said hi and hugged. And as it turns out, Steven Weber was an old friend from NYC, where we had been in a theater company together 14 years earlier. So, we laughed and hugged. Rebecca Schull was also an actor that I knew from NYC. I'd been in a play with her at the Public Theater in 1981, and several play readings after that. I give her a hug and we caught up a little. Tony Shalhoub got up from his chair and we hugged. He'd gone to Yale School of Drama with my wife, Eve Gordon, and our families were good friends. Then, I go right over to Amy Yasbeck and give her a big kiss, because she and I starred in *Splash, Too* together. At this point, I can see that David Schramm is trying to place me. I go over to him, and say, 'We met in 1973. You had just graduated from Juilliard, and the Acting Company came up to Saratoga Springs to do their very first repertory season. The company also had a month-long workshop for area high school students, and I was one of those kids.' Actually, all I got out was, 'We met in 1973...' and he jumped up to give me a hug. I didn't know Crystal Bernard, but nodded anyway. A bit of trivia: When they were casting for the leads of *Wings*, Steven Weber was up for Brian, of course, and Tim Daly was up for Joe. But also, NBC had flown me out to Los Angeles from NYC for the final network auditions. I was up for *both* parts. (I can still remember the three of us sitting outside the frosted-glass office waiting for each other to go in.) So when I was circling back to my seat, I gave Brandon Tarkikoff a hug too, because what the hell. As I reach my chair, I see there are two other guest stars on the show that week already seated. I believe they were Sibel Ergener and Bruce Thomas. They were both staring at me like, 'Who ARE you?' One of them said, 'Should we know you?' I sat and said, 'Nope. Just the right guy at the right time.' During all this, Tim Daly had not arrived yet. But a minute or two later he shows up, scans the room, and says, 'Hey. Todd.' About ten years prior Tim Daly and my wife, Eve, had starred together in a series called *Almost Grown*. I turned to the other two guest stars, shrugged, got up, and gave Tim a hug."

When the ousted Antonio returns for more of his belongings, Matthew recognizes him as the man staying across the hall from where he lives now. Matthew says Antonio always sings "Cherish," stinks up the building with his garlic-infused cooking and cries a lot. Reluctantly, Brian and Casey's conscience gets the better of them and they tell Matthew, the ideal roommate he can't have the room after all, and they ask Antonio to return.

The credits roll over Fay and Roy finding a website with nude photos of Joe and Helen in the hot tub and cleaning the gutters all posted by those mischievous boys in Joe's neighborhood.

"Ms. Write" (Season 8 Episode 18) Aired March 19, 1997
Written by Ellen Byron and Lissa Kapstrom
Directed by Leonard R. Garner, Jr.

The episode begins with Casey and Helen watching horror films in the living room and screaming. Still on edge from the movie, Joe comes home earlier than expected from a charter flight to Vermont and Helen thinks he's a prowler and gives him a black eye. The gang razzes Joe the next day at work when they find out Helen gave him the shiner. Joe realizes after this incident that the house needs a burglar alarm system. Antonio offers to install one for $75, but his work is shoddy and unsightly with visible wires leading all over the house. The way in which Antonio installs the alarm sensors also gets under Joe and Helen's skin as they must walk through every room very gingerly lest they set off the sirens.

Meanwhile Brian is dating Casey's boss at the department store, Beth. Kaitlin Hopkins, who portrayed Beth shared, "The cast was full of just awesome humans. They were full of joy in the work and grateful for the opportunity they had. Just a lot of laughter - it was a happy set, and it was especially fun for me and Steven Weber, as we had done a play together very early in both our careers off Broadway - *Come Back, Little Sheba* at The Roundabout Theatre Company, and had been friends for years. Playing opposite each other again was a blast. Years after that, 2002, we were both on Broadway at the same time. He was doing *The Producers*, I was doing *Noises Off*, and we would meet for drinks now and then after our shows and catch up. It is one of the best things about being an actor is often you cross paths again with people you have worked with and known for decades, and those are friendships you travel with throughout your career." Hopkins also got to work again with, "The great David Lee, co-creator of *Wings* and *Frasier*. He was directing a production of a Noel Coward play called *Present Laughter* at the Two River Theatre. He offered me one of the lead roles. David is one of the most respected comedic writer/directors in our industry. I had the most wonderful adventure being reunited with him all those years later. He taught me so much about comedy, a true visionary in sitcoms, and also an amazing theater director."

About her character on the show, Hopkins recalled, "She was self-centered and unaware of how her energy impacted others. Someone who doesn't listen, interrupts people and thinks the world revolves around her. Even though my character wasn't a fan of *Catcher in the Rye*, I loved it. Read it in high school." Beth experiences some unexpected and unwelcome competition, as Brian is intrigued by the letters being left in his mailbox addressed to a Kyle Vane, likely a former resident. By the way, Kyle Vane is the name of the son of one of the show's writers Christopher Vane. Vane shared, "Until you brought it up, my son never knew about his name being a big part of an episode of the series. He's well into his 20s now and

I found the episode on CBS All Access on-line and had him sit down and watch it with me. This discovery brought about the biggest smile from Kyle." Vane added, "Steven Weber thought Kyle Vane sounded like the name of a great hard-hitting third baseman." After a few letters accumulate on the Kyle pile, Brian gets the nerve to open one of them and finds that it's a mysterious love letter to Kyle from someone who signs simply "R." Brian becomes infatuated with "R" and opens and reads every one of the letters. Even though he is still seeing Beth, he's become obsessed with "R." In fact, Brian breaks it off with Beth because of the mysterious "R" letters. Casey was relying on the relationship between Brian and Beth working out to advance her career to the men's boxers and briefs section of the department store, but this breakup certainly doesn't bode well for a promotion. A post card that arrives for Kyle has a return address that finally allows Brian to meet the elusive "R" who is really Rebecca (Ashley Johnson) and she's twelve. "R" was very mature for her age for having written those letters to Kyle who stayed with neighbors on Nantucket the past summer. Brian has botched yet another good relationship while in search of an even better one – he still has some growing up to do. Although not credited, the voice of "R" in Brian's head as he reads the steamy letters is that of Lillian Adams according to casting director Jeff Greenberg.

The episode was directed by Leonard R. Garner, Jr., about whom Hopkins said, "Is a genius at comedy and I was so excited to have the opportunity to work with him, I mean…he's a genius, one of the best comedy directors out there. I felt so lucky to watch and learn from the work that was happening around me." The credits roll over the traditional Schubert theme.

"Dreamgirl" (Season 8 Episode 19) Aired April 2, 1997
Written by Michael Sardo
Directed by Leonard R. Garner, Jr.

The episode opens with Fay finally going on a paid vacation – a traveling murder mystery weekend. Joe and Brian still haven't found anyone to take Fay's place in the interim, and every applicant for the temp job has been, shall we say, unfit. One of the applicants was very intimidating (Vince Lozano) - he recently had a homicide conviction overturned (formerly inmate #72144). Even more unnerving – the homicide involved the applicant's former boss. About the role, Lozano shared, "I think this was my second TV gig. I just remember Steven Weber being the coolest guy in the world and so fucking hilarious on the show. He was so cool with me and I'll never forget that. I ran into him last year at Ed Asner's celebrity poker tourney and we spoke for a while and it made me feel good because he remembered me right away. Tony Shalhoub was so awesome and was brilliant on the show. Also, he would take time to talk to me about the biz and I'll be forever grateful. I remember filming in front of live audience, Tim Daly went up with his line and the audience laughed because Tim made a joke - something about nerves. But it relaxed me. I was fired up ready to box twelve rounds. Then we did an amazing job with the scene in the next two takes. And director Lenny Garner definitely understood comedy. *Wings* was one of the greatest shows on television and maybe a little underrated. But wow what a great cast right up there with *Cheers* and *M*A*S*H*! Great writing, great acting and a great ensemble. You felt the love." For a while, the former inmate was Joe and Brian's leading candidate. That is, except for Shannon (Samantha Smith) – a gorgeous blonde whom Brian fears will keep him from concentrating on work. Helen encourages the Hackett boys to hire her, but then has second thoughts. Shannon is so attractive that both Hackett Brothers are actually relieved when Fay returns, although she comes back even more surly than when she left – her vacation was horrible – a hot mess.

Meanwhile a new airport shuttle is seriously hurting Antonio's taxi business. He's seeking a second job to get him through this rough patch. Casey gets him a part-time job at minimum wage at Henley's department store. Antonio works diligently, unlike Casey, and is quickly promoted, much to her annoyance. Antonio continually rubs Casey's nose in his newfound success. Over the credits we discover that Casey has gotten even by placing stolen goods in Antonio's locker, getting him fired.

"Heartache Tonight" (Season 8 Episode 20) Aired April 16, 1997
Written by Lori Kirkland
Directed by Leonard R. Garner, Jr.

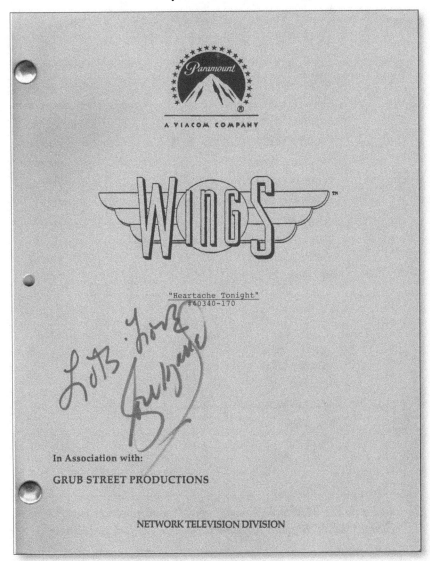

The "Heartache Tonight" script's cover page signed by guest star Rose Marie. (Courtesy of Jack E. Herman).

```
                            WINGS
                      "Heartache Tonight"

                        #40340-170



                            CAST


        JOE HACKETT...............................TIMOTHY DALY

        BRIAN HACKETT............................STEVEN WEBER

        HELEN CHAPPEL...........................CRYSTAL BERNARD

        FAY EVELYN COCHRAN......................REBECCA SCHULL

        ROY BIGGINS.............................DAVID SCHRAMM

        ANTONIO SCARPACCI.......................TONY SHALHOUB

        CASEY DAVENPORT.........................AMY YASBECK

        ELEANOR BIGGINS.........................ROSE MARIE

        JACK GORDON.............................BILLY DEAN

        CAMILLA.................................

        JANICE LYNN.............................DULCY ROGERS

        CUSTOMER................................



                            SETS



        INT. TERMINAL

        INT. OFFICE

        INT. BRIAN & CASEY'S HOUSE

        INT. ROY'S HOUSE

        INT. CAB
```

The cast list for the "Heartache Tonight" episode with guest star Rose Marie as Eleanor "Bluto" Biggins, Roy's mom. (Courtesy of Jack E. Herman).

The episode title is inspired by a big hit song by the Eagles. The action begins with Antonio carrying some heavy luggage in from his cab only to have the passenger tip him a mere quarter. Fay suggests that Antonio become more of a suck up like her.

Elsewhere Brian is unwell and Joe sends him home to recuperate. He then infects Casey who proceeds to scare away her date, Jack Gordon (played by country singer Billy Dean) by coughing on him and then passing out.

In other action, out of the blue Roy asks Helen and Joe over to his house for a chicken dinner on Saturday night. Roy wants some friends to be around when he introduces his mother, the acerbic Eleanor Bluto Biggins (Rose Marie) to the woman he loves, Pauline. Pauline breaks up with Roy on the phone just before Mrs. Biggins arrives and Roy begs Helen to pose as Pauline, and Joe pretends to be the houseboy Arturo. The evening gets more nightmarish by the minute because Mrs. Biggins was told that Roy's girlfriend was an exotic dancer and met Roy during a lap dance. Mom doesn't approve of Pauline (aka Helen) and calls her a floozie. However Mom does say she loves Roy, something he hasn't heard her say in many years. The credits roll over the traditional Schubert theme.

"Oedipus Wrecks" (Season 8 Episode 21) Aired May 7, 1997
Written by Ellen Byron and Lissa Kapstrom
Directed by Darryl Bates

About directing one of the final episodes of a long-running sitcom, director Darryl Bates shared, "I was aware of two distinct feelings. One feeling was that, in a series that's in its eighth season, and especially toward the end of that season, everyone gets a little antsy to just get it done. By season eight, the actors have other things to do during the week besides rehearse the show, and so everyone wants to get the work done quickly and then just get out of there. You're *very* aware of that as a director. And that happens without fail on any show that makes it past five seasons. At the same time, there was also a recognition that we were coming to the end of something very special, something that was a big part of all of our lives for many years, akin to the breakup of a family. So at the same time, I think that we also all felt that we wanted to slow things down a bit and savor the moments that were rapidly coming to an end."

The episode begins with the announcement that Colonel Shulkraut's Happy Time Circus is in town. Roy is excited, Antonio has never been to the circus and has a wide-eyed curiosity about it, and Joe is simply terrified saying, "Bad, bad things happen at the circus." Joe is haunted by an event from his youth involving an elephant who inhaled his Orange Crush at the circus, and then sneezed on him.

Elsewhere Brian hopes to bond with the child of a woman named Emily Palmer (Shannon Tweed) whom he's dating. He has gifts for the young man and tickets to the circus. Turns out, her son is not a little boy, but a grown man named Shawn (Christopher Wiehl) who falls for Casey. An awkward moment arises come morning when Brian and Emily find out that Shawn and Casey spent the night together in the same house, thus the episode title, "Oedipus Wrecks." To avoid more awkward moments it is recommended that whomever is in the apartment first should put a tie on the door-knob as a signal for others to stay away. It gets even more clumsy when Shawn and Casey reveal their plan to bum around South America for a year as Shawn takes times off from medical school. This news greatly upsets his mother, but she has the last word and makes an offer to Shawn – if he will stay in school, she'll buy him a new car. Game, set, match.

Meanwhile, Antonio enjoyed going to the Shulkraut circus quite a lot, but not Roy. Roy was humiliated and insulted by Bippy the Clown (Chip Zien). Joe encourages Roy to head back to the circus to demand an apology from Bippy. Roy asks Joe to come along to confront his fear of pachyderms – two birds, one circus. Roy and Bippy become friends, and for a while Joe has a good time at the circus, until the incident with the Orange Crush happens a second time as the credits roll.

"Raging Bull*&@!" (Season 8 Episode 22) Aired May 14, 1997

Written by Christopher Vane
Directed by Jeff Melman

The episode opens with Joe in a boxing ring in black and white pumping himself up for a big fight. That sets up what comes next as Joe enters the terminal and breaks the news to Brian and Antonio who are having lunch that he has scheduled a boxing match against a guy named Mac O'Malley who tormented him in high school. Unfortunately, when O'Malley heard who he would be fighting he laughed so hard he threw his back out, so Brian is then scheduled to take Mac's place. Brian had signed up as an alternate not expecting to fight at all. Helen dubs this "the Thrilla in Vanilla." She is Joe's trainer, Antonio is Brian's. It was supposed to be a friendly competition until Joe received a letter from the I. R. S. that Sandpiper forgot to file income tax. Joe blames it on Brian and a huge argument ensues, even after it's discovered to be Fay's fault, not Brian's. It then becomes a revenge fight. Brad Blaisdell plays the referee. Writer Christopher Vane remembered, "When I was in high school, someone got the bright idea to hold a boxing tournament among the boys. I was pitted against a good friend of mine. It was such an awkward position to be in. I didn't want to hit him, but I didn't want to lose either. And you couldn't chicken out. Luckily, they canceled the tournament, but I thought it would be an interesting situation for Joe and Brian. The trouble is, how do you end it? We knew neither one should win, and we debated them knocking each other out, but in the end we went for sentimentality and I think it was satisfying."

When the bell rings, Joe and Brian dance around the ring for a time but no actual punches are ever thrown. They each have flashbacks to their childhood good times together and find they can't hit one another after all. They meet center ring and raise their arms in a tie, but while raising those arms they knock out Antonio. The credits roll over the same black-and-white scene that opened the episode.

"Final Approach Parts One and Two" (Season 8 Episodes 23 and 24) Aired back-to-back May 21, 1997

Written by Michael Sardo (Part One), and Ian Gurvitz (Part Two)
Directed by Leonard R. Garner, Jr. (Part One) and Jeff Melman (Part Two)

One of the most unique aspects of this episode is that the original opening credits with the Franz Schubert theme (not used since the middle of Season Three) make one last triumphant return. It's the first time we see the name Amy Yasbeck in those credits. The episode begins with Joe proudly displaying his "NIFTY" (the Nevers Field Tenant of the Year Award). It's also time for lease renewal and Helen is unsure she wants to sign for another three years of working behind the lunch counter. Helen does eventually sign for

Background actors in the holding area, getting blocking directions from Second A. D. Sheila Stewart for the penultimate episode titled "Final Approach Part One." (Courtesy of Jack E. Herman).

Extras talent coordinator Jack E. Herman (rear center with headset and tie) and Second A. D. Sheila Stewart (also with headset) are surrounded by the regular group of background performers. (Courtesy of Jack E. Herman).

*Executive Producer
Dave Hackel (sunglasses)
and Extras Talent
Coordinator Jack E.
Herman in front of
the Aeromass counter.
(Courtesy of Jack E.
Herman).*

another term but is down in the dumps thinking that the lunch counter is where she will be for the rest of her life.

Joe surprises Helen by creating a music room in the attic of their new home where she can still pursue her dreams of being a great cellist. Helen is reluctant at first, but then opts to go for it and secures an audition with the New England Chamber Ensemble. While creating the music room in the attic, Joe found a few of Brian's belongings, including the old suitcase from the pilot episode left behind by their late and loony father - the suitcase that had been full of keys. Brian doesn't want any of these things, but just as Joe is about to toss the suitcase out the Hackett boys find something they missed the first time around - $1,000 in the lining and another note saying there's a lot more where this came from. They also find yet another key (to a pawn shop in Boston). The pawn shop yields another suitcase filled with lots of paper – old newspaper and nothing else except a map of Nantucket. A treasure map at that. Supervising Producer Christopher Vane said, "I got to be in that scene as an extra. While the brothers are looking at the treasure map, I'm seen sitting on a city stoop." Joe and Brian try to keep the treasure map under their hat, but Fay demands to know what's going on, why flights are being canceled. To find out she hides Joe's car keys but then doesn't remember where, so they now have to involve Antonio who has to drive them in his cab (with shovel) to Surfside Beach for the dig. That then leads them to a locker in Penn Station in New York, back to Boston, then to Providence and

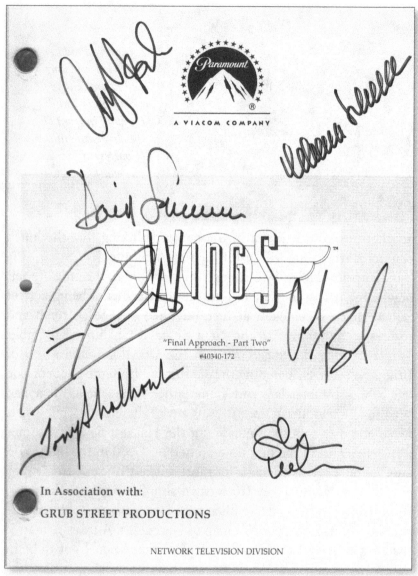

The cast-signed cover page of the script for the Series Finale titled "The Final Approach Part Two." (Courtesy of Suzanne Holmes).

back again only to find more keys. Just as all hope seems lost, Fay recognizes one of the keys as a key to one of the upstairs lockers in the terminal. This time they hit paydirt, emphasis on the *pay* part. It's a suitcase full of cash that's been in the terminal for eight years. It contains $250,000 to be exact. Of course Joe wants to use the money wisely to fix up the plane while Brian wants to escape

```
                            WINGS

                   "Final Approach, Part 2"

                        #40340-172




                        Written by

                        Ian Gurvitz


                  Created and Developed by

                      David Angell
                      Peter Casey
                      David Lee



                      Directed by

                      Jeff Melman




          Copyright 1997 Paramount Pictures Corporation.
          All Rights Reserved.

          This script is the property of Paramount Pictures
          Corporation and may not be copied or distributed
          without the express written permission of Paramount
          Pictures Corporation.  This copy of the script
          remains the property of Paramount Pictures.  It may
          not be sold or transferred and it must be returned to
          Paramount Pictures promptly upon demand.

          THE WRITING CREDITS MAY NOT BE FINAL AND SHOULD NOT
          BE USED FOR PUBLICITY OR ADVERTISING PURPOSES WITHOUT
          FIRST CHECKING WITH TELEVISION LEGAL DEPARTMENT.


      Return to Script Department
      PARAMOUNT PICTURES CORPORATION        FIRST DRAFT
      5555 Melrose Avenue
      Hollywood, California 90038           March 12, 1997
```

The cover page for the Series Finale titled "The Final Approach Part Two."

Nantucket and his boring pilot job and live on an island where *not* being naked is a crime. Casey wants to go with, but Brian says no (at least at first), and then softens when she says that she would miss being with him. Because of the windfall, generous Joe grants Fay five percent of Sandpiper Air.

Helen then gets a phone call that Klaus Sternberg was so impressed with her at a recent audition he wants her to study with him for a year in Vienna, but she initially opts to keep it a secret from Joe because he would have to give up Sandpiper. The good

56.
(K)

```
                          ROY
          (OVER P.A.)  I didn't mean it.  Your
          plane isn't really stupid, and...
          (EMOTIONAL)  Oh, good luck.
                          HELEN
          Thanks, Roy.
                          JOE
          Yeah, thanks.
                          ANTONIO
          That was nice, Roy.  You're getting a
          kiss.
ROY EXITS QUICKLY TO HIS OFFICE.  ANTONIO FOLLOWS.  JOE TURNS
TO HELEN.
                          JOE
          Well...
                          HELEN
          Wait a minute, where's Casey?  I have
          to say goodbye to Casey!
CASEY COMES DOWNSTAIRS, CALLING BACK UP.
                          CASEY
          ...and another thing, Walter.  That
          toupée?  It looks like you're wearing
          a Danish on your head!  Everyone
          thinks you're a joke!  Ha-ha-ha-ha-
          ha!  (TO BRIAN)  Okay, let's get to
          the Caribbean, mon!
                          BRIAN
          Uh, Casey.  Trip's off.  I'm staying.
```

Another page near the end of the script for the Series Finale titled "The Final Approach Part Two."

fortune of everyone else around him raises the ire of Antonio who never seems to get a break. His streak of bad luck continues as he develops a big wart on his finger as well as a rash on his neck and his cab gets swallowed by a sinkhole. Wallowing in self pity, Antonio accidentally spills the beans about Vienna to Joe. Well, since Joe already fulfilled his dream of running an airline, now he feels it's Helen's turn so he agrees to sell Roy the business. Roy is thrilled to finally be acquiring Sandpiper. Brian overhears the conversation

```
                           CASEY

              WHAT?!

                           HELEN

              Brian's going to stay and run

              Sandpiper.  Isn't that great?

                           CASEY

              But-but-but... you can't do that!  I

              burned all my clothes!  I quit my

              job!  I told off everyone on this

              island!  What am I supposed to do for

              work?

      BEAT.  ALL LOOK AT HELEN'S COUNTER.  THE BLOOD DRAINS FROM
      CASEY'S FACE.

                           CASEY (CONT'D)

              Oh, no!

                           JOE

              Come on, Helen, we'd better get

              moving.

      HELEN PUTS HER ARM AROUND HER SISTER.

                           HELEN

              'Bye, Casey.

                           CASEY

              Take me with you!

      JOE HUGS CASEY.

                           CASEY (CONT'D)

              Take me with you?

                           HELEN

              Thank you, Brian.
```

Still closer to the end of the script for the Series Finale titled "The Final Approach Part Two."

between Roy and Joe and decides not to flee to his naked paradise but rather stay in Nantucket and run the business while Joe's away for that year in Vienna. He also helps pay for Antonio's cab being extracted from the sinkhole and all his medical bills. The irresponsible, carefree Brian Hackett has finally grown up. Casey's the last

```
                                                           58.
                                                           (K)


                    BRIAN

          (TO JOE AND HELEN)  Ready?

                     JOE

        Let's do it.

JOE AND HELEN TAKE ONE LAST LOOK AT THE TERMINAL AND EXIT OUT
GATE ONE.  BRIAN STARTS TO EXIT, THEN TURNS BACK TO CASEY.

                    BRIAN

        By the way, just because you'll be at

        the counter and I'm at Sandpiper,

        doesn't mean anything's going on

        between us.  Got it?

                    CASEY

        Oh, please, who are you kidding?

        It's inevitable.  We're doomed.

        (THEN)  Up for a mud bath later?

                    BRIAN

        Hey, where am I going?

BRIAN STARTS TO EXIT.  CASEY STARTS TOWARD THE COUNTER.  THEY
EACH LOOK BACK.  MAYBE...  BRIAN EXITS OUT GATE ONE.

                              DISSOLVE TO:
```

Next to last page of the script for "The Final Approach Part Two."

one to know about Brian's decision not to leave Nantucket (after she told off everyone on the island she didn't like, gave numerous others the finger, burning every bridge imaginable). With Helen away in Vienna, the lunch counter job is wide open and now belongs to Casey. Fay has the last word of the series, announcing the reopening of Sandpiper Air on the terminal microphone. Most of the large crowd in the terminal for that final scene consists of crew, writers, directors, producers all as extras – so many of the

```
                                                              59

                              L



   EXT. AIRPORT - CONTINUOUS
   (Air Traffic Controller(V.O.))

   WE HEAR THE VOICE OF AN AIR TRAFFIC CONTROLLER.

                          AIR TRAFFIC CONTROLLER (V.O.)
                Sandpiper, you are cleared for take-
                off... Have a nice flight.
   AS THE SANDPIPER PLANE TAKES OFF, WE:
                                           FADE OUT.


                      END OF ACT THREE

                      END OF PART TWO

                      END OF SEASON

                      END OF SERIES
```

The final page of "The Final Approach Part Two."

wonderful people who made *Wings* an American treasure. About the series finale and the final scene director Leonard R. Garner, Jr. said, "I didn't do anything on camera but many people did come back to be extras in those final scenes. There were some tears but for the most part I think the show had probably run its course and folks were eager to move on. However, if the show had been

The souvenir Series Finale tee shirts. (Courtesy of Suzanne Holmes).

renewed for a ninth season I certainly would have been back." Even though they had left to create and work on *Frasier, Wings* creators David Lee and Peter Casey said, "Yes, we were there. We wouldn't have missed it." Rebecca Schull stated, "When the show was over I had a new grandchild I wanted to spend more time with, and being from New York I wanted to get back there. But if NBC had decided to do a ninth season I would've stayed on. But so many members of our wonderful cast went on to other great things – Thomas, Tony, Tim, Steven." Dave Hackel, the executive producer for the first half of the show's run said, "Yes, we all came back on set and they let many of us do walk-ons as extras just to be on camera. That was fun. And yes, I'm in that final scene walking through the terminal." Ken Levine said, "My writing partner David Isaacs and I are sitting at Helen's counter during one scene." First assistant middle camera operator Kevin Haggerty said, "It was so nice to have everything all buttoned up in this episode. I've worked on several shows, including *Two Broke Girls* and *Just Shoot Me* that didn't have this opportunity. My wife even teared up a bit reading the final script for the episode. It was nice to have closure – a nice way to end a wonderful experience and a wonderful time in my life." Tim Daly stated, "I was ready to be done at that point. Many of us were kind of running on fumes. I didn't even think about a second wind because we were all actors who could do a lot of different things from drama to comedy and we needed to stretch. Some were eager to move on. It

You are cordially invited, one last time, aboard Sandpiper Air. (Courtesy of Jack E. Herman).

became tough on the writers, too. I do miss that medium, though. It was so good. I fully appreciate it now." Conversely Steven Weber shared, "Was I relieved it was ending? Hell no. I would have continued forever. Jobs like that are hard to come by, ones that are so much fun and are of great quality. I would have gladly continued."

Supervising Producer Christopher Vane shared, "When the writers were pitching ways to end the series, there was one idea I really liked. Borrowing from the famous *Newhart* ending, we envisioned a tag where Joe bolts up in bed from a nightmare and says, 'I just had the worst dream!' Then the camera pulls back to reveal that he's in bed with Brian. Joe: 'I just dreamed we were brothers.' Brian responds, 'Oh god, that's awful. Come back to bed, honey.' As the two guys spoon together, we fade out. Of course, we couldn't do it, but to see Steven and Tim shoot that scene would've been priceless."

The credits then roll one final time over the traditional Schubert theme.

Hugs after shooting "Final Approach Part Two" – Co-Creator David Angell center (with glasses) facing the camera. (Courtesy of Jack E. Herman).

Hugs galore after completing the Series Finale, March 18, 1997 – Left to right Steven Weber, Tony Shalhoub, Rebecca Schull. (Courtesy of Jack E. Herman).

Happy tears at the curtain call for the Series Finale – Rebecca Schull, Amy Yasbeck and David Schramm (left). (Courtesy of Jack E. Herman).

Applause from Tim Daly and Steven Weber at the curtain call near the Sandpiper counter. And that's a wrap.

One last look – Sandpiper's Cessna surrounded by the crew. (Courtesy of Jack E. Herman).

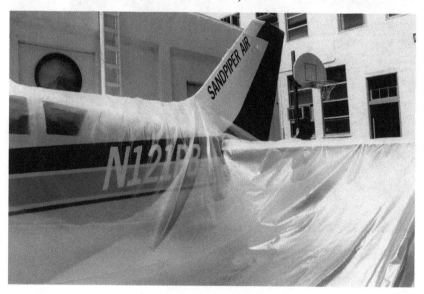

The Sandpiper Plane covered up and in storage. (Courtesy of Suzanne Holmes).

The *Wings* Yearbook

Just in time for the filming of the Series Finale, Suzanne Holmes and Lori A. Moneymaker compiled a *Wings* Yearbook. Here are some selected pages from that behemoth undertaking (courtesy of Suzanne Holmes).

The cover art for the Wings *yearbook given to cast and crew after the last scenes of the Series Finale were filmed.*

Cast and crew discuss the scripts.

AUDREY BANSMER - COSTUME DESIGNER
ROGER STRICKER - SET COSTUMER
TONI LOMBARDO - PICCIOLO - COSTUME SUPERVISOR

ROY CHRISTOPHER - PRODUCTION DESIGNER
RICHARD FERNANDEZ - ASSISTANT ART DIRECTOR

SHEILA GUTHRIE - CASTING DIRECTOR
ERICA ARVOLD - CASTING ASSISTANT
JEFF GREENBERG - CASTING DIRECTOR
RICHARD FONTENOT - CASTING INTERN

Meet the crew.

**JEFFREY RICHMAN
CO-EXECUTIVE PRODUCER**

**CHRISTOPHER VANE
SUPERVISING PRODUCER**

**ELLEN BYRON & LISSA KAPSTROM
SUPERVISING PRODUCERS**

WINGS 13

Meet the producers.

ROBIN CHAMBERLIN
PRODUCER

LORI A. MONEYMAKER
CO-PRODUCER

SUZANNE HOLMES
ASSOCIATE PRODUCER

Would you believe still more producers?

MICHAEL SARDO
PRODUCER

LORI KIRKLAND
EXECUTIVE STORY EDITOR

JOYCE GITTLIN
CREATIVE CONSULTANT

BOB ELLISON
CREATIVE CONSULTANT

14 WINGS

Meet more of the beautiful people behind the scenes. They wore many hats.

ANDY ACKERMAN   PETER BONERZ

NOAM PITLIK   DAVID LEE

AMES BURROWS   JUDY ASKINS   KEN LEVINE   RICK BEREN

I really want to direct – Meet the directors.

LEONARD R. GARNER, JR.
DIRECTOR

JEFF MELMAN
DIRECTOR

DARRYL BATES
DIRECTOR

JOYCE GITTLIN
DIRECTOR

18 WINGS

Meet the Directors Part Two.

**HOWARD GEWIRTZ
EXECUTIVE PRODUCER**

**MARK REISMAN
EXECUTIVE PRODUCER**

**IAN GURVITZ
EXECUTIVE PRODUCER**

Lots of power on this page – the Executive Producers.

TOMMY COLE
MAKE-UP

DORI ANDERSON
MAKE-UP

VALERIE SCOTT
HAIRSTYLIST

RENEÉ DIPINTO
HAIRSYLIST

22

Making the already pretty people even prettier — Hair and Makeup.

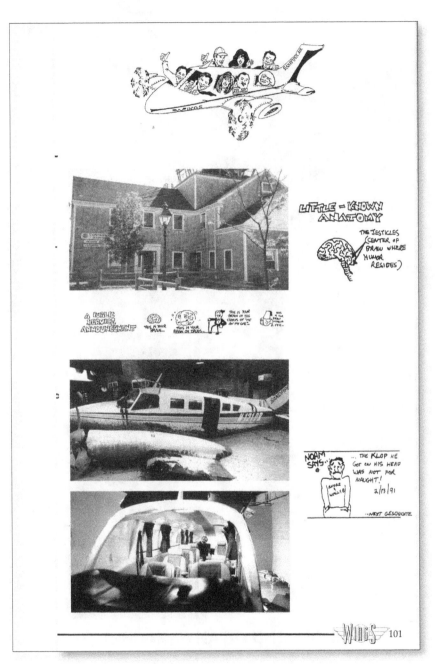

Tom Nevers Field and some "not so plain plane" pictures.

MEAL TICKET

HAVE YOU SEEN THIS WOMAN?
CALL ANTONIO SCARPACCI
555- 1812

MY WINGS MEMORY:

WHEN I PLAYED NANCY IN SHOW #164.
- LYNN DEE SMITH

SQUEEZE IT!

BEFORE

AFTER

MR. GOOGIE

STEVEN WEBER'S CALL SHEET CARTOONS

BEEVO! BEEVO! BEEVO! BEEVO! BEEVO! BEEVO!

IT'S THE END OF AN EARACHE

Part one of "the Weber Doodles." Steven Weber loved to draw on the scripts and call sheets, and some of his fine artwork has survived.

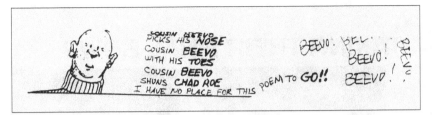

More classic "Weber Doodles." (Courtesy of Suzanne Holmes).

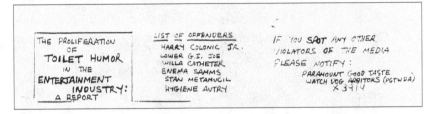

Still more "Weber Doodles." (Courtesy of Suzanne Holmes).

And even more "Weber Doodles." (Courtesy of Suzanne Holmes).

TAKING THEIR FINAL BOWS

THE TAPE IS PULLED...   THE SETS ARE STRUCK...

THAT'S A WRAP!

The cast and crew take "wing" after final bows and the wrap party.

**BILL NUZZO - CRAFT SERVICE
BRUCE MOORE - CRAFT SERVICE**

**THE WRONG BROTHERS
BOB MOORE
LARRY ANTONINO
MICHAEL HAKES
JON GREATHOUSE**

**DARRYL BATES - EDITOR
DAVE KARSON - ASSISTANT EDITOR**

DON HULETT - PROP MASTER

ROBERT LEE - WARM-UP

24 WINGS

Still more very important and very key behind-the-scenes faces, including warm-up guy Robert G. Lee.

"Wings Things" — a glossary

Ace – Alex's nickname for Joe Hackett.

Adele – Alex's mother's name.

Aeromass – Roy Biggins' Airline.

Ahab's Fast Fish – Kenny's other place of employment.

Air – Something Brian thinks is sexy.

Al Weinpur – Hefty man obsessed with whales.

Al's Crapshoot Motel – Where Joe's bachelor party was held.

Alfred – Casey's pet rock.

Algonquin Indians – Native to Nantucket.

Altar Linen – Something as white as a tourist's legs.

America's Wackiest Videos – The TV show on which Lowell wants to win the grand prize.

American Flyer Magazine – The magazine cover on which Joe wants to appear.

Angelo – What Carlton Blanchard always calls Antonio.

Angel of Flight 28 – Brian after taking over for the ailing pilots on a jet full of people.

Ann-Margret – Lowell's answer to every Trivial Pursuit question.

Antonio Bolonio – One of Antonio's childhood nicknames.

Antonio Scarpukey – One of "Dead End" Connelly's nicknames for Antonio.

Antonio Sockpuppet – Another of "Dead End" Connelly's nicknames for Antonio.

Antwerpio – Yet another of "Dead End Connelly's" nicknames for Antonio

Aunt Fay's Frozen Falafel – Fay's idea of a good business venture.

Aunt Freda – A relative of Lowell's who did a great impression of a chicken and once laid an egg.

Backdraft – Roy's name for Lowell when his hat was smoking.

Bad Mogambo – Bad luck or a bad omen.

Barbuda – Where Brian took a vacation after an IRS windfall.

Basil's – Bar on Mustique.

Be-Bop-a-Lula Burger – Available at Helen's Doo Wop Diner, same as the Sumo Burger.

Beach People – Joe and Helen after moving into their new house.

Beevo – Lowell's cousin with three thumbs who shaves animals for surgery, mentioned in many episodes.

Belly Button – Brian's code word to escape the Singles Mingle.

Bert – You don't mess with men named Bert, according to Antonio.

Biedermeier Furniture – Expensive pieces owned by Carlton Blanchard.

Big Dot – Woman who works at the gas station.

Big Pat – Woman who works in the bait shop.

Big Pencil – A wedding gift from Joe's side of the family.

Big Sandwich – Something no party should be without. Available in different sizes, the All-American, the Fiesta and the biggest big sandwich, the Cordoba.

"Big Strong Man" – Lowell's childhood TV idol.

The Big Ugly – Someone getting fired.

Binder Boy – A nickname for OCD Joe, who had binders, graphs, charts and notes on everything.

Blackout Biggins – Roy's nickname after singing the National Anthem.

BLT – What Joe orders from Helen every Tuesday.

Blue Skies – The program's original working title.

Bob the Mailman – Ate too many of Dee Dee's chocolate chip pancakes and died.

Bosom – A funny-sounding word.

Boyd Wiggins – Roy's name in the newspaper article in which he was pictured with Mary Pat Lee.

"Brian with an I" – What Mimsy called Brian.

"The Bri Guy" – What Ted Cobb calls Brian.

Brother P-Touch – Joe's labelmaker.

Brutus – Roy's dog.

"Bry Bry" – What Dani calls Brian in the "Maybe It's You" episode.

Buck Naked Line Dancing – One of Antonio's favorite cable TV programs.

Butt Boil – What Joe calls Danny "Dead End" Connelly.

"Buttons and Bows" – The song Roy dances to when allegedly hypnotized.

Captain Andy's – Famous for their big seafood platter called the Super Tanker.

Captain Jazzbo – A figurine on Lowell's blimp.

Car-B-Cue – Item sold by Lowell for cooking chicken or ribs while one drives.

Carragnas – Breasts in Khirinan.

Cart Blanche – Helen's food vending airport competition.

Casa Kielbasa – Roy's favorite Polish restaurant.

The Century House – A local hotel and restaurant where Joe and Helen were married.

Check Please – Something Brian says when surprised or grossed out.

Chickage – One of Brian's many terms for the opposite sex.

Chocolate Donut – NOT Bob's donut.

Chopper – Alex's dog.

Christmas Eel – Antonio's traditional family holiday dish.

The Christmas House – How Helen wants her house to be known.

Christmas Teddy – The Hackett Brothers' favorite holiday ornament.

Church of Universal Harmony – Roy is a mail-order minister of the church, a tax dodge, and he can perform wedding ceremonies.

Cindy – One of Joe's childhood nicknames.

Circle of Safety – No closer than ten feet at any time.

Circus – Where bad, bad things happen.

The Club Car – The name of a real restaurant/nightspot on Nantucket Island.

The Club Shangrila – Where Tracy Hayes danced naked.

Colonel Shulkraut – The man who runs the Happy Time Circus.

Come Hither – Fay's offensive perfume made from sheep pheromones.

Cousin Dominic – Antonio's leather goods cousin.

"The Crane Train to Mental Well-Being" – Frasier's seminar.

The Culinary Killer – Florence Chambers, Fay's doppelganger.

Cupcake – A frequently used term of endearment or sarcasm from Roy.

"D" – Antonio's nickname for maître D's.

Dagmar – Frederick Crane's big-bosomed nanny.

Danielle – Pretty woman who works at the tire store.

Deke Braverman – Pilot who gave Joe a plastic wing pin.

Deke Slayton – The astronaut with whom Fay did shooters.

Deviled Eggs – Roy's suggestion for Joe and Helen's wedding.

Devlin Twins – Strippers at Jim Bartow's bachelor party.

Dewey – Lowell's friend with a piece of extra ear skin that looks like an earring.

Dr. Dickens – The top Faulkner's man.

Dr. Jim – Joe's late childhood doctor.

The Doodletown Pipers – Offered Joe a job to sing with them (not really).

Dotman – One of Lowell's guesses in Pictionary.

Dry Socket – Something to avoid after having wisdom teeth pulled.

Dry Wall Roulette – The game Ace Galvin plays in the hotel room.

"Dumped" – Joe's poem, read on stage at the Cup.

Dwayne – A stupid name for a hurricane.

Earl – Roy's fake big brother.

Easy Casey – Casey's high school nickname.

Easy Casey's Fat Sister – Helen's high school nickname.

Eat-a-Holics – The over-eaters group therapy session to which Helen brings Brian.

Ed – Lowell's favorite golf ball.

Edna – The big-faced girl – Antonio's moon-faced mama.

Eighty-three Dollars – The amount on Dee Dee's check for Joe and Helen.

Emptyyyyyyy – Carlton Blanchard's bedside plea.

Engelbert – Fay's pet rock.

Engineer Willy – Sarcastic host of Roy's twelfth birthday party.

Ermo – Fay's pool boy with the six-inch thumbs.

Ernest Frean – Writer of *Phantom of the Oprah*.

Eunuch – The Magic Word.

Evangeline – Stripper at Walter's bachelor party.

Excuse Number 11 – Honesty.

Excuse Number 9 – I can't go out with you because of the flesh-eating bacteria.

The Eye Thing – A trick performed by old friend Meriwether.

Fancy Mather – The possible name of Lowell's godchild.

Fat Fat the Water Rat – What Carol used to call Helen.

Fat Tony's Meatball Dream House – The eatery where Roy won a free hoagie.

Faulkner's – Helen's made up syndrome that allegedly causes fainting.

Fayland – Where the little elves and leprechauns watch over everyone.

Fay's Foggy Day Fun Box – A box behind the counter filled with games, crafts and time killers for foggy days when the planes are grounded.

Felix – The wonderful, wonderful contractor.

Fitsy – Mimsy's dog.

508-555-0174 – Casey's office number.

508-555-4010 – The phone number for Alex's Helicopter Service.

Flight 211 – The one on which Fay and Joe met, New York to Honolulu.

Florence Chambers – The Culinary Killer.

The Flower Basket – Florist shop on Nantucket.

Food-a-Holics – Where Roy and Mary Pat Lee met.

Forrest Hump – X rated movie being made in the woods.

427 Madaket Way – The address of Joe and Brian's childhood home.

Frank – God's first name.

Fred Scoggins – Loves to talk about his hip replacement.

Fudgy – The wedding cake at Walter's wedding.

Fugitives from Justice – Reality show with Maury Povich.

"Get in the box, Joe" – What Brian and Fay said to Joe.

Gland Boy – Nickname for Brian.

Glandzilla – Another nickname for Brian.

Grub Street Productions – The name of David Angell, Peter Casey and David Lee's company named for a London street where 18th Century writers would turn out anything for money.

The Guy with the Hole in His Cheek – Jerry in air freight at Logan Airport.

The Hack – Joe Hackett's baseball nickname.

Hackel – The surname of one of the program's Executive Producers, and the surname on the tuxedos in "Here It Is, the Big Wedding." Brian gets the tuxes for the Hackel bar mitzvah by mistake.

Harrison Kingsbury – The dead rich guy whose body Joe and Brian lost in Miami.

Harvey Millbank – Faxes Roy pictures of his butt.

Headboard Heaven – One of Roy's euphemisms for making love.

Heart of the Jungle – The movie that exposed Grandpa Jack as a fraud.

Hekekia – Lowell's uncle who worked in a meat packing plant and lost his thumb.

Helen Heads – Devotees of Helen Chappel, rock cellist.

Helen's Doo Wop Diner – A new name for Helen's lunch counter to compete with the lunch cart.

Helen's Taste of Tokyo Café – Another new name for Helen's lunch counter.

Henley's – The department store in which Casey works.

Homer Pathett – Editor-in-Chief of *The Nantucket Herald*.

Homunculus – What Joe calls Lewis Blanchard.

Hoohah – What Brian took a picture of with Joe's camera.

Hosemaster – Vacuum cleaner with whisper drive, one step below Hosemaster 2000.

Howard Crawley – A guy Joe and Brian went to school with who became a cop.

Hunk-a-Doodle-Doo – What Helen calls Lowell's cousin Beevo.

HW's – Hot Wings.

"I Can't Stop Loving You" – Alex's favorite song, performed by Ray Charles.

Idi Amini Martini – Available at Brian's.

Iguana Air Lines – Brian's former place of employment on Mustique. Their motto, "We're ugly but we'll get you there."

Indian Point – Nantucket's make out spot.

"Isn't It Romantic" – Joe and Helen's song, and also one of Lowell's favorites.

"Itsy Bitsy Spider" – The song Cupcake the rat can play on a touchtone phone.

"Itsy Bitsy Teeny Weeny Yellow Polka Dot Martini" – Available at Brian's.

Janie Jordan – Joe's real prom date.

Jacqueline Cochran – The famous female aviator whose surname might have inspired Fay's.

Jed – Joe's alias on Christmas Eve in Debbie's hospital room.

Jelly donut – Bob's donut.

Jerry – The name of Joe's nose zit, also a possible nickname for Lowell.

Jingles – Helen's childhood pet.

Joe and Helen – The first names of Tony Shalhoub's real life parents.

Joe Talk – The way Joe does and says things.

"Joey Bear" – Sandy Cooper's secret nickname for Joe Hackett.

Joey O's – The cereal Joe dreams of, had he become a big baseball star.

July 15, 1973 – The date the time capsule was buried.

Jumbo Turkey Leg - What Roy very often orders for lunch.

June 5, 1978 – The imaginary date of Joe and Sandy's prom.

The Just Washed Inn – Where Antonio stayed after breaking up with Elise.

Kadota Fig – One of Lowell's favorite foods.

Katherine – A name Fay likes a lot.

Keramandu – Ancient art of face reading.

Kerblotten – What Fay is called by the woman who called Roy patatata.

Khirinan – Nantucket's proposed sister city, one of the Top Three producers of talcum powder.

King Arthur's Bar and Grill – Where Alex moonlights.

The Knight and Castle – A gay bar on Nantucket Island.

Knobs – The sleazy theater across from where *Rent* was playing in New York.

Koalachakti Tribe – A Brazilian tribe that believes everyone has an animal spirit guide.

Krista Purcell – The first girl Brian ever asked out. He was eight.

Kyle Vane – Received love letters from "R."

La Maison – Expensive restaurant on Nantucket Island.

Lard Lady – Another of Helen's old childhood nicknames.

Larry – Roy's childhood pet turtle which he painted blue. Also the first name of Joe and Helen's sad sack contractor.

Lars – Mimsy's lackey.

Las Cruces, New Mexico – Where Carlton's brother used to live.

Laundromate – Singles' laundromat in Boston frequented by Brian and Casey.

Leg of Lamb – What Fay has in her freezer.

Leonard – Sylvia's brother.

"Life: Grab It, It's Yours" – The title of John Gold's self-improvement tapes.

Lift – What Joe teaches over and over at his flight school.

Lloyd the Councilman – Had a heart attack, paving the way for Roy's campaign.

Lobster Bucket – Popular restaurant on the island.

Lot 49D – Where Brian's burned down house used to stand.

Love at 30,000 Feet – The title of Roy's unfinished novel.

The Lovely Helena – Helen's name in Brian's magic act.

Lowell Slaw – Lowell's suggestion for the lunch menu item named for him.

Lowelly – What Brian calls Lowell.

Lucky – A three-legged blind Chihuahua.

Lulu – The fire cat who drew attention away from the Angel of Flight 28.

Mac O'Malley – Tormented Joe in fourth grade, gave everyone nicknames, was supposed to spar with Joe in the ring.

Madam Zola – Reads the bumps on Antonio's head.

Madam Zorko – Fay's fortune teller name.

Maggot – One of Antonio's childhood nicknames.

Magneto – A generator for Joe's plane.

Main Street Lumberyard – Carlton Blanchard's old place of business.

The Marching Mules – Siasconset High School's band.

Margaret – Kenny's middle name.

Martha Blankenship – Former winner of the chowder cookoff.

Martha's Vineyrad – How Martha's Vineyard was spelled on the board, left column behind Fay from the middle of Season Eight to the very end. When asked about this, Steven Weber said, "Robert, it may very well have been me who did this. Thanks for your diligent efforts at seeking truth!"

Martini Navratilova – Available at Brian's.

Mavis Lynch - Davis' mom.

Maynard and Jocko – Act with a monkey who plays cello with his feet and a banana.

May 27th – Joe and Helen's wedding date.

Melen – Helen's name inscribed incorrectly on her engagement ring.

Mercenary Monthly – Where Ted Cobb used to work.

Meriwether – The guy who does "the eye thing," first name Phil.

Mexican Beanbag Chair – Weeb Gilroy's invention.

Milford Blanchard – Carlton's estranged brother.

Miss Sarcastic Pants – What Fay once called Helen.

Mr. Duffy – Elderly man who sits on his porch and shouts out crude remarks.

Mr. Dull Man – Where Brian says Joe shops for clothes.

Mr. Googie – The doll Joe squeezed to relieve stress.

Mr. LeBeau – Lowell's old perverted math teacher.

Mr. Squishy – Lowell's bath toy accidentally left behind in South Carolina.

Mr. Thirty Seconds – Davis Lynch.

Mr. Toupee Man – Aka Mr. Tupperman.

Mrs. Babcock – Fay's dead neighbor.

M. I. T. – Murray's Institute of Tools.

Momo – A dumb guy.

Monday, August 17, 1974 – The day Miss Jenkins left the island to get married.

Mooch – One of Antonio's childhood nicknames.

"Moon River" – One of Lowell's favorite songs.

Mount St. Helen – Another of Helen's old childhood nicknames.

Murray Cum Laude – Lowell at graduation.

Mustique – The Island where Brian used to fly for Iguana Airlines and where Joe escapes to.

My Big Buddy – Roy's very dark children's book.

"My Goat Knows the Bowling Score" – Antonio's version of "Michael."

Nakedland – Brian's realm (Brian is president).

Nancy Ferguson – A girl's name in Joe's address book with a star next to it.

Nancy Fletcher – The woman Joe planned to go with to opening day at Fenway.

Nanhackett – What Joe dreams the island's name should be.

Nantucket Airport – According to Lowell Mather, it was built in 1970, renovated in 1988 and recently painted by Bill the Painter Man.

Nantucket Hair and Nails – Where Cynthia and Shirley work.

Natty Stewart – Fay's friend, a 70-year-old Hungarian woman with arthritis.

Nebuchadnezzar – An extra large bottle of wine named after the King of Babylon.

Nelson's Heart – Written on the canister in the cooler left at the airport.

NIFTY – The Nevers Field Tenant of the Year Award.

"Nostrils are the window to the soul" – Lowell's credo.

"Nothing Rhymes with Alex" – The song Brian sings in the terminal to try to get Alex back.

Num Num – Similar to a Hoohah.

Ocupado – The alternate title of Roy's unfinished novel.

Oenophiles – Wine lovers.

Oil Drum Dave – Who Pencil Patty left Antonio for.

Old Dude – Joe while dressed as Pinocchio.

Old Seabrook Clam Chowder – The canned chowder with which Roy tried to enter a contest.

Ollie Andersen's Little Taste of Oslo – One of Roy's favorite restaurants.

Ollie's Drugs – Sandpiper Air uses their fax machine.

Omelet – What it looks like when Fay writes the word "overdue."

1,078 – The number of ceiling tiles in the terminal.

$1,002 – The amount of Antonio's refund check.

112 Navy Street, Room 5 – Where Ariel (aka Gretchen), Antonio's mystery woman lives.

Orange – Brian on Joe's chart.

Pant Load – An insult the Hackett boys like to use.

Paolo – Antonio's toy parrot.

Pasta Head – Another nickname Roy has for Antonio.

Patches – Along with Jingles, another former pet.

Pearl Nadelman – The woman inside Kingsbury's casket.

Peeper – Another of Antonio's childhood nicknames.

Peggy Springer – A girl over whom the Hackett boys fought in high school.

Pencil Patty – Lives under the bridge, occasionally dates Antonio.

Phantom of the Oprah – The play Fay, Roy, Antonio and Lowell were to be putting on.

Phil and Deedee Chappel – Helen and Casey's parents.

Phil and Lou's Delicatessen – The business that led to a 30-year estrangement of brothers Phil and Lou.

The Pickens/Pellateri Fight – The short fight seen on a big screen TV in the hangar.

Pilgrim Rent-a-Car – Seen in the background to the left of Helen's lunch counter.

Plasma Boy – What Antonio called Brian while he was driving his cab.

Plymouth Barracuda – 1968 muscle car owned by Carlton Blanchard.

PMS – The initials on the lost piece of luggage.

Poathing – A combination of pity and loathing.

Pontrelli's – The Italian restaurant in which we first saw Antonio, named for a crew member on the show, Gina Pontrelli.

The Pope – Joe, when on his high and mighty Pope perch.

Poppo the Clown – A favorite local kid's TV show clown.

The Princess Casey – Stuart's yacht.

Quahog – The local name for clams, something to which Antonio is allergic.

R. Fimmel – Fay's neighbor.

Raging Stallion – Roy's walkie talkie handle.

Ramona – Roy's inflatable girlfriend.

Ranger – The name of Joe and Brian's dog from their childhood.

Raoul – Omelet chef.

Ray Biggins – How Roy is introduced for the National Anthem the second time.

Ray Wiggins – Roy's character in his kids' book, *My Big Buddy*.

Really Big Idea – Cord's non-idea.

Red Hastings – A man obsessed with the color red who dated Helen.

Red Raider – Lowell's walkie talkie handle.

Regis Philbin – A rascal.

Rico's Fish Hut – The only other part-time job available to Brian other than bank guard.

Rigazzo con Veste – The boy in the dress.

Ring fund – A nest egg created by Joe.

Rob's Kabobs – Company whose motto is "If you grill it they will come."

Robin Hood and His Merry Women – A film rented by Roy.

Rock Springs, Wyoming – Where Carlton's brother lived.

Romance Connection – The dating service recommended by Antonio.

Room 412 – The room at the Harbor House where Joe and Helen had their engagement party.

Roy Buggins – How Roy is introduced for one of his two performances of the National Anthem.

Roz Doyle – The *Wings* line producer. Peri Gilpin's character on *Frasier* was named for her as a tribute after she passed on.

Saint Swithin's Day – A half day at Sandpiper Air.

Sandpiper – Joe Hackett's Airline.

Sandpiper Scair – What Sandpiper Air became on Halloween 1996.

Scab O'Neill – One of Lowell's friends.

Scary Mel – Weird guy who works on the fuel dock.

Schmagratulations – Joe Hackett's made up Nantucket wedding greeting.

Schmoozola – Kissing up, schmoozing people, wining and dining them.

Sconset – Short for Siasconset.

Sconset Sal – Lowell's godmother, and the woman who almost married Antonio.

Sconset Tattler – Local newspaper.

Senator Fred Bourneman – The man waiting for the heart at Boston University Medical Center.

Senor Pepe – Helen's contact in Tampico for a Mexican divorce.

Sgt. Whiskers – Budd's cat who couldn't pee.

17B – Joe's seat on Flight 211 on which he met Fay.

Shannon Moss – The color of Fay's kitchen, and also a woman Brian used to date.

Sheldon DeVane – Shelled and de-veined from Fay's scampi recipe, Lowell thought it was a person's name.

Short-eared Owls – The birds Fay attempts to save.

Siasconset Seafood Company – Where Helen gets a part-time job.

Sidney Rosenbear – The stuffed teddy bear who psychoanalyzed Joe.

Sir John Speed – Mapmaker who discovered the source of the Nile.

SISST – The Society for Inter Solar System Teamwork.

"Sitting in Butter" – Uttered by the bank robber whom Brian later recognizes on a Sandpiper flight.

Skippy – What Roy occasionally calls Joe.

Skirts – Another of Joe's childhood nicknames.

Skoogeritas – Served at Al Skoog's Bar.

Skoogerizing – A feature of Al Skoog's steam cleaning service.

Slackass – Roy's nickname for Lowell.

Slick – Alex's nickname for Brian Hackett.

Smelly Boy – One of Antonio's childhood nicknames.

Sneakerphone – One of Helen and Joe's wedding gifts from his side of the family.

Snitken, Snitken and Katz – The lawyers who worked on Casey and Stuart's divorce.

So Sue Me – Brian's credo.

Sounds Good – One of only three responses a cabbie should make.

South Bay Fudge Factory – Helen was their best customer.

Spaghettihead – One of Roy's nicknames for Antonio.

Sparky – Occasional nickname for Brian.

Speech Four – Career opportunities only come to those who deserve them.

Speech Six – You were right, you gave me good advice, I should have listened to you, it was a mistake for me to ever get involved.

Speech Three – Every Barry Manilow song is different, if you can't tell them apart it's because you haven't been listening closely enough.

Sphinx Brothers – What Roy calls Joe and Brian after they were both punched in the nose and bandaged.

Stan – Helen's very sensitive date.

Step One – Brian meets a woman.

Step Three – Phone rings, Brian tells Joe to tell the woman on the other end he moved to Arizona because of his sinuses.

Step Two – Brian sleeps with her.

Stinky Timmy – Works at the gas station.

Strychnine – A word Fay can spell and the poison of choice for Florence Chambers.

Sugar Buns – Nickname for Joe by the policewoman.

Sugar Ray Sheraton – Brian's boxing name.

Suicide Hill – Where Joe, Brian and Helen went sledding in Winter.

Sumo Burger – Same as the Be-Bop-a-Lula Burger.

Sweetcakes – Roy's nickname for Helen.

Sylvia – Roy's ex.

Tangelo – Half tangerine, half orange. Joe's fruit.

Taste of Warsaw – The Polish restaurant Brian goes to with Roy and Lydia.

Tater Time – A French Fry vending machine.

Taterville – Formerly a town in Iowa. Budd is blamed for its demise.

Tequila Nights – Book written by Brian's friend Danny Quinn.

Theresa Flahive – A girl from school over whom the Hackett boys fought.

31 ½ - The age at which the Mather boys become men and receive an inheritance.

Thrilla in Vanilla – The boxing match between Joe and Brian.

Thunder – Mr. Lundy's chick magnet dog.

Tim Daly – The way in which the show's star is credited beginning in Season Three (prior to that it's Timothy).

The Tin Whistle – Nantucket nightclub where Brian met Gwen.

Tinkerbell Issues – Something from which Brian suffers.

Toby's House of Wieners – Named a bratwurst after Brian.

Toilet Water – Involved in many of Brian's high school pranks – his trademark.

Tortilla – The word that makes Joe cluck like a chicken.

Transitions – The senior group Helen is sent to in order to get over her anger over losing Joe.

Traumatic Head Injury – A drink named for Brian Hackett.

The Trout Quintet – Helen's favorite classical piece by Franz Schubert.

Tubbo – One of Helen's old nicknames.

Tube of Death – What Brian calls a hot dog.

Turtle Shoals – The golf course/timeshare in South Carolina.

22 – The number on Joey Hackett, baseball hero's jersey.

$262.00 – The meager amount Joe got from his insurance company after the plane crash.

213 Church Lane – Where Lowell lived, an inside joke as his real last name is Church.

Ty Warner – Broke Joe's old baseball record.

Uh Huh – One of only three responses a cabbie should make.

Uncle Funtime's Petting Zoo – Where Roy had his eleventh birthday.

Uncle Larry – Joe and Brian's uncle with spaghetti sauce on his chin.

Uncle Sal – Antonio's relative who owned a girdle shop.

Uncle Wayne – Brian and Joe's uncle who often made a beard out of his mashed potatoes at dinner.

Unified General – The insurance company under which Joe's plane is covered.

Vineyrad – The word Vineyard on the Sandpiper departure chart behind Fay is often spelled as Vineyrad, left column beginning in the middle of season eight.

Waffails – How Lowell fits the word waffles into the eulogy for Weeb.

Waffles – Weeb's favorite food.

Wahiners – Island boys.

Wahinis – Island girls.

Wait – Antonio's nickname for waiters.

"Waiting for a Fare" – Antonio's angry and dark poem.

Wally – Brian's alias at the Singles' Mingle.

Water Street Gym – Where Alex works out.

Weeb Gilroy – The elderly man who taught Lowell how to be a mechanic.

Whaling Museum – Where Fay used to go to meet men.

Wham Bam Pam – Pam Chase, health inspector and old school-mate of Helen's.

Wharf Tavern – Another bar on the island.

Whispering Pines Mortuary – Where Antonio was moonlighting.

Whitewood Insurance – Brian's house was insured by them.

Wilson "Banana Head" Kingsbury – Eleanor Kingsbury's son.

Windsurfer – The name of the island's ferry company.

Winkerstinker – What Fay calls Frank who enters the boat parade each Christmas.

Winston Catlow – Helen's first cello teacher, and the man who disrupted Helen's recital.

Woo Woo Stuff – Weird wedding rituals.

Yankee Doodle Donuts – A donut shop on the island.

Yankee Doodle Scissors – Where most people on Nantucket Island get a haircut.

Yard Demon 742 – Antonio's neighbor's loud gardening equipment.

You Don't Say – One of only three responses a cabbie should make.

You You – Similar to a hoohah and a num num.

Other Sitcoms with an Airline Connection
(Listed Chronologically)

The Jeannie Carson Show (1958) - This was the revamped version of *Hey, Jeannie* starring Scottish actress Jeannie Carson. Season one focused upon a Scottish girl adjusting to the ways and mores of America. In the truncated second season she becomes a flight attendant with co-star William Schallert in a pre-*Patty Duke Show* role.

The New Bob Cummings Show (1961) – This series was similar to the old *Bob Cummings Show* (aka *Love that Bob*). Bob was still a playboy, but also a pilot with an Aerocar – a car that was also capable of flight.

Wendy and Me (1964) – This series attempted to bring George Burns TV success without Gracie. It co-starred Connie Stevens (Wendy) who was married to a Trans-Globe airline pilot named Jeff played by Ron Harper. Jeff's womanizing buddy across the hall, Danny played by James Callahan was also a pilot.

The Tycoon (1964) – After *The Real McCoys*, Walter Brennan attempted sitcom success again on this ABC single-season entry. He portrayed Walter Andrews, one of the world's richest men and many scenes took place in his private plane, piloted by Van Williams, later TV's *The Green Hornet.*

The John Forsythe Show (1965) – In between successes on *Bachelor Father* and *Dynasty*, Forsythe starred as an Air Force pilot who inherits an all-girls' school in this eponymous series. Co-stars included Ann B. Davis and Elsa Lanchester.

The Tim Conway Show (1970) – This sitcom reunited Tim Conway with his *McHale's Navy* co-star Joe Flynn as inept pilots for Triple A Airlines with their lone plane, the "Lucky Linda."

From a Bird's Eye View (1971) – This Sheldon Leonard sitcom focused upon two bumbling stewardesses in London played by Millicent Martin and Patte Finley, and their temperamental boss Mr. Beauchamp (Peter Jones).

The Bob Newhart Show (1972-1978) – Bob Newhart played a psychologist, Suzanne Pleshette played his schoolteacher wife. Their neighbor, Howard Borden played by the late Bill Daily was a divorced, needy and daft airline navigator.

M*A*S*H (1972-1983) – Based upon the movie of same name, many helicopters were featured in the show's eleven season run (including the opening credits). It instantly made stars out of Alan Alda, Loretta Swit, Wayne Rogers, Gary Burghoff, Larry Linville and McLean Stevenson.

Flying High (1978) – An hour-long sitcom that was, for all intents and purposes, *The Love Boat* in the sky. It starred Connie Sellecca and it was the story of three stewardesses from diverse backgrounds and different parts of the country all working for Sun West Airlines.

The Crew (1995) – This one was set in Miami's Regency Airport and consisted of a diverse crew including an unstable pilot, and the quirky flight attendants practical Maggie and her roommate Jess, good old boy Randy, and Gay Paul.

L. A. to Vegas (2018) – This one centered around the crew and parade of passengers for discount Jackpot Airlines with weekend flights from Los Angeles to Vegas. It starred Dylan McDermott. The show was produced by Steven Levitan but lasted only one season.

WING FLAPS — Inconsistencies Over 172 Episodes and Eight Seasons

Unlike many other earlier sitcoms, *Wings* had quite an efficient continuity department. Only a small list of inconsistencies can be found within the 172 episodes spread over eight seasons.

1. "The Big-Faced Girl" – She was Antonio Scarpacci's last resort date on several occasions. Although never seen on camera, she was described as a woman with a face so big it took two people to carry her retainer and romancing her was like making love to a jack-o-lantern. The inconsistency is that in most episodes her name is Edna, but in one, for some reason, she is named Denise.

2. In one episode Lowell says that he is deathly afraid of spiders, while in another he claims to love spiders.

3. In the series' first of many holiday episodes, "A Terminal Christmas," Helen speaks of a sister named Lorraine, but when that sister returns to Nantucket and joins the cast as a regular in Season Six she is named Casey (short for Cassandra).

4. In one episode, it is revealed that Helen Chappel's birthday is August 3, but in another she claims to be a Libra.

5. Joe only has one airplane, but what is seen on camera is not always N121PP (Nevada 121 Papa Papa). Occasionally it's N121PB, and even N160PB when it's in flight.

6. There are two totally different characters over the series run nicknamed "Tuck." One is Lowell's rat-shooting friend portrayed by Tracey Walter and one is half of a couple that Joe and Helen hang out with in the "Have I Got a Couple for You" episode as portrayed by Tony Carreiro.

7. Helen's cameo pin previously belonged to Joe's mother in one episode, but Helen says she got it on her own grandmother's death bed in another.

8. In the three-episode arc "Wingless" in Season Eight Mitchell Ryan's character is listed in the credits as Jonathan Clayton in all three parts, but in part two of the arc he's referred to in the dialogue as Edgar Clayton by Antonio and Roy.

9. Fay spreads her husband's ashes that were in a cookie jar into the ocean from Sandpiper's plane in an early episode of the series titled "A Terminal Christmas." In the episode titled "Ms. Write" from the final season, those ashes are still in the cookie jar.

10. In one episode Lowell says he can't sleep if he can't see the ocean. In another when looking for his own apartment he doesn't like the place because it has a view of the ocean.

11. Antonio gives Brian a camcorder for Christmas in "'Twas the Heist before Christmas" but Brian already had one from "The Life and Times of Joe and Helen" episode (bought with petty cash).

12. Roy only has a mom, Eleanor "Bluto" Biggins, but in one episode he buys a Car-B-Cue for his "parents'" anniversary.

13. Lowell has great difficulty balancing his own books in one episode and asks Fay to help him. In another, he is seen balancing the books for Sandpiper Air.

14. In one episode Lowell has two sisters - one is said to be very fertile, the other has webbed toes. However, in another episode Fay says that Lowell doesn't have any sisters.

15. In "Hey, Nineteen" Alex mentions having seen Brian's grandfather, however in "B. S. I Love You," Brian and Joe forgot what their grandfather looked like and thus fall for an imposter portraying him.

The Wings Alphabetical Guest List

Caroline Aaron as Mary Pat Lee
Brooke Adams as Sister Mary (Mrs. Tony Shalhoub in real life)
Kirstie Alley as Rebecca Howe
Carol Alt as Tracy Hayes
Teri Austin as Shannon Moss
Barbara Babcock as Mae Hackett
Diana Bellamy as Albie's mother
Craig Bierko as Matt Sargent
Andrew Bilgore as Carl Torley
Clint Black as himself
Peter Brown as Dr. Lasker
Phil Buckman as Carter
Jane Carr as Claire Bennett
Dan Castellaneta as George Wexler
Ray Charles as himself
Gordon Clapp as Phil
Lana Clarkson as Janine
Robert Colbert as Deke
Kevin Connolly as Scotty
Robert Culp as Ace Galvin
Tyne Daly as Mimsy Borogroves
Billy Dean as Jack Gordon
Calvert DeForest as the club patron
Gabe Dell, Jr. as the pizza boy
Roy Dotrice as Pete
John Ducey as the board member
Steven Eckholdt as Connor McDevitt
Chris Elliott as Steve
Richard Erdman as Howard Banks
Tim Fall as Trevor
Dann Florek as Bob
Matthew Fox as Ty Warner

Jonathan Frakes as Gavin Rutledge
Anne Francis as Vera
George Furth as Frank
Peri Gilpin as Barbara
Jack Ging as Coach Mattay
Gilbert Gottfried as Lewis Blanchard
Kelsey Grammar as Frasier Crane
Scott Grimes as Marty
Edward Hermann as Y. M. Burg
Pat Hingle as Grandpa Jack Hackett
George Kennedy as himself
Phil Leeds as Lou
Jay Leno as himself
Rick Lenz as Jerry
Peggy Lipton as Miss Laura Jenkins
Norman Lloyd as Lyle Bartlett
Valerie Mahaffey as Sandy Cooper
Rose Marie as Eleanor "Bluto" Biggins
Jenny McCarthy as Dani
Sam McMurray – Dennis Lundy
Stuttering John Melendez as Albie
Josh Mostel as Dave Gardner
Megan Mullally as Cindy
Brian Doyle Murray as Coach Snyder
Don Murray as Donald Hackett
Craig Richard Nelson as the auctioneer
Bebe Neuwirth as Lilith Crane
Steve Nevil as Frank Guttman
Edwin Newman as himself
Oliver North as himself
George Plimpton as Dr. Grayson
Michael J. Pollard as Benny
Matthew Porretta as David
Maury Povich as himself
John Ratzenberger as Cliff Claven
Debbie Reynolds as DeeDee Chappel
Robert Ridgely as "Big Strong Man"

John Ritter as Stuart Davenport
Charles Rocket as Danny Quinn
Soupy Sales as Fred Gardner
Gene Schull – Man in lederhosen (husband of Rebecca Schull)
Marian Seldes as Eleanor Kingsbury
Cathy Silvers as Phoebe
Real Don Steele as the Radio Contest DJ
David Ogden Stiers as Edward Tinsdale
Peter Tork as himself
Amy Van Nostrand as Gwen Tucker (Tim Daly's real-life wife at the time)
Lucky Vanous as himself, the shirtless Diet Coke commercial guy
Liz Vassey as Courtney
Abe Vigoda as Harry
Ally Walker as Melissa
Tracey Walter as Tucker
Todd Waring as Matthew
George Wendt as Norm Peterson
Teddy Wilson as John
Steve Young as himself
Chip Zien as Bippy the Clown

Famous People Mentioned (but not appearing) on Wings

Buzz Aldrin
Ann-Margret
Neil Armstrong
Desi Arnaz
Fred Astaire
Red Auerbach
Gene Autry
Pearl Bailey
Lucille Ball
Ellen Barkin
Count Basie
Ned Beatty
Warren Beatty
Jack Benny
Ingrid Bergman
Joe Besser
Joey Bishop
Humphrey Bogart
Shirley Booth
Ernest Borgnine
Marlon Brando
Christie Brinkley
David Brinkley
Charlotte Bronte
George Burns
LeVar Burton
Gary Busey
Barbara Bush
George H. W. Bush
Albert Camus
Wilt Chamberlain

Jackie Chan
Coco Chanel
Cher
Andrew Dice Clay
Perry Como
Alistair Cooke
Kevin Costner
Jacques Cousteau
Walter Cronkite
Scatman Crothers
Tom Cruise
Macaulay Culkin
Jamie Lee Curtis
Miles Davis
Robert DeNiro
Catherine Deneuve
Bob Denver
John Denver
Gerard Depardieu
Angie Dickinson
Walt Disney
Placido Domingo
Phil Donahue
Hugh Downs
Michael Dukakis
Olympia Dukakis
Bob Dylan
Amelia Earhart
Buddy Ebsen
Mamie Eisenhower
Ella Fitzgerald

Jane Fonda
Gerald R. Ford
John Forsythe
Michael J. Fox
Eva Gabor
Mitch Gaylord
Mel Gibson
Kathy Lee Gifford
John Glenn
Eydie Gorme
Melanie Griffith
Oliver Hardy
David Hartman
Goldie Hawn
Katherine Hepburn
Alfred Hitchcock
Abbie Hoffman
J. Edgar Hoover
Bob Hope
Howard Hughes
Ice Cube
Ice T
John Irving
Shoeless Joe Jackson
The Jacksons
Mick Jagger
Peter Jennings
Elton John
Ladybird Johnson
Donna Karan
Charles Keating
Ted Koppel
Harvey Korman
Stan Laurel
Jerry Lewis
Abraham Lincoln
Charles Lindbergh

Art Linkletter
Rich Little
Gina Lollobrigida
Ida Lupino
Madonna
Barry Manilow
Meat Loaf
Ethel Merman
Liza Minelli
Mr. T.
Isaac Mizrahi
Claude Monet
Ricardo Montalban
Demi Moore
Jan Murray
Jack Nicholson
Pat Nixon
Manuel Noriega
Ken Norton
Deborah Norville
Al Pacino
Rosa Parks
Dolly Parton
Jane Pauley
Pearl Jam
Ross Perot
Tom Petty
Regis Philbin
Pablo Picasso
Elvis Presley
Princess Caroline
Princess Margaret
Monty Python
Mary Lou Retton
Paul Revere
Debbie Reynolds
Buddy Rich

The Rolling Stones
Andy Rooney
Hermann Rorschach
Richard Roundtree
Babe Ruth
Robert Ryan
Jonas Salk
Colonel Harlan Sanders
Wally Schirra
Willard Scott
Alan Shepard
Maria Shriver
Bugsy Siegel
Carly Simon
Roger Smith
Bruce Springsteen
Sylvester Stallone
Sharon Stone
Barbra Streisand
John Sununu
Patrick Swayze
Danny Tartabull
Dylan Thomas
The Three Stooges
Franchot Tone
Pete Townshend
Spencer Tracy
Alex Trebek
Lee Trevino
Leon Trotsky
Francois Truffaut
Vincent Van Gogh
Vanilla Ice
Otto Von Bismarck
Mike Wallace
George Washington
John Wayne

Andrew Lloyd Webber
Richard Widmark
Simon Wiesenthal
Jo Beth Williams
Oprah Winfrey
Deborah Winger
Orville Wright
Wilbur Wright
Chuck Yeager
Henny Youngman

Episodes Missing in Syndication
(but Available on the complete DVD set)

Of the 172 filmed episodes of *Wings* 23 are not syndicated. Tim Daly said it's likely because of music licensing issues, and it does appear that all of the episodes in question contained either "Isn't It Romantic," "Call Me Irresponsible," "Moon River," "That Old Black Magic," or holiday tunes. However, composer Bruce Miller said, "It may be music related, then again it may just be that the syndicators wanted a nice round number of episodes in the package to be shown and streamed." The only way to see the entire 172 is on the DVD box set. As of this writing, *Wings* can be seen on CBS All Access and on Pluto TV's *Wings* Channel.

Those missing from syndication are as follows:
"The Puppet Master"
"A Terminal Christmas"
"My Brother's Back and There's Gonna be Trouble"
"Try to Remember the Night He Dismembered"
"Exit Laughing"
"The Gift Part One"
"The Gift Part Two"
"I Love Brian"
"Another Wedding"
"Twisted Sister"
"All's Fare"
"Gone but Not Faygotten"
"The Love Life and Times of Joe and Helen"
"She's Gotta Have It"
"'Twas the Heist before Christmas"
"Lynch Party"
"A Tale of Two Sister Cities"
"Life Could be a Dream"
"Maybe It's You"
"Olive or Twist"
"Fay There, Georgy Girl"

"Escape from New York"
"House of Blues"

The Author's Top Twenty Favorite Episodes
(Listed Chronologically)

"Legacy"
"The Puppetmaster"
"Love Is Like Pulling Teeth"
"Murder She Roast"
"Ladies Who Lunch"
"The Bogey Men"
"Das Plane"
"Blackout Biggins"
"It's So Nice to Have a Mather around the House"
"The Houseguest"
"2 Good 2 Be 4 Gotten"
"The Faygitive"
"Miss Jenkins"
"Have I Got a Couple for You"
"Ex Lies and Videotape"
"Death Becomes Him"
"The Person Formerly Known as Lowell"
"Life Could Be a Dream"
"The Gift of Life"
"Just Call Me Angel"

About the Author

Author Bob Leszczak donning his treasured Wings tee shirt.

Bob Leszczak was born and raised in Elizabeth, New Jersey. An only child, the phonograph and the family's television set became his favorite toys before the age of two and are the focus of his many books. He is a lifetime vinyl record collector and music and TV historian. Bob got his bachelor's degree in communication at Seton Hall University in South Orange, New Jersey, and while still in college, he toured as a member of the vocal group, the Duprees, most famous for the Top Ten hit called "You Belong to Me" and sang tenor. He also worked on the college radio station, WSOU-FM. He released recordings with numerous doo wop vocal ensembles, such as the Infernos, the Autumns, Retrospect, and the James Myers Quintet. Some were a cappella, and some had musical accompaniment. Bob paid his dues in radio broadcasting and eventually became a popular on-air personality in great radio markets such as Boston, Washington, D.C., Tampa/St. Petersburg (where he garnered a coveted Air Award in 1999), Orlando, Hartford, Denver, and Riverside/San Bernardino, California (all under the alias of Bob O'Brien). He was also a panelist on the weekly TV talent show titled *Lucky Break* in 2006, and is a SAG/Aftra extra, appearing regularly in *The Marvelous Mrs. Maisel* and *Gotham*, as well as in countless films and miniseries such as *Joker, Marry Me,*

The Plot against America, The Loudest Voice, When They See Us and CNN's *History of Sitcom* documentary. Bob was the writer/producer of a weekly five-hour music trivia program called *Solid Gold Scrapbook* for the United Stations Radio Network in the 1980s. In recent years, Bob has returned to writing and is the author of *Who Did It First? Great Rhythm and Blues Cover Songs and Their Original Artists; Who Did It First? Great Pop Songs and Their Original Artists; Who Did It First? Great Rock and Roll Songs and Their Original Artists; Dynamic Duets – The Best Pop Collaborations 1955-1999; The Encyclopedia of Pop Music Aliases 1950-2000; From Small Screen to Vinyl – A Guide to TV Stars Who Made Records 1950-2000; The Odd Couple on Stage and Screen: A History with Cast and Crew, Profiles, and an Episode Guide; Single Season Sitcoms 1948-1979, A Complete Guide; Single Season Sitcoms of the 1980s, A Complete Guide;* and *Single Season Sitcoms of the 1990s, A Complete Guide.* He is an avid jogger and a fervent fan of football and baseball. At the present time, Bob is a DJ on WKXW-FM (New Jersey 101.5 FM).

Placque at present day Paramount Stage 19. (Courtesy of Jack E. Herman).

Present day Stage 19, the home of Wings. (Courtesy of Jack E. Herman).

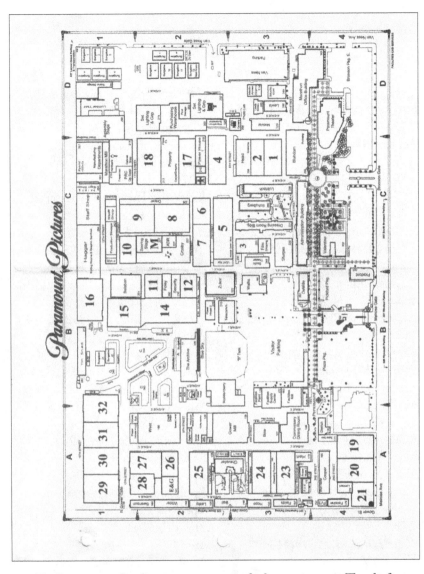

The Paramount Studios map, so you can find your way out. Thanks for coming. I hope you'll fly with us again. (Courtesy of Suzanne Holmes).

INDEX

Printed in the USA
CPSIA information can be obtained
at www.ICGtesting.com
LVHW012318081223
765728LV00006B/188